The Const
Roman Republic

The Constitution of the
Roman Republic

ANDREW LINTOTT

OXFORD

UNIVERSITY PRESS

OXFORD
UNIVERSITY PRESS

Great Clarendon Street, Oxford OX2 6DP

Oxford University Press is a department of the University of Oxford.
It furthers the University's objective of excellence in research, scholarship,
and education by publishing worldwide in

Oxford New York

Auckland Cape Town Dar es Salaam Hong Kong Karachi Kuala Lumpur
Madrid Melbourne Mexico City Nairobi New Delhi Shanghai Taipei Toronto

With offices in

Argentina Austria Brazil Chile Czech Republic France Greece
Guatemala Hungary Italy Japan South Korea Poland Portugal
Singapore Switzerland Thailand Turkey Ukraine Vietnam

Oxford is a registered trade mark of Oxford University Press
in the UK and in certain other countries

Published in the United States
by Oxford University Press Inc., New York

First published 1999
First published in paperback 2003
Reprinted 2004

British Library Cataloguing in Publication Data
Data available

Library of Congress Cataloging in Publication Data
The constitution of the Roman Republic / Andrew Lintott.
Includes bibliographical references and index.
1. Constitutional history–Rome.   2. Rome–Constitutional law.
3. Rome–Politics and government–510-30 BC.
4. Political science–Early words to 1800.
5. Rome–History–Republic, 510-30 BC.
I. Title.
JC88.L588   1999   342.37'029–dc2   98-30-30456
ISBN 978-0-19-815068-8
ISBN 978-0-19-926108-6 (pbk)

Typeset by Regent Typesetting, London
Printed in Great Britain
on acid-free paper by
Biddles Ltd., King's Lynn, Norfolk

Preface

THE study of the constitution should be central to the study of the Roman Republic, as I argue more fully in the Introduction. One object of this book is to provide a work in English to which teachers of ancient history can refer pupils on this topic. However, I have also sought to rescue Roman constitutional studies from the stigma of being old-fashioned, smelling of the attic of nineteenth-century scholarship, and out of tune with modern approaches to the analysis of society. It is of course true that the constitutional approach is not the unique route to understanding the way ancient societies worked, but that was recognized by Mommsen, when he was writing the *Staatsrecht* — a work that is much less narrowly legalistic than is often supposed. And the same may be said of earlier constitutional studies reaching back to Machiavelli and indeed to Polybius.

I am extremely grateful to the many scholars, largely outside the United Kingdom, who have helped me by sending books and offprints. In England I owe a special debt to John Crook and Duncan Cloud, who read the book in typescript, saved me from a number of errors, and made many interesting suggestions. The British School at Rome elected me their Hugh Last Fellow and provided me with a valuable base at an important stage in my research. My study of the Republican constitution began and has reached a conclusion at Oxford, and it is a pleasure to be once again publishing under the imprint, especially as this book will soon be accompanied by a second edition of *Violence in Republican Rome*, where the reader will find a fuller discussion of certain issues raised in it.

Worcester College, Oxford   A.L.
May, 1998

Contents

Abbreviations

Abbreviations of periodicals in general follow the system of *L'Année Philologique*, with one important exception: ZSS for *Zeitschrift der Savigny-Stiftung für Rechtsgeschichte, romanistische Abteilung*.
   Abbreviations of papyri in general follow those in E. G. Turner, *Greek Papyri: An Introduction* (Oxford, 1980), pp. 159 ff.

ANRW	*Aufstieg und Niedergang der römischen Welt*, Festschrift J. Vogt, ed. H. Temporini and W. Haase (Berlin and New York, 1972–)
Braund, *AN*	D. C. Braund, *Augustus to Nero: A Sourcebook on Roman History 31 BC–AD 68* (London/Sydney, 1985)
Bruns	G. Bruns and O. Gradenwitz, *Fontes Iuris Romani Antiqui* (7th edn., Tübingen, 1919)
CAH	*Cambridge Ancient History*
CIL	*Corpus Inscriptionum Latinarum*
De Martino, *SCR*	F. de Martino, *Storia della costituzione romana*, 5 vols. (Naples, 1958–67)
EJ²	V. Ehrenberg and A. H. M. Jones, *Documents Illustrating the Reigns of Augustus and Tiberius* (2nd edn. with addenda, Oxford, 1975)
FGH	F. Jacoby, *Die Fragmente der Griechischen Historiker*, 3 parts, 11 vols (Berlin and Leiden, 1923–58)
FIRA	S. Riccobono, *Fontes Iuris Romani Anteiustiniani* (2nd edn. Florence, 1968)
HRR	H. Peter, *Historicorum Romanorum Reliquiae* 2 vols. (2nd edn., Stuttgart, repr. 1993)
IG	*Inscriptiones Graecae*
IGRR	R. Cagnat *et al.*, *Inscriptiones Graecae ad Res Romanas Pertinentes*, 3 vols. (Paris, 1906–27)
ILLRP	A. Degrassi, *Inscriptiones Latinae Liberae Rei Publicae*, 2 vols. (2nd edn., Florence, 1966)
ILS	H. Dessau, *Inscriptiones Latinae Selectae*, 4 vols. (Berlin, 1892–1916, repr. 1954)
Imp.Rom.	A. Lintott, *Imperium Romanum: Politics and Administration* (London and New York, 1993)

Inscr.Ital.	A. Degrassi, *Inscriptiones Italiae, xiii Fasti et Elogia*, 3 vols. (Rome, 1947–63)
JRLR	A. Lintott, *Judicial Reform and Land Reform in the Roman Republic* (Cambridge, 1992)
MRR	T. R. S. Broughton, *The Magistrates of the Roman Republic*, vols. i and ii. (2nd edn., New York, 1960); vol. iii (Atlanta, 1987)
OGIS	W. Dittenberger, *Orientis Graeci Inscriptiones Selectae*, 4 vols. (Leipzig, 1903, repr. Hildesheim, 1960)
ORF	H. Malcovati, *Oratorum Romanorum Fragmenta*, 2 vols. (4th edn., Turin, 1976–9)
RE	Pauly-Wissowa, *Real-Encyclopaedie der classischen Altertumswissenschaft*
RDGE	R. K. Sherk, *Roman Documents from the Greek East* (Baltimore, 1964)
RRC	M. H. Crawford, *Roman Republican Coinage*, 2 vols. (Cambridge, 1974)
RS	M. H. Crawford, ed. *Roman Statutes*, 2 vols. (London, 1996)
SEG	*Supplementum Epigraphicum Graecum*
Smallwood, GCN	E. M. Smallwood, *Documents Illlustrating the Principates of Gaius, Claudius and Nero* (Cambridge, 1967)
Staatsr.	Th. Mommsen, *Römisches Staatsrecht*, vols. i and ii, 3rd edn., vol. iii, 1st edn. (Leipzig, 1887–8)
Strafr.	Th. Mommsen, *Römisches Strafrecht* (Leipzig, 1899)
*Syll.*³	W. Dittenberger, *Sylloge Inscriptionum Graecarum*³, 4 vols. (3rd edn., Leipzig, 1915; repr. Hildesheim, 1960)
VRR	A. W. Lintott, *Violence in Republican Rome* (Oxford, 1968)

The following legal texts may be referred to without further reference:

Frag.Tar.	*Fragmentum Tarentinum*, R. Bartoccini, *Epigraphica* 9 (1947), 3–31; *RS* i. 8
Lex agr.	*Lex Agraria, CIL* i². 585; *FIRA* i. 8; *JRLR*, pp. 17 ff.; *RS* i. 2.
Lex Ant.Term.	*Lex Antonia de Termessibus, CIL* i². 589; *FIRA* i. 11; *RS* i. 19
Lex de Delo	*Lex Gabinia Calpurnia de insula Delo, CIL* i². 2500; *RS* i. 22; C. Nicolet, ed. *Insula Sacra* (Rome, 1980)
Lex Gen.Urs.	*Lex Coloniae Genetivae Ursonensis, CIL* i². 594; *FIRA* i. 21; *RS* i. 25
Lex Irn.	*Lex Irnitana*, J. Gonzalez, *JRS* 76 (1986), 147–243
Lex Iul.agr.	*Lex Iulia agraria* (or *Mamilia Roscia Peducaea Alliena Fabia*), *FIRA* i. 12; *RS* ii. 54
Lex lat.Bant.	*Lex latina tabulae Bantinae, CIL* i². 582 (cf.i.2.iv² (1986), pp. 907–8); *FIRA* i. 6; *RS* i. 7

Lex mun.Mal.	*Lex municipii Malacitani, CIL* ii. 1964; *FIRA* i. 24
Lex osca Bant.	*Lex osca tabulae Bantinae, FIRA* i. 16; Bruns, 8; new fragment, D. Adamesteanu and M. Torelli, *Arch.Class.* 21 (1969), 1–17; *RS* i. 13
Lex portorii Asiae	H. Engelmann and D. Knibbe, 'Das Zollgesetz der provincia Asia. Ein neues Inschrift aus Ephesus', *Epig.Anat.* 14 (1989), 1–206
Lex prov.praet.	*Lex de provinciis praetoriis (de piratis), FIRA* i. 9; new fragments, M. Hassall, M. Crawford, J. Reynolds, *JRS* 64 (1974), 195–220; *RS* i. 12
Lex rep.	*Lex Repetundarum, CIL* i². 583; *FIRA* i. 7; *JRLR*, pp. 88 ff.; *RS* i. 1
Lex Rubr.Gall.	*Lex Rubria de Gallia Cisalpina, CIL* i². 592; *FIRA* i. 19; *RS* i. 28
SC Asclep.	*Senatus Consultum de Asclepiade, CIL* i². 588; *FIRA* i. 35
SC Bacch.	*Senatus Consultum de Bacchanalibus, CIL* i². 581; *FIRA* i. 30
SC Calvisianum	*FIRA* i. 68, v (pp. 409–14); *SEG* ix. 8
Tab. Heracl.	*Tabula Heracleensis, CIL* i². 593; *FIRA* i. 13; *RS* i. 24

I

Introduction

Who is there so feeble-minded or idle that he would not wish to know how and with what constitution almost all the inhabited world was conquered and fell under the single dominion of Rome within fifty-three years?

(Polybius, 1. 1. 5)

Polybius' association of Rome's phenomenal military success with the excellence of her constitution may surprise twentieth-century readers, but it was almost self-evident for a Greek intellectual from within the governing class in his period. It was Herodotus who first made the connection between political systems and their military capacities. In his view an important result of the reforms (*eunomia*) of Lycurgus was the victory of the Spartans over their neighbours; again, when the Athenians acquired democracy (*isēgoria*) through Cleisthenes, the immediate consequence was their victory over the Boeotians and Chalcidians. This is of course also the theme of Pericles' funeral oration, as reported by Thucydides. In Plato's *Republic* the starting-point of the discussion of the ideal constitution (as opposed to the utopian primitivism first described in Book 2) is the need for the city to be victorious in war.[1] As far as I know, there is no specific text of this kind in our Roman sources: the closest parallel is in Livy, who ascribes Roman success to their skills in civil and military affairs (*artes domi militiaeque*) as well as their way of life (*vita* and *mores*). For other Romans their military success was the outcome of good *mores* and the favour of the gods.[2] Nevertheless, the Livian narrative of the Second Punic War, for example, places in relief not only the effectiveness of Roman political activity but also the

[1] Hdt. 1. 65–8; 5. 77–8; Thuc. 2. 36. 4–37; Plato, *Rep.* 2. 373d–374a. Herodotus' point about Athenian democracy was picked up approvingly by Machiavelli, *Discorsi*, 1. 58. 30.

[2] Livy, *Praef.* 9. In Sall. *Cat.* 7. 3 success follows the founding of the Republic. For *mores* see e.g. Sall. *Cat.* 9. 1; *Jug.* 41. 2; *Hist.* 1. 11M; for divine favour Cic. *Mur.* 75 (referring to a speech of Scipio Aemilianus); *RDGE* 34, lines 11ff. (the letter of the praetor Messalla to Teos).

constitutional innovations that the war brought about. We shall see in
the next chapter how political activity is used in a later book of Livy to
frame the story of military success.

Nowadays, when historians study the republican constitution, it is not
so much because it is the key to understanding Roman success abroad,
but because they wish to evaluate Roman politics and society in this
period. The fact that the constitution was, as Polybius saw, a natural
growth,[3] rather than the creation of a legislator at a specific point in time,
arguably justifies us in treating it as a true reflection of forces in Roman
society and of Roman ideology concerning the conduct of politics,
although even here there may have been a conflict between traditional
norms and current practice (I shall have more to say about this later). In
the study of Roman history understanding of the constitution is also
helpful in various ways. Politics in the Republic were a game played
according to complex rules. Without knowledge of these it is hard to
grasp the behaviour of the contestants. Moreover, knowledge of constitutional norms may help us to choose between accounts given by ancient
(or modern) authorities or to fill gaps in our evidence. Again, a proper
understanding of constitutional norms is a safeguard against anachronistic political judgements based on subjective principles. How otherwise
can we properly evaluate the deaths of Tiberius Gracchus and Julius
Caesar or Cicero's actions against the Catilinarians? There is a further
justification of a quite different type. Polybius' and Cicero's view of the
Republic as a mixed constitution, in which, at its acme, the balance of
elements produced harmony and stability, has had an important effect
on Renaissance and post-Renaissance political theory (see Chapter XIII).
It may be, however, that recent generations have been more impressed by
the myth than the reality. Without an attempt to grasp the reality, this
cannot be assessed.

The fact that the Republic was a natural growth creates also the fundamental problem in analysing it. It was not a written constitution, nor was
it entirely unwritten. Two questions may make the problem clearer.
First, how could Romans during the Republic find out what was proper
constitutional practice in any particular political situation? Secondly,
what were the sources of law, i.e. what was the authority which sanctioned a given constitutional practice?

---

[3] Pol. 6. 9. 10–14, 10. 12–14.

Sources of Legal Authority

By the second century BC the Romans were regularly publishing copies of statutes on bronze in public places, probably 'in a position where it can be correctly read from ground level', as the texts of the statutes themselves say, when referring to the publication of essential notices.[4] Copies were also kept on tablets or papyrus in the treasury or its associated record-office. The purpose of publication has been much discussed recently. To what extent was it merely symbolic, to what extent genuinely intended for information?[5] Clearly, in a certain sense it was the assertion of the law's existence. At the same time it is unlikely that the majority of the Roman people had the capacity to read, still less to understand legal texts. Nevertheless, men with skill in legal language could have understood them and told the others, and those in public office were obliged to read either the public copies on bronze or those in the treasury. The same is true of *senatus consulta*, the minutes of senate-meetings, after a decree had been made and had not been vetoed by tribunes (those vetoed were on occasion written down,[6] but it is unlikely that they were ever displayed in public places). We have copies of a number of senatorial decrees published for diverse reasons in what is intended to be a readable form. Especially important were those which urged magistrates to penalize certain kinds of activity, such as the decree about the Bacchanals of 186 BC and the imperial decree found at Larinum forbidding senators and *equites* to become gladiators.[7]

The authority behind a law was that of the *populus Romanus* or *plebs Romana* voting in an assembly: 'Titus Quinctius Crispinus the consul lawfully asked the people, and the people lawfully resolved.'[8] Polybius reports that the people had the right to make or rescind any law (6. 14. 10) and, he implies, no other body. The authority behind a *senatus consultum* under the Republic was different and less absolute. The decree stated the senate's view on a question put to it, usually recommending a certain course of action to the magistrate who consulted it and perhaps to other magistrates as well. In executing the decree the magistrate enjoyed the legal and moral standing consequent on senatorial approval.

---

[4] *Lex rep.*, lines 65–6 (*JRLR*, p. 104); *frag. Tar.* (*RS* i. 8), 14; *Tab. Heracl.* (*RS* i. 24), 16. See also Jos. *AJ.* 19. 291.   [5] Harris, 1989, 164 ff., 206 ff.; Williamson, 1987, 160–83.

[6] Cic. *de Orat.* 3. 5; *Fam.* 1. 2. 4, 7. 4; 8. 8. 4–8; *Att.* 5. 2. 3.

[7] *CIL* i². 581 = *FIRA* i. 30; Levick, 1983.

[8] *RS* ii. 63 (= Frontinus, *de aquis*, 129). This—from an Augustan law—is the only complete prescript of a Roman statute surviving; for fragments of Republican prescripts see *JRLR*, p. 202.

Although it was dangerous to consider a decree of the senate to be a justification for overriding a law, if there was no conflict with a law, a magistrate, who executed a decree of the senate, added to it his authority as one elected by the people, and this had obvious implications for those subject to him.

A source of public law which was less defined, but essential, was tradition and precedent. Many of the fundamental rules of the constitution were not based on written statutes, for example, the annual election of two consuls, the convening of different types of assembly for different purposes, the very existence and functions of the senate. However, although these elements of the constitution were not based on specific legislation, they may well have been referred to in written laws or *senatus consulta* as existing institutions. They would also have been mentioned in the books of the religious colleges, especially those of the augurs, which were concerned with rules for assemblies. When Cicero was considering in March 49 BC the elections which Caesar planned to hold, he refers to the authority of books ('nos autem in libris habemus . . .') for his assertion that while consuls could preside over the elections of consuls or praetors, praetors could not preside over the election of either consuls or praetors. These books are generally and plausibly identified with augural commentaries, which collected previous augural decisions. There were also the commentaries on constitutional practice written in the later second century BC by C. Sempronius Tuditanus, which would not have any special authority in themselves but doubtless exploited augural lore. Hence we have evidence in the late Republic for written exegesis and consolidation of unwritten constitutional tradition.[9] In other words, there were rules which were written down but did not derive their authority from the writing in which they were recorded.

Constitutional tradition (*instituta, mos, consuetudo*) had under the Republic an enormous spectrum ranging from basic unwritten laws— *ius*, even if not *scriptum*—to what one may term mere *mos*, the way things happened to be done at the time. We may be reminded of the English Common Law, especially in so far as this was held to be the charter for a particular relationship between the crown, parliament, and the people.[10] However, this parallel cannot be pressed, for one reason in

---

[9] Cic. *Att.* 9. 9. 3; also *Div.* 2. 42, 73; *Dom.* 39 on augural commentaries, from which Marcus Messala would have derived his book, *De Auspiciis* (Gell. 13. 15. 3–16. 3). On Tuditanus' commentaries see ibid. 13. 15. 4; *HRR* i. 146–7, frr. 7–8. Note also Iunius Gracchanus' *de potestatibus* (*Dig.* 1. 13. 1. *pr.* (Ulpian); F. B. Bremer, *Iurisprudentia Antehadriana* I, p. 37 ff.).

[10] Pocock , 1987; Weston, 1991. See also Nippel, 1980, 230–6.

particular, that, by contrast with Common Law for which a clearly defined antiquity was a necessary qualification, Roman *mos* was regarded as something in continuous development. 'This also will become established, and what we now defend by precedents (*exempla*) will itself join the ranks of precedents.' So Tacitus in his version of the emperor Claudius' speech on the Gallic senators—and the emperor himself in the preserved text of his speech had included constitutional changes in his panorama of Roman growth. Furthermore, we find in the next book of the *Annals* a much more serious breach of tradition— Claudius' marriage to his niece—justified by the need to accommodate *mos* to the times. This sort of argument was treated as commonplace by Cicero in 66 BC when replying to those who claimed that Pompey's proposed command under Manilius' bill was a breach of precedent and the practices of their ancestors: 'I will not point out here that our ancestors have always followed precedent in peace, but expediency in war and have always adapted the ideas of new policies to suit changing circumstances.'[11]

The ambiguous nature of *mos* is best illustrated by an incident from the period of the Second Punic War. In 209 BC the *pontifex maximus* Publius Licinius Crassus forced a dissolute and prodigal young man, Gaius Valerius Flaccus, to be inaugurated as *flamen Dialis* (an ancient priesthood subject to numerous taboos). The latter, the story goes, immediately threw off his wicked ways and then claimed a seat in the senate in respect of his priesthood—a tradition which had fallen into disuse, allegedly because of the poor calibre of previous incumbents. He was expelled from the senate by Lucius Licinius Crassus, the brother of the *pontifex maximus*, who happened to be praetor at the time, and in consequence he appealed to the tribunes. The praetor's argument was that 'law did not depend on obsolete precedents from ancient annals but on the usage established by all the most recent customs'. However, the tribunes decided that 'it was equitable that the negligence of previous holders of the priesthood should detract from them and not from the status of the priesthood itself', and they brought Flaccus back into the senate amid the approval of both the senators inside and the crowd outside. The implication of the praetor's conduct was that recent precedent tended to prevail over what was more remote and that *mos* was expected to change. The young *flamen Dialis*, however, showed that one could win

---

[11] Tac. *Ann.* 11. 24; *ILS* 212, col. I, 24 ff.; Tac. *Ann.* 12. 6; Cic. *Imp. Pomp.* 60 (in the '*praeteritio*' the argument is emphasized by being passed over).

arguments by citing ancient tradition, if other circumstances were favourable.[12]

Jochen Bleicken has tried to create a theoretical model for the development of *mos*,[13] which is usefully provocative, even if it cannot do justice to all the complexities. For him the early Republic was a period, in which *lex*—written law, such as the Twelve Tables—and *mos* were not in conflict, but were complementary aspects of an aristocratic regime based on consensus—a golden age, one might say. *Mos* and *consuetudo* described simply practice—whatever was done for whatever reason with whatever authority. We may object immediately that it is doubtful if such a golden age ever existed. Bleicken's picture of an ideal consensus, social unity, and internal peace does not correspond well with the Romans' own conception of the early Republic. However, for the sake of argument at least, we may concede that there was a time when there was no essential conflict between written statute (*lex*) and unwritten tradition.

Bleicken's second stage is one in which drastic changes in law (*ius*) were required in order to cope with the ever more complex demands on the regime. New norms tended to be introduced by statute (*lex*), but, when this did not occur, recent *mos* came to supplement, even supplant, earlier *mos*. Bleicken's example is the process by which the capital trials for treason (*perduellio*) laid down by the Twelve Tables were supplemented by tribunician prosecutions for a fine (*multa*).[14] I myself am not sure that prosecutions by a magistrate for a fine were not envisaged in the Twelve Tables. However, what does seem to have been an important development in this field, not dependent on statute, is the regular appearance of the tribune as the prosecutor in both capital and non-capital cases, which must have been the result of the evolution of the tribune into an element of the government from the fourth century onwards.

By this time *mos* appears as something which is separate from and hence potentially may be in conflict with *lex*.[15] Moreover, in the revolutionary period which followed, when aristocratic consensus was fragile,

[12] Livy, 27. 8. 4–10. See also Sall. *Cat.* 51. 37–40 for the argument that tradition was expected to change, deployed in the speech assigned to Julius Caesar.

[13] Bleicken, 1975, 368 ff.

[14] *RS* ii. 40, *Tab.* IX. 1–2 = Cic. *Leg.* 3. 11 and 44; cf. Livy, 26. 2. 7–3. 9. See Lintott, 1987, 44–8.

[15] See e.g. Livy, 26. 3. 8. One might usefully compare here the process whereby English Common Law developed from being simply the law regularly enforced by the King's courts to something distinct from the law of statutes (Pollock and Maitland, 1968, i. 176–8).

it became the norm to deal with new needs by legislation (when this was resisted, we find legislators even requiring oaths of obedience from magistrates and senators).[16] The consequence was that *mos* by contrast came to be regarded as preponderantly ancient tradition, idealized by conservatives as a counterpoise to new developments which, in their view, were rooted in corrupt statutes. This point of view lies at the heart of Tacitus' sketch of the growth of legislation in *Annals* 3. 27–8, where the Twelve Tables are the end of equitable law, and legislation subsequent to them is inspired by ambition and jealousy with a view to self-promotion or injury to rivals. Custom tended to become a conservative catchword in so far as it was used to describe actions in opposition to the *populares*, even those taken after new expedients like the *senatus consultum ultimum*.[17]

It should be clear from this that the constitution of the Republic was not something fixed and clear-cut, but evolved according to the Romans' needs by more means than one. It was also inevitably controversial: there were frequently at least two positions which could be taken on major issues. What must also be evident is the most likely way that young Romans from the élite learnt about the constitution. Occasionally, they might have referred to the text of a law or *senatus consultum* or part of a religious commentary, but for the most part they would have learnt from the daily practice of political life and from what was said by orators on controversial issues. A further source of education for them from the early second century BC onwards was the annals of Rome, which, even in the works of the early Roman historians (*c.*200 BC), contained stories of political crises, some of which seem shaped, if not invented, to explain difficult constitutional problems. This to a great extent foreshadows how scholars since the Renaissance have studied the Republic. We read the texts of laws and decrees of the senate, we study the fragments of learned commentaries to be found in antiquarian sources, but frequently our best guide to constitutional practice is to read in ancient narratives what actually happened over a period, and, where there was conflict, to discover, as far as we can, in what terms the issues were formulated at the time.

It may be helpful to differentiate between possible approaches to the constitution of the Republic. One is an analysis of how things worked in the last two centuries of the Republic, which can be achieved by a positivistic study of political history. A second is to trace developments

---

[16] See VRR 139–40; JRLR 243–4.

[17] See e.g. Cic. *Cat.* 1. 27–8; 2. 3.

from their origins in the early Republic or even before. This will inevitably have a large component of myth, as it does in our basic sources, Livy and Dionysius of Halicarnassus, both on account of the lack of sound information available to the earliest Roman annalists and because those who wrote history tended to have a contemporary political agenda. A third approach is to theorize about the nature of the constitution. Whatever the merits of his actual achievement, Polybius deserves the credit for being the first to have actually attempted to put Roman political behaviour in a conceptual framework. Without such a framework we are likely to lose our way in a mass of data; with the aid of one we may make fruitful comparisons with other constitutions. It is significant that the best known and fundamental modern attempt to give an account of the constitution, Theodor Mommsen's *Römisches Staatsrecht*, is highly theoretical, in spite of the assembly of source-material in the footnotes.

All three approaches will be used in what follows. In view of the uncertainties about the origins of the Republic, I will commence the story, homerically, in the middle—that is, in the first half of the second century BC, where one can tread on fairly solid ground, thanks to the existence of Polybius' analysis and of a major part of the annalistic tradition in surviving books of Livy.

Additional Note: Because this is a book about politics and public life I do not discuss here what were for lawyers important sources of private law—the edicts of magistrates and the legal opinions of those skilled in the law (*responsa prudentium*). Regarding the former, in addition to the general freedom conferred on magistrates to exercise their authority in the public interest (to be discussed in Chapter VII), at an ill-defined point in the middle Republic a *lex Aebutia* seems to have conferred on praetors the right to adapt the legal processes laid down in the Twelve Tables and later statutes and to create new legal actions. However, there is no equivalent to this authority under the Republic in public matters.

II

A Roman Political Year

Livy's narrative ebbs and flows between politics at Rome and war or diplomacy overseas. Towards the end of a Roman year, which until the last day of December 154 BC ran from the Ides of March to 14 March following,[1] the tide flowed in the direction of Rome. So at the beginning of the winter of 190/89 two proconsuls made their way to Rome, Manius Acilius Glabrio, fresh from his victories in Greece, and Quintus Minucius Thermus from Liguria. The senate granted the supreme military honour of a triumph to the former (he had defeated Antiochus the Great in Greece as well as the Aetolians), but not to the latter (37. 46. 1–3).[2] Further news was brought to the senate and people of a defeat in Spain and complaints from the colonists at Placentia and Cremona about the depopulation of the towns. The senate decreed that the consul Laelius should enrol six thousand new families for the colonies and that the praetor Cotta should see to the election of a commission of three to settle them on the land (37. 46. 7–11). Laelius, when he returned from Gaul to hold the consular elections, not only recruited new colonists for Cremona and Placentia but secured the approval of the senate for the foundation of two more colonies (47. 1–2).[3] Letters then arrived from Lucius Aemilius Regillus, a praetor commanding the fleet in the Aegean, about a naval victory over Antiochus and the crossing of the consul Lucius Scipio into Asia, which were duly celebrated by sacrifices (Antiochus was to be decisively defeated on land shortly after the beginning of the new Roman consular year and five to six further weeks would have been needed to bring that news to Rome).

At the end of the Roman year elections were held for the consuls and

---

[1] For the change in the start of the consular year see Cassiodorus, *Chron. sub anno a.u. c.*601, contrast e.g. Livy, 33. 43. 1.

[2] The Roman calendar, on account of the failure to insert sufficient intercalary months, was about four months in advance of the solar year at this point. See Briscoe, 1981, 22–26; Derow, 1973.

[3] Their actual foundation required a law passed by the people and the election by the people of a commission (see below).

praetors.[4] One candidate for the consulship, Marcus Aemilius Lepidus, was allegedly unpopular because he had left his province in Sicily without asking the senate's permission. Only Marcus Fulvius Nobilior achieved a majority of the centuries in the election and he was duly returned. The following day, as consul, he secured the election of a colleague.[5] Six praetors were elected. The first business of the consular year was the rejection of an embassy from the Aetolians seeking a negotiated peace rather than a surrender. Following a motion by the commander who had defeated them, Acilius Glabrio, the ambassadors were told to leave Italy within fifteen days and not to return except with the permission of the Roman commander who was in their area and the escort of a Roman envoy (37. 49).

The consuls then consulted the senate about the provinces. The senate decided that the consular provinces were to be Asia and Aetolia, the consuls to draw lots to decide which should have which. These were the areas of most important military activity.[6] Further decrees were made permitting the consuls to levy Roman, Latin, and allied troops in Italy and to re-equip the fleet which had been prepared against the Aetolians. Specific instructions were also given for the Aetolian war to be extended into the island of Cephallenia. The consul who was to undertake the Aetolian war was also urged, in so far as the public interest allowed, to return to Rome for the elections not only of the next round of annual magistrates but of censors: he was to let the senate know if he could not come.

Lots were then drawn not only for the consular provinces but for those of the praetors. There must have been some preliminary discussion of the latter, not mentioned by Livy, because, although there was a

---

[4] Down to Sulla's dictatorship these elections seem to have been usually left to the last moment—i.e. the month preceding the new consular year, February–March, and later, with the change of the beginning of the consular year, December. In the late Republic the normal date was July. (Bibulus' delay of the elections of 59 to 18 Oct. (Cic. *Att.* 2. 20. 6) was exceptional.)

[5] If a consul found himself without a colleague, he was not compelled to hold an election to fill the vacancy (Mommsen, *Staatsr.* i. 29). For example in 68, after the death of one of the originally elected consuls, L. Caecilius Metellus, and of the suffect, Cn. Servilius Vatia, Q. Marcius Rex remained sole consul for most of the year (Dio 36. 4. 1). Nevertheless there would usually be pressure on the surviving consul to fill the vacancy (see App. *BCiv.* 1. 78. 359 for pressure on Cn. Papirius Carbo in 84), unless the time involved was short. Occasionally in the first three centuries of the Republic the consul chose to nominate a dictator instead. Although *dixit*, an emendation for the MS *duxit*, might indicate direct nomination, the language of the rest of the passage, suggesting the unpopularity of the other candidates, is an argument for a second election.

[6] Before Sulla's dictatorship the consul's principal duty was to undertake Rome's major wars (*Staatsr.* ii. 1. 93–4; Giovannini, 1983, 66 ff.). See below, Chap. VII with nn. 49 ff.

regular pattern of praetorian posts—two branches of jurisdiction in the city and the overseas administration of Sicily, Sardinia (with Corsica), and the two Spanish provinces—some variation occurred when there was a need for magistrates elsewhere. On this occasion the two juris-dictions at Rome (those of the *praetor urbanus* and *peregrinus*)[7] were combined to allow a praetor for the fleet and the replacement of all the governors of the permanent overseas provinces. Provision was made for supplementary levies for the Spanish governors; the governors of Sicily and Sardinia were required to raise two extra tithes of corn from their provinces for the supply of the armies in Aetolia and Asia. (37. 50)

Before the praetors could set out for their provinces a political crisis was created by the fact that the new governor of Sardinia, Quintus Fabius Pictor, held the priesthood of *flamen Quirinalis*. The *pontifex maximus*, who held ultimate authority over all other priesthoods, pre-vented Fabius leaving his priestly duties at Rome, following a precedent from the last year of the First Punic War, when the then *pontifex max-imus* had prevented the departure of one of the consuls to the fleet in Sicily. Livy's account of what followed is summary (37. 51), but we can to some extent deduce what happened from other parallel disputes.[8] After discussion in the senate and public meetings and attempts by magistrates and the *pontifex maximus* to use their legal powers on each other, the *pontifex maximus* seized pledges from the praetor and inflicted a fine on him, against which the latter appealed to the tribunes and also to the people (*provocare*). An assembly was held, probably convened by the tribunes, which resolved that the praetor should obey the *pontifex max-imus* with the consolation of the remission of the fine. When the praetor in pique tried to abdicate his office, the senate decreed that he should not, and allocated him the jurisdiction between citizens and foreigners, which had earlier been amalgamated with the jurisdiction between citizens.

After a succession of rumours firm news arrived about the victory over Antiochus. Subsequently, an embassy came from the king escorted by Marcus Cotta, and there were further embassies from allies of Rome, the Rhodians and king Eumenes II of Pergamum in person. In

---

[7] The *praetor urbanus* ('qui inter cives ius dicit') undertook jurisdiction over legal actions brought by one Roman citizen against another, the *peregrinus* ('qui inter peregrinos ius dicit', according to the terminology of our Republican texts) over those where one of the parties was not a Roman. See *Staatsr.* ii. 1. 196 ff.; Chap. VII with n. 59.

[8] Cf. Val. Max. 1. 1. 2; Livy, *Per.* 19; Festus, 462–4L; Livy, 40. 42. 8–13; Cic. *Phil.* 11. 18; on which see *Staatsr.* ii. 1. 57–9; Bleicken, 1959, 341 ff.; Kunkel, 1962, 21 ff.; Chap. VIII with n. 21.

consequence, there were first solemn thanksgivings to the gods, *supplicationes*, on the instructions to the senate. The senate then heard the king and the embassies. The chief issue in dispute was the future status of the Greek cities liberated from the hegemony of Antiochus. Eumenes argued that, unless the Romans were to take over the area as a province, he should have them as his subjects, as a reward for the loyalty of his dynasty to Rome; the Rhodians argued that it was in line with previous Roman policy towards the Greeks, and would confer immense honour on Rome, if they were to be declared free. In consequence the domains of Antiochus were divided into two dependencies, one being granted to Eumenes, the other to the Rhodians, with the proviso that only those formerly subject to Pergamum should pay tribute to Eumenes and that the rest should have local autonomy, and freedom from tribute and corvées.[9]

The senate was again in action replacing the governor of Further Spain, when news came that the original appointee, Baebius, had been killed after a Ligurian attack on his way to Spain. During the summer arrangements went forward for settling one of the colonies in Boian territory proposed the previous year. This was Bononia (Bologna). We only hear in Livy of the foundation itself, but a popular vote would have been required, following the previous year's *senatus consultum*, to elect the customary three-man commission (*triumviri coloniae deducendae*) and to create a constitution for the colony (37. 57. 1–8).[10]

Towards the end of the year politics were dominated by the contest for election to the censorship. There were six candidates for two places, among them Acilius Glabrio, consul in 191 and victor over Antiochus and the Aetolians. He is said to have been the favourite, thanks to his distribution of money deriving from his victories to the people. Allegedly prompted by his rivals, two tribunes accused him before the people of having retained money and booty seized in Antiochus' camp, without solemnly bringing it to the Capitol in his triumph or handing it over to the treasury in some other way. (There was as yet no statute about peculation and norms regarding the disposal of booty were a matter of

---

[9] 37. 52–6. Livy's account of the terms (56. 1–6) contains detail not to be found in the parallel account of Polybius (21. 18–24), which must derive from a conflicting annalistic source.

[10] Such a constitution in this period would in many ways reflect that of the mother city, Rome. This may be exemplified in the *lex Osca* on the tablet from Bantia (*RS* i. 13), if it is to be dated before the Social War, since it is likely to be modelled on the constitution of the Latin colony of Venusia. On Livy's omission here see Badian, 1996, 188; on the formalities of colonization Gargola, 1995, chs. 2–4.

dispute. However, Glabrio was not the first to have been accused of improperly appropriating too large a share of the proceeds of a victory.)[11] One of Glabrio's competitors, Marcus Porcius Cato, was conspicuous among the witnesses. Although a fine of 100,000 *asses* was proposed (i.e. 10,000 *denarii*), the main thrust of the accusation was to bring Glabrio into disrepute and, when he desisted from his candidature, the accusation was dropped in the course of the third hearing.[12] Titus Quinctius Flamininus and Marcus Claudius Marcellus were in consequence elected censors at the end of the consular year, when Fulvius Nobilior returned from Greece.[13]

During the early part of the winter L. Aemilius Regillus returned from the Aegean to be voted a naval triumph, and later L. Scipio returned from Asia to hold a particularly spectacular triumph for his victory on land over Antiochus in the last days of the consular year 189/8 (37. 58–9). About the same time M. Fulvius Nobilior returned to hold the consular and praetorian elections, in which he is said to have prevented the election of his enemy Lepidus. He subsequently returned to Greece, when the provinces of the consuls were both prorogued.[14] Livy's final notices for the year concern dedications of statues and ornamental shields—among them a number by aediles who had secured the condemnation of grain-dealers for causing corn-shortages—and the repetition of the two most important Roman games, presumably as result of unfavourable omens observed (38. 35. 4–6).

As Tacitus was later to remark (*Ann.* 4. 32), the traditional matter of the annalists was immense wars, the storming of cities, the routing or capture of foreign kings, or, if on occasion they turned their attention to internal matters, it was the struggles of consuls with tribunes, agrarian and grain laws, and strife between aristocracy and plebs. The domination of the political narrative by war and its needs is in part the convention of the historian, but not entirely. The chief function of the consuls, and an important function of the praetors, was that of being military leaders. The authority of the senate was most clearly demonstrated when it acted as a forum for the discussion of foreign and military policy. As the preceding narrative has suggested, Rome's military needs determined

[11] The story of the election is in Livy, 37. 57. 9–58. 2. On M. Livius Salinator, *cos.* 219, see Livy, 22. 35. 3; *de Vir. Ill.* 50. 1; on the rights and wrongs in the distribution of booty, Shatzman, 1972.

[12] Astin, 1978, 3 f.

[13] See Livy, 38. 35. 1–3. The need for a magistrate with consular authority for the election of censors may be inferred from Messala's account of the auspices (Gell. 13. 15. 4).

[14] Livy, 38. 35. 1–3. This follows a long section on war and diplomacy abroad.

the shape of the political year. This was, moreover, a year in the miraculous period, when, in Polybius' words 'almost all the inhabited world was conquered and fell under the single dominion of Rome'. It was also the time when in Sallust's view the Romans lived in the greatest political unity (*concordia*).[15] Nevertheless, we do find glimpses of the working of the constitution in domestic matters.

Overseas it is the great authority of the individual commander that takes the eye, not only in the field but in diplomacy. Roman allies may make approaches to the senate at their own discretion; defeated enemies like Antiochus send representatives under an escort provided by the commander; when the Aetolians try to do so without escort they are rebuffed. The combination of political and military authority in the senior magistrates means that they not only constitute a strong executive but can exercise a powerful influence on policy at Rome both in office and in its immediate aftermath, as Laelius did over colonization in Cisalpine Gaul and Glabrio over the Aetolians. At Rome it appears that the senate is the focus of politics. It is here that not only issues of foreign policy are debated but also matters like the quarrel between the praetor and the *pontifex maximus*. The senate is an accepted sounding-board and referee over the boundaries between the authorities of the members of the executive, who would also for the most part be members of it.

However, it would be wrong to think it a unique or supreme authority. Indeed, it is characteristic of the Republic that there were multiple points of legitimate decision-making, which were normally not to be overturned by some higher authority (something which was largely to disappear under the monarchy of the Caesars). The magistrates—including the aediles, tribunes, and quaestors, whose annual elections are not usually mentioned by Livy, and the commissioners for founding or refounding colonies—owe their position to the people in an assembly. The story of the censorial election shows how the popular vote might be subject to what were considered improper influences,[16] but it also shows that such influences were not necessarily decisive. In the consular elections of 189/8 the presiding consul himself is said to be responsible for the failure of one of the candidates. We do not know whether this simply refers to persuasion of the electorate or to the exploitation of some technicality of the constitution. It is in any case clear from other evidence that presiding magistrates did not always get their way.[17]

---

[15] Pol. 1. 1. 5; Sall. *Hist.* 1. 11M.

[16] See Lintott, 1990a.

[17] See Livy, 35. 10. 9 (and contrast 39. 32. 5–12), with Rilinger, 1976, 143ff.

The assembly was the forum of the political accusation directed against Acilius Glabrio. Earlier, as a result of Fabius Pictor's appeal to the tribunes and his *provocatio*, it was in the assembly that his dispute with the *pontifex maximus* was finally resolved. Moreover, the accusations by the aediles against hoarders of grain, briefly alluded to by Livy, would have been conducted in an assembly. As for legislation by the assembly, we have no example in Livy's text for this year, but a law would have been required for the foundation of Bononia. Another source tells us of a *lex Terentia* granting full citizenship to the children of freedmen, which seems to have been passed in this year.[18] Matters of citizen-rights were reserved for the assembly, as Livy's account of the following year shows. A bill to give full Roman voting rights to the citizens of Fundi, Formiae, and Arpinum, proposed by the tribune Gaius Valerius Tappo, was threatened with a veto by four of his colleagues on the ground that it had not been discussed in the senate. The obstructing tribunes were informed that the grant of voting rights was a matter for the assembly, not the senate, and they abandoned their veto.[19]

By contrast, we should realize that Livy's account at best gives a brief impression of the powers granted to magistrates in the city. We have a single instance of the tribunes acting as legal referees and the focus for appeals and only a hint of the aediles' function as supervisors of the welfare of the city of Rome. Nor is Livy concerned here with the regular functions of the censors in assigning status and determining matters of public finance.

Finally, although the evidence is not so rich in this year as it is in others, the interweaving of religion in political life is patent. Apart from the *cause célèbre* of Fabius Pictor, Livy mentions *supplicationes* to the gods voted in response to military successes—rites which were carried out by the consul—triumphal processions, the repetitions of the games, and a number of dedications of statues to gods. Although the importance of the annals as a source for the constitution is cumulative, and the historian is forced to extrapolate from one year and one period to another, the narrative of even a single year is indicative of the character of the Republic.

---

[18] Plut. *Flamininus* 18. 2. [19] 38. 36. 7–9; cf. 27. 5. 7; 41. 9. 9.

III

Polybius and the Constitution

Polybius' analysis of the Roman constitution is an excursus, placed in his sixth book as an explanation of why the Romans did not collapse after their series of devastating defeats at the hands of Hannibal at the beginning of the Second Punic War. He remarks that there had been some changes between then and his time of writing but they were not significant (6. 11. 13). My present chapter has more than one purpose. Polybius provides a theoretical schema, a map of the constitution, which may be criticized in the light of facts otherwise known to us, and thus help us to construct our own map.[1] We may also in my view see reflected in it Roman discourse and perception of their constitution[2]—something of which Polybius would have been well aware through his enforced stay at Rome and friendship with Roman aristocrats. It may be thought that Polybius' form of analysis, based as it is on constitutional organs and their relationships, is inadequate to tackle the realities of the Roman Republic. However, if one sees it as an analysis based on centres of power (monarchic, aristocratic, and democratic), such an objection seems invalid. Nor can one accuse Polybius of being narrowly legalistic, when he gives space to the Roman army and religion. He himself warns us that his account is a simplification and that we should judge him by what he actually says and not by what he leaves out (6. 11. 3–8).

Polybius conceived the Roman constitution as nearly unique in being a 'mixed constitution' which had not been created by a lawgiver, as Sparta's had been by Lycurgus, but had developed over time in a biological fashion, the only parallel being the constitution of Carthage. After his explanation of the cycle of 'pure' constitutions—which proceeded from a monarchy based on force through constitutional monarchy, aristocracy, oligarchy, democracy, brutalized democracy (*cheirokratia*) to tyranny—and the now largely lost sketch of the Roman constitution's

---

[1] Fundamental for this approach are Walbank, 1957, 673–97 (a more summary overview in Walbank, 1972, 130–56), and von Fritz, 1954, 155–83, 220–57.

[2] See especially Nicolet, 1974.

past history, Polybius comes to its present nature. (I shall discuss the relation of this to other political theories about the mixed constitution in a subsequent chapter).[3] For Polybius the powers of the consuls, the senate, and the people are respectively the monarchic, the aristocratic, and the democratic elements of this mixed constitution.

The consuls are described in two spheres of action, at home, before they lead out an army, and as commanders in the field (6. 12. 1–8). They are said to be in charge of everything, when in Rome. The other magistrates are their subordinates and obey them, except the tribunes. The consuls control the approach of embassies to the senate; they select business to be discussed by the senate, and they carry out its decrees. In war they have almost arbitrary power over Roman soldiers of all ranks and over allies, with full authority to punish and to spend as much money as they think fit. The picture is, as Polybius has warned us, simplified, but is it over-simplified to the point of being misleading?

About the consuls' powers in the field there is little need for argument except over one point. The ability to draw money at will from the treasury through the quaestor—something which Polybius reiterates (6. 12. 8; 13. 2; 14. 3)—is not something attested as a norm by other evidence.[4] Moreover, if we assume that the consul possessed this ability when in the field, as the order of Polybius' argument suggests, this seems inconsistent with his later point that the consul is dependent on the senate for supplies when in the field (6. 15. 5). On the whole consuls would have consulted the senate, and anyone who expected to stay in command after the lapse of his original annual magistracy would have been unwise to take money without consultation. Regarding the consul's position at Rome more questions arise. First, the omission of any mention of the praetors means that Polybius has passed over a magistrate who can act in place of the consul in convening the senate and the assemblies and in passing decrees and laws. This substitution for the consul by the praetor is attested as a norm in Polybius' time.[5] There is also a clear example of a bill brought to the assembly by a praetor, when the consuls had not yet left Rome in 208 BC.[6] One cannot therefore

---

[3] See below, Chap. XII.

[4] Polybius was probably influenced by the example given by Scipio Africanus (probably in his second consulship of 194), when he seized the keys of the treasury from his quaestor at a time when a law or tradition (*nomos*) required the doors to be shut—a story recounted by Polybius himself (23. 14. 5–6). See *Staatsr.* ii. 1. 131–2.

[5] Livy, 24. 9. 5; 27. 5. 16; 33. 21. 9; *Staatsr.* ii. 1. 129–30.

[6] Livy, 27. 23. 7. See also 42. 21. 8. Later, there is the example of Q. Fufius Calenus passing a law about the separate registration of jury-votes in 59 (Dio 38. 8. 1), when both Caesar and Bibulus were at Rome.

defend Polybius by arguing that, since praetors took no political initiatives when either consul was available at Rome, their power did not detract from that of the consuls.

A more important point is that Polybius leaves the impression that the other magistrates were subordinates to the consuls in everything they did, as if they were their subordinates on campaign, and this is clearly not so. The praetor's jurisdiction was essentially autonomous, even if appeal could be made to the consul or tribunes against it (see Chap. VII with nn. 30 and 67, Chap. VIII with nn. 24 ff.). The aediles might find that they needed the support of consular authority in managing the games, but, in principle, here—as in their supervision of markets, roads, water, fires, and funeral arrangements—they had a particular sphere of authority, in which the consuls normally had no part (see Chap. VIII with nn. 37 ff.). The only true subordinate of a consul in civil administration was his own quaestor.

And yet one is forced to ask whether Polybius' simplified picture is not what some Romans in his day claimed to be the dimensions of consular power (one might cite as a parallel the extremely tendentious statements by Cicero during the period of the civil wars about the consul's powers in the provinces—argued by certain scholars to explain the later powers assumed by Augustus between 27 and 23 BC).[7] And this brings us close to the concept of an all-powerful *imperium*, which was the foundation of Mommsen's view of the Roman Republic.[8] For him this power was originally only bounded by annual tenure and collegiality; later it came to be diffused by the multiplicity of magistracies and weakened by the obstruction of the tribunes. Yet it is uncertain whether there had ever been an authentic tradition at Rome for a consul to give orders like a monarch within the city boundary, as he was permitted to do in the field. Indeed, one reason given for the invention of the dictator in the Roman Republic was that, irrespective of the fact that he had no colleague, he could behave in an authoritarian way in the city, where a consul could not.[9]

The power of the senate for Polybius (6. 13) is first illustrated by its power over what went in and went out of the treasury—absolute, apart from the overriding discretion of the consul. It is unlikely that he

---

[7] Cic. *Phil.* 4. 9; *Att.* 8. 15. 3; Pelham, 1911, 66–8; Jones, 1960a, 6.

[8] *Staatsr.* i. 6 ff.; 24 ff.

[9] It is Dionysius of Halicarnassus (*AR* 5. 70–7) who stresses the dictator's capacity to repress civil unrest. For Cicero (*Rep.* 1. 63, 2. 56) and Livy (2. 18 ff.) his job is to provide a single commander in major wars. However, according to Livy (2. 18. 8–9, cf. 29. 11) the effect of the office was to instil fear into the plebs. See also Chap. VII with n. 71.

believed that the senate could prevent money due to the treasury—from taxation, sales, or fines—being actually deposited there. It would seem rather that he is thinking about general policy over taxation. Yet taxation and other matters of finance were sometimes governed by legislation passed by the assembly.[10] Polybius, then, has stated a norm as if it was an absolute, following perhaps a polemical statement by some Roman authority, to which a contrary position could be taken.[11] Regarding outgoings, it was indeed the rule that magistrates were dependent on the senate for financial provision in their provinces. As for the senate's determination of the grants made to the censors for public works contracts, this is confirmed as at least current practice in Polybius' day by annalistic evidence relating to 179 BC and later.[12]

The second aspect of the senate's power is its authority in Italy over crimes requiring public supervision—treachery, conspiracy, poisoning, and assassination. This is an obvious allusion to the senate's intervention over matters like the Bacchanals, the alleged poisoners, and the *sicarii* in southern Italy.[13] A further concern is the problems of individuals or cities which require censure or physical support or a garrison. This too is well documented in evidence of the period. We hear of censure in the *senatus consultum de Tiburtibus* of 159 BC; physical assistance against outside attacks, civil strife, slave-revolts, even a plague of locusts, not to mention the settling of disputes between cities.[14] The interesting point here is that these powers, which amounted to instructing magistrates to take the appropriate action in the relevant area, seem to have constituted a recent accretion of senatorial authority, since the senate took cognizance of matters outside as well as inside the *ager Romanus*, largely in response to requests from those in trouble, but not entirely, as the Bacchanal investigation showed.

The third aspect of the senate's power in Polybius' account is the reception of embassies in Rome and the despatch of embassies overseas

---

[10] e.g. the laws about the leasing of the *ager Campanus* in 210 and 172 (Livy, 27. 11. 8; 42. 19. 1), the *lex Minucia de triumviris mensariis* (Livy, 23. 21. 6), the *lex [?Fla]minia minus solvendi* (Festus, 470L), the *lex Sempronia de pecunia credita* of 193 (Livy, 35. 7. 4–5).

[11] See Cic. *Vat.* 36 for a similar exaggerated claim.

[12] Livy, 40. 46. 16; 44. 16. 9.

[13] See *SC de Bacchanalibus* (*FIRA* i, no. 30); Livy 39. 14–19 and 41. 5–6; 40. 19. 9–10, 37. 4, and 43. 2; *Per.* 48. The evidence is collected and discussed by McDonald, 1944. A later example of senatorial intervention is attested by Cic. *Brut.* 85 ff. (the murders by the slaves of the *publicani* in the Silva Sila).

[14] Censure attested by *SC de Tiburtibus* (*FIRA* i, no. 33); physical assistance by Livy, 30. 1. 10; 32. 26. 4–18; 33. 36. 1–3; 41. 27. 3; 42. 10. 8; 43. 1. 5–6, 17. 1; settling of disputes by Livy, 45. 13. 10–11; Cic. *Off.* 1. 33; Val. Max. 7. 3. 4; *ILLRP* 476–7. See McDonald, 1944.

to solve problems, reconcile peoples, give instructions, receive sur-
renders, and to declare war.[15] This is indeed a well-chosen illustration.
For what is characteristic of the embassies sent out is that the senate or
its representatives, the *legati*, are not merely acting as a deliberative but
as an executive body. One might object to this point that, although it is
indisputable that the senate made policy, any executive action is carried
out by the ambassadors or by magistrates in the area. Moreover, ambassadors had discretion and did not merely act as the senate's mouthpieces:
in 168 BC Popilius Laenas forced Antiochus IV to agree to leave Egypt
before moving from the spot on which he stood—a procedure which can
hardly have been foreseen in the senate; in 196 BC the commission
appointed to settle Greece developed a policy of freedom for the Greeks
which exploited to the full the discretion they had been granted by
the senate.[16] However, it remains true that senatorial decisions in
these matters were generally regarded as authoritative and not mere
advice.

Polybius then turns to the powers of the people (6. 14). With the
senate having so much power over matters of detail, especially over
income and expenditure, the consuls having full discretion in war-
preparations and in the field, what part, he asks, is left for them?
Something of the greatest weight—the control of honour and punishment (*timē* and *timōria*).[17] For Polybius honour and punishment
controlled *dunasteiai* (i.e. tyrannies and narrow oligarchies), republics,
and in short the whole of human life. Any community which did not
take measures to achieve this discrimination between those deserving
honour and those deserving punishment was not able to handle properly
anything subject to its authority. The people, he says, try men often for
fines, whenever the amount is significant, and especially those who have
held the highest offices, and it alone tries for the death-penalty (6. 14. 6).
Here, in my view we must supply as object 'those who have held the

---

[15] The evidence for these activities is enormous. Chap. II illustrates the richness of a
single year. For a recent discussion of foreign embassies with earlier bibliography see
Linderski, 1995. For the senate's functions in declaring war see Rich, 1976.

[16] Pol. 29. 27. 1–8; 18. 44 and 46. 5–7 and 15. On the activities of commissions of ten *legati*
see Schleussner, 1978, 34 ff., who stresses their capacity for executive action as well as
negotiation: they did have freedom to manoeuvre but within guidelines laid down beforehand.

[17] According to Cicero (*Ad Brut.* 23. 3) it was a maxim of Solon's that a community was
held together by two things, *praemium* and *poena*. Walbank on Pol. 6. 14. 4 cites as a precedent, Plato, *Laws* 3. 697a–b referring to *timē* and *atimia*. It is interesting that in the
Discorsi Machiavelli immediately after introducing a discussion of the Roman Republic as
a mixed constitution in chapters (1. 2–6) clearly influenced by Polybius moves on to the
theme of criminal justice (1. 7–8). See below, Chap. XIII with nn. 12 ff.

highest offices'.[18] After a brief digression on how defendants about to be condemned, 'with only one tribe left to vote', can go into exile,[19] Polybius talks briefly of the people's power over elections, the ratification and abrogation of laws, and decisions of war, peace, and alliance.

The following three chapters (6. 15–17) are an analysis of the powers of opposition and co-operation available to the three parts of the constitution. The consul (15), though he appears to have full powers when he goes out to war, needs senatorial co-operation if he is to get clothing and supplies in the field. If the senate shirks its duty and is obstructive, he is paralysed (15. 4–6). He is in the senate's power when he seeks prorogation (6–7)—or a triumph (7–8), since he cannot carry out the latter properly if the senate denies him support and funds. Furthermore, he requires popular good will, if his settlements are to be ratified and he is to survive prosecution. The senate (16), with all the power that it has, has still to rely on the people to ratify the most wide-ranging and important penal investigations of political crimes, for which the punishment is capital (16. 1). The people can also pass laws limiting senators' powers and privileges (16. 2–3). Moreover, the senate's policies cannot be executed and it cannot even hold meetings, if there is a single tribune's veto, and the tribunes are obliged always to carry out the people's decisions and set their sights on its wishes.

As for the people, they are dependent on the senate because of the enterprises contracted out by the censors throughout Italy for construction or management—harbours, market-gardens, mines, country-estates. These are all undertaken by the common people and almost everyone is involved in the buying of these contracts and their execution. The senate has the power to grant extra time and lighten the terms of a contract, if there is a disaster, and to release people from contracts, if

---

[18] Otherwise this statement will be inconsistent with what Polybius has said at 6. 13. 4, which asserts that the senate handles capital jurisdiction in Italy (this last term encompasses allied peoples but must include also the Roman countryside and Rome itself, the original focus of the Bacchanal inquiry). Note also 6. 16. 2, stating that the senate cannot complete the greatest and most all-embracing investigations, involving the death-penalty, without the ratification of the people, which shows that the senate is not permitted to act alone. See also Lintott, 1972, esp. 257–8 and Chap. IX with nn. 30 ff.

[19] Although in the late Republic the final votes in capital trials before the people were expected to take place in the *comitia centuriata* (Cic. *Dom.* 45), we cannot presume that 'tribe' here is simply an error for 'century', since the picture of successive voting, while plausible for the tribal assemblies, is only conceivable in the *comitia centuriata*, if the vote was tied after all the *classes* and their associated centuries had voted and only the century of *capite censi* was left to vote (see Chap. V with nn. 77 and 91). Plautus (*Capt.* 475) also depicts condemnation of defendants in a tribe, but he may have in mind non-capital trials.

they are incapable of fulfilling them (6. 17. 1–6).[20] Most important, the senate provides judges in most public and private matters which give rise to major complaints (ibid. 7–8).[21]

In consequence of the power that each of the elements has to damage or co-operate with the others, this structure performs as it should in face of all circumstances. For when an external threat forces them to act with a common purpose, their instinct to compete means that nothing is left undone and their co-operation ensures that it is done in time. Again, when they are free from danger and wallowing in success and prosperity, so tending to insolence and arrogance, the constitution provides a remedy. For any overpowerful and overambitious element finds that it is not independent but is checked by the countertension and opposition of the other elements (6. 18).

Such is the core of the analysis. Polybius goes on to consider the Roman military systems and subsequently to make comparisons with the constitutions of Crete, Sparta, and Carthage. In this last section he expands his conception of Rome in several important respects. By comparison with Sparta, the Roman constitution was better suited to empire-building and more 'dynamic'; that is, productive of power (6. 50). By comparison with Carthage, the Roman system was still at its peak (*acme*), while that of the Carthaginians had passed its peak. For at Carthage already the people had the greatest power in deliberation, while at Rome the senate was at its peak, and so in the former it was the policies of the masses which prevailed, while in the latter it was those of the best men (6. 51). The aristocratic aspect of Rome is further stressed in the account of funerals of distinguished men at Rome, which Polybius sees as a vital stimulus for the young towards virtue and patriotism (6. 53–54. 3), and the treatment of religion, which Polybius believes that the Romans had dramatized and introduced into public and private life to the utmost, in order to control the masses (6. 56. 6–12). Hence it is evident that Polybius sees Rome not only as a mixed constitution but one in which in his day the aristocratic element had *de facto* predominance, and both these features in his view contributed to it success. Its aristo-

[20] The most notorious example of a request for such a dispensation occurred in 61 (Cic. *Att.* 1. 17. 9, 18. 7; 2. 1. 8, 16. 2; Suet. *Jul.* 20. 3; App. *BCiv.* 2. 13. 47–8). Polybius has without doubt here produced a drastically oversimplified and misleading picture of the *dēmos*, because he has equated it with the artisans and their bosses who were involved with construction and other state-financed enterprises, ignoring independent farmers, businessmen, and their free wage-labourers. I cannot believe that he has taken the *publicani* by themselves to be representative of the *dēmos*.

[21] See Brunt, 1988, 194 ff., esp. 227–36 for arguments that C. Gracchus broke this senatorial near-monopoly of important civil judication.

cratic nature is later reaffirmed in the obituary notice on Scipio Africanus, where Polybius points to Scipio's influence with both the masses and the senate, and this contrasts with the obituary on Polybius' own fellow-citizen Philopoimen, who pursued his ambitions in a 'democratic and many-faceted constitution', that of the Achaean League.[22]

However, in spite of all its desirable qualities, this constitution could not escape the change and corruption inherent in every existing thing. How would this occur? Polybius suggests that in the light of his previous explanation of the cycle of constitutions his readers should be able to supply the conclusion of the theory themselves. When the constitution had thrust aside external threats to reach a position of unchallenged superiority and dominion, then wealth and well-being would make men more ambitious about office and other enterprises, there would be more pomp and luxury, and the people would cross the border into the next stage of the constitution. For, believing itself wronged by the greed of some of its superiors, and flattered by the vain proposals deriving from the ambitions of others, it would become indignant, unwilling to obey, and unwilling merely to be an equal element in the constitution to the other two. At this stage, it would have the best and finest of names, freedom and democracy, but in fact the worst, mob-rule.[23] The general impression given by this chapter is one of prejudice against the *dēmos*, such as characterized both Plato, the originator of the theory of the constitutional cycle, and the average Roman aristocrat. Nevertheless, Polybius did not abandon his belief in balance. What in his view was about to go wrong was that the people would want more than their equal part in the system and it was the aristocrats themselves who would have corrupted them.

The problems arising from this account are much debated. Comparison with other source-material shows it to be generally well-informed about the Roman constitution of its period, but it is also frequently held to be marred by omissions and misconceptions.[24] It is hard to criticize the analysis in a methodical fashion without having some explanation of the

---

[22] Pol. 23. 14. 1–2 and 12. 8. See also 2. 38. 6 for his description of the political nature of the Achaean league and his emphasis on free speech (*parrēsia*).

[23] 6. 57. 1–9. *Ochlokratia* in 6. 57. 9 seems to be the equivalent of *cheirokratia* in Polybius' account of the cycle at 6. 9. 7–10—created by the ambition and lavish spending of the rich which creates expectations among the poor that can only be fulfilled by a tyrant.

[24] Among recent writers, Walbank in his commentary (1957) makes plain how in detail Polybius' account is borne out by other sources, but in his overview (1972, 155–6) treats it in effect as a gallant failure; balanced, though critical, analyses are to be found in Nicolet, 1974, and Nippel, 1980, 142–53, an enthusiastic appreciation in Millar, 1984.

source of any distortion, whether this is the views passed on to Polybius by his aristocratic Roman friends or the prejudices which derived from his own Greek background.

As I have suggested earlier, Polybius does not seem to have been hampered by a straitjacket of Greek constitutional thought. He certainly bases his account on what the Greeks held to be the basic constitutional organs—the magistrates, council, and assembly—but he does so in a far from traditional way. This is evident if we compare 6. 12–18 with the section of the Aristotelian *Athenaiōn Politeia* (*Constitution of the Athenians*) beginning at chapter 42, which describes in detail the Athenian democracy after 403 BC. Whereas the *Constitution of the Athenians* describes the rules governing the activities of the magistrates and the various public bodies, Polybius talks of the power of the various elements in relation to one another, and this power is not simply that given constitutionally but that deriving from the exploitation of constitutional power in sectional interests. Moreover, Polybius emphasizes the obstructive nature of each element's power. The idea that the constitution is not only mixed, but founded on checks and balances, does not emerge gradually from the discussion, but is a presumption at the start or, if you like, a theorem which is proved. The result is that the ability of the elements of the constitution to co-operate, although it is the subject of a resumptive chapter (6. 18), is not something which is highlighted before, and, when it is discussed, is ascribed first to external danger and secondly to the mutual threat which each element poses to the others, in so far as the excessive ambitions of any one are resisted by the others.

In my opinion Polybius' approach has an originality which is not in the mainstream of Greek political thought, as we know it, even if he starts from two Greek ideas, the cycle of constitutions and the mixed constitution (in fact the latter seems to have been already known to the Romans).[25] What has influenced him? At the risk of sounding simplistic, I would say first that it is contact with things and ideas Roman. The Romans had almost certainly already constructed their own political mythology which portrayed their constitution emerging out of conflict (see chapter IV below).[26] This general presumption would have assisted

[25] Cato, fr. 80P, found in Servius' commentary on Aeneid 4. 682: '*populus patresque* . . .', where the commentator points out that some people thought that the Carthaginian constitution had three parts, the people, the *optimates*, and royal power; among them was Cato. He would no doubt have been reluctant to see a monarchic element in the Roman republic in the light of his hostility to monarchic behaviour by his contemporaries.

[26] Von Ungern-Sternberg (1990), while arguing against the concept of the 'Struggle of the Orders', has suggested that neither Polybius nor the earliest Roman writers believed it

Polybius in creating his antagonistic model, which places the emphasis on power rather than function. A second factor is the impression made on Polybius by the more dramatic constitutional acts. Most power exercised by the senate over the plebs was unspectacular, but that which operated through the letting of contracts had an eye-catching focus, the auction, and one which had produced its share of controversy. Foreign policy frequently crystallized round the appearance of an embassy or a foreign potentate (one of the most spectacular in Polybius' time was the appearance of king Prusias II of Bithynia dressed as a freedman).[27] The departure of the consul as a general to war or his return in triumph was much more splendid than his presidency over items of domestic administration in lengthy senate-debates. A lengthy treason-trial would have seemed a more powerful demonstration of popular authority than a routine election.

It is hard to say whether a further feature of the account is the result of Polybius' own rhetoric or that of his informants, I mean the fact that constitutional rights tend to be expressed in absolute and unqualified terms. When he claims (6. 14. 6) that the people alone try for a capital penalty, even if, as I think we should, we supply 'those who have held the most distinguished offices' as the object of the verb, he is oversimplifying the position, as he himself shows (16. 2), where he attributes to the people the right to ratify investigations of political crimes entailing a capital penalty, which are undertaken by the senate. Although this confirms the ultimate sovereignty of the people over capital crimes, it shows that they do not try alone such crimes. Again, the claim that the

to have extended after the time of the Twelve Tables. To leave aside the issue of how the story of early Roman history was constructed (where I am in considerable sympathy with Ungern-Sternberg), I do not think that the beginning of the Vatican excerpt in 6. 11, which is abrupt and hard to translate (see Walbank, 1957, 674, and 1972, 148, n. 116), justifies the conclusion that Polybius thought that no important political developments took place between (apparently) the Valerio-Horatian laws ('thirty years after Xerxes' crossing to Greece') and the Second Punic War. To be sure, the chief elements in the constitution had now been put in place, but Polybius believed that the ideal constitution of the time of the Second Punic War had been achieved through natural evolution, which on his view would have continued to involve conflict between the three elements. As to Ungern-Sternberg's other evidence, Sallust (*Hist.* 1. 11M) is too summary to provide a secure argument, and in any case he regards the Second Punic War as the end of conflict between the *patres* and plebs; one cannot draw *ex silentio* arguments from Diodorus' brief excursus (12. 24–5) into Roman political history at the time of the Twelve Tables—where measures normally ascribed to the Valerio-Horatian laws are mingled with those of the fourth century (25. 2)—while Cicero's treatment of early Roman history in *De Re Publica* is distorted by his desire to erase or minimize any plebeian achievement (see below, Chap. XII with nn. 33 ff.).

[27] Pol. 30. 18. Another example was the arrival of Eumenes II in winter 190/89 (Pol. 21. 18–22. 1 and see above, Chap. II with n. 9).

tribunes are bound always to carry out the decisions of the people and set their sights on their wishes was an expression of one attitude to the tribunate not universally shared by all tribunes. Indeed the presentation of tribunician behaviour obscures the extent to which, although not slaves of the senate, they nevertheless frequently co-operated with the majority view in the senate.[28]

Polybius' account is a good introduction to the problems that face a modern scholar when he seeks a firm footing on which to discuss the Roman constitution. As a theoretical analysis of the functioning of the constitution, it is unique in our surviving sources (although Cicero treated the Republic as a mixed constitution in *De Re Publica*, he played down the notions of conflict and obstruction and did not follow the constitution's development beyond the fifth century BC).[29] On the other hand, in so far as Polybius' treatment is focused on the conflicts and the dramatic demonstrations of power in Republican politics, it is at one with another major source—the annalistic tradition preserved in Livy and Dionysius of Halicarnassus. Here the nature of the constitution emerges from colourful stories, as it did no doubt in their predecessors, the annalists of the Republic, the earliest of whom would have been read by Polybius. The constitution of the Republic consisted of far more than statutes: it was based on traditional institutions defined by precedents and examples. These were above all embodied in stories, whether these related to more recent events and had good claims to historicity or were reconstructions of distant events with a strong element of myth. Thus the constitution did not stand above politics like a law-code: it is what the Romans thought to be right and did, and in more senses than one it was product of history.

---

[28] 'Mancipia nobilium'—a rebuke made to tribunes by L. Postumius Megillus in Livy, 10. 37. 11. For tribunician activity in the senate's interests, see Bleicken, 1955, 54 ff. (his view of the tribunate has been significantly nuanced in a later article, Bleicken, 1981).

[29] See below, Chap. XII with nn. 28 ff.

IV

The Story of the Origin of the Constitution

Polybius' ideas, in particular the notions that the Roman republican constitution was the product of a natural growth and that it drew its strength from conflict and co-operation between rival forces, were based not only on contemporary politics at Rome but on the portrayal of the early history of Rome, which he summarized in a now missing part of Book 6. This in turn must have been based on the earliest Roman annalists, no doubt supplemented by the comments of his Roman friends. Though the texts of the earliest annals are almost entirely lost, we can disentangle with some plausibility the outlines of the tradition which we possess in a greatly elaborated form in the work of Livy and Dionysius of Halicarnassus. To do so is clearly important for understanding Polybius' thought, but more important for understanding the way the Romans themselves conceived their constitution, and this will be true, to whatever extent we believe that the Romans contaminated their early history with ideas and material from a later era.

It is neither necessary nor possible to examine thoroughly here the credibility of early Roman history.[1] When the earliest annalists got to work at the time of the Second Punic War, they would have had access to only limited written material from the past. Of prime importance were the consular *fasti*, a list of the consular pairs going back to the beginning of the Republic (corrupt though this may have been at some points): in its final version this placed the beginning of the Republic in 509 BC.[2] The *pontifices* are likely also to have retained material which had formed their annual records—wars, triumphs, famines, and pestilences: whether these survived from the time before the sack of Rome by the

---

[1] For recent surveys of the problem, still as controversial as when B. G. Niebuhr wrote his *Römische Geschichte* (1826–30), see *CAH* vii. 2, 2nd edn., esp. ch. 1, pp. 1–29 (R. M. Ogilvie and A. Drummond) and ch. 3, pp. 52–112 (A. Momigliano); also Raaflaub, 1986, chs. 1 (K. Raaflaub) and 2 (T. J. Cornell), pp. 1–76; Cornell, 1995.

[2] *Inscr. Ital.* xiii. 1.; *MRR* i with the note on chronology in ii. 637–9. The suggestion of Wiseman (1979, ch. 2), that the *fasti*, as we have them, are largely a creation of the second century BC, seems to me to tip the scales too far against their historical value.

Gauls (390 or 386 BC) is debatable.[3] There were some early inscribed documents, such as the treaty with the Latins, still known in Cicero's day, and the fundamental Roman law-code, the laws of the Twelve Tables.[4] By the fourth century BC historical Roman events were being recorded by Greek writers, and early in the following century Timaeus of Tauromenium (Taormina) seems to have included a significant treatment of Rome in his history (there were also references to Rome in Etruscan works, but there is no sign that any Roman used them before the emperor Claudius).[5] Nevertheless, for much of what they inserted into their work the early annalists must have depended on oral tradition, especially that transmitted by aristocratic families,[6] consolidated perhaps in the written records of the *laudationes*. These were the funeral panegyrics, delivered in the ceremonies of which Polybius so heartily approved, but no more reliable for that reason, as later Roman writers recognized.[7]

Rome was once ruled by kings, as Tacitus remarked in the first sentence of the *Annals*. Even if they had no further information, the Romans could have inferred this from the existence of the priest entitled *rex sacrorum*, the institution known as *interregnum*, which occurred during the Republic when no consuls, praetors, or dictator remained in office, and the building at the south-east end of the forum called *regia*, used by the *pontifex maximus* under the Republic.[8] There had been, according to Roman tradition, seven kings—not counting Romulus' two associates, Remus and Titus Tatius—the last three of whom, beginning with Tarquinius Priscus, comprised two Etruscans and a Roman related to them by marriage (Servius Tullius): an Etruscan influence on the conduct of Roman higher magistrates was evident in the insignia of the *fasces* and the practice of augury. It was believed in the late Republic that after Romulus, kings required some kind of popular ratification for their accession (the belief may well have derived from the antique and poorly understood institution of the *lex curiata*, the law confirming the rights of higher magistrates, which ultimately was passed in an assembly that

---

[3] Testimonia and possible fragments in *HRR* i. 3–29; doubts about their later availability and value in Frier, 1980, and Rawson, 1971; greater confidence about the authenticity of the record in Bucher, 1987.

[4] Cic. *Balb.* 53 with *CAH* vii. 2². 271–6, cf. 253–7 on the first treaty with Carthage; *FIRA* i, pp. 23–75 = *RS* ii, no. 40, on the Twelve Tables.

[5] On Timaeus (*FGH* 566) see Momigliano, 1977, 37–66, and the bibliography in Hornblower, 1994, 35; on Etruscan works Cornell, 1975.

[6] See now Wiseman, 1994; von Ungern-Sternberg, 1988.

[7] Pol. 6. 53–5; Livy, 8. 40. 4; Cic. *Brut.* 62; *HRR* i. 30–59.

[8] Brown, 1974–5.

existed only in name because of the disappearance of the political units called *curiae*): this confirmation by the people, however, was neglected by the last two kings.[9] It was also assumed, not implausibly, that under the kings some kind of senate existed, though there was only a small part for this aristocratic council in the reconstructed story.

With a greater or smaller degree of probability the origins of a number of institutions were referred by annalists to the regal period: the rituals involved in a treaty, a declaration of war, and the surrender of a foreign people (Livy, 1. 24, 32, and 48); the social system of *clientela* (Dion. Hal. *AR* 2. 9); land-division, priesthoods, appeal to the people from a judicial verdict (Livy, 1. 26. 5–14); above all, the census and *comitia centuriata* (the military assembly whose classes were under the Republic distinguished by a property-qualification) (Livy, 1. 42. 5–44. 1), these last being a characteristic feature of Roman society. Antiquarians, by contrast, found early Roman legal formulae relating to murder attributed to the kings.

To what extent has the annalists' picture of the Roman monarchy been confirmed by archaeological discoveries?[10] A cautious answer would be that the stories of the annalists and of the archaeologists are parallel accounts which to some extent can be made consistent with each other. For the archaeologist Rome begins as a group of villages whose existence goes back well beyond the traditional date of the foundation of the city *c.*750 BC; these produced a luxurious élite from the late eighth century onwards and were linked together into a city with a paved forum and public buildings (mainly religious) a little after 600 BC. A building which probably combined political and religious functions was the *regia*, in which the word *rex* was conveniently found scratched on the foot of a bucchero cup.[11] Hoplite armour is depicted on fragments of terracotta friezes from neighbouring Etruria and Latium, though nothing depicts the method of fighting in formation as we find it on the protocorinthian 'Chigi' jug imported into Etruria from Greece in the seventh century.

[9] Servius Tullius ruled 'primus iniussu populi, voluntate patrum' (Livy, 1. 41. 6); Tarquinius Superbus 'neque populi iussu neque auctoribus patribus' (1. 49. 3). According to Cicero (*Rep.* 2. 38), however, Servius consulted the people after the funeral of Tarquinius Priscus 'iussusque regnare legem de imperio suo curiatam tulit'. On the *curiae* and the *lex curiata* see *Staatsr.* i. 609ff.; iii. 1. 92ff.; 318ff.; Momigliano, 1963, at 108–12; Giovannini, 1983, 44ff., and Ch. V below with n. 48.

[10] The largest recent collection of archaeological material is Gjerstad, 1953–73. For overviews of the evidence see M. Torelli, *CAH* vii. 2². 30–51; Cornell, 1979–80; Ross Holloway, 1993; Smith, 1994 and 1996. A great deal of the material is conveniently assembled in the exhibition catalogues, *Civiltà del Lazio primitivo* (Rome, 1976) and *La Grande Roma dei Tarquinii* (=*GRT*) (Rome, 1990). On the forum area see Coarelli, 1983, and the article 'Forum Romanum' (G. Tagliamonte and N. Purcell) in Steinby, 1995, 313–36.

[11] See *GRT*, pp. 22–3, 1. 9 = *CIL* i². 4. 2830 = *CAH* vii. 2². 76.

Hence it would be hard to tell from archaeology alone how broad the social base of the Roman army was.[12]

There have been discovered recently stone footings of the walls of aristocratic houses on the north-east slope of the Palatine, which would have been used in what is in literary tradition the Etruscan period. Etruscan nobles connected with Rome appear in the exploit depicted on the wall of the François tomb. Most explicitly, an inscription from Satricum of *c.*500 BC shows companions of Poplios Valesios (Publius Valerius), called *suodales*, making a dedication to Mars, thus giving us a glimpse of an élite warrior group, perhaps similar to those described in Lesbos in the poems of Alcaeus or to Cleisthenes' *hetairoi.*[13]

There is little doubt that in the last two centuries of the pre-Republican era Rome was ruled by a king surrounded by a wealthy warrior aristocracy. This in turn may be related to the connection of certain of the patrician *gentes* of the Republic with religious cults and of others with the voting districts (*tribus*) into which Roman territory was later divided.[14] The general picture thus obtained is, however, of little value in assessing the tradition about the political achievement of the kings.

The annalists' picture of the founding of the Republic is more satisfying as a philosophical object-lesson or a piece of tragic drama than as history. Tarquinius Superbus seizes power through the assassination of Servius Tullius, is highly effective in promoting Roman power in Latium but arbitrary and tyrannical at home, and finally, after his son has provoked outrage by the rape of the wife of another Tarquinius from Collatia, succumbs to a coup d'état engineered by a group of nobles with popular backing. According to the story known in the late Republic, there was no good reason to dispense with the kingship except the character of Tarquinius, who had in his own person changed monarchy into tyranny. Moreover, the aristocracy had constituted a dangerous precedent which inspired revolutionary ideals in the common people.[15] The behaviour of the nobles seems inadequately motivated, and the importance of the plebs perhaps anachronistically exaggerated.

---

[12] See *CAH* vii. 2². 45 for Acquarossa frieze (ibid. 36 for painted ostrich-egg from Vulci), and Torelli, 1993, 88; for Tuscania Torelli, 1993, 103–4; for Cisterna, ibid. 98–9. See also *GRT*, p. 94, 4. 1. 26 for Palatine fragment.

[13] Houses—*GRT*, pp. 97–9, 4. 2; Carandini, 1986. Etruscan nobles—*GRT*, pp. 18–19, l. 1–2; Alföldi, 1965, 212 ff. with plates 8–12. Satricum—Stibbe, 1980; *GRT*, pp. 23–4, l. 10 = *CIL* i². 4. 2823a. For Greek parallels see e.g. Lintott, 1982, 51–5.

[14] For discussions of the *gentes* see A. Drummond, *CAH* vii. 2². 143 ff., Smith, 1996, 198 ff.; for the *tribus*, Taylor, 1960.   [15] Cic. *Rep.* 2. 45–7, 53, 57–8; Livy, 2. 1. 4–6.

It is not surprising that some modern scholars, finding the story unconvincing, have held that there was no revolution at all, rather an evolution from the leadership of kings to the leadership of annual magistrates.[16] Others have taken their lead from the Etruscan traditions known to the emperor Claudius, which gain some visual corroboration from the scene in the François tomb: according to this view Rome in the latter part of the sixth century fell into the hands of a series of Etruscan *condottieri*, Caelius Vibenna, Mastarna (whom Claudius equated with Servius Tullius), and the Tarquinii themselves; indeed after Tarquinius Superbus' fall, Porsenna actually took control of the city.[17] The traditional founding-date of the Republic, moreover, was close in time to the defeat of the Etruscans at Aricia in Latium by the tyrant of Cumae, Aristodemus, which led to the general collapse of Etruscan power southeast of the Tiber.[18] Thus on this view, in spite of the material prosperity, there had been a high degree of political instability in the late sixth century, and the end of the monarchy at Rome was a by-product of its liberation from direct Etruscan political control.

In spite of its problems, it is hard to abandon the picture of the beginning of the Republic as violent change. In the later Republic the political overtones of the word *rex* were close to those of the Greek word *turannos*. Valerius Poplicola, one of the first pair of Republican consuls, was held to have passed a law declaring *sacer* (in this context the word means 'open to seizure and destruction') the person and property of anyone who plotted to seize a tyranny.[19] The annals also contained three stories of men overthrown for aspiring to *regnum*, even though they had not actually undertaken any violent coup (see below). On the other hand, the annals also give an impression of continuity. An assembly had been used to ratify the election of the kings. With the expulsion of Tarquinius the new annual magistrates were immediately elected in the *comitia centuriata*, the military assembly invented by Servius Tullius, and, in Livy's account, according to the commentaries of that king.[20]

[16] Gjerstad, 1962; Mazzarino, 1947.

[17] *ILS* 212 (trans. Braund, *AN*, no. 570), col. I, 16 ff.; Tac. *Hist.* 3. 72; Momigliano, 1963; Alföldi, 1965, 72 ff.; 212 ff.; Harris, 1971, 10 ff.; Cornell, 1995, 143 ff.

[18] Dion. Hal. *AR* 7. 5. 1–6. 3 (in the twentieth year after Miltiades' archonship at Athens).

[19] Livy, 2. 8. 2; Dion. Hal. *AR* 5. 1. 3. Valerius himself is said to have moved his house from the summit of the Velia through accusations of being tyrannical (Cic. *Rep.* 2. 53; Livy, 2. 7. 6–12; Plut. *Popl.* 10. 1–6; Dion. Hal. 5. 19. 1–2). A new treatment of *sacratio* is provided by Fiori, 1996, in which ch. 6, pp. 325 ff., deals with Publicola.

[20] Livy, 1. 60. 3—allegedly under the presidency of the *praefectus urbi*, whereas we find in Cicero (*Rep.* 2. 23) and Dionysius of Halicarnassus (4. 75. 1–2, 76. 1, 84. 5) the institution of the *interregnum*.

The resulting regime was dominated by an aristocracy, and in the annals, as soon as the Romans had finally defeated Etruscan attempts to restore the monarchy, conflicts between *patres* and plebs dominate the narrative. The *patres* are the senate, viewed not only as a ruling political order but also as a supreme and oppressive social order, who are depicted as supporting creditors against debtors and monopolizing public land.[21] A ban on intermarriage between patricians and plebeians, which entrenched the patricians as a ruling caste, becomes an issue later, after it was incorporated into the Twelve Tables.[22]

The scene is thus set for the struggles between patricians and plebeians, which are one of the salient features of the annals of the early Republic, alternating with stories of foreign wars. Essentially this is a story of patrician resistance to popular unrest—in the earliest stage the unrest provokes the creation of a dictator, a magistrate whose invention a little earlier is associated with cowing the plebs—but resistance is followed by timely concession and compromise. There is for the most part only small-scale violence which is not represented as having led to bloodshed, still less to anything approaching the *stasis* familiar in the Greek world.[23] It is not a story which could have been transposed into Roman history from that of other ancient cities. This is above all true of the first major event in the struggle, which provided the foundation of later developments—the first secession of the plebs, assigned to the year 494 BC. In reaction to the harsh measures of creditors, those plebeians who were under arms refused to participate in a campaign and withdrew to a hill outside but near the city—either the Mons Sacer across the river Anio or the Aventine which was at that time beyond the city boundary.[24]

The threat of a combination of civil strife and external threats to their security constrained the *patres* to recognize plebeian spokesmen, the *tribuni plebis* (the number originally chosen is disputed). These were

[21] See e.g. Livy, 2. 23, 27 and 41; Dion. Hal. *AR*. 5. 63–9; 6. 22–9, 34–44.

[22] Cic. *Rep*. 2. 63, presented as an innovation rather than the formalization of previous practice. Differing interpretations by J. von Ungern-Sternberg, R. E. Mitchell, and J. Linderski in Raaflaub, 1986, 82 ff.; 171 ff.; 252 ff.

[23] On the dictator see Livy, 2. 29. 11–30. 5, (cf. 18. 4 and 8–9 for the effect on the plebs); Cic. *Rep*. 1. 63; 2. 56; Dion. Hal. *AR* 5. 70–7, and Chap. VII with nn. 71 ff. For a comparison with Greek *stasis* of the archaic period see Lintott, 1982, 72–5.

[24] Sall. *Hist*. 1. 11; 3. 48. 1M; Cic. *Corn*. fr. 49 Puccioni = Asc. 76C; Festus, 423–4L; Livy, 2. 23–33; Dion. Hal. *AR* 5. 63 ff.; 6. 22 ff. The plebs is said to 'occupy' the hill, *insidere* or *considere*. The departure from Rome is termed *secedere (secessio)*. The word *sed-itio* has the same root meaning as *se-cessio*, 'a going apart', but in the Latin known to us is a general term for unrest and rebellion with no particular connection with the *démarche* of the plebeians. This suggests that *secessio* became the term for this particular act early in Latin tradition.

declared sacrosanct: that is, their persons were to be inviolate and any physical harm done to them would be avenged by the plebs. This became the basis of the the tribune's power to interpose his person, whether to obstruct some political act (where it was known as *intercessio*) or to lend aid (*auxilium*) to an individual threatened with injustice by a magistrate or a private citizen. The tribunes were not yet treated as regular magistrates, but remained representatives of a section, albeit the greatest part, of the people.[25]

Appeals to the tribunes in the annals are sometimes associated with cries of help to the people. Citizens in trouble cry 'Provoco ad populum' or 'Provoco et fidem imploro'. This is in fact portrayed as happening before the creation of tribunes; later, the appeal to the tribunes may be regarded as a substitute for the appeal to the people or vice versa, or both may be used together.[26] *Provocatio* was later regarded as one of the principal rights of the individual Roman citizen, a theoretical guarantee against execution without trial and, after the *lex Porcia* of Cato the Censor, against flogging.[27] There are major problems concerning the exact legal significance of this cry for help and the date at which it received the backing of legal sanctions directed against those who overrode it. Livy portrays the cry of *provoco* being used in the Horatius case under king Tullus Hostilius. A law about *provocatio* was attributed to Valerius Poplicola and, according to Cicero, *provocatio* was frequently mentioned in the Twelve Tables; the first undisputed evidence, however, of any legal sanction is in a *lex Valeria* of 300 BC.[28] The development of criminal justice will be examined in a later chapter. For the present discussion it is sufficient to point out that, although *provocatio* may be used in the context of a legal process, this is not its only function nor is it a necessary part of an assembly trial.[29] As portrayed in our sources, it remains a cry for help without specific content, which may or may not lead to some kind of judicial hearing. As such it has parallels in Greek society and in later European societies.[30] It seems more likely that it won recognition at Rome originally as a fact of life, a measure employed among the Roman people to rally support round a threatened individual,

[25] Richard, 1978, 559 ff.; Bleicken, 1955, 5 ff.; 1959, 347 ff.; Fiori, 1996, 293 ff.; Chap. VIII with nn. 1 ff.

[26] Lintott, 1972, esp. 228–31; Bleicken, 1959—with earlier bibliography. See also Chap. VII with nn. 17 ff.; Chap. VIII with nn. 17–18; Chap. IX with nn. 22 ff.

[27] Cato, *ORF*, fr. 117; Cic. *Rab. Perd.* 12; Sall. *Cat.* 51. 21.

[28] Livy, 1. 26. 8 ff.; 10. 9. 3–6.

[29] This point was first made by Brecht, 1939, 300 ff., and developed by Heuss, 1944, 106 ff.; Bleicken, 1959, and Kunkel, 1962, 21 ff. See also Chap. IX with nn. 22 ff.

[30] *VRR* 11 ff.; Lintott, 1972, 228–9, 232–3; id., 1982, 15–28.

rather than as a creation of legislation. Nevertheless, in the long run, in conjunction with appeal to the tribunes it was the main achievement of the struggles of the plebs in the direction of individual liberty.

Some time after their creation the tribunes were reinforced by the election of two plebeian aediles as their subordinates. As leaders of the plebs, the tribunes are portrayed holding public meetings, which were the precedent for the formal procedures of the *concilium plebis*, though such meetings are unlikely to have had constitutional recognition before the Twelve Tables. Here they passed resolutions (*plebiscita*), which at first only bound the plebs, and they also conducted a form of trial, as a means of putting pressure on a political opponent—threatening him with death or a fine. Capital trials in these assemblies were later specifically restricted by a law of the Twelve Tables.[31]

These were the first Roman law-code (451–450 BC), indeed the only codification of law ever produced in classical Rome. They are presented in the annals as a compromise after plebeian pressure. What we know of the code is largely concerned with private law; it did, however, deal with trials in the public interest before an assembly. Although Livy calls it the source of all public and private law, it is not taken in the late Republic as an authority about the powers and duties of magistrates, assemblies, and the senate, and the argument from silence here seems overwhelming.[32] The code is said to have recognised the existence of *provocatio*, but we should not understand this to mean that it gave it a constructive part in the legal system (see Chap. IX with nn. 22 ff.). In general, the activities of the ten law-commissioners (*decemviri*) are not said to have furthered the political aims of the plebs and in one respect may have obstructed them, if indeed they enshrined in law the ban on intermarriage between patricians and plebeians.[33] Furthermore, the second college of ten, allegedly elected to create the last two tables, are said to have acted tyrannically in office and illegally prolonged their authority into a second year. In the

---

[31] On aediles see Zon. 7. 15. 10. XII Tab. (*RS* ii. 40) IX. 1–2 (= Cic. *Leg.* 3. 10 and 44) deals with capital trials. See also Cic. *Sest.* 65; *Rep.* 2. 61.

[32] Against the statement of Livy, 3. 34. 6, stands Cicero's failure to refer to the Twelve Tables in *De Legibus* Book 3, where he is drawing up detailed constitutional rules, except for the provision cited in n. 31. The only other political provisions we know to have been ascribed to the Tables are :—(i) that declaring the last directive of the assembly valid over all previous directives (Livy, 7. 17. 12 = Tab. XII. 5, *RS* ii, p. 721), (ii) a clause concerning treason (Tab. XI. 5, *RS* ii, p. 703), and (iii) the ban on nocturnal gatherings mentioned in an early imperial declamation (Porcius Latro, *In Cat.* 19). The authenticity of all these has been challenged, see *RS* ii ad locc.; Guarino, 1988, at 330–5.

[33] Cic. *Rep.* 2. 63 = XII Tab. XI. 1 with Livy, 4. 1–6, esp. 6. 2–4. See the discussions by J. Linderski, W. Eder, and M. Toher in Raaflaub, 1986, 245–326.

Livian version the story becomes a moral fable, proving to plebeians that hatred of the nobility should not lead them to entrust themselves to magistrates with arbitrary powers.[34]

After the second college of *decemviri* were overthrown through a second secession by the army, the consulate was restored and laws are said to have been passed by the consuls Valerius and Horatius confirming the rights of the plebs. This legislation, as it is presented, to some extent anticipates later developments, but it is clear in any case that the position of the tribunes was thought to have been constitutionally entrenched at this point, perhaps for the first time.[35] There follows a period in which there was no major strife between patricians and plebs, but some reforms and constitutional developments: the ban on inter-marriage between patricians and plebeians is removed by Canuleius, there are restrictions placed on fines, quaestors and censors are elected for the first time (in 446 and 443), and the election of the latter is said to be a concomitant of the creation of tribunes of the soldiers with consular power as a replacement for the two consuls—a larger college of military commanders, which is only attested as operating in the late fifth and early fourth centuries.[36]

The next major constitutional conflict and consequent reform is attributed to the next century, in the period following the sack of Rome by the Gauls. However, it is appropriate to consider here a feature of Rome's early political history which stands outside the main tradition of constitutional reform stimulated by plebeian pressure, that is, the stories of the three demagogic would-be tyrants, Cassius, Maelius and Manlius.[37] Spurius Cassius was one of the consuls of 486 BC, Spurius Maelius a wealthy man outside the senate in 439, Marcus Manlius Capitolinus a charismatic soldier who had saved the Capitol from the Gauls at the time of the sack of Rome in 390 (386). All three are said to have taken active measures to alleviate the economic distress of the poor, Cassius by proposing through legislation to distribute land or money, Maelius by privately buying grain for distribution to the poor, and Manlius by rescuing debtors from servitude to their creditors through largesse from his own funds.[38] No open incitation to riot or rebellion

---

[34] See esp. Livy, 3. 36–7.
[35] Livy, 3. 55; Dion. Hal. *AR* 11. 45. See also the confused passage in Diod. 12. 25. 2.
[36] Tac. *Ann.* 11. 22; Livy, 4. 6. 8–9 and 8. 1–7; *Staatsr.* ii. 1. 180–92.
[37] See Lintott, 1970; Fiori, 1996, 375 ff. with earlier bibliography.
[38] The chief sources are on Cassius—Livy, 2. 41. 1–9; Dion. Hal. *AR.* 8. 69–70; on Maelius—Livy, 4. 13. 2–3 and 10; Dion. Hal. *AR* 12. 1–4; on Manlius—Livy, 6. 11–20, esp. 18. 6, 20. 6.

could be laid to their charge; their tyrannical designs seem largely to have been inferred from their pursuit of popular favour and the large support that they managed to gather around them (though Maelius is said to have collected weapons in his house). We can also detect a development of the annalistic tradition in accounts of their suppression. What seem to be later versions show Cassius and Manlius being tried for treason and Maelius being killed by Gaius Servilius Ahala in his capacity as a *magister equitum*, the second-in-command to the dictator allegedly elected in the crisis (see Chap. VII with nn. 83–4). In the earlier versions Maelius is killed out of hand by Ahala as a private citizen, Cassius is executed by his own father by virtue of his *patria potestas*; there is also some evidence for an alternative story of Manlius' end.[39] The moral of the stories was that it was right to kill anyone who aspired to a *regnum* even before they used force to obtain it, and that assistance to plebeians by individuals without the general consent of the élite was tantamount to seeking a tyranny. Whereas the tradition about the secessions to a great extent sanctified the plebeians' pursuit of legal and political rights, that about the tyrant-demagogues was a charter for aristocratic solidarity in face of any serious attempt to overturn the social order.

The alleged sedition by Manlius occurred in the uneasy period when Rome was being rebuilt and secured against hostile neighbours in the period following the Gallic sack of Rome. Not long afterwards there was agitation over debt, the distribution of public land, and the admission of plebeians to the consulship (it was proposed to end the substitution of tribunes of the soldiers for the consuls). This led to an anarchy, when regular magistracies of the people were not elected. The anarchy of ten years recorded seems implausible and the result of annalists' attempts to fill a gap in the consular lists resulting from inaccurate chronology.[40] Nevertheless, there is no reason to doubt the genuineness of the crisis. Eventually the tribunes Licinius Stolo and Sextius secured the plebeian demands: there was relief on debt-payments, and the first law was passed restricting the amount of public land tenable by an individual; moreover, one consulship a year was opened to plebeians. This in turn led the patricians to create the first praetorship and the two posts of curule aedile, a counterpart to the pair elected by the plebs.[41]

[39] For Maelius' weapons see Livy, 4. 13. 9; on the fate of Cassius Cic. *Rep.* 2. 60; Livy, 2. 41. 10–12; Dion. Hal. *AR* 8. 77–9; on that of Maelius Livy, 4. 13. 11–15. 1; Dion. Hal. *AR* 12. 2. 1–4. 4; on that of Manlius Livy, 6. 19. 5–20. 1; Dion. Hal. *AR* 14. 4; Dio 7. 26. 1–3; Zon. 7. 24; Diod. 15. 35. 3.

[40] See *MRR* ii. 637–9.

[41] Livy, 6. 35 and 38–42; 7. 1. See Chap. VII with nn. 58 ff., Chap. VIII with nn. 31 ff.

After this we hear nothing more of agitation or secession for about eighty years. It was a period when Roman military success led first to the control of Latium, Campania, and the land in between, then, by stages, to the domination of all Italy south of the Arno, with the exception of a few Greek cities in the southernmost part of the peninsula. At intervals during the same period there is an account of some reform which weakens patrician control of the constitution or improves the social conditions of the plebs. These are not on the whole related by Livy with the degree of elaboration (*ornatio*), which characterized the stories of political conflict earlier. This may be thought to improve their credibility, and indeed, the nearer the history is to the time when annals were first written, the greater the probability of an authentic tradition. It would be unwise, however, to assume that all the reforms took place without a considerable political struggle. What were they?

In 356 we find the first plebeian dictator, in 351 the first plebeian censor. Then in 342 it was enacted that one consul must be plebeian and that both could be, while in 339 Publilius Philo, a plebeian dictator, is said to have enacted that the same should apply to the censors; further laws of his provided that the senate should not retain a veto over legislation in the *comitia centuriata*, but should give its view beforehand, and that plebiscites should be binding on the whole people. This public recognition of the resolutions of the plebs as laws cannot have been as complete as that enacted later by the *lex Hortensia*, and we must assume that some conditions were attached.[42] Two years later the praetorship was opened to plebeians. Then, in 311, it was enacted that the military posts of *tribunus militum* and *duumvir navalis* should be filled by popular election.[43]

Meanwhile, we hear of measures about interest-rates and debt-repayments in 357 and 355, a further law of 342 allegedly making loans at interest illegal (though later we only hear of limits on interest-rates), and finally the *lex Poetelia* of 326, which is said to have abolished debt-bondage, but seems only to have banned privately contracted bondage, not that which followed from failure to discharge a legal judgement.[44] In 300 BC a *lex Valeria* was passed about *provocatio*, which, in Livy's phrase, protected it more carefully. In fact it declared that the execution of a Roman citizen in face of *provocatio* was illegal ('improbe factum'). We

---

[42] Livy, 8. 12. 14–16; cf. the texts in n. 50 below. On the problem of the validity of plebiscites see de Martino, *SCR* i. 337 ff.; ii. 132 ff.; Cornell, 1995, 277–8; Hölkeskamp, 1988.
[43] Livy, 9. 30. 3–4.
[44] Livy, 7. 16. 1, 21. 5, and 42. 1; 8. 28; Varro, *LL*. 7. 105; *VRR*, 26–7, 33 n. 2.

have no evidence of a fixed penalty or of any specific legal procedure to deal with offences against this law. The innovation seems to have been that, whereas previous laws recognized *provocatio* as a fact of life and suggested ways of dealing with it, this was the first law which forced a magistrate to yield to it willy-nilly.[45] In the same year a *lex Ogulnia* was passed doubling the membership of the major priesthoods and opening them to plebeians.[46] It is probably to this period that we should attribute the *plebiscitum Ovinium*, known to us from Festus,[47] which obliged the censors to draw up the roll of the senate from the *curiae* on the basis of merit, and the admission of the tribunes to sit inside the senate (before this they are said to have sat outside and blocked the exit, when they wished to veto a decree).[48]

Cicero tells in passing of a *lex Maenia*, which removed the senate's veto on the results of elections, probably shortly after the controversy over the election of M'. Curius Dentatus to his first consulship.[49] Finally in 287 occurred what is usually regarded as the end of an era: a long period of serious unrest led to the last secession of the plebs, on this occasion to the Janiculum. The reason given in the brief surviving source-material is debt. But the dictator Q. Hortensius who brought the secession to an end also legislated to the effect that plebiscites were now to be binding on the whole Roman people without qualification, and this remained the constitutional position as long as Roman assemblies continued to function.[50]

The historiography of the early Republic explains why Polybius saw the republican constitution as a natural growth. The story is of slow, piecemeal development, with a general tendency in favour of the democratic element in spite of some setbacks. Major developments arise from confrontation between the aristocracy and the people, which, if not entirely non-violent, at least involve no major violence. However, the outcome can be fairly seen as a compromise between opposing forces.[51]

---

[45] Livy, 10. 9. 3–5; Lintott, 1972, 238–9.

[46] Livy, 10. 6. 4–6.

[47] Festus, 290L.

[48] Zon. 7. 15. 8; Val. Max. 2. 2. 7; and see below Chap. V with n. 13, Chap. VIII with nn. 5–6.

[49] Cic. *Brut.* 55; de Martino, *SCR* ii. 129.

[50] Livy, *Per.* 11; Pliny, *HN* 16. 37; Gell. *NA* 15. 27. 4. For an interpretation of the *lex Hortensia* as an exceptional response to popular pressure that contrasted with the process of patricio-plebeian compromise of the previous half-century, see Hölkeskamp, 1988.

[51] For the view that the 'Struggle of the Orders' is essentially a modern conception see von Ungern-Sternberg, 1990, and my comments in Chapter III, n. 26. See also his contribution, 'The End of the Conflict of the Orders', in Raaflaub, 1986, 353–77, arguing convincingly that we should not regard 287 BC as a significant terminal date (on which see also

The outcome of the political struggles of the early Republic was to remove the privileged position of the patricians in almost all their functions (the chief exception was the administration of an *interregnum*).[52] A new aristocracy was created which in principle was dependent on popular election and merit rather than birth. The plebs as a whole gained recognition for their own officers, the tribunes and plebeian aediles, without the former resigning their extraordinary privilege of sacrosanctity, which had been forged in the struggles and which was the basis of their right to veto and to protect individuals. The reformed senate had not lost its importance; it was arguably stronger as a result of becoming a gathering of all those who had achieved eminence. However, the ultimate sovereignty of the assemblies in elections and legislation was now a cornerstone of the constitution. The question which immediately arises is, how democratic these assemblies were; and this is the subject of the next chapter.

Lintott, 1987, 52). It has even been argued that any early political struggles in the Republic have been wrongly framed as a conflict between *patres* and *plebs*, see R. E. Mitchell, 'The Definition of *patres* and *plebs*' in Raaflaub, 1986, 130–74. But, however sceptical we may be about the Roman tradition, we must nevertheless accept that those who lived at the time of the Second Punic War had present experience of social conflict backed by a comparatively secure memory of conflict in the previous century (see Ungern-Sternberg, 1990, 100–102). They also had heard stories from the past, e.g. about secession and would-be tyrants, without having a secure grasp of the events which gave rise to those stories. They had finally the living traditions of the tribunate and *provocatio*, which must have (rightly) seemed the products of a conflict. The annalistic account which emerged was a gallant attempt to do justice to these data.

[52] Livy, 1. 17; Dion. Hal. *AR* 4. 75. 1–2; 76. 1; 84. 5; Cic. *Rep.* 2. 23; *Leg.* 3. 9; Asc. 31, 33 and 36C; *Staatsr.* i. 649 ff. (with further references).

V

The Assemblies

Under the developed Roman Republic, as Polybius pointed out, it was the people who conferred magistracies, enacted or rejected laws, had the ultimate say in capital punishment and (though this ceased to be true *de facto* after his day) in decisions of war, peace, and alliance.[1] The people were not the only source of political power, but they may be reasonably described as a sovereign authority, if one considers that they were in theory permitted to abolish the Republic by legislation or by the conferral of extraordinary powers on a magistrate: indeed it is arguable that they did just that, first when they voted extraordinary powers to Julius Caesar as dictator, then when the *lex Titia* created the triumvirate in 43 BC, and finally when the assembly confirmed Augustus' unprecedented package of powers in 23 BC.[2] What prevented this occurring in the period between the *lex Hortensia* and Caesar's dictatorship were the traditions of behaviour built up over centuries and a concept of basic republican principles, which we saw illustrated in the last chapter in the form of hostility to tyranny and the protection of the liberty of the plebs. Thus the assemblies were restricted by a concept which Mommsen described as theoretically illogical and practically vague, but, as he went on to remark, it is such concepts that make history.[3]

Any equation between a Roman assembly and popular sovereignty needs nuancing further. There were two components to any assembly, the magistrate who convened it and those citizens who assembled in response to his call. Without the magistrate the assembly could not meet, and it only heard discussion and voted about proposals put forward by that magistrate.[4] The word 'heard' should also be stressed: although

[1] Pol. 6. 14. 4–6, 9–12.
[2] Dio, 43. 14. 3–5; Cic. *Phil.* 7. 16, cf. Suet. *Jul.* 41. 2; App. *BCiv.* 4. 7. 27; Dio 47. 2. 1; *Res Gestae* 1. 4; 10. 1. The last passage does not mention Augustus' *imperium proconsulare*, but see *P. Colon.* I. 10 = EJ² 366 for the popular vote to Agrippa of an *imperium* equal to that of other magistrates but valid throughout the Roman empire.
[3] *Staatsr.* i. 15.
[4] As Mommsen pointed out (*Staatsr.* iii. 1. 304). I am not, however, convinced by

other magistrates and private citizens were asked to speak by the president of an assembly (and on occasion an open invitation was issued),[5] there was no general right to participate in the discussion, such as obtained in a Greek democracy like that of Athens. It is symptomatic that the space specially constructed for public meetings at Rome and in her colonies, the *comitium*, was designed for standing, rather than sitting.[6] Republican meetings of the *comitia centuriata* (and ultimately those of all electoral assemblies) took place in a military parade or exercise-ground in the *campus Martius*; even the monumental Saepta Julia, completed by M. Agrippa, would probably at most have provided seating for officials. In general, Roman assemblies, formal and informal, took place in a number of settings, not specifically designed for public meetings, and, although it is likely that some of the audience found something convenient to sit on during the proceedings (perhaps the slope of the Capitoline hill or a piece of a monument), no specific provision was made for this: in fact Cicero stresses that the members of Roman assemblies, unlike their Greek counterparts, remained on their feet.[7]

Finally, an assembly was far from being the whole *populus Romanus*, still less the inhabitants of Rome. Only adult male citizens were qualified to participate; slaves could not, and, even at the end of the Republic, there were restrictions on the capacity of newly manumitted freedmen to vote (see below with nn. 52ff.). Until the Social War Rome's Italian allies—who were a vital part of her military strength—like other foreigners had no right to participate; a limited right was, however, conceded to Rome's Latin allies. As for the *Quirites*,[8] the Roman citizens themselves, even in the days when Rome was nothing but a city with a limited area of surrounding countryside attached, an assembly was at best a representative group of the population. This does not necessarily subvert the principle of a primary assembly open to all citizens: even in

Bleicken's (1975, 288ff.) interpretation of this relationship as a kind of concordat between the aristocracy and the people, since the magistrate did not necessarily represent the aristocracy.

[5] Livy, 45. 21. 6; 36. 1ff.; Dio 39. 35. 1–2. On *contiones* see Pina Polo, 1996, esp. 34ff., on the opportunities for non-magistrates to speak.

[6] For the Roman *comitium* see Coarelli, 1985, 11–21; for those in Rome's colonies see Gros and Torelli, 1992, 141–2; Torelli, 1988, 41–7 (Paestum); Mertens, 1969, 98–101 with plans III F and IV (Alba); Brown, 1980, 22 and figs. 22–3 (Cosa); Coarelli, 1997, 162 (for Fregellae).

[7] See esp. Cic. *Flacc.* 15–17; *Brut.* 289; *Leg. Agr.* 2. 13 with *Staatsr.* iii. 1. 396; Botsford, 1909, 144, n. 1; Taylor, 1966, 29–30, 123–4. On the nature of the *villa publica* and the voting area in the Republican Campus Martius see Coarelli, 1997, 155ff.

[8] The order to divide into voting units at the end of discussion was given to the *Quirites* (Livy, 2. 56. 12).

democratic Athens in the fourth century the Pnyx could only accommodate a fraction of those entitled to vote. One might argue, as
Mommsen did, that even an assembly consisting of all those living
entitled to vote would have been, not the city, but merely a body representing the city, since it would have been deciding on behalf of former
members now dead and of those not yet born or adult.[9] Nevertheless, as
Rome expanded, the disparity between the numbers who attended
an assembly and the current population of the city, not to mention the
hundreds of thousands of Romans living up and down Italy or abroad,
became immense (see further Chap. XI with n. 37).

Comitia, *Contio*, and *Concilium*

Two types of assembly must be distinguished at the start—those
normally designated by the word *comitia* (or *comitiatus*) and those
designated by *contio* (or *conventio*), the two words meaning respectively
a 'going together' and a 'coming together'. *Comitia* (the plural of the
word *comitium*, which meant a specially constructed meeting-place) was
used for an assembly convened in an appropriate place to take a substantive decision, whether this was an election, a piece of legislation, or
a judicial verdict. Because of its frequent use for electoral assemblies, it
became a synonym for an election, but its range of meaning remained
much wider, including both assemblies of the *populus* and of the *plebs*.[10]
The term *contio* was perhaps occasionally used for such meetings in the
late Republic, but it normally designated by contrast those meetings
where nothing was legally enacted. These were summoned with little or
no restriction on venue to listen to public pronouncements, including
magistrates' edicts, to hear arguments in speeches, to witness the
examination of an alleged criminal or even to see his execution.[11] (The
term *contio* will be used in this, more usual, sense in what follows.) A
contio might elicit an impression of popular feeling through applause
and shouts, but did not create any decision. Any consensus evinced in a
contio had no more constitutional validity than the cheers and boos of a

---

[9] *Staatsr.* iii. 1. 305. See also Hansen, 1987, 14–19.

[10] Farrell, 1986; Botsford, 1909, 119–38.

[11] For *contio* designating a formal meeting, though not necessarily one that came to a
decision, see Cic. *Att.* 4. 3. 4 *ad fin.*; *lex gen. Urs.* (*RS* i. 25), cap. 81; Varro, *LL* 6. 88; Macr.
1. 16. 29 (citing L. Iulius Caesar's work on the auspices). See Botsford, 1909, 142 on it being
normally a 'listening assembly'. For *contiones* being held on days in February that were not
according to the calendar (Michels, 1967) *comitiales*, i.e. legitimate for voting assemblies,
see Cic. *QF* 2. 3. 1–2. It is also the most natural interpretation of *Att.* 1. 14. 1 that Fufius'
contio was held on a (non-comitial) *nundinae*.

theatre audience, though obviously it might be of considerable political importance.[12]

The solemnity of the procedure in *comitia*, on the other hand, lay in the use by the presiding magistrate of an inaugurated tribunal (that is, one set aside as a hallowed space or *templum*),[13] and in the adherence to established procedures—matters on which the augurs seem to have been the authority when there was a dispute.[14] Hence the prescript of a law claimed that the magistrate had asked the people 'lawfully' (*iure*) and the people or plebs had resolved 'lawfully'. This was one of the ways in which the sovereignty of the assembly was limited.[15]

A further term for meeting was *concilium*. This was both a general term for political gatherings, frequently applied to those of non-Roman peoples, which became associated (probably because of its close resemblance to the word *consilium*) with deliberative assemblies. It was the common word for meetings of the plebs at Rome, but might on occasion refer to assemblies of the whole people. Unlike *comitia* or *contio* it is rare as a technical legal term: it was used, however, when emphasis was laid on identifying the membership of an assembly (for example, a *concilium* of the plebs or of the Latins), rather than on the formal structure or function of an assembly (as when one spoke of *comitia tributa* or *comitia quaestoria*, the latter meaning elections for the quaestorship).[16]

Assembly Procedure

Among regular magistrates, consuls, praetors, aediles and tribunes all had the right to summon assemblies, as did the dictator and, probably, his second in command, the master of the horse. Although there were days on which assemblies were forbidden for religious and other reasons,

---

[12] *Staatsr.* iii. 1. 305. On the reactions of Roman theatre audiences see Cic. *Att.* 2. 19. 3; 14. 2. 1; *Sest.* 117–24. For orators in *contiones* deliberately extracting a reaction from their audience see Cic. *QF* 2. 3. 2; *Sest.* 126; Plut. *Pomp.* 48. 11–12; *VRR* 10; Pina Polo, 1996, 21–2.

[13] Val. Max. 4. 5. 3; Varro *LL* 6. 86–7 and 91.

[14] For formal references of problems to the augurs see Livy, 8. 23. 14; 23. 31. 13; 45. 12. 10; on augural authority Cic. *Att.* 9. 9. 3; *Leg.* 2. 21 and 31; *Phil.* 2. 83; and note the importance of works on the auspices such as those by Messala (Gell. 13. 15. 3–16. 3) and by L. Caesar (n. 11 above).

[15] Cicero in his comparison of Roman and Greek practice (*Flacc.* 15–17) stresses the formality and discipline at Rome. On the limitations to popular sovereignty see Nocera, 1940, 30 ff.

[16] For *concilium* referring to assemblies of the whole people, contrary to the definition of Laelius Felix in Gell. 15. 27. 4, see Livy, 1. 26. 5 and 36. 6; 2. 7. 7; 3. 71. 3; 6. 20. 11. For the use of the term in the text of statutes see *lex lat. Bant.* (*RS* i. 7) 5; *Tab. Heracl.* (*RS* i. 24) 132. For *comitia quaestoria* see e.g. Cic. *Fam.* 7. 30. 1. The evidence is set out and investigated in Botsford, 1909, 119–38, and Farrell, 1986.

there was no fixed calendar for meetings.[17] For this reason there might be competition between magistrates seeking to hold assemblies on the same day, whether these were *comitia or contiones*. A formal voting assembly had precedence over trials in a *quaestio*, and hence probably over *contiones*. According to the rules set out by the augur Marcus Valerius Messalla (*cos.* 53 BC), if a formal assembly (*comitiatus*) had begun, it could not be supplanted by another formal assembly under a rival magistrate. However, before proceedings began, a consul could call away (*avocare*) either a *comitiatus* or a *contio* from any other magistrate, while a praetor could call away an assembly from any other magistrate but a consul.[18] The status of the tribunes in this respect is uncertain, but we have examples of tribunes complaining that their rights were being infringed when a *contio* was called away from them, even when a praetor did so to carry out jurisdiction.[19]

The procedure for holding a Roman assembly has to be reconstructed from diverse sources. The first necessity, if the assembly was to be formal, was for notice to be given beforehand. Before elections it is said to have been originally customary for candidates to present themselves to the electorate on three market-days before the election; later it was established that there should be a *trinundinum*, a time-lapse of at least three market-days (in effect seventeen days or more) between the announcement and the election, during which no legislation was permitted.[20] Similarly, the *lex Caecilia Didia* of 98 BC required the elapse of a *trinundinum* between the promulgation of a law and its enactment in the assembly.[21] A magistrate conducting a prosecution before the assembly gave notice (*diem dicere*) to the accused of the first day of investigation (*anquisitio*) in his trial, then at the end of each hearing

---

[17] See Macr. 1. 16. 30 (citing Granius Licinianus) for a *lex Hortensia* making market-days *fasti*—but not *comitiales*, i.e. licensed for formal assemblies (see ibid. 40).

[18] *Lex rep.* 71–2; Gell. 13. 16. 1.

[19] Livy, 43. 16. 9 and 11; *De Vir. Ill.* 65. 5; 73. 2.

[20] Macr. 1. 16. 34 (citing a Rutilius—? P. Rutilius Rufus, but misinterpreting *nundinae* in a way a late-republican senator could never have done); Cic. *Fam.* 16. 12. 3; *Att.* 1. 16. 13. For the interpretation here see Lintott, 1965, criticizing Mommsen's view (*Staatsr.* i. 375–6) that a *trinundinum* was an interval of 24 days—anticipated, unknown to me at the time, by Lange, 1875. Michels, 1967, 88 and 191ff., proposed a 25-day *trinundinum*, accepting my argument that three Roman weeks were 25 days according to their method of counting, but arguing that Cic. *Pis.* 8–9 does not entail that Clodius' first legislation as tribune (three days later than the Compitalia on 1 Jan.) was on 4 Jan., 58 and hence technically illegal on her interpretation. See also Lintott, 1968, on the actual dates of *nundinae* and the consequences of this.

[21] Cic. *Dom.* 41; *Sest.* 135; *Phil.* 5. 8; *Schol. Bob.* 140St. See VRR 134–5, 140–3. The complexity of late-Republican statutes made it especially desirable to have an interval sufficient for the study of their texts by those who might wish to criticize or oppose.

announced the adjournment until the next (*diem prodicere*), and finally allowed an interval of a *trinundinum* before the final vote in the assembly.[22] Before the actual assembly the magistrate had to take the auspices in the inaugurated area (*templum*) from which he was to conduct the proceedings. If these were favourable, and if no other magistrate announced unfavourable omens, he requested the presence of colleagues, other magistrates, and senators and instructed a herald to summon the people. [23] This, according to the ancient commentary cited by Varro, was carried out not only from the *templum* to be used but also from the walls; an announcement was made from the *rostra* in the forum, even when these were not to be used as the *templum*, and the shops of the money-changers were shut; furthermore, in the case of an accusation before the *comitia centuriata* a horn was sounded on the citadel and in front of the house of the accused.[24]

A voting assembly began with a prayer.[25] The magistrate himself would then introduce the subject of the assembly. In electoral *comitia* we have no evidence of introductory remarks by the presiding magistrate, only of an intervention, once the proceedings had started, but the possibility of a short prefatory address should not be excluded. Indeed, if, as has been recently argued with considerable plausibility, *professio* under the Republic was self-advertisement to the people at large, not a formal declaration of candidature to a presiding officer, then this might have been the moment for the president to invite candidates finally to ask for election (*petere*).[26]

Informal assemblies were taken up with speeches. Moreover, on the final day of the vote on a bill there could be debate before the actual legislation. Private citizens had to be given an opportunity to speak about a bill before it was either put to the vote or vetoed. This on one occasion entailed that two tribunes were not allowed to speak against a

[22] For *diem dicere*, see e.g. Cic. *Mil.* 36; *Div. Caec.* 67; *diem prodicere*, Cic. *QF* 2. 3. 2; *trinundinum* Cic. *Dom.* 45. Compare the republican municipal law from Bantia which prescribes a thirty-day interval before the final stage of assembly trials (*lex osca Bant.* (*RS* i. 13), lines 15–17. The trials prescribed by this law seem to have involved one more hearing than those at Rome in Cicero's day. See Chap. IX, n. 21.

[23] Varro, *LL* 6. 91. On *nuntiatio* of omens see Cic. *Phil.* 2. 81; Cato in Festus, 268L; Pliny, *HN* 28. 17; Serv. *Ad Aen.* 12. 260; *de Vir. Ill.* 73. 6–7; Wissowa, 1912, 529–34; de Libero, 1992, 56 ff.

[24] Varro, *LL* 6. 92–3, cf. 87–8 for the procedure for holding a census.

[25] Cic. *Mur.* 1; *Ad Herenn.* 4. 68; Dion. Hal. *AR* 7. 59. 2. See also Livy, 39. 15. 1, for it being used before a *contio* in which *senatus consulta* were to be solemnly announced.

[26] For a prefatory speech see *Staatsr.* iii. 1. 392; for intervention Livy, 24. 8. On *professio* see Levick, 1981.

tribunician bill of their colleague on the first day of debate.[27] Before the vote a bill was formally read, normally by a herald, and, in the assemblies organized by tribes, an urn was brought, into which lots were cast to determine the order of voting and the tribe in which any Latins present were to vote. This was the last point at which the tribunes were allowed to exercise their right to veto.[28]

At the injunction, 'Discedite, Quirites',[29] the voters in a tribal assembly left the neighbourhood of the tribunal to form themselves into their appropriate voting units in specially fenced-in spaces (*saepta*); in the *comitia centuriata* they were summoned into an area defined by a *licium*, probably a rope. They then were called into the *templum* on the tribunal to deliver their votes. It has been convincingly inferred from a passage of Varro that up to 145 BC tribal voting in the forum was based on the *comitium* and the associated Republican *rostra*, but, when this became too cramped, the focus was shifted to the opposite, south-east, end of the forum and steps of the temple of Castor were used as the tribunal.[30] By the late second century BC *pontes*, elevated gangways, were erected as a route. A *lex Maria*, usually attributed to C. Marius as tribune in 119, made the *pontes* narrow, presumably to limit the possibility of intimidation.[31]

The magistrate selected distinguished men to act as *rogatores*. From this term it is generally inferred that before the introduction of written ballot the voter was asked about his choice and his verbal response was translated into marks pricked on appropriate tablets (*puncta* is a term used for votes in the late Republic).[32] There is no direct evidence for this

[27] Asc. 71C; Livy, 45. 21. 6 and 36. 1; Dio 39. 35. 1–2; Plut. *Cato mi.* 43. 2–3.

[28] On the reading of bills see Cic. *Leg.* 3. 11; Asc. 58C; Plut. *Cato mi.* 28. 1; on the allotment Cic. *Dom.* 50; *Leg. Agr.* 2. 21; Asc. 71C; *Ad Herenn.* 1. 21; Livy, 25. 3. 16. On the timing of vetoes there are recent contributions by Rilinger, 1989, and de Libero, 1992, 38 ff. In fact, there seems to have been no standard moment for a veto, but the *sortitio* was the last opportunity and, on the other hand, it was not acceptable for bills to be vetoed without discussion.

[29] The phrase (Livy, 2. 56. 12; Asc. 71C) is normally translated as 'Depart into your separate groups', but may have originally meant 'Clear the voting area'. See Vaahtera, 1993*a*, 113–14.

[30] See Cic. *Mil.* 41; *lex Val. Aur.* (*RS* i. 37 = EJ² 94a) *tab. Heb.* lines 10–11; Serv. *Ad Eclog.* 1. 33; on the *licium* (Varro *LL* 6. 88, cf. 86 and 94–5) see Taylor, 1966, 56, 136 n. 61, 156 n. 41; Vaahtera, 1993*a*, 112–15. The phrase '*intro vocare*' is found in Livy, 10. 13. 11 and *lex rep.* 72. On the move of tribal voting assemblies see Varro, *RR* 1. 2. 9; Cic. *Amic.* 96; Taylor, 1966, 21 ff.; Coarelli, 1985, 11 ff., 163 ff. The purpose of the *saepta* would have been not only to separate voting units but to prevent voters voting twice.

[31] *Ad Herenn.* 1. 21; Cic. *Att.* 1. 14. 5; Suet. *Jul.* 80. 4; *RRC* 292. 1—a coin of P. Nerva of 113 or 112 BC; on the *lex Maria*, Cic. *Leg.* 3. 39; Plut. *Mar.* 4. 2.

[32] On *rogatores* see Cic. *Leg.* 3. 33 ff.; on *puncta* Cic. *Planc.* 53; *Mur.* 72; *Tusc.* 2. 62; Hor. *AP* 343 (in a metaphor, after references to the *equites equo publico* and the *centuriae seniorum*, on which see below with nn. 74 ff. and 89).

view. The standard Latin term for a vote, *suffragium*, perhaps derives from an even earlier period, reflecting the fact that the assembly did not originally vote at all but made a crash with its arms in approval.[33] It has recently been suggested that Dionysius of Halicarnassus was not being completely anachronistic, when he refers to the casting of *psēphoi* in Rome's early history, provided that this word is interpreted as pebbles, such as used in classical Athens, rather than the written ballots of the late Republic. The placing of pebbles under supervision in appropriate jars would have been a more reliable form of registration of votes than the translation of speech into points on tablets.[34]

Written ballot was introduced into assemblies by a series of plebiscites in the late second century BC—the *lex Gabinia* of 139 about elections, the *lex Cassia* of 137 about non-capital trials, the *lex Papiria* of 131 about legislation, and the *lex Coelia* of 106 about capital trials. From Cicero's presentation of these reforms in the *De Legibus* it is evident that it was thought that they diminished the influence of the élite, inasmuch as the citizens were no longer required to reveal to a *rogator* how they were voting. The same concern for propriety and secrecy can be seen in the *lex de repetundis* of 123–2 BC, where judges are required to cast their ballot openly with their arm laid bare, so making plain that they are only casting one vote, but concealing with their fingers the letter which remained on the ballot.[35] Secrecy before the act of voting in an assembly may also have been prescribed by law (in the Gracchan *lex de repetundis* the jury in a *quaestio* are required to swear that they will do nothing to enable any of their number to find out in advance about his colleagues' votes): moreover, the *lex Maria* (above) shows that there was concern about improper pressure and intimidation on the voter before he cast his vote.[36] However, he may well have needed help with preparing his ballot, even when it was only a matter of choosing between VTI ROGAS ('aye', abbreviated to V on coins of L. Cassius Longinus, of 63 BC) and ANTIQVO, ('nay', perhaps abbreviated to A).[37] One celebrated passage of Cicero reveals the existence of prepared ballots for a vote on legislation, and it has been argued that this was common, whether there was a single type of ballot with two alternative signs, or there were two different types. It is conceivable that the practice spread to elections, with

---

[33] See Vaahtera, 1993*b*.
[34] See Dion. Hal. *AR* 7. 17. 4; 7. 59. 2–10; 10. 36. 1 and 41. 3; 11. 52. 3–4, with Vaahtera, 1990.
[35] Cic. *Leg.* 3. 34–9; *lex rep.*, lines 50–4.
[36] Cic. *Leg.* 3. 38; *lex rep.* 44–5.
[37] See *RRC* 413. 1. For the marks on judicial ballots see ibid. 428. 2 (Q. Cassius) with 'A(bsolvo). C(ondemno)' and 437. 1a–b (C. Coelius Caldus) with 'L(ibero). D(amno)'.

tablets inscribed in advance with shortened versions of the candidates' names (a rough parallel would have been the preparing of sherds in advance for an Athenian ostracism). The coin of P. Nerva appears to show a voter being handed a tablet, when already on the *pons* leading to the voting baskets. However, we are told that Cato Uticensis had an election for aediles annulled because he found a number of tablets with the same handwriting, and this suggests that prepared ballots were unusual and suspect.[38]

The baskets (*cistae*) containing the votes delivered were watched over by *custodes*, who in the late Republic were drawn from the album of jurors for the *quaestiones*: under the Principate those at Rome were called 'the nine hundred' (*nongenti*).[39] These *custodes* were also responsible for counting (*diribitio*) and reporting the votes to the presiding magistrate.[40] Decisions were not taken according to total votes cast but according to the majority in each voting unit, whether century or tribe. In the *comitia centuriata*, whose complexities I discuss later (see the text with nn. 72 ff.), voting followed a hierarchy of classes, while within classes the lot may have decided which century's vote was announced first. In the tribal assemblies, when votes were taken successively according to the order of tribes established by lot, they were announced in that order. In a yes/no decision, as soon as eighteen of the thirty-five tribes had voted the same way, the matter was finished. In an election, moreover, it was not a matter of who received most votes, but who could be the first to register the approval of eighteen tribes. Hence it was perfectly possible for a candidate who had obtained as many as or more tribes than his competitors individually to lose a close election because of the order in which the returns were made. This would have been particularly likely in the elections for tribunes, where with ten vacant places there were potentially three hundred and fifty tribal votes to be registered.[41] In late-Republican elections, when tribal voting took place simultaneously, a magistrate who wished to avoid accusations of prejudice would have decided by casting lots the order in which the tribes were to be

---

[38] Cic. *Att.* 1. 14. 5; *RRC* 292. 1; Plut. *Cato mi.* 46. 3; *Staatsr.* iii. 1. 402; Luisi, 1993.

[39] On *cistae* see Sisenna, fr. 118P; *Ad Herenn.* 1. 21; *lex Val. Aur.* (*RS* i. 37 = EJ² 94a) *tab. Heb.* 17 ff., cf. *RS* i. 38 = EJ² 94b, *Tab. Ilic.* 14 and 20; on *custodes* Cic. *Red. Sen.* 28; *Pis.* 36; Pliny, *HN* 33. 31; *lex mun. Mal.*, ch. 55.

[40] Cic. *Planc.* 14 and 49; *Pis.* 36; Varro, *RR* 3. 5. 18.

[41] On the use of lot to determine the order of returns see *lex Val. Aur.* (*RS* i. 37 = EJ² 94a) *tab. Heb.* 40 ff.; Cic. *Leg. Agr.* 2. 21; on the resulting order Gell. 10. 1. 6 (Varro); Cic. *Pis.* 2; *Mur.* 35; Plut. *C. Gr.* 3. 3; *Caes.* 5. 1; Suet. *Vesp.* 2. 3; on the complications Hall, 1967 and 1972. For the completion of a vote in a trial before the assembly see Livy, 43. 8. 9, where all 35 tribes voted unanimously.

announced, and this probably became the norm.⁴² Finally, it was the presiding magistrate's task to have the assembly's decision declared. The procedure had to be completed in a day: if a vote was interrupted or abandoned, it had to be repeated from the beginning.⁴³

The Organization of the Different Assemblies

Curiae and Comitia Curiata

Some assemblies in the later Republic existed only in a symbolic and ritualized form. These were the assemblies based on *curiae*—held to be thirty ancient divisions of the Roman people created by Romulus and named after the Sabine women—which were now represented by 30 lictors.⁴⁴ One form of this assembly, termed the *comitia calata*, which met under the presidency of the *pontifex maximus*, was employed for religious purposes, such as the inauguration of priests and selection of Vestal virgins, and for the making of testaments, which originally would have had religious implications in so far as authority over family rituals was transmitted.⁴⁵ The *comitia curiata* was used for the kind of adoption known as *adrogatio*, whether in the lifetime of the adoptive parent or as a result of a will,⁴⁶ but more regularly to pass the *leges curiatae* ratifying the status of elected magistrates and of promagistrates.⁴⁷ What precisely was conferred by the *lex curiata* was obscure in the late Republic. A magistrate could claim that he had no need of it to exercise command; a legislator could include in his bill a provision whereby it was made redundant. An oddity was that for the censors the same measure was carried out in the *comitia centuriata*. It seems to be a confirmatory ritual, whose origin lay in the time where the Romans were involving new assemblies in their election procedure beside the original *comitia curiata*.⁴⁸

⁴² *Lex mun. Mal.* ch. 57; cf. Cic. *Planc.* 35 for the selection of the first voter by lot.
⁴³ Cic. *Phil.* 2. 82; App. *BCiv.* 1. 14. 62.
⁴⁴ See on the *curiae* Cic. *Rep.* 2. 14; Livy, 1. 13. 6; 9. 38. 15; Festus, 180–2 and 503L; Dion. Hal. *AR* 2. 50. 3; Cic. *Dom.* 77; on the lictors Cic. *Leg. Agr.* 2. 31.
⁴⁵ On the *comitia calata* see Gell.; 15. 27. 1–3; cf. 1. 12. 9ff.; on inauguration Cic. *Brut.* 1; *Phil.* 2. 110; Macr. 3. 13. 11.
⁴⁶ See in general Gell. 5. 19. 4–10 and, on the adoption of C. Octavius into the Iulii Caesares after Caesar's death, App. *BCiv.* 3. 94. 389–91; Dio 45. 5. 3. This last has been held to be an exceptional procedure by Schmitthenner, 1973, 39ff., 51ff., 114–15, and Linderski, 1996, 149–54. However, our lack of evidence may be misleading and the procedure quite normal, see Schulz, 1951, 144–6; Crook, 1967, 112.
⁴⁷ Cic. *Leg. Agr.* 2. 26ff.; *Fam.* 1. 9. 25; *Att.* 4. 17. 2 and 18. 4; Livy, 5. 52. 16; Gell. 13. 15. 4.
⁴⁸ Cic. *Leg. Agr.* 2. 26. Giovannini (1983, 51–5) has argued that the *lex curiata* conferred

Tribus and *Comitia Tributa*

There were two important forms of assembly employed in the middle and late Republic—*comitia centuriata* and *comitia tributa*. The second may well be later in origin, but for convenience I will examine it first.

The word *tribus* had nothing etymologically to do with kinship groups: it meant simply a division or district into which people were distributed. In practice almost all the original rural *tribus*—for example Aemilia, Claudia, Cornelia, Fabia, Papiria—have names associated with the groups Romans termed *gentes*, but we have no secure explanation of the connection: perhaps these *gentes* and their clients provided the original membership of the *tribus*, perhaps the *gentes* once owned all the land in their respective *tribus*, perhaps they were simply dominant groups in the area. It is hard to weigh up these speculations when we are not sure what united members of *gentes* apart from their *nomen*, that is, the second name of men and the first or only name of women—for example Gaius *Iulius* Caesar and his daughter *Iulia*.[49]

According to tradition there were four urban districts and seventeen rural in the old Roman territory in 495 BC, before the expansion under the Republic. Fourteen rural tribes were added down to 241 BC, ending with the Velina and Quirina in that year, to bring the total to thirty-five. After this time, the Italian territory that became Roman—after the Social War of 90–89 BC this amounted to all Italy south of the Arno and Rubicon rivers—was eventually distributed among the existing tribes, although measures were experimentally taken in 90–89 BC to increase their number in order to cope with the influx of citizens.[50]

The Gracchan *lex repetundarum* required the names of jurors in the album to be written down 'by father, tribe, and *cognomen*' (lines 14, 18). In a man's official name the tribe followed the patronymic and the *cognomen* came last—for example, M(arcus) Tullius M(arci) f(ilius)

on all magistrates the right to take the auspices, but the patrician monopoly of the *curiae* that he assumes is a doubtful foundation for the argument, nor can he explain the parallel procedure for the censors in the centuriate assembly where there cannot have been a patrician monopoly. As for pro-magistrates, there seems no evidence for a specific right to take military auspices (Chap. VII with nn. 43–4). However, it seems to have been thought that they had lost the right to take auspices with the lapse of their urban magistracy. Thus for them the *lex curiata* did not have the specific effect which Giovannini supposes. For the notoriously embittered controversy between Sigonio and Nicolas de Grouchy in the sixteenth century over the nature of the *lex curiata* see McCuaig, 1989, 183–202, and 1986.

[49] On *tribus* see Staatsr. iii. 1. 11ff.; Taylor, 1960, 11ff.; and Chap. X with nn. 42ff.; on *gentes* see the recent overviews of A. Drummond, *CAH* vii. 2². 143ff.; Smith, 1996, 198ff.

[50] App. *BCiv.* 1. 49. 214–15 and 53. 231; Sisenna, fr. 17P.

Corn(elia tribu) Cicero. The tribe was the critical indicator of Roman citizenship, not only for the sons of Roman fathers when they grew up, but for those incorporated into the citizen body from outside. The *lex repetundarum* made specific provision about this for the benefit of those winning citizenship through a successful prosecution.[51] Tribes were allocated in the census, a newly enrolled adult normally taking the tribe of his father, which he would only lose if he changed his family through being adopted. The tribe might, therefore, come to bear little relationship to the whereabouts of the citizen's domicile and property.

A group of people whose tribal status fluctuated over the centuries was freedmen and their descendants (who were of course freeborn). Political dispute about their location in the citizen body was said to have begun with the censorship of Appius Claudius in 312 BC, who allegedly 'corrupted the forum and campus (that is, the voting places of the tribes and the centuries) by distributing the lower class (*humiles*) among all the tribes'. It appears that the people in question were freedmen, probably not allowed to be registered at random, but allocated to the rural tribe of their patron.[52] The freedmen were put back in the following censorship into the four urban tribes, where they would have had less political influence. In the early second century BC the votes of freedmen and their descendants again became an issue. According to Plutarch, the tribune Q. Terentius Culleo passed a bill in 189 forcing the censors to 'accept' all those born of free parents. It was not for the censors to bar wholesale a class of citizens from the means to exercise their citizen status, or so it was argued later, and one plausible interpretation of the passage is that the descendants of freedmen were to be treated like any other free-born Roman and hence enrolled in a rural tribe where appropriate.[53] We later hear of a reform—perhaps the work of the censors of 179, who seem to have been flexible in their attitude to the tribes—whereby liberated slaves themselves could enrol in a rural tribe, if they had a five-year-old son or a property of 30,000 sesterces in the country.[54] Later there was a conflict between the censors of 169–8, Gaius Claudius Pulcher and Tiberius Sempronius Gracchus (father of the famous tribune), concerning former

[51] *Lex rep.* 77, where important details are lost in a lacuna. The commonly accepted supplement refers to enrolment in the tribe of the condemned man, but a plausible alternative would allow a free choice of tribe, see *JRLR* 156–7.

[52] Livy, 9. 46. 11; Diod. 20. 36. 4.

[53] Plut. *Flamin.* 18. 2 with Livy, 45. 15. 4, for the argument (the Livy passage occurs shortly after a lacuna caused by the loss of a folium in the MS, but its context is clear); Taylor, 1960, 132 ff.   [54] Livy, 45. 15. 1–3, cf. 40. 51. 9.

slaves, though not, it appears, about their descendants, which led to their being confined to one of the urban tribes chosen by lot.[55]

The issue of the status of ex-slaves continued to be raised in the late Republic. A law was passed by Marcus Aemilius Scaurus improving their electoral position in 115, another by Publius Sulpicius in 88, which was annulled by Sulla, reinstated under the Cinnan regime, but presumably annulled under Sulla's dictatorship.[56] In 66, Gaius Manilius passed a bill that freedmen should be allowed to vote in their patrons' tribes, but it was annulled on procedural grounds. Finally, Publius Clodius seems to have been planning a bill to enhance the voting rights of former slaves, when he stood for the praetorship of 52.[57]

Throughout this series of disputes two tendencies can be seen. The most fundamental is the anxiety about the influence of newcomers to the citizen body, especially those of non-Italian stock.[58] This would have been exacerbated by the exponential increase in the number of ex-slave citizens during the late Republic. The other is the political exploitation of new citizens by their patrons to secure influence where it counted most, in rural tribes. Even if the treatment of Appius Claudius the censor in our sources is anachronistic, it reflects concerns which would have been surfacing in the early second century BC. The same hopes and fears would have attended the proposals to give the suffrage to the Italians and aroused suspicions of men like Marcus Fulvius Flaccus, Gaius Gracchus, and Marcus Livius Drusus, the tribune of 91. Although we hear of the creation of new tribes after the *lex Iulia* of 90 BC, by 88 the new Italian citizens were only being included in eight of the old tribes. In the end it seems that the Italians were absorbed without such extreme restriction, but their registration was a slow process and the allocation of new districts to the tribes has an unevenness which suggests that their political power was being manipulated.[59]

We know of other subdivisions of the Roman citizen body—*vici* and *pagi*, that is, districts inside the city and in the neighbouring countryside, and *collegia*, organizations based on professions involved

---

[55] Livy, 45. 15. 3–7; contrast Cic. *de Or.* 1. 38 and *de Vir. Ill.* 57. 3, according to which the freedmen were to be confined to the four urban tribes.

[56] See *de Vir. Ill.* 72. 5; Cic. *de Orat.* 2. 257 on Scaurus; Asc. 64C; Livy, *Per.* 78 and 84 on Sulpicius.

[57] See Asc. 45, 64C; Dio, 36. 42. 2, on Manilius; Cic. *Mil.* 87; Asc. 52C on Clodius.

[58] Cic. *de Orat.* 2. 257 has a quotation of words apparently used by Scaurus; Vell. 2. 4. 4 and Val. Max. 6. 2. 3 an *obiter dictum* of Scipio Aemilianus (other versions collected by Astin, 1967, 265–6).

[59] Vell. 2. 20. 2; App. *BCiv.* 1. 49. 214–15 and 53. 231; Sisenna fr. 17P; Taylor, 1960, ch. 16.

with cult[60]—but the tribes remain the only fundamental and comprehensive constituent parts. They had officials, *curatores* and *divisores* (treasurers), and are likely to have had their own registers (the *curatores* were involved in the census). Thus, in spite of the military organization based on *centuriae*, they would even have had a function in military recruitment. It is unlikely to be a coincidence that military officers were called *tribuni* and the military treasurers, who were supposed to have acted as paymasters to the army, were *tribuni aerarii*.[61] Nor in view of the tribes' general importance in the organization of the people is it surprising that the chief plebeian officials were *tribuni plebis*.

How many kinds of tribal assembly? Assemblies based on the tribes are attested as having been convened both by tribunes and aediles of the plebs and by major magistrates of the people—consuls, praetors and curule aediles (so-called because, like the consuls and praetors, they had the right to a curule chair). In our ancient sources the term *comitia tributa* is chiefly used to describe the structure of the assembly and is on occasion used for a plebeian meeting. Since Mommsen's time, most modern scholars have used this term exclusively for a meeting by tribes of the whole *populus*, including the patricians, while reserving the term *concilium plebis* for meetings of the plebeians. This orthodoxy has come under attack.[62] It has been argued, first, that this terminology is merely a modern convention, and, secondly and more controversially, that there were no meetings of the tribes, apart from plebeian meetings presided over by tribunes: references to legislation by consuls or praetors must, therefore, either refer to meetings of the *comitia centuriata*, or be the results of late-Republican deviation from correct procedure, or be in fact allusions to consuls and praetors getting tribunes to propose bills for them.[63]

The proposition that there was no assembly based on the tribes but the *concilium plebis* runs counter to certain solid pieces of evidence. We have texts of laws which show consuls legislating before the tribes not only under Augustus (the *lex Quinctia* of 9 BC) but also in 58 BC (the

---

[60] Dion. Hal. *AR* 4. 14. 3–15. 5; Cic. *Dom.* 74; *Comm. Pet.* 8. 30. On the republican *collegia* see e.g. Waltzing, 1895, i; Ausbüttel, 1982; *VRR* 78–83.

[61] Varro *LL* 6. 86; Cic. *Verr.* 1. 22; *Att.* 1. 16. 12, 18. 4; *de Orat.* 2. 257; *Corn.* I, frr. 40–41 Puccioni; Dion. Hal. *AR* 4. 14. 1–3; *Staatsr.* iii. 1. 161ff. (189ff. on *tribuni aerarii*); Taylor, 1960.

[62] For '*comitia tributa*' describing a plebeian assembly see Livy, 2. 56. 2, and more generally on the terminology Farrell, 1986. For restatements of the criticism of orthodoxy see Develin (1975 and 1977) and Sandberg (1993).

[63] Develin, 1975, 335; Sandberg, 1993, 89ff.

lex Gabinia Calpurnia de Delo); the law about creating and supporting twenty quaestors, which our sources attribute to Sulla as dictator, was passed before a tribal assembly.[64] Since, moreover, the epigraphic text of the *lex de provinciis praetoriis* of 101–100 refers to actual legislation by the praetor Marcus Porcius, it is questionable to reinterpret texts in literary sources which, when taken naturally, mean that consuls and praetors legislated.[65] Consuls held elections of aediles before the tribes. Not only plebeian aediles, but curule aediles conducted before the people prosecutions leading to a fine, which would have normally come before a tribal assembly.[66]

Hence it cannot be properly argued that there were no *comitia tributa* apart from the *concilium plebis*. It may well be that the term *comitia tributa* was commonly used both for assemblies convened by curule magistrates and for those convened by tribunes. This does not preclude these two kinds of assemblies differing in certain respects, even if our lack of knowledge prevents precise definition of this. One important uncertainty is whether, after the *lex Hortensia* gave plebiscites the force of laws, patricians were admitted to plebeian assemblies. We find recorded a speech by a former military tribune of patrician rank in an assembly convened by a tribune to discuss the rejection of L. Aemilius Paulus' request for a triumph in 167. It may have seemed impractical and undesirable to exclude patricians from informal assemblies, but when for example a vote was actually taken on a law, it would surely have been improper, even repugnant, to include patrician votes in a decision which would be described as 'X . . . plebem rogavit plebesque iure scivit'.[67] Moreover, the person presiding over a Roman assembly, which was a co-operative function of the magistrate and the meeting he had gathered, would have affected the nature of that assembly. For this reason it seems best to continue to distinguish between tribal assemblies convened by a curule magistrate and those convened by a tribune (it is not clear whether assemblies convened by plebeian aediles in the later Republic for judicial purposes remained exclusively plebeian).[68]

Tribal assemblies were characterized by flexibility of venue. Formal

---

[64] *RS* i. 14 and 22; *RS* ii. 63.

[65] *RS* i. 12, Cnidos III, lines 4 ff.

[66] On elections see Varro, *RR* 3. 2. 2 and 5. 18; on prosecutions *Staatsr.* ii. 1. 491 ff.; *VRR* 96–8.

[67] See Zon. 7. 17. 6 for the patricians' exclusion, *contra* Botsford, 1909, 271 and 276, relying on passages of Livy on the fifth century. Sandberg, 1993, 77–9 raises doubts about the admission of patricians to the *concilium plebis*.

[68] See *VRR* 96–8. Both curule and plebeian aediles undertake prosecutions for the same kind of offences.

assemblies might take place in the forum—at first based on the *rostra* and *comitium*, later on the temple of Castor at the south-east end. They are also attested in the *area Capitolina* by the temple of Jupiter Optimus Maximus.[69] Elections, which at least until the time of Ti. Gracchus involved the tribes voting in succession, originally took place in the forum or on the Capitol. In the late Republic they took place in the Campus Martius, which would have been able to accommodate the simultaneous voting of the tribes and thus speed up the process.[70] In legislative assemblies we find the practice of selecting a first tribe by lot, *principium*, whose vote would be announced before the others cast their votes.[71] Such was the comparatively simple organization of the assembly in which almost all legislation took place and the election of all magistrates except consuls, praetors, and censors.

Comitia Centuriata

Beside the tribal assemblies the Romans retained an assembly which appeared archaic in conception and in form, but whose subdivisions, unlike those of the *comitia curiata*, had not become obsolete. This was the assembly based on property classes, whose unit was the *centuria*. The Roman sometimes called it *exercitus*.[72] It met in the military parade and exercise ground, the Campus Martius; *centuriae* was a term also used for the smallest infantry units in the Roman army; and the assembly's creation, attributed to king Servius Tullius, is seen by the annalists as a means of exacting military and civil duties from citizens in proportion to their means, while granting them voting privilege in proportion to the services thus demanded.[73] It is tempting to see it in origin as a single '*classis*' of heavily armed infantry (what in Greece would have been hoplites), with a small group of cavalry and other specialist military units, these fighting men being the citizens with full rights, by contrast with the poor and landless who formed the *proletarii*. This would explain

---

[69] For the *comitium* see Varro *RR* 1. 2. 9; for the temple of Castor *lex de Delo* (*RS* i. 22), 3; Cic. *Dom.* 54, 110; *Sest.* 34; *Pis.* 23; Plut. *Cato mi.* 27. 5; also *lex lat. Bant.* (*RS* i. 7), 17, for the temple as the locus for the taking of an oath; for the election of colonial commissioners in the *area Capitolina* Livy, 34. 53. 2; in general Taylor, 1960, 27–8.

[70] App. *BCiv.* 1. 14–16; contrast Varro, *RR* 3. 2. 2; Cic. *Att.* 1. 1. 1; 4. 16. 8. Note also Plut. *C. Gr.* 3. 2—a reference to the *pedion*, perhaps the *campus*, in a description of C. Gracchus' election to his first tribunate.

[71] On the *principium* see *lex agr.* 1; *lex Corn XX quaest.* (*RS* i. 14) praef. 2; for the first voter (*preimus sceivit*) *lex agr.* 1; *lex Ant. Term.* (*RS* i. 19), praef. 4; *lex de Delo* (*RS* i. 22), 4; Cic. *Planc.* 35.

[72] Varro *LL* 6. 88; Livy, 39. 15. 11; Gell. 15. 27. 5; Macr. 1. 16. 15; Serv. *ad Aen.* 8. 1.

[73] Livy, 1. 42. 5 and 43. 10; Dion. Hal. *AR* 4. 19. 2–3 and 21. 2.

satisfactorily some functions of the assembly—the election of consuls and praetors who would be its commanders and the election of censors who took the census on which its membership was based.[74]

Nevertheless, this assembly as we find it in the middle and late Republic can no longer be regarded as a mirror of the Roman army. There was no place in it for legions, cohorts, and maniples, nor was there any necessary match between centuries in the assemblies and centuries in the army. Thus the principle, enunciated by Dionysius of Halicarnassus, that because the rich, though fewer, were divided into many more centuries than the poor, they had to do proportionately more military service, could no longer obtain—if indeed it ever did obtain at Rome and was not merely a philosophical justification discovered when the assembly was obsolete as a military formation. Cicero has no doubt about the purpose of the assembly in the eyes of Servius Tullius: it was that 'the greatest number of people should not have the greatest influence'.[75]

Both Livy and Dionysius give us more or less identical reconstructions of the assembly allegedly created by Servius Tullius, based on 193 or 194 centuries, including 18 centuries of cavalry and 170 of infantry, which, they state, was no longer in existence in their own day. (According to Livy, the reason for the change was the 'inclusion of the full number of thirty-five tribes and the doubling of that number by centuries of seniors and juniors'. However, neither author has left us an account of the later version.)[76] Cicero ascribes to Scipio Aemilianus, the protagonist of his dialogue *De Re Publica* (whose dramatic date is 129 BC), an encomiastic, but enigmatic, account of the assembly created by Servius Tullius:

If this system of division had been unknown to you, it would have been explained by me. Now you see the calculation to be such, that the centuries of cavalry with the six *suffragia* and the first class, with the addition of the century which has been assigned to the carpenters for the greatest advantage of the city, have eighty-nine centuries; if these have been joined by only eight out of the one hundred and four centuries (for this is the number that remain), the total strength of the people has been achieved, and the much more numerous

---

[74] See Fraccaro, 1929; Last, 1945; de Martino, *SCR* i. 144–8; Momigliano, *CAH* vii. 2.² 103–4. See Fascione (1981) for doubts about the orthodox view that the *comitia centuriata* had the monopoly of declarations of war, which have validity even for those who do not trust the evidence for the early Republic.

[75] Dion. Hal. *AR* 4. 19. 2–3 and 21. 2; Cic. *Rep.* 2. 39 (cf. 40 for the view that the men who had the greatest voting power were those who had the greatest stake in the excellent condition of the community) ; see also Livy, 1. 43. 10.

[76] Livy, 1. 43. 12; Dion. Hal. *AR* 4. 21. 3.

remainder of ninety-six centuries would not be excluded from the vote, to avoid insolence, nor would it be having excessive power, to avoid danger.[77]

Cicero seems to be describing a system which was in force in 129 BC but, as he believed, originated with Servius Tullius. In this there were eighteen centuries of cavalry (including six '*suffragia*'), seventy centuries in the first class plus a century of carpenters (these last privileged because of their military function), and one hundred and four others. The brief description of the voting in the abandoned consular election held by Marcus Antonius after Caesar's murder, in which the business is finished after the second class have voted,[78] reinforces the impression of *De Re Publica* that this is the *comitia centuriata* with which Cicero is familiar in his own day. The seventy centuries of the first class suggest a connection with the thirty-five tribes, and other passages of Cicero show that he considered the *tribus* to be in some way the voting unit in this assembly of centuries. It is, however, obvious to us, though it may not have been so obvious to Cicero, that a system based on the thirty-five tribes could only have come into being after the creation of the last two tribes in 241 BC.[79]

The descriptions provided by Livy and Dionysius are perhaps nothing more than antiquarian reconstructions of the reform attributed to Servius Tullius, based on the number of 193 centuries (though the figures in the manuscripts of Livy produce a total of 194) and the principle that the cavalry and the first class must have a majority. In these there are

---

[77] Cic. *Rep.* 2. 39. It is generally held that the contrast between the 97 centuries (*equites*, first class, *fabri* + 8 more) and the remaining *multo maior multitudo sex et nonaginta centuriarum* explains the contrast between the *locupletes* and the *multitudo* or *plurimi* earlier in 2. 39. Yakobson, however, (1992, 48–9) has argued that the *locupletes* in 2. 39 are identical with the *locupletes* in 2. 40 (that is, the *assidui* in the *classes*, as opposed to the *proletarii*), concluding from this that the imbalance in voting between the richer and poorer *assidui* was relatively unimportant, compared with the confining of the votes of more than half the citizen body to a single century of *proletarii*. But it appears that this view cannot be sustained and that *locupletes* in 2. 39 cannot cover the same social group as in 2. 40. For in the latter part of 2. 40 Cicero argues that a single century from among his hypothetical 96, the bulk of classes 2 to 5, had almost more members than the whole first class. This not only shows that the contrast he is making is between the higher and the lower centuries of the *assidui*, but that Yakobson's reconstruction of his demography would be impossible (in the proportions of 1st class—7,000; rest of *assidui c.*650,000; *proletarii—c.*750,000, where the first class would be 0. 5% of the total voting population, though its poorer members would not have possessed more property than a farm of reasonable size).

[78] Cic. *Phil.* 2. 82. For 12 centuries of *equites* voting with the first class before the senators in an assembly trial see Livy, 43. 16. 14.

[79] On the *tribus* as part of the *comitia centuriata* see Cic. *Phil.* 11. 18; *Planc.* 49 *ad fin.*; on the last two tribes Livy, *Per.* 19.

eighteen centuries of cavalry and one hundred and seventy centuries of infantry; the latter are divided into five property classes, the qualifications being respectively 100,000, 75,000, 50,000, 25,000, 12,500 or 11,000 *asses* (it is not clear whether these *asses* are thought each to have had the original value of a pound of bronze or to have been the devalued currency from the period of the Second Punic War onwards). In addition there are in Livy five centuries of military support personnel—smiths and carpenters, trumpeters and horn-players, of which the former two are brigaded with the first class and the latter two with the fifth—one of attendants (*accensi velati*), and one century of those free from obligation to military service, except in an emergency—known elsewhere as *proletarii* or *capite censi*.[80] Each class shows a progressive decline in equipment: the first class are fully armed hoplites; the defensive armour is then reduced through the classes until the fourth class has none, only a thrusting and a throwing spear, and the fifth class are slingers. There were indeed differences in arms and functions in the Roman infantry described by Polybius, but these depended on age and do not corroborate the gradations of equipment supposed here. It is hazardous to associate the assembly thus described with any particular period in Roman history.[81]

It is none the less probable that in some form the *comitia centuriata* goes back to the early Republic at least. It follows that it will have changed, how much and how often we cannot tell, before reaching the form, based in some way on the 35 tribes, known to Cicero. The number of infantry centuries (170) does not relate mathematically to 35 and probably derives from the period before the incorporation of the tribal element. This reform must be dated after 241 BC and before the Second Punic War, if we trust the references in Livy to centuries of *iuniores* named after tribes in this period.[82] It has been associated with Q. Fabius Maximus on the basis of a partially preserved stone from Brindisi, engraved in the second century AD, commemorating someone (anonymous owing to a lacuna) active in 230 BC and the Hannibalic war. The man celebrated here 'first selected the senate and . . . the assembly'. Livy's account of the twenty years before the Second Punic War has not survived, but it would be surprising if this achievement of Fabius had

[80] Livy, 1. 43. 1–8 with the commentary of Ogilvie, 1965; Dion. Hal. 4. 16–17 (note the division into *seniores* and *iuniores*) and 4. 20. 3–5 (20. 5 for *proletarii*); 7. 59. 2–8; Cic. *Rep.* 2. 39–40.

[81] Pol. 6. 19 ff. On the development of Roman military organization before Polybius' day see Sumner, 1970.

[82] Livy, 24. 7. 12 and 8. 20; 26. 22. 2 and 11; 27. 6. 3.

been omitted in Plutarch's biography. The reference to the senate in particular suggests that the stone is more likely to refer to a man who created the political institutions in the recently founded colony of Brundisium.[83] We must be satisfied, therefore, with having a plausible time-bracket for the reform at Rome.

Before the palimpsest of Cicero's *De Re Publica* was published in 1822, it was inferred from Livy that the tribal reform of the assembly had led to five classes, in each of which there were two centuries, one of *seniores*, the other of *iuniores*, assigned to every one of the 35 tribes. Hence, with the 18 centuries of cavalry, 4 centuries of technicians, and the *capite censi*, the assembly would have had 373 centuries. This view was first proposed by Ottavio Pantagato in the mid-sixteenth century, and has been maintained by many scholars even after the discovery of the *De Re Publica* palimpsest.[84] It may in fact have been true of the Augustan period, when Livy and Dionysius were writing, but it would not have permitted the election of a suffect consul in 44 BC to terminate as soon as Cicero claimed.[85]

Mommsen sought to reconcile the discrepant data by arguing that what would have been 350 units was reduced to 170 by the combination of the centuries in classes 2 to 5 in groups of two or three. This interpretation, which had been thought incredible, received unexpected support when the discovery of the *tabula Hebana*, with its description of voting in special centuries in advance of the main election in the *comitia centuriata*, revealed how by a system of allotment centuries could be made to combine their votes in a single basket.[86] There still remain problems. A number of late Republican texts suggest that *centuriae* were permanent, not *ad hoc* combinations on the day of the vote. So at best the *tabula Hebana* is a model of how *centuriae* might be permanently formed on the basis of tribes in the lower classes of the *comitia*.[87] It is likely in any case that tribes, which were the units in which citizens were registered initially, helped to determine the *centuriae* to which they were allocated. Each tribe may have kept a list of its members, divided into *seniores* and *iuniores*, in each of the five classes, and this may have led to their automatic allocation to a particular *centuria*. Such a procedure

---

[83] Vitucci, 1953; Cassola, 1962, 268–75, 289–92; Taylor, 1957; *contra MRR* i. 585; Gabba, 1958*b*.   [84] Livy, 1. 43. 12; Taylor, 1966, 88; McCuaig, 1993.   [85] Cic. *Phil.* 2. 82.

[86] *Staatsr.* iii. 1. 270 ff., esp. 275–9; *lex Val. Aur.* (*RS* i. 37) *tab. Heb.* (= EJ 94a), 23–31; Tibiletti, 1949.

[87] Varro, *LL* 7. 42; Cic. *Red. Sen.* 27; *Red. Quir.* 17; *Comm. Pet.* 18, 29, and 56; Suet. *Jul.* 19. 1. Among those who reject a direct application of the system of the *Tabula Hebana* to the Republic are de Martino, *SCR* ii. 1. 142–8; Staveley, 1972, 126–7, and 1956, 112 ff.; Grieve, 1985.

would have simplified the work of the censors in their mammoth task of registration during the middle and late Republic.

The purpose of the reform which introduced the 'tribal' element remains unclear. The bias of the assembly towards the wealthy was not significantly altered. Although the system seems bafflingly complex to us, it may have been regarded by the Romans as a rationalization, inasmuch as both the major assemblies would have been now based on the same unit. Moreover, the centuriate assembly now reflected through the *tribus* the extension of the domicile of Roman citizens across Italy and, in so far as this was an innovation, this may have given relatively greater voting power to those in more remote rural tribes.

The military function of the registration in the late Republic would have been confined to separating infantry from cavalry and *seniores* from *iuniores*, since any differences in equipment among infantry had disappeared at, or before, the time of Marius and the bar on *proletarii* undertaking military service had become obsolete.[88] The connection between membership of the equestrian centuries and military service on horseback had not entirely disappeared in the late Republic, but they did not serve any longer as cavalry units.[89]

Some special features of procedure in the *comitia centuriata* have already been mentioned. What is at issue here is a formal assembly. A *contio* which preceded a meeting of the *comitia centuriata*, for example as part of a capital trial before an assembly, need not have differed from other *contiones* in venue or procedure. At formal *comitia*, however, the magistrate, after taking the auspices in a *templum*, summoned, by means of heralds in the forum and on the walls, the *exercitus* (that is, the military assembly) to a meeting *in licium* (that is, in a roped off area).[90] It is possible that the assembly met in the first place in its formal divisions. When a vote was called, at least in elections, it appears that a century of *iuniores* from the first class was selected as *praerogativa* and its vote was taken and announced.[91] After that, in Cicero's time, the first class came to vote and the result was announced, then the cavalry, then the second class, and so on. If a majority for a legal or judicial decision, or

---

[88] Gabba, 1949.

[89] *Staatsr.* iii. 1. 480–6; Stein, 1927, ch. 1; Harmand, 1967, 39–41. The latest example of Roman cavalry in combat provided by our sources is in Sall. *Jug.* 46. 7 and 50. 2 (109 BC).

[90] Varro, *LL* 6. 88, cf. 86, 94–5; Taylor, 1966, 56, 136 n. 61, 156 n. 41; Vaahtera, 1993, 112–15.

[91] Cic. *Phil.* 2. 82; *Planc.* 49; *QF* 2. 15. 4; *Div.* 1. 103; Livy, 5. 18. 1; 24. 7. 12 and 9. 3; 26. 22. 2 and 13; 27. 6. 3; Festus, 290L (Varro, *rer. hum.* VI, arguing that its purpose was to inform *rustici* who could not have benefited from the *professio* of the candidates); *Staatsr.* iii. 1. 397–8.

majorities for the appropriate number of candidates in an election were reached, then the result was declared and business was over. This might be quick or involve the votes of the lowest classes, but in any case the sheer number of votes available to the wealthy and comparatively wealthy would have often produced a different result from that which would have resulted from the same number of people voting in tribes.

There was also a bias in favour of age in the assembly—in the first class and in any other class where the *seniores* were given an equal number of centuries to the *iuniores*. The number of male citizens aged from about 17 years (when they were given the *toga virilis*) to 45 would have outnumbered those aged 46 or more, on the life expectancy we can reasonably project for them, by more than two to one. To judge from Cicero's treatment of the *comitia centuriata* in the *De Re Publica*, the privilege granted to wealth and age satisfied an ideology which was well-established in Roman republican thinking. However, it should be remembered that the *comitia centuriata*, at least by the second century BC, was of comparatively limited importance. Legislation was largely reserved for the *concilium plebis*; capital trials in the assembly were rare; it was only the elections to higher magistracies which regularly exercised this assembly.

The complexity of the assemblies is in sharp contrast with the simple executive structure provided by the magistracies. Clearly, to some extent this was the product of the natural growth of the constitution and of the parallel development of the organization of the plebs and that of the people as a whole in the early Republic. Nevertheless, the preservation of the *comitia centuriata*, however modified, suggests a desire to retain an institution in which worth, wealth, and age predominated, for the purposes of expressing the will of the people in some constitutional functions. We may also see the elaborate rules governing procedure in assemblies in general as a reflection of a certain caution about popular self-expression and decision-making.

Obstruction, Abrogation, Annulment

A tribune might veto the proceedings in an assembly before the vote was actually called (see above with n. 28). This usually happened in legislative assemblies, but we have evidence of obstruction being threatened to an electoral assembly. As for assemblies passing judicial verdicts, we know of no instance of such obstruction, though it is not unthinkable in a situation where the presiding magistrate was disregarding correct procedure.[92] There were certain understandings in the middle Republic. A tribune, as Polybius remarked, was expected to set his sights on the wishes of the people, and we have an example of a veto being abandoned in face of protests that the tribune had no right to obstruct the people's will in this situation.[93] Such understandings do not seem to have counted for much in the turbulence of the late Republic. Obstruction might also be made on religious grounds on account of unfavourable omens. In theory, any private citizen might announce an unfavourable omen to a magistrate, but the latter was not bound to take notice of it: an augur, however, seems to have been accepted as an authority.[94] The announcement of an unfavourable omen by another magistrate (*obnuntiatio*) was expected to be effective, especially after the passing of the *leges Aelia* and *Fufia* at some point in the middle of the second century. These were later reinforced by the *lex Caecilia Didia* of 98 BC, which provided that the senate could declare that the people were not bound by a law passed improperly. Such grounds were failure to observe promulgation over a *trinundinum*, tacking disparate measures together in a single proposal (described by the phrase *per saturam*), and violating the auspices (with which the use of violence came to be associated).[95]

A magistrate who had been elected improperly or who had disgraced his office could be forced to abdicate. Where co-operation was not forthcoming, a magistracy might be abrogated by the assembly, though there are no examples of this from the middle republic. On one well-known occasion in 133 the plebs voted to deprive one of their tribunes of his office, and the same measure was threatened in 67. Even curule magistrates occasionally found themselves deprived of office in the periods of civil strife in the late Republic. Pro-magistrates operating after their year of office outside Rome could be deprived of their *imperium* by a popular vote.[96]

[92] Veto on election threatened in Livy, 27. 6. 3–11; for an appeal to tribunes against praetorian jurisdiction see Asc. 84C and in general *Staatsr.* i. 274–87.

[93] Pol. 6. 16. 5; Livy, 38. 36. 7–9.

[94] Cato in Festus (268L); Cic. *Phil.* 2. 81 and 83; also Cic. *Att.* 2. 16. 2 for Cicero imagining Pompey passing an augural judgement on Caesar's legislation. See Botsford, 1909, 111 ff.; Wissowa, 1912, 529 ff.; de Libero, 1992, 53 ff. (though her belief that the mere announcement of an intention to watch the heavens (*de caelo servare*) was in itself valid obstruction, is dubious, even if some Romans, such as Cicero and Bibulus, maintained this view).

[95] On the *leges Aelia et Fufia* see Nocera, 1940, 108 ff.; Astin, 1964; Sumner, 1963; on annulment see *VRR* 132–48; Bleicken, 1975, 466 ff.; de Libero, 1992, 87 ff.; Heikkila, 1993, 117–42. It still seems to me safest to hold that the senate's controversial right to annul laws was created precisely by the *lex Caecilia Didia*.

[96] App. *BCiv.* 1. 12. 51–4; Plut. *Ti. Gr.* 12. 1–5; Cic. *Mil.* 72; *Leg.* 3. 24; Oros. 5. 8. 3; Asc. 71–2C; Dio, 36. 30. 2; *Staatsr.* i. 629–30.

Any legislation which had been passed by an assembly could in theory be rescinded, partially rescinded, or rendered ineffective by later legislation, according to a principle which allegedly was enshrined in a law of the Twelve Tables.[97] A legislator could attempt to bolster his law by including in the enforcement clause (*sanctio*), which contained penalties for transgressing it, a similar measure against proposing its repeal:[98] in the late second century BC the practice also developed of requiring oaths from magistrates and senators that they would obey certain laws.[99] It was, however, argued that once a law was repealed or declared invalid, any oaths prescribed by it also became invalid.[100] As for penalties for proposing a law's repeal, these would only come into question if the attempt to repeal failed. Thus they were a deterrent against seeking repeal without adequate support—it was perhaps this that influenced the tribunes of 58 BC who first proposed Cicero's recall—but no complete protection for the law under attack.[101] A legislator nervous about offending, wittingly or unwittingly, against the sanctions in previous laws might include in his own bill a clause asserting that, if his law collided with previous laws so protected, it should not be held valid. This clause could be combined with the regular one indemnifying the legislator against collisions with sacred law.[102]

The Nature of Roman Legislation

As the previous discussion has shown, Rome had no distinction corresponding to that developed in post-403 Athens between a law and a decree of the assembly, *nomos* and *psēphisma*. Many of the most fundamental principles of the Republic were not embodied in written law, but they could be overridden by a single statute (*lex* or *plebiscitum*) passed by an assembly. Equally, the oldest laws going back to the Twelve Tables or earlier could be repealed as a whole or in part by a single *lex* or

[97] Livy, 7. 17. 12 = RS ii, 40 *Tab.* XII. 5; Cic. *Att.* 3. 23. 2; *Balb.* 33. See above, Chap. IV with n. 33.

[98] *Dig.* 1. 8. 9; 48. 19. 41; Cic. *Att.* 3. 23. 2; *Verr.* 4. 149; *lex lat. Bant.* (RS i. 7), 7–13; *frag. Tar.* (RS i. 8), 25–6; *lex prov. praet.* (RS i. 12), Delphi C15 ff.; *lex de Delo* (RS i. 22), 34–5; *lex Irnitana*, ch. 96, tab. XC, 11 ff. See also *lex rep.* 56 with JRLR 137–8. Bibliography on *sanctiones* is conveniently collected by E. Bispham, *Epigraphica* 59 (1997), 128.

[99] *Lex agr.* 40–42 with JRLR 243–4; *lex lat. Bant.* (RS i. 7), 17–22; *frag. Tar.* (RS i. 8), 20 ff.; *lex prov. praet.* (RS i. 12), Delphi C. 10 ff.; App. *BCiv.* 1. 29. 131; 2. 12. 42; Cic. *Clu.* 91; *Att.* 2. 18. 2; Plut. *Cato mi.* 32. 5–6; Dio, 38. 7. 1–2; VRR 139–40; Tibiletti, 1953, 57–66.

[100] App. *BCiv.* 1. 30. 136.

[101] Cic. *Att.* 3. 23. 2–4.

[102] Cic. *Att.* 3. 23. 3; *frag. Tar.* (RS i. 8), 26; *lex de Delo* (RS i. 22), 36; Val. Prob. 3. 13; Cic. *Balb.* 33; *Caec.* 95.

plebiscitum. On the other hand, the apparent vulnerability of Roman law to sudden change was to some extent compensated by the fact that it required a lengthy and elaborate procedure to pass any statute in the first place.

The more complex the rules of the Roman republic became, the more necessary it was to incorporate them in written law. Furthermore, the initiative for reform in the later Republic frequently derived from individuals or small groups operating outside the consensus of the élite. This gave rise to immensely lengthy and complex statutes, mainly plebiscites passed by tribunes in their tribal assembly. Such were for example the *lex de repetundis* and the *lex agraria*, partially preserved on bronze, to which I have devoted another work. It is hard to imagine laws as long as these being read to an assembly—still less Caesar's *lex Iulia de repetundis*, whose chapter 101 was dealing with matter that appears only a little over half-way through the *lex de repetundis* which we possess on bronze.[103] Yet it is difficult to see how else such complicated legal instruments could be enacted, except by an autocrat's edict or a legal commission (and the *decemviri* who had drawn up the Twelve Tables were believed to have turned into tyrants). The regulations about promulgation over a *trinundinum* (see above with nn. 20 and 95) would have at least ensured that there was time for ordinary citizens to become acquainted with the text of a proposed law, and, even if the debate in *contiones* was limited, it did create publicity.

The assembly, in elections and legislation, was an unparalleled generator of power and of change. It is not surprising that the élite, recognizing its potential, sought to restrain it with safety-devices and regulators, some of which were not only in their own interest but in those of good government in general.

---

[103] Cic. *Fam.* 8. 8. 3, cf. *lex rep.* 57.

VI

The Senate

Polybius believed that in his time the aristocratic element was predominant within Rome's mixed constitution. Although the consul was a commanding figure both in the field and at Rome, although the people had supreme authority in elections, legislation, and criminal trials, it was the senate which controlled money, administration in Italy, and the details of foreign policy. Thus, in Polybius' eyes the power of the senate lay not in any theoretical sovereignty but in the management of so many aspects of the day-to-day government of the empire. The last word should be stressed, because it is the administration of Rome's external affairs which most interests Polybius: apart from matters of finance, he is not concerned with the domestic management of the city of Rome and the *ager Romanus.*[1] He is not alone in this, however: even the annalistic record tends to highlight foreign policy and thus senatorial activity.[2]

We have no text, equivalent to an article in a modern constitution, which describes the functions and powers of the Roman senate, nor indeed anything resembling the chapters in Roman municipal laws which deal with the functions of local senates and their relation to local magistrates.[3] These might at first sight be thought a useful guide, but it must be remembered that they deal with constitutions where the power of assemblies is strictly limited, and where in any case the priorities of the makers of the constitution were different from those underlying the Roman republic. A local constitution was intended, it seems, to be stable, grand initiatives were to be discouraged, and, above all, magistrates were to be subject to checks from the local senate, in order that they should have little room for corruption.[4] It might be thought that it

---

[1] See above, Chap. III with n. 5, for Polybius' neglect of the functions of the praetors and aediles in his account of the magistrates. He does, however, allude to civil (6. 17. 7) and criminal jurisdiction (6. 13. 5, 16. 2) and to censorial contracts (6. 17. 1–6).

[2] See Chap. II.

[3] *Tab. Heracl.* (*RS* i. 24), 83–8; 108–40; *lex mun. Tar.* (*RS* i. 15), 26–31; *lex Gen. Urs.* (*RS* i. 25), chs. 69, 82, 91–2, 96–7, 101, 103, 105, 124–5, 129; *lex Irn.* chs. 30–31, A–G, 61–2, 66–73, 76–80, 86.

[4] *Imp. Rom.* 139–43, 152–3.

would have been better for the Republic if the same principles had been followed there, but, apart from the weight of tradition, this would have conflicted both with aristocratic pride and with the ultimate right of assemblies to make major changes. It would also have been against the ethos of the Republic, as a society which achieved and maintained greatness by allowing its most able citizens wide scope to fulfil themselves, and which accepted that within limits vigorous conflict could be creative.

The powers of the Roman senate under the Republic rested for the most part on *consuetudo* and *mos* and, furthermore, to a considerable extent on comparatively recent tradition, being a response to the administrative demands of Roman expansion. Two main lines of interpretation have been employed by modern scholars. In the eyes of Mommsen, in spite of the growth of its *de facto* authority, the senate remained the body which advised the magistrates, the task it had performed for the kings and would in due course perform for the emperors.[5] On this view, it was the magistrate with *imperium*, his authority deriving from the people, who carried most weight in the constitution, with the result that it was changes in the nature of the magistracy that were determinative of changes in the constitution. A different view, which goes back to the early nineteenth century, has been maintained by scholars in spite of Mommsen's *Staatsrecht*. In a more recent work on the Roman constitution Mommsen's interpretation has been denounced by F. de Martino as an over-schematic misrepresentation: the senate was the true government of Rome, not merely an advisory body like the judicial *consilia* of magistrates.[6] This opinion is, moreover, shared by many who are more concerned to discount the popular element in the constitution *vis-à-vis* the senate and conceive the Republic as an aristocracy.[7]

What is not always noticed is that this conflict of view is rooted in Roman politics and not merely a conflict in scholarly interpretation. Cicero may have pictured the senate in *pro Sestio* as an eternal council (*consilium sempiternum*) in charge of the *res publica*, to which the magistrates were servants (*ministri*), but others had different ideas. We are told that L. Postumius Megillus (*cos.* 291) claimed that the senate did not rule him, while he was consul, but he ruled the senate. L. Philippus in 91, in

---

[5] This was also the view of Rubino, 1839. On 19th-cent. scholarship on the Roman senate see now Ormanni, 1990, 59–135.

[6] De Martino, *SCR* i. 410, cf. 417–18; on his 19th-cent. predecessors, B. G. Niebuhr, E. Herzog, P. Willems, see Ormanni, 1990, 71 ff., 91 ff.

[7] e.g. Gelzer, 1912; Bleicken, 1955 and 1975.

fury over the senatorial support for the policies of M. Livius Drusus, declared that he needed an alternative *consilium*. What is more, when he was reproached for this by L. Crassus, it was not in anger for insulting the majesty of the senate, but in sorrow that he had forgotten his paternal responsibilities as consul towards that body.[8] As Polybius saw, if a consul fell foul of the senate, it could be obstructive and make it difficult for him to achieve what he wanted. But in the last resort, it lacked means of coercion, unless it had the support of the tribunes: it was through these that, for example, it tried to bring pressure on Scipio Africanus in 204 and M. Popillius Laenas in 173–2.[9]

The two attitudes to the relationship between the senate and the consul were reflected, and confirmed, in differing approaches to the senate's early history. Cicero saw the senate, though created by the kings, as a self-sufficient body at the time of the fall of the monarchy, one which could take charge of the situation and set in motion consular rule: it was in this sense superior to the consuls, because prior.[10] This view could find support in the concept of *interregnum*, the arrangement still used in the late Republic, whereby, if there were no curule magistrates (that is, no consuls, praetors, or dictator) 'the auspices returned to the *patres*'. This meant 'to the patricians', but, if you believed that the senate and the patrician order were more or less identical at the beginning of the Republic, the creation of an *interregnum* at the time of the expulsion of the last king (as narrated by Dionysius, but not by Livy) was a charter for the priority of the senate to the magistrates.[11]

On the other hand, if you asked the question, how did senators get chosen, rather than, how did magistrates get elected, a different perspective resulted. So, according to Festus, 'as the kings used to choose and replace those that they had *in publico consilio*, so also, after the kings had been expelled, the consuls and tribunes of the soldiers with consular power used to choose those most closely tied to them of the patricians and then of the plebeians, until the Ovinian tribunician law intervened, requiring the censors to select all the best men from every order.' A similar perspective can be seen in the explanation of *conscripti*, in which Valerius Publicola is said to have supplemented the 164 patrician senators available in 509 BC by conscribing plebeians to bring the total

---

[8] Contrast Cic. *Sest.* 137, 143 (and *Att.* 1. 14. 2 which shows Pompey professing allegiance to this view) with Dion. Hal. *AR* 17. 4; Dio, 8, fr. 36. 32; Cic. *de Or.* 3. 2–3.

[9] Pol. 6. 15. 2–8; Livy, 29. 20. 4–11; 42. 8–9, 10. 9 ff., and 21–2.

[10] Cic. *Rep.* 2. 56—with discussion of *patrum auctoritas*, 61; *Leg.* 3. 6; *Sest.* 137, 143.

[11] Cic. *ad Brut.* 13 (=1. 5). 4; *Rep.* 2. 23; *Leg.* 3. 9; Asc. 33, 43C; Dion. Hal. *AR* 4. 75. 1–2, 76. 1, 84. 5; Livy, 1. 17. 5–10; 22. 34. 1; *Staatsr.* i. 649 ff.

up to 300.[12] Neither statement has necessarily any strong claim to historicity concerning the situation before the *plebiscitum Ovinium*, but they show how the senate could be portrayed as a creation of a consul, indeed almost as his appendage.

As it is, arguments from origins are of doubtful value, when we seek the essential nature of the senate, since the starting-point and the amount of change the institution underwent are both uncertain. It is likely that the senate as an institution was an inheritance of the Republic from the kings; it is possible that an originally patrician membership was diluted by plebeians even before the consulship was opened to plebeians in the fourth century; the institution of the *patrum auctoritas* shows that the patrician element was once an important element in legislation. However, inevitably speculative views of the senate of the early Republic do not help to explain the nature of senatorial authority in the period that followed. The converse is nearer the truth.

Membership of the Senate

Whatever principles had been followed in the two centuries before the *lex Ovinia*, one consequence of it was that patricians could no longer expect to be chosen senators automatically, another was to establish the unique authority of the censors over membership. It is not clear whether the corrupt word '*curiati*' in the Festus text (290L) should be emended to '*curiatim*', thus suggesting that in some way the selection should be made by *curiae*: in this case the method would have become obsolete at the same time as the *curiae*. Another possibility is that it is a reference to the censors taking an oath, '*iurati*'.[13] It is likely in any case that about 300 BC tenure of the offices of consul, praetor, dictator, master of the horse (*magister equitum*) or, probably, curule aedile would have automatically placed a Roman among 'all the best men', and this remained true down to the Second Punic War. Then the casualties in the battles up to Cannae led to emergency measures to replenish the senate from those who had not yet held a curule magistracy by considerations of rank (*ordo*) rather than individual merit: former aediles (presumably plebeian) were the first to be admitted, and it is perhaps from this time onwards that both aedileships became a regular qualification. In the clauses of the *lex repetundarum* of 123–2 BC, which barred magistrates, senators, and their connections from serving on the juries, the minor magistrates from tribune of the plebs downwards are all listed, but the higher magistrates,

[12] Festus, 290L, 304L.   [13] Cf. Cic. *Clu.* 121 and see Willems, 1878, i. 169–71.

including aediles, are indicated in the phrase, 'anyone who has or shall have been in the senate'.[14] According to the Augustan jurist Ateius Capito, tribunes, although they had the right of convoking the senate (by virtue of their office), were not senators before the Atinian plebiscite. If, as it seems, this *lex Atinia* gave tribunes an automatic qualification for senate membership, it will belong to the period between 122 and 102 BC. For in the latter year we find the censor Metellus Numidicus refusing to ratify the former tribune Saturninus as a senator.[15] In 81 Sulla granted quaestors senate membership, and so we find M. Tullius Cicero, quaestor in 75, a member of the senatorial subcommittee which examined the dispute between Oropos and the tax-collectors in 73.[16]

Our antiquarian sources tell us that when senators were summoned to a meeting the phrase 'and those who are permitted to state their opinion in the senate' was added. The explanation offered in Festus is that this phrase covered those of the *iuniores* who had held a magistracy since the last census and were not senators before they were registered among the *seniores* in the census.[17] It appears first that membership of the senate was thought to carry with it the status of a *senior*, otherwise only attained at the age of 46. Secondly, the full status of senator required the approval of the censors and until that time former magistrates were 'those permitted to deliver their opinion in the senate'. This phraseology is still found in late Republican legal texts—in Sulla's *lex de sicariis et veneficis* and, though it has to be largely restored, in the Latin law from Bantia.[18] Thus the principle of censorial confirmation of the status of senator seems to have been retained even after Sulla's legislation (unless we suppose that the retention of the distinction was a legal draughtsman's oversight). Nevertheless, those who had the right to deliver their opinion were in practice treated like senators, albeit junior ones, as Cicero's participation in the committee investigating Oropos in 73 BC shows.

A number of sources suggest that in the later Republic before Sulla's dictatorship the number of senators was 300, though this may well not have been the original number at the beginning of the Republic. It is not evident how important this figure was for the censors, whether it was a

---

[14] Livy, 23. 23. 5–6; *lex rep.* 13, 16, and 22.
[15] Gell. 14. 8. 2; App. *BCiv.* 1. 28. 126.
[16] Tac. *Ann.* 11. 22; *lex Corn. XX quaest.* (*RS* i. 14); *RDGE* 23, lines 11–12. See also, for Cicero's future colleague Caesonius functioning as a senatorial juror before the censors reviewed the senatorial roll in 70–69 BC, *Verr.* 1. 29.
[17] Festus, 454L; Gell. 3. 18. 8.
[18] Cic. *Clu.* 148; *lex lat. Bant.* (*RS* i. 7), 23. See also Livy, 36. 3. 3.

maximum or a rough target.[19] Moreover, the effective membership, given the number of senators who might at one time be 'absent on behalf of the *respublica*' or have other excuses for non-attendance, would have been considerably less. We find quorums of 100 and 150 required for certain senatorial meetings in 186 and 172.[20] If we assume that the six men who were elected praetor each year in the early second century achieved this on average at age 35, and if we also assume, a little optimistically, that they lived on average another 25 years, this accounts for 150 senators. If we add to them about twenty men who had been elected aedile but had not yet become praetor (or never attained that office), this would leave about 130 senators of a total of 300 who were selected by the censors without being qualified by virtue of a higher magistracy. The probability is that the censors still operated in part by criteria of birth, enrolling members of patrician and distinguished plebeian families who were either too young for the offices of aedile or above or had declined to pursue them. Tenure of a priesthood could also have been a qualification for membership.[21]

Sulla, is said to have added three hundred men of equestrian standing to the senate, when it was short of men after the Italian and civil wars, as well as providing that the quaestorship should be a sufficient qualification for membership.[22] This probably led to a total membership of somewhat over 500. The quorum laid down by the *lex Cornelia de privilegiis* in 67 BC was 200. The maximum attendances known to us in the late Republic are 415 in 61 BC, 417 in 57 BC, and 392 in 50 BC. If we assume that each cohort of 20 who became quaestors were elected at the minimum age of 30, as Cicero was, and that they on average lived to age 60, it would then follow that the total membership of the senate would have been 600. But these assumptions are optimistic.[23]

[19] Plut. *C. Gr.* 5. 3, App. *BCiv.* 1. 35. 158, and Festus, 304L, give 300 senators; 1 *Macc.* 8: 15 gives 320. *Staatsr.* iii. 2. 849 ff. and Willems, 1878, i. 303 ff., assume that 300 was a strict maximum.   [20] *SC Bacch.* (*FIRA* i, no. 30), 18; Livy, 42. 28. 9.

[21] For an example of a young priest in the senate see Chap. I with n. 12. On the likely survival of senators see K. Hopkins and G. Burton in Hopkins, 1983, 146–9—in this case discussing the Principate, but the conclusions are transferable. Willems, 1878, i. 168, argued on the basis of Livy 22. 49. 16–17 that there had been before 216 BC an obligation on the censors to enrol even former holders of lower magistracies, but this contradicts the implications of Livy, 23. 23. Livy 22. 49 may only be summarizing the men of senatorial rank killed, including those who had not survived to be formally enrolled by the censors ('octoginta *praeterea*' in 22. 49. 17 may be the result of a Livian misunderstanding). In fact the enrolment at age 30 of all quaestors, who probably numbered 12 by the early second century, and former quaestors would have produced a senate of about 300, but this does not seem to have been the principle followed.

[22] App. *BCiv.* 1. 100. 468; Tac. *Ann.* 11. 22.

[23] Asc. 59C; Cic. *Att.* 1. 14. 5; *Red. Sen.* 26; App. *BCiv.* 2. 30. 119. Hopkins and Burton,

We hear of no specific property-qualification for membership of the senate before the time of Augustus. A few scattered texts suggest that senators were drawn from the equestrian order, that is, those placed in the centuries of cavalry by the censors, and it is likely that senators at least possessed the equestrian qualification (the sum of 400,000 sesterces, which is attested for the late Republic, may well go back to the second century, perhaps even to the time of the reform of the *comitia centuriata* in the third century).[24] The censors under the Republic would have been concerned with the financial standing of senators, but there was the complication that any senator who was still in the *potestas* of a living father could not hold property in his own right and would have presumably depended on his father's status rather than any property qualification of his own.[25] Augustus' requirement of a million sesterces for senatorial status may have been an innovation not only in amount but in being a fixed qualification.

Senators were also required to be of good character. A censor who either 'passed over' (*praeterire*) a new member or 'shifted' (*movere*) an established member was expected to allege some specific failing, such as corruption, abuse of capital punishment, or the disregard of constitutional practice, the auspices, or a colleague's veto.[26] In the late Republic expulsion from the senate was prescribed as a penalty for failing to obey certain laws. We also find in the *lex repetundarum* of 123-2 BC men excluded from service as a *patronus* or a juror, who had been condemned in a *quaestio* or *iudicium publicum* (that is, for a criminal offence) with the result that it was illegal for them to be enrolled in the senate.[27] A similar principle can be seen in a text excluding from local senates a wide

1983, 146-9, applying their most generous model life-table reckon an average of 30 years survival from age 25.

[24] Cic. *Rep.* 4. 2; Livy, 42. 61. 5; Gell. 3. 18. 5 (Varro, *Hippokuōn*), and see Nicolet, 1976, 20-30. Pol. 6. 19. 4 states only the requirement of ten prior years of military service of some kind as a qualification for any magistracy. The 400, 000 HS figure may have been used in the form of *asses* (1,000,000), before the sesterce became the standard unit of accounting from *c.*140 BC onwards (Livy, 24. 11. 7-8 (214 BC) shows that the senatorial order was ranked above those possessing more than a million asses). Mommsen, *Staatsr.* iii. 2. 876-7 and i. 498, n. 1, and Willems, 1878, i. 189 ff. both held that there was no precise qualification, though none of the latter's texts strictly prove this, only the existence of poor senators—one cannot deduce much from the contrast between 'superior . . . ordine' and 'inferiorem . . . fortuna' in Cic. *Fam.* 13. 5. 2.

[25] Festus, 50L, states that only property which can be bought and sold according to *ius civile* can be registered, but does not not say by whom.

[26] *Staatsr.* ii. 1. 377, 421.

[27] *Lex lat. Bant.* (*RS* i. 7), 19-20, cf. 1-2; *frag. Tar.* (*RS* i. 8), 21; App. *BCiv.* 1. 29. 131; *lex rep.* 11, 13 and 16-17.

range of persons tainted with ignominy—including bankrupts, those condemned in civil suits involving *infamia*, former gladiators, prostitutes, pimps, and those who had been degraded for military offences.[28] These considerations would also have been relevant to a censor judging Roman senators. In practice the consequence was that a man became a senator for life, unless he was convicted of a crime for which expulsion was one of the penalties, or the censors held his conduct to have been so disgraceful that a mark (*nota*) was put against his name, and they removed him from the list. This was considered by some Roman writers a contrast with the early Republic, when the consuls, tribunes of the soldiers with consular powers, and ultimately the censors had absolute discretion as to whom they chose.[29] We have evidence of some kind of hearing before such censorial decisions, and in the last years of the Republic this was made compulsory by legislation of P. Clodius.[30]

The Place and Time of Meetings

Whatever view we hold of the origins of the senate and its relationship to the magistrates, especially the senior ones, the location of its meetings shows that it was something more than the *consilium* of a magistrate: it was, like the assemblies, an institution of the Roman people. The senate met in an inaugurated space, a *templum*, and the meeting was preceded by both sacrifice and the taking of the auspices.[31] The venues known to us under the Republic are both inside and outside the formal, augurally constituted, boundary of the city, the *pomerium*,[32] but within the mile beyond that boundary which was regarded as the limit to the city as a piece of political geography. Apart from the Curia Hostilia next to the *comitium* and its successors, the Curia Cornelia and Curia Iulia (if the latter may be regarded as Republican), a number of temples of the gods were used and certain other more specialized locations. On the Capitol and its slopes there were meetings in the temple of Jupiter Capitolinus itself (the regular venue at the beginning of the consular year), the temple of Fides (the site of the notorious meeting before the killing of Ti. Gracchus) and the temple of Concord. Another site in this area is the

---

[28] *Tab. Heracl.* (*RS* i. 24), 108 ff.; Willems, 1878, i. 213 ff.

[29] Festus, 290L; Cic. *Clu.* 118, 120, and 131 ff.; Zon. 7. 19. 7–8; on the *nota* Staatsr. ii. 1. 384 ff.; 418 ff.; Willems, 1878, i. 234 ff.

[30] Plut. *C. Gr.* 2. 8; Asc. 8C; Dio, 38. 13. 2.

[31] Gell. 14. 7. 7; Varro, *LL* 7. 10; Serv. *Ad Aen.* 7. 153 and 174; Staatsr. iii. 2. 934–5; Bonnefond-Coudry, 1989, 25 ff.

[32] On which see Varro, *LL* 5. 143.

Atrium Libertatis, whether it was on the saddle between the Capitol and the Quirinal (the traditional view) or in fact what we call the Tabularium on the Capitol.[33] At the far end of the forum the senate met in the temple of Castor and Pollux, on the summit of Palatine in the temple of Magna Mater and in the temple of Jupiter Stator at its foot, and in the Velia-Carinae area in the temples of Tellus and of Honos et Virtus (if the latter is rightly located there).[34]

Outside the *pomerium* the environs of the Circus Flaminius, which were only a short distance from the Capitol, provided locations where magistrates with military *imperium* could attend, without having to surrender and renew it: these were the temples of Bellona and Apollo. The senate met in these buildings to discuss requests for triumphs, and also to meet with foreign legations which it did not wish to welcome into the city.[35] Beyond this, in the Campus Martius the building of Pompey's theatre in the late Republic included an associated *curia*.[36]

There is also a not entirely clear tradition about *senacula*, of which there were said to have been three, one on the Capitol by the temple of Concord, one by the temple of Bellona, and one at the *porta Capena*. Their basic function was apparently to provide senators with a place to meet when they were not on duty in a senate-meeting; it is said that the *senaculum* by the temple of Bellona was itself used for meetings, but we have no instance of a meeting there, as opposed to inside the temple itself.[37] Sessions of the senate frequently began at dawn, but it was possible to begin after some other public activity was over, and of course there might be emergencies.[38] Given that meetings might last from dawn to dusk, it would have been convenient for senators to have somewhere to retire during the day. The institution of these places of waiting provides indirect evidence that the Romans treated the senators as in principle always available for duty.

Until the second century BC there seems to have been no legal requirement for senators to have a house at Rome, but senatorial life was based on the assumption that they did. At the beginning of the war with

---

[33] See Purcell, 1993.

[34] See Bonnefond-Coudry, 1989, 31–185 with the tables at 32–45 and 47.

[35] Ibid. 137–56.

[36] Asc. 52C; Suet. *Iul.* 88. 3; Plut. *Brut.* 14. 2; Pliny, *HN* 35. 59; Bonnefond-Coudry, 1989, 161–8.

[37] Festus, 470L; Varro, *LL* 5. 156; Val. Max. 2. 2. 6; Livy, 23. 32. 3; 41. 27. 7; Bonnefond-Coudry, 1989, 185–92.

[38] See Gell. 14. 7. 8; Livy, 44. 20. 1, with *Staatsr.* iii. 2. 919–20 for the normal timetable; Cic. *QF* 2. 3. 2 for an example of a late start; Livy, 26. 9. 9 and 10. 2, for senators being kept ready in the forum in 211, when Hannibal marched on Rome.

Antiochus in the consular year 191/0 senators, those with speaking rights, and minor magistrates were forbidden to go further from Rome than a point from which they could return the same day, and only five senators were permitted to be absent at once. Then, during the war with Perseus in 170 a further edict forbade senators to live outside the first milestone from the centre of Rome (the same restriction was later applied to local senators at Urso).[39] They were expected to be available, when summoned, on days when meetings could be held, unless they had a justification for being away from Rome.

Public service as a magistrate, *legatus* to a magistrate, or an ambassador (also termed a *legatus*) obviously could excuse their absence. In the last century of the Republic we also hear of the *libera legatio*, whereby senators were permitted to leave Italy to fulfil a vow at some foreign shrine. In practice this was used frequently for private business—to recover a debt or accept an inheritance. Cicero tried to abolish the practice as consul in 63 BC but only succeeded in reducing the maximum absence to one year.[40] In the late Republic senators tended to absent themselves from Rome during the regular vacations from public business and law-suits, *res prolatae* (the earliest reference to the existence of these vacations is in the judicial law from before the Social War on the *fragmentum Tarentinum*). In Cicero's time there was one vacation in the spring, beginning shortly after 5 April and ending before mid-May (this was the period in which the famous meeting at Luca was held, in which Caesar, Pompey, and Crassus were allegedly joined by 200 senators); another began at the end of November.[41] Nevertheless, these were not strictly senatorial vacations and indeed contradicted the notion of the senate as a perpetually available council. In fact, urgent business entailed that these vacations were ignored by the senate, for example in 63 BC at the time of the Catilinarian conspiracy and in 43 BC at the time of the Mutina war.[42]

It is a further reflection of the concept of the senate as a permanent council that senate-meetings might originally be held on any day—

[39] Livy, 36. 3. 3; 43. 11. 4; *lex gen. Urs.* (*RS* i. 25), ch. 91.

[40] Cic. *Att.* 2. 18. 3; 4. 2. 6; 15. 8. 1, 11. 4, 29. 1; *Phil.* 1. 6; *Leg.* 1. 10; 3. 9 and 18; *Flacc.* 86; *Fam.* 12. 21; *Leg. Agr.* 1. 8; 2. 45; Plut. *Mar.* 31. 2, and see *Dig.* 50. 7. 15 (Ulpian).

[41] See *Frag. Tar.* (*RS* i. 8), 24; Cic. *QF* 2. 6. 3; 3. 6. 4; *Att.* 14. 5. 2; on Luca Plut. *Pomp.* 51. 4–6; *Caes.* 21. 5–6; *Crass.* 14. 6–7; App. *BCiv.* 2. 17. 62–3. In the *lex Irnitana* (Chap. K) we find provision for local *res prolatae* 'messis vindemiae causa', not to exceed two periods, each of a maximum of 30 days. On the senate's calendar in the late Republic see Stein, 1930.

[42] See the tables in Bonnefond-Coudry, 1989, 206–7 and 217–18. See also ibid. 378 ff. on the contrast between the Ciceronian theory of participation and the practice of the late Republic.

including *dies nefasti*, days on which no jurisdiction could be performed on the ground that they were unlucky or subject to a religious restriction. On some festival days meetings would have begun after the ceremonies were over, and clashes with meetings of the *comitia* would have been in general avoided. However, the senate was summoned to the temple of Fides by the consul during the assembly which led to the death of Ti. Gracchus in 133, and the same occurred on the day of C. Gracchus' last assembly. The senate forbade meetings on one assembly day (*dies comitialis*) in Cicero's consulship in order that it might have freedom to meet and discuss the Catilinarian conspiracy.[43] In the late Republic a *lex Pupia*, most plausibly dated to 61, prohibited senate-meetings on *dies comitiales*, at least until the assembly business was over. We also hear of a *lex Gabinia* requiring the sessions in the month of February to be reserved for hearing of foreign embassies, until these were completed.[44]

Procedure

The Introduction and Discussion of Business

Apart from the religious preliminaries, any magistrate who wished to consult the senate had to summon it formally. The term often used for this (*cogere*) suggests compulsion, and we are told that fines and the taking of pledges might be inflicted on those who failed to attend without reasonable excuse. M. Antonius once even threatened to go further and demolish Cicero's house. However, there is little, if any, evidence for such measures being actually executed.[45] It was not necessary to specify the issues that were to be discussed, and on some occasions, for example on the first day of the consular year, there was no fixed agenda: the magistrate asked the senate's opinion about public affairs without further definition, *de re publica infinite*.[46]

'Lucius Cornelius the praetor consulted the senate three days before

---

[43] App. *BCiv.* 1. 16. 67; Plut. *Ti. Gr.* 19. 2–5; Diod. 34/5. 28a; Cic. *Mur.* 51; *Staatsr.* iii. 2. 921 ff.; Bonnefond-Coudry, 1989, 220–44.

[44] Cic. *QF* 2. 12. 3; *Fam.* 1. 4. 1. As Bonnefond-Coudry (229–56, 333–46) rightly argues, both these measures aimed to forestall obstruction, the *lex Pupia* that of comitial legislation, the *lex Gabinia* that of business with foreign embassies.

[45] Cic. *Fin.* 3. 7; *Fam.* 5. 2. 3; *QF* 2. 11. 1; *Phil.* 1. 6, 12; Livy, 3. 38. 12; Gell. 14. 7. 10. Failure to summon senators formally might have led to challenges to the validity of the meeting (Dio, 55. 3. 1–2; *Staatsr.* iii. 2. 915). Magistrates entitled to summon the senate were, according to Gellius 14. 7. 4 (Varro), the dictator, consuls, praetors, tribunes, the interrex, and the *praefectus urbi*—to whom we should add the *magister equitum* in the light of M. Antonius' activities in 48 BC (Dio, 42. 27. 2).

[46] Gell. 14. 7. 9; Livy, 22. 1. 5; 26. 26. 5.

the nones of May in the temple of Castor.' Such is the prescript of a typical text of a *senatus consultum* found on an inscription. Sometimes a consular date might precede the notice of consultation.[47] After a list of those present at the drafting of the *consultum*, the text proper began with a statement about the introduction of the matter. One frequent form of preface alluded to a speech by the presiding magistrate: 'Inasmuch as Quintus Lutatius, son of Quintus, consul made words (*verba fecit*) . . .' This might be followed by a brief reference to the subject, or the content of the magistrate's speech might be summarized: 'that Asclepiades . . ., Polystratus . . ., Meniscus . . . had come to our aid in their ships at the beginning of the Italic War, they had given courageous and loyal service to our public interests and they wished him to discharge them to their homes, if he thought fit, so that account should be taken of their fine actions and noble exploits on behalf of our public interest'.[48]

An alternative preface referred to a request or complaint made by an embassy: 'inasmuch as the Prienian ambassadors . . . (fine, good and well-disposed men from a fine, good and well-disposed people which is our ally) made a speech in our presence about the land which the Magnesians abandoned and ceded the possession of this land to the people of Priene, asking that arbitration should be given'.[49] Whichever type of preface is used, it is followed by a standard link phrase, 'about this matter the senate resolved as follows', which in turn introduces the actual decree. Here we find a precise minute of what had been ultimately resolved. The separate items might be given headings, e.g. 'concerning harbours, revenues, and mountains', 'concerning magistracies, sacred things, and revenues'; the ins and outs of the debate were not recorded.[50]

The close structure of introductory speech followed by itemized decree in the inscribed texts gives the impression of a tightly controlled debate, and it is only our literary authorities, especially Cicero, that allow us to see something of the turmoil that might actually occur. They are important, not only because we can obtain from them an imaginative

---

[47] *SC Tib.* (*FIRA* i. 33); consular dates are to be found e.g. in *FIRA* i. 32; *SC Asclep.* (*FIRA* i. 35 = *RDGE* 22).

[48] *SC Asclep.*, *RDGE* 22, Greek 5 ff. For brief references to the subject of debate see e.g. Cic. *Fam.* 8. 8. 5; *RDGE* 1C, 24, and 25.   [49] *RDGE* 7, 43 ff.

[50] *RDGE* 2, lines 18, 20, etc. The addition of '*C(ensuere)*' or '*edoxen*' to the end of the decree—in many texts closely related to the preceding syntactical structure—seems simply to have been a confirmation that the decree was carried (see e.g. *RDGE* 5, 37; 9, 72; 10, A11, B14; 15, 66; 22, Latin 16 = Greek 31; 23, 69; also *FIRA* i, no. 45, i. 20, ii. 47 (these decrees from the Principate). The subject of '*Censuere*' must be the senators, not the tribunes (Badian 1996, 192, *contra* Val. Max. 2. 2. 7), but it was apparently not attached to decrees that were vetoed (Cic. *Fam.* 8. 8. 6–7).

'feel' for what went on, but also for the concept we derive of the senate as a constitutional organ. Mommsen presented the senate as a body that in theory was directed by and responded to the presiding magistrate: deviations from this norm were abuses.[51] This remains the standard received view, but it has been recently objected that the variations to be found in senatorial procedure reveal a body which was not prepared simply to jump through hoops, and which possessed an authority which could be used even against the magistrate who had convened it.[52] Thus analysis of procedure contributes to the modern argument over whether the senate was simply an especially large *consilium* for magistrates or the real government of Rome.

What then was the nature of debates? As we have seen, the presiding magistrate might begin by making a speech (*verba fecit*). This need only have been a brief introduction, but a longer oration was also permissible. Cicero complained about Marcus Brutus' version of the great debate about the fate of the Catilinarian conspirators on 5 Dec. 63 BC: 'He is going to praise me because I raised the matter, not because I made everything plain, I encouraged, because in short I made my own judgement before I consulted.' In other words, Cicero claimed that he had not made a neutral reference to the senate on this question but had strongly indicated the line he expected the senate to take. The presiding magistrate or magistrates might also intervene in the middle of a discussion.[53] On occasions the presiding magistrate simply introduced ambassadors,[54] or letters were read.[55] The magistrate then normally referred to the senate the problem that he had outlined or the information that had been brought before them. We hear occasionally under the Republic of proposals brought ready drafted to the senate. In the *senatus consultum de Oropiis*, it seems that the report of a senatorial sub-committee on the dispute between Oropos and the tax-collectors was put to the senate without further ado, perhaps *per discessionem* (see below with n. 78). After Caesar's murder we find both Marcus Antonius and Gaius Vibius

[51] *Staatsr.* iii. 2. 942 ff., 961 ff.

[52] Bonnefond-Coudry, 1989, 351 ff.

[53] Cic. *Att.* 12. 21. 1. See also *Mur.* 51; *Phil.* 5. 1; *2 Verr.* 2. 95 ff.; *Prov. Cos.* 39 for presidents' introductory speeches; Livy, 27. 9. 14–10. 2; App. *BCiv.* 2. 128. 535 for speeches by the president after the debate had started. In my view it is likely that Cicero's fourth Catilinarian is a combination of his introductory speech, up to *vindicandum est* at the end of para. 6, and an intervention in the debate after Caesar's speech but before Cato's.

[54] Apart from the epigraphic examples such as *SCTib* (n. 47 above) and a great number to be found in *RDGE* see e.g. Livy, 29. 17–19. 2; 30. 21. 12–23. 5; 37. 49. 1–7; Bonnefond-Coudry, 1989, 296 ff.

[55] Caes. *BCiv.* 1. 1. 1; Cic. *Fam.* 10. 12. 3 and 16. 1; 12. 19. 2 and 25. 1; *ad Brut.* 2. 3; Livy, 35. 6–7. 1; 40. 25. 8–26. 2.

Pansa bringing detailed proposals for ratification. Usually, however, when the senate was asked its views, it was assumed that there was room for manoeuvre and its range of decison was in no wise limited.[56]

A consul did not ask his colleague, if the latter was present, first, but addressed the ex-consuls (*consulares*) in order—traditionally beginning with the *princeps senatus*, the man selected as senior senator by the censors, but in practice in Cicero's day demonstrating his own ranking-order both in his first choice and the subsequent order of precedence within each senatorial grade. In the late Republic, when a man might be elected consul five and a half months before entering office, it seems to have been regular practice to ask a consul-elect first.[57] After calling those of consular rank, the president then proceeded to the ex-praetors, praetors, and other senators in descending order of rank. 'Dic, M. Tulli', 'Speak, Marcus Tullius, what you think should be done.'[58] The senator's reply would culminate in a recommendation, which would be expressed by *uti* with the subjunctive following *censeo*, but it might also contain an appreciation of the situation, for example that certain men had served the *res publica* well (see above) or that certain actions were against the public interest (*contra rem publicam*).[59] The 'interrogation' had, once begun, to be completed by the president asking all senators present, before a vote could be taken.[60] Since each meeting had to be completed by nightfall, this created the possibility of a filibuster (*diem consumere*), a tactic employed, for example, by Cato against the *publicani* and by Clodius against Cicero.[61]

A senator was required to answer. In 205, when Quintus Fulvius Flaccus threatened to remain silent in protest against the treatment of the senate by the consul Scipio, he asked the tribunes for protection against any punishment.[62] The senator in question might simply state his agreement with a previous speaker, as Cicero imagined himself doing—

---

[56] *SC Orop.* (*RDGE* 23); other drafted proposals Cic. *Phil.* 1. 3; 10. 17; *Staatsr.* iii. 2. 962. Contrast Cic. *Cat.* 4. 6.

[57] On *princeps senatus* see Gell. 4. 10. 2; 14. 7. 9. with Bonnefond-Coudry, 1993; also Cic. *Att.* 1. 13. 2; 10. 8. 3; and Gell. 4. 10. 2–3 for discretion in the ranking order; *Att.* 4. 2. 4 and 3. 3; Sall. *Cat.* 50. 4 for preferment of the consul-elect.

[58] Cic. *Att.* 7. 3. 5 and 7. 7 (where Cicero imagines being asked a question in the senate); Bonnefond-Coudry, 473.

[59] Cic. *Fam.* 8. 8. 6; *Att.* 2. 24. 3. The *tumultus* decree (*VRR* 153–4) was also essentially the registration of an emergency, which gave rise to further instructions.

[60] Cic. *Att.* 1. 17. 9; Livy, 29. 19. 10; Bonnefond-Coudry, 477.

[61] See Cic. *Att.* 1. 17. 9; *Fam.* 1. 2. 3; *Amic.* 12 for the terminus. On filibusters see *Att.* 1. 18. 7; 4. 2. 4 and 3. 3; *QF* 2. 1. 3; 2*Verr.* 2. 96; Caes. *BCiv.* 1. 32. 3; Gell. 4. 10. 8. Other evidence and discussion in de Libero, 1992, 15 ff.

[62] Livy, 28. 45. 1–7. See also Cic. *Pis.* 26; Tac. *Ann.* 11. 4.

'Cn. Pompeio adsentior'. The emperor Claudius was to complain, in a speech about the conduct of his contemporaries, that the first senator asked merely repeated word for word the proposal in the consul's *relatio*, and the rest said 'adsentior'. However, their reaction was arguably not so unreasonable in the light of the fully drafted proposals characteristic of the Principate.[63] Those of lower rank might not have had either the courage or the competence to do more than agree with a previous speaker. Even before they spoke, the lower ranks were accustomed to show their inclinations by walking across the senate to stand by a speaker whom they supported. 'In a rush the *pedarii* ran to support that proposal', wrote Cicero about a *senatus consultum* which damaged Atticus' business interests in Sicyon. The more normal phrase seems to have been *ire pedibus in sententiam alicuius*.[64] By the second century AD this practice seems to have died out, and ingenious explanations were being sought for the term *pedarius* which by now referred to a senator who had not held high office. Whether we regard *pedarius* as a technical term or not under the Principate, it seems merely to have been a humorous name under the Republic arising from the means by which humbler senators showed their attitude.[65] The debate about the Catilinarians on 5 December 63 BC was striking in that two important interventions were made by a former aedile and praetor-elect (Caesar) and by a former quaestor and tribune-elect (Cato). In 60 BC Cicero had to explain to Atticus how the younger P. Servilius Isauricus, who cannot have been more than a *quaestorius* at the time, was responsible for a rider to a motion, which forbad a Roman magistrate exercising jurisdiction over loans to a free city: the resulting *senatus consultum* was voted through by the *pedarii* without the support of the consulars. Nevertheless, the evidence of the Ciceronian period generally suggests that it was the consulars who dominated discussion (Cicero's indignation in 60 over the *pedarii* seems largely genuine, though it also may have had the purpose of mollifying Atticus), and it is likely that this was even more true of the second century BC and earlier.[66]

---

[63] Cic. *Att.* 7. 3. 5 and 7. 7; *FIRA* i. 44 = Smallwood, *GCN* 367, col. III, lines 19–23.

[64] On *pedarii* see Cic. *Att.* 1. 20. 4, cf. 19. 9; for *ire pedibus* Livy, 9. 8. 13; Gell. 3. 18. 1.

[65] Gell. 3. 18. 3–10; Front. *de aq.* 99. 4; also *ILS* 6121 = *CIL* ix. 338 for *pedani* ranked after *quaestorii* in the album of the local senate at Canusium. I take the joke in Varro's *Hippokuōn* (Gell. 3. 18. 5) to be an allusion to the new senators from the equestrian order who filled the lower ranks of the senate after Sulla's reform (see Bonnefond-Coudry, 1989, 655 ff.).

[66] Cic. *Att.* 12. 21. 1; Sall. *Cat.* 51–2; Cic. *Att.* 1. 19. 9 and 20. 4 (with *Prov. Cos.* 6–7). On the importance of the former censors and consulars see the tables in Bonnefond-Coudry, 1989, 596–8, 621–32. The evidence becomes significant in the period from 63 onwards,

Debates did not always follow a straightforward course, however. A senator had the right to digress from the topic proposed (*egredi relatione*). In January 43, Cicero began a speech: 'We are consulted on small, but perhaps necessary matters, senators. The consul brings before us the matter of the Appian way and the Mint, a tribune brings before us the Luperci. Although the solution of these matters seems easy, my mind wanders from the proposed agenda, in suspense over greater problems.' And what results is his seventh Philippic against Antonius. At the end he remarks, 'As to the matters which you are raising, I agree with Publius Servilius (Isauricus).'[67] In 204 BC two important questions seem to have surfaced in the course of debates about other topics: the treatment of the colonies which had in effect mutinied in 209 was raised during a discussion of reinforcements for the legions, and the repayment of those who had lent money to the *res publica* in 210 was brought up unexpectedly by M. Valerius Laevinus in another debate. Tacitus later recorded an assertion of Thrasea Paetus that senators, whenever they were given the right to speak, were permitted to put forward whatever they wanted and demand that this matter be formally referred.[68] Even if no proposals emerged, speeches might range far beyond the matter in hand. In February 61 there was a meeting in one of the temples by the circus Flaminius, in which the consul Messalla raised the questions of the sacrilege at the Bona Dea ceremony and the bill proposed providing extraordinary judicial procedure. Pompey in his *sententia* gave a blanket endorsement of decrees of the senate, including those of 63 BC ('de istis rebus'). This stimulated Crassus to make a long speech about Cicero's services as consul on themes previously favoured by Cicero himself. Whereupon Cicero in his turn took up the themes of 'the authority and responsibility of the senate, its harmony with the equestrian order, the unity of Italy, the half-dead relics of the Catilinarian conspiracy, cheap grain and peace.'[69]

Senatorial initiative might go further. A special opportunity was provided by meetings which began with a report or request—letters from abroad, a returning pro-magistrate recounting his exploits and requesting a triumph, a foreign embassy asking for help or terms of peace, the investigation of an informer.[70] Not only were senators free to ask

where, thanks largely to Cicero's correspondence, we can be sure that minor senators have not been filtered out of the historical record.

[67] Cic. *Phil.* 7. 1 and 27; see also Gell. 4. 10. 8.
[68] Livy, 29. 15 and 16; Tac. *Ann.* 13. 49; Bonnefond-Coudry, 1989, 476.
[69] Cic. *Att.* 1. 14. 2–4.
[70] Examples of information laid are Sall. *Cat.* 48. 3–8; Cic. *Att.* 2. 24. 2–3.

questions and to make informal comments, but the interrogation of the informer, the ambassadors, or the returning commander could lead to speeches. So in 210 Marcus Claudius Marcellus attacked the Sicilian ambassadors for their disloyalty and demanded that his settlement of the island's affairs should be ratified, before both he and the ambassadors finally left the chamber and a *relatio* was made to the senate. C. Manlius Vulso found himself in a debate with his own former *legati* over whether his Galatian campaign deserved a triumph.[71] What frequently resulted from these situations was a demand from the floor of the senate for a *relatio*. When Publius Aelius Paetus returned to Rome from his Gallic province late in the consular year of 201/0, the senators demanded at his first senate-meeting that he should make his priority a decision about war-preparations against Philip V of Macedon. In 211 the consuls were pressed to raise the question of the status of Lucius Marcius, the tribune of the soldiers who had usurped the title of pro-praetor in Spain.[72] A request for a specific *relatio* might even emerge in the course of a debate. When the informer Tarquinius accused Crassus of complicity in the Catilinarian conspiracy, the senate burst into shouts of protest and Cicero yielded to demands for a motion that this evidence was false and that Tarquinius should be put in chains and give no more testimony. In 56 BC senators requested a special motion allowing Cato to stand in advance for the praetorship as a reward for his services in Cyprus.[73]

Even if the debate remained focused on the *relatio* of the consul, it might develop in different ways. Senators might find themselves choosing between an early proposal by a leading senator and its negative, or a variety of proposals might emerge, or a proposal became gradually modified.[74] A senator might return to the debate to reveal that he had changed his *sententia*, as Decimus Iunius Silanus did in the final Catilinarian debate after hearing Caesar's speech. However, he might also come back to refute a subsequent speaker and sustain his original view—one of the technical meanings of the term '*interrogatio*'—as Quintus Lutatius Catulus did after that same speech of Caesar's. It was also permisssible to intervene in order to reply to a personal attack, as Clodius did to Cicero's denunciations in 61 and Pompey did to Gaius

[71] Livy, 26. 30. 1–32. 8; 38. 44. 9–50. 3; Bonnefond-Coudry, 1989, 461 ff.
[72] Livy, 31. 3. 1; 26. 2. 1–5; Bonnefond-Coudry, 1989, 454 ff.
[73] Sall. *Cat.* 48. 5–6; Val. Max. 4. 1. 14; Dio, 39. 23. 1.
[74] Contrast Cic. *Att.* 1. 14. 5 with *Fam.* 1. 1. 3 and 2. 1 and with *ad Brut.* 13 (= 1. 5). 1; *Prov. Cos.* 1 and 17. See Bonnefond-Coudry, 1989, 499 ff., on the plasticity and dynamism of the debate.

Cato's in 56.[75] Nor should we ignore the part played by applause, heckling, or indeed silence in the chamber. We hear of applause and jeers in a debate about Clodius' trial in 57, and shouts in the discussions about the *ager Campanus* in 56, while by contrast the tribune Publius Rutilius Lupus was greeted with a cold silence when he raised the restoration of Ptolemy Auletes.[76] There might even be interruptions from outside. Senate-debates were normally public, in so far as the doors of the building used were left open and people could look in. This allowed Clodius' supporters on one occasion to terrorize a senate meeting in the *curia* by shouts from the Graecostasis in the *comitium*. We even hear of a senate-meeting being frustrated because of intruders.[77]

It would be wrong to draw too strong a distinction between the delivery of opinions about a *relatio* according to the order determined by the president and the variant procedures we have been discussing. Both formed part of the formal procedures of the senate. Nevertheless, they were expressions of two different tendencies—the former following the principle of the senate being the magistrate's *consilium*, the latter that of the senators being autonomous persons of status with a right and duty to act in the best interests of Rome, as they saw them. It is also clear that senate-debates had a momentum of their own, which it was hard for a presiding magistrate to control. Once he had referred a matter to the senate, he was expected to go on asking for opinions until either there were no more senators to ask or it was night. He was also subject to pressure from the men of greatest authority in the city regarding the matters to be discussed. He only recovered control of the situation when he was able to call a vote, and even then not entirely.

Voting and the Publication of Decrees

One kind of vote was taken without the president seeking verbal opinions from senators at all. This was the *senatus consultum per discessionem*, so called not because other decrees did not require a division (*discessio*), but because this decree followed a division without dis-

---

[75] See Sall. *Cat.* 50. 4 on Silanus; *Schol. Bob.* 169–70St. and Plut. *Cic.* 21. 4 for *interrogatio*; Cic. *Att.* 1. 16. 8–10; *QF* 2. 3. 3 for *altercationes* (cf. Suet. *Aug.* 54. 1 for Augustus' problem with the *immodicas disceptantium altercationes*).

[76] Cic. *QF* 2. 1. 1–3, 6. 1.

[77] On the open door see Cic. *Phil.* 2. 112, 5. 18, *Cat.* 4. 3; on the exploitation of the *comitium QF* 2. 1. 3 (with Varro, *LL* 5. 155 on the Graecostasis); Dio, 39. 28. 2–3; also *QF* 2. 11 (10). 1 with the MS reading, '*populi convicio*' (on which see Lintott, 1967). For occasional debates in secret see Livy, 22. 60. 2; 42. 14; Val. Max. 2. 2. 1; Dion. Hal. *AR* 12. 2. 1; *HA XX Gord.* 12. 1–3.

cussion. Such were the votes to abolish the dictatorship after Caesar's murder and, with more dubious justification, that concerning a thanksgiving (*supplicatio*) for Marcus Aemilius Lepidus later in 44 BC.[78] However, a magistrate who wished to cut short senatorial business in this way could be frustrated by the cry of 'consule' ('consult'), which required him to ask for verbal *sententiae*. Other cries of tactical importance in the senate were the request for a count of those present ('numera') and the request that the motions should be divided ('divide').[79]

When the presiding magistrate was in a position to call for a vote, he had discretion over which proposal or proposals he put. He would have heard the various *sententiae* and could have seen where the *pedarii* clustered in the greatest numbers. However, his choice might be determined by personal considerations or indeed tactical calculations in order to achieve the result he wanted. The vote in each case was between a proposal and its negative. 'Those who have this view, go over to that side, those who think anything else (*alia omnia*), to this side.' So ran the formula preserved by Festus. (Hence the phrase *in alia omnia ire* came to mean 'to reject'.) Pliny the younger opined later that the method was crude and he would have preferred that senators should be told to go to whatever part of the senate corresponded to their view. However, that would have only been of value in a straw-poll: it would not have in itself produced a final decree in accordance with genuine majority opinion.[80]

If one motion failed, another might be put. There were no ground rules about the order in which motions should be ranked. On two occasions it is clear that the president made his selection with the object of avoiding a particular result. In the first the historian Polybius had a personal interest. Ambassadors came from the Achaean League in 155, requesting the release of the hostages taken to Italy on Aemilius Paulus' orders in 167. Three motions emerged, one to let them go, a second to retain them, a third to release them but not to allow their return to Greece for the moment. The consul Aulus Postumius put the extreme motions first. The motion for total release was rejected with the help of those who wished a delay before return of the detainees; the motion for

---

[78] Gell. 14. 7. 9–12 (getting unnecessarily confused); Cic. *Phil.* 1. 3; 3. 24. See also *SC Orop.* (*RDGE* 23); Dio, 41. 1. 2–2. 1, though the account is suspect, if the debate is meant to correspond with that in Caes. *BCiv.* 1. 1. 2–7; Bonnefond-Coudry, 1989, 484 ff.

[79] Festus, 174L; Cic. *Att.* 5. 4. 2. On '*divide*' see below with n. 83.

[80] Festus, 314L; Pliny, *Ep.* 8. 14. 19. On *in alia omnia . . .* see Cic. *Fam.* 1. 2. 1; 8. 13. 2; 10. 12. 3; Caes. *BG* 8. 53. 1.

retention was similarly passed with their support.[81] The second example is the debate on 14 January 57 BC about the restoration of Ptolemy Auletes. We are told that, because the matter had been discussed the previous day, the senate had decided that spoken *sententiae* should be brief, and this demonstrates how the senate could agree to curtail debate in order to reach a decision. Four motions had emerged the previous day; the consul Lentulus Marcellinus now ranked three of them.[82] First was that of Bibulus, who proposed that no army should be used, but that the king should be restored by three ambassadors chosen from those currently without office; Hortensius' motion, which Cicero himself supported, was that the governor of Syria, Lentulus Spinther, should restore the king without an army; the third motion, that of Volcacius Tullus, was that Pompey should undertake the task. It was demanded that Bibulus' motion should be divided, that is, that separate items within it should be subject to separate votes.[83] It was agreed that no army should be used, but the use of three ambassadors was rejected. Then the tribune Rutilius Lupus, who had raised the question of assigning the task to Pompey the previous day, claimed that Volcatius' motion should be taken next, and a fierce procedural dispute emerged which exhausted the day. According to Cicero, who may have been optimistic as he was writing to Spinther, Hortensius' motion was likely to have succeeded, but the consuls who had put Bibulus' motion first, because they preferred it, did not mind the debate running into the sand.

If a motion was passed, it still had to clear the hurdle of a possible veto (*intercessio*) by a consul or tribunes before it could be registered as a *senatus consultum*. We know of a few instances of consular *intercessio* being made or threatened, belonging to the period between the close of the Second Punic War and the Social War, in all of which there seems to have been a conflict between the public interest and the aristocratic pride of one of the consuls.[84] If a decree was vetoed by tribunes, it could be brought back in the hope it might escape a veto on another occasion.[85] Alternatively, the veto itself might be made the subject of a debate, as it

---

[81] Pol. 33. 1. 5–7; Bonnefond-Coudry, 1989, 544.

[82] Cic. *Fam.* 1. 1. 3–4; 1. 2. 1–3. On the ranking of *sententiae* see *Fam.* 10. 12. 3; *Phil.* 8. 1.

[83] Cic. *Fam.* 1. 2. 1, and compare for the division of motions *Mil.* 14 with Asc. 43–5C, where half a decree was vetoed by tribunes.

[84] See Livy, 30. 40. 8 and 43. 1; 38. 42. 8–13; 39. 38. 8–9; 42. 10. 10–11; Asc. 15C. Bonnefond-Coudry (555 ff.) follows Mommsen (*Staatsr.* i, 282 n. 7) in arguing that consular *intercessio* against another consul in the senate had become a dead letter in the late Republic (note the contrast in Suet. *Jul.* 29. 1 between *intercessores tribunos* and *alterum consulem*.

[85] See Bonnefond-Coudry, 562–3, comparing Asc. 36 with 43C and Cic. *Fam.* 10. 12. 3 with *ad Brut.* 2. 3.

was on a fateful occasion immediately preceding the civil war in the first week of January 49.[86] A vetoed decree was termed *senatus auctoritas* and might be recorded as such.[87]

In the actual drafting of a decree the presiding magistrate was dominant. As we can see from the preserved texts of decrees, he was assisted normally by a small group of senators, whom presumably he chose himself—usually of no great distinction under the Republic, being for the most part of no more than praetorian rank. Until the last years of the Republic there is nothing to suggest that the presiding-magistrate had assistance from secretaries or short-hand writers. On 3 Dec. 63 BC at the preliminary investigation of the Catilinarian conspirators Cicero chose three senators to record the proceedings 'whom I knew could most easily keep up with what was said through their powers of memory, knowledge, and speed of writing'. Four years later Caesar in his consulship commenced the publication of the *acta senatus* as well as the *acta diurna*. This should have entailed some form of secretarial recording, but may not have resulted in more than the regular circulation of all *senatus consulta* and *auctoritates* and the names of those who proposed motions and amendments—not a complete transcript of *sententiae* delivered. This published gazette of the senate was to be discontinued by Augustus.[88]

In any case, the responsibility for the texts published would still have rested with the man who presided over a particular session. Even before the mass-production of decrees in the period before and after Caesar's murder Cicero was accused of falsifying a *senatus consultum*, and we hear of a corrupt pact in 54 BC, in which one item was the invention of a decree with the aid of two consulars who would claim to have been present when it was drafted.[89] Securing the passage of a *senatus consultum* was not as cumbersome a business as legislation through the assembly, but it could be time-consuming if there was no crisis demanding urgent measures or if there was a will to obstruct. Nor could one be certain of getting the desired result. For those whose authority was hard to challenge the temptation to take short cuts was considerable.

[86] Caes. *BCiv.* 1. 2. 7–8 and 5. 1. See also Cic. *Fam.* 8. 8. 6–7, 13. 2; *Att.* 4. 2. 4.

[87] Cic. *Fam.* 1. 2. 4 and 7. 4; 8. 8. 6–7; *Att.* 5. 2. 3; *Leg.* 3. 10; Dio, 41. 3. 1; 42. 23. 1.

[88] Cic. *Sulla* 41–2; Suet. *Jul.* 20. 1; *Aug.* 36. See also Cic. *Fam.* 8. 1. 1 for the information collected by Caelius' writers for Cicero in Cilicia.

[89] Cic. *Dom.* 50; *Att.* 4. 17. 2; *Fam.* 9. 15. 4; 12. 1. 1 and 29. 2; *Phil.* 5. 12; 12. 12.

The Authority of the Senate

First, it should be said that, since under the Republic the constitutional powers of the senate were for the most part not a matter of written law but of accumulated tradition, it makes little sense to seek to distinguish between *de iure* and *de facto* powers. The most that can be done is to distinguish between earlier custom and more recent innovation, and to notice which innovations were accepted without being contested and which gave rise to disquiet.

Magistrates elected by the people could not operate without support. After it was no longer necessary to obtain ratification by the *patres* of decisions by the people, the magistrate needed the *consilium* of the senate for a number of reasons. It was the only political council at Rome where free, or largely free, political discussion could take place, as opposed to the delivery of speeches to an audience. It was a repository of accumulated experience of political office and military command. It was the natural forum for the resolution of disputes between magistrates and for arranging that their spheres of operation did not conflict: hence the senate's power over the allocation of provinces and the public resources of men and money. Equally, as the only political council at Rome, it was the natural focus for representatives of foreign communities. Furthermore, the senate was both the political form taken by the Roman aristocracy and also an important means of social self-expression by that class, in so far as it constituted a form of club, indeed the only significant aristocratic club (the *sodalitates* of Rome never seem to have achieved the importance of the *hetaireiai* of Athens as social gatherings).

Of course, all these considerations did not necessarily imply a freedom of decision without further reference. One could imagine a constitution where all senate resolutions had to be ratified by an assembly. But there would have been obvious practical difficulties. Assembly procedure was formal and slow, while a nation, like the Romans, regularly involved in war frequently needed quick decisions. Moreover, the authority permitted to the senate was grounded in more than practical necessity. The Roman people, though by no means deferential in all respects, trusted in the abilities of their aristocracy and accepted the need for a strong executive. This was one reason for the importance of the concept of *auctoritas* at Rome. The magistrates received office from the people and were responsible to the people for their conduct in office, as Polybius pointed out. In the mean time they were expected to carry out their tasks to the best of their ability without further reference to the assembly, except when there was a question of a war with a major power.[90] Thus the discretion accorded to the magistrates was a major contribution to the senate's authority, since it made room for the discretion of the senate.

Over the centuries successive senates made the most of the space granted them. They did not merely take decisions about particular situations, but produced decrees which were intended to be normative over a period, for example in 200 over the *ager in trientabulis*, in 193 over the repayment of debts to Latins, in 186 over the Bacchanals, and in 64 over the *collegia*.[91] The senate even had specific responsibilities incorporated in legislation, as with C. Gracchus' law about the allocation of consular provinces, or the *lex Caecilia Didia* of 98 BC, which granted to the senate the power to declare legislation invalid.[92] However, these resemblances to a modern parliament do not entail that the senate ever became a supreme legislative body. Nor could it easily have done so. The nature of its debates rendered it in fact ill-suited to producing elaborate legislation, such as that incorporated in late-Republican statutes, unless this was simply a matter of ratifying a complex motion brought to it with no more than minor amendment. Although the texts of a number of the decrees of the Republic preserved in inscriptions appear complex, this usually derives from what was actually presented to the senate in the first place—in the form of either speeches by ambassadors, preliminary discussions with individual senators, the report of a sub-committee, or the proposal of a magistrate. On a number of occasions, such as the granting of a treaty or special privileges to foreign communities or individuals, the items would have been sufficiently standard for a presiding magistrate to draft a decree following an outline produced in a debate.[93] It is in any case unlikely that a *sententia* produced on the floor of the senate amounted to much more than an explanatory preamble and four or five items.[94] Perhaps the most assertive and dramatic decree, with sweeping

[90] Pol. 6. 14. 10. This principle seems to have been abandoned by the late Republic, though it is not clear which was the last example of a declaration of war by the assembly, since our sources are not sufficiently precise over matters like the declaration of the First Mithridatic War (App. *Mith.* 22. 83). For the evidence see Rich, 1976, 14–15, 49–50.

[91] See e.g. Livy, 31. 13. 2–9, 35. 7. 1–3; *SC Bacch* (*FIRA* i. 30); Asc. 7C, with Crifò, 1968, esp. 55 ff.

[92] See on the *lex Sempronia*, Sall. *Jug.* 27. 3; Cic. *Dom.* 24; *Prov. Cos.* 3; *Fam.* 1. 7. 10; on the *lex Caecilia Didia* Cic. *Dom.* 41 and 50; *Sest.* 135; *Phil.* 5. 8; *Schol. Bob.* 140St.; *VRR* 133 ff.

[93] See *RDGE* 2; 23; also 16, 21, 26 c–d—decrees regarding treaties.

[94] In Cic. *Phil.* 5 there are five proposals—in paras. 34, 36, 40–41, 46, and 53. See also ibid. 3. 37–9 (four items); 8. 33; 9. 15–17; 10. 25–6; 11. 29–31 (four to five items); 13. 50; 14. 36–8.

and ultimately catastrophic implications, the so-called 'ultimate decree' which entrusted the consuls and other magistrates with the defence of the city, was drafted in a completely general and imprecise fashion (see the appendix to this chapter). It was for the magistrate who received it to fill in the details.

APPENDIX TO CHAPTER VI

The So-Called Last Decree

In the late Republic the senate developed a tradition, when faced with what it regarded as a violent threat to the security of the *res publica* originating among the citizens themselves, whereby it urged the consuls or other magistrates in office to take any measure necessary to counter this threat. The *res publica* was entrusted to these magistrates; they were urged to defend it and to ensure that it came to no harm.[1] These vague and reassuring phrases were understood by the senators who endorsed them to be an encouragement to the magistrates to use force against fellow-citizens without concerning themselves with the strict legality of what they did.

Normally the person of a citizen, who was not a manifest or condemned criminal, was protected from physical harm or manhandling on a magistrate's orders by the right of *provocatio* and the capacity of the tribunes to offer physical protection. The effect of this decree was to deter the tribunes from intervention: indeed on occasions they were enlisted as supporters of its execution.[2] *Provocatio* itself, at least in the middle and late Republic, was protected by law: that is, there was the sanction of a subsequent prosecution against those who rode roughshod over it. Probably the critical step in the establishment of this decree as an institution was the acquittal of the consul of 121 BC, L. Opimius, on the charge of killing citizens without proper trial, and thus in defiance of the *provocatio* laws. This had happened during and after the suppression of C. Gracchus, M. Fulvius Flaccus, and their supporters, when for the first time a decree of this kind had been formally put to the vote by the presiding magistrate.[3] However, Opimius' acquittal was controversial, and the interpretation of the decree itself continued to be the subject of dispute during the late Republic up to the time when it was fatefully used against the tribunes defending the proconsul of Gaul, Julius Caesar, on 7 January 49 BC—in spite of the fact that they were offering no violence, as Caesar himself was at pains to point out later.[4] It was then that he described it as 'that last decree'. (On the basis of this phrase, and this phrase alone, it is generally termed in modern scholarship the *senatus*

---

[1] Cic. *Phil.* 5. 34; 8. 14; *Rab. Perd.* 20; Sall. *Hist.* 1. 77. 22; Asc. 34C; *VRR* 151–2.
[2] Cic. *Rab. Perd.* 20; Asc. 34C; Cic. *Fam.* 16. 11. 2; Caes. *BCiv.* 1. 5. 3.
[3] Livy, *Per.* 61; Cic. *de Or.* 2. 106 and 132 ff.; *Part. Or.* 104; *Sest.* 140; *VRR* 167–8.
[4] Caes. *BCiv.* 1. 5. 3 and 7. 5.

consultum ultimum, although a more precise title, reflecting the actual terms of the decree, would be the *senatus consultum de re publica defendenda*.[5])

Caesar did not denounce the decree itself as a breach of the constitution either in 49 or in 63 BC, if we can trust the speech assigned him in Sallust's *Catiline*. He questioned its appropriateness in the circumstances of 49; in 63 he urged the consul, Cicero, not to transgress the laws too blatantly by executing the leading Catilinarians in the city without formal trial.[6] It is illustrative of the position of the senate in the Republican constitution that there seem to have been no limits on the decrees that it could pass—not through any absolute sovereignty, nor because, as a body, it could not be held legally responsible for its actions, but because in form a decree was no more than a recommendation, which could only be put into force by the magistrates.[7] This particular decree was, moreover, exceedingly vague in its language. It was not clear, for example, whether it was simply recommending a limited use of force to restore the rule of law or the extermination of those who were thought to have disturbed the peace. A large part of the bitterness to which the decree gave rise derived from the interpretation placed by the magistrates on it, especially when it was held to justify extraordinary forms of trial after order had been restored.[8]

Apart from the important part it played in the political history of the late Republic, the decree is of more general constitutional interest for more than one reason. First, it is an example of an institution created by *mos* over a period (cf. Chap. I with nn. 11ff.), that not only owed nothing to *lex* (statute) but had the precise object of rendering temporarily void certain *leges*. Secondly, it raises the perennial question, how far can one save law and order by using illegal violence, how far can *ius* be based on *vis* without ceasing to be *ius*—a subject which I have discussed elsewhere.[9] Thirdly, it has elicited unusual theories about the nature of the senate.

For Mommsen the function of the senate in passing this decree was curiously marginal. In his view the temporary neglect of legal process in a crisis was necessary and, because necessary, unproblematic. The very threat to the community both justified and required not only the magistrates but the whole citizen-body to go to its defence, following the principle of *Selbsthilfe*, self-help. The senate's job was to signal the crisis and to suggest practical steps to be taken. Now it is arguable that, whether or not one accepts the principle of self-help as universally valid, there is a fair amount of evidence that it was so accepted by and large by Romans under the Republic.[10] However, the Romans also clearly

---

[5] The title preferred by Plaumann, 1913.

[6] Caes. *BCiv.* 1. 7. 5; Sall. *Cat.* 51, esp. 17–26, 35–6.

[7] To this extent Mommsen's view of the senate (*Staatsr.* iii. 2. 1025 ff.) must be right. The senate does not give orders; it formulates a view that something should happen—and this in answer to a question put to it by a magistrate, to which it is bound to give a reply.

[8] Sall. *Jug.* 31. 7–8 and see *VRR* 162–4, 166–8; Lintott, 1972, 259–62.

[9] *VRR*, esp. chs. 2–4.

[10] *Staatsr.* i, 690 ff.; iii. 2. 1240 ff. On 'self-help' see *VRR*, chs. 1–3; Lintott, 1972, 228–34;

thought that this decree centred on a relationship between the senate and certain magistrates, not the community as a whole, and that the approval of the senate was far more important than some generally understood principle.

More representative are the views of G. Plaumann and H. M. Last, which are focused on the leading magistrates.[11] They resemble Mommsen to some extent in believing that in a sense the decree was superfluous. Decree or no decree, in a crisis it was the magistrate's duty to save the *res publica* in any way that he could. For Last the decree did not in any way alter the legal powers the magistrate possessed: it was merely an offer of senatorial support, which implied that supra-legal measures were necessary. In Plaumann's eyes the development of the decree as an institution was important in that it rendered the supra-legal measures taken less arbitrary: nevertheless, the decree arguably ran counter to the principles of the Roman constitution.

One palliative of the illegality was suggested by Last, that the senate at the time of the decree designated certain men *hostes*—enemies and therefore not deserving the rights of citizens—and this view has been followed with varying nuances by Bleicken and J. Ungern-Sternberg.[12] There are, however, problems. It is not that we have no evidence of such declarations: we have, but in no case are they closely connected with the 'last' decree. The first known targets were Marius, Sulpicius, and their followers in 88; the last was M. Antonius, first in 43 and later, it appears, in 32–1.[13] In all cases except perhaps one (in 83) these were people who had been in arms or might be thought to present a military threat. In 63 Catiline and Manlius were formally declared *hostes*—but after Catiline's departure to Etruria and thus three weeks or more after the 'last' decree; the Catilinarians in the city were never formally so declared. However, Cicero in the first Catilinarian speech—with Catiline present in the senate—claimed that he had discovered him to be an enemy, and later argued that the arrested conspirators were *hostes*.[14] This should alert us to the dangers of taking Ciceronian rhetoric too literally or legalistically.

On the occasions when the decree was passed, there usually could have been little doubt who were the targets. In 121, C. Gracchus and M. Fulvius Flaccus were described as tyrants in the senate, according to Plutarch (as Ti. Gracchus had been in 133, when the consul Scaevola had refused to be moved by informal representations by senators). In 100 Servilius Glaucia and Saturninus were pointedly passed over by the consuls when they were urged to enlist support from those they thought appropriate.[15] Yet this is not to say that the targets were

on its inappropriateness as a justification for the 'last' decree, see *VRR* 158–9, especially for the implications of Cic. *Rab. Perd.* 20.

[11] Plaumann, 1913; Last, *CAH* ix (1st edn.), 82 ff.

[12] Bleicken, 1962, 23; von Ungern-Sternberg, 1970, 55 ff., on which see the critical reflections of Crifò, 1970, 1–15.

[13] Evidence in *VRR* 155.

[14] Sall. *Cat.* 36. 2–3. Contrast Cic. *Cat.* 1. 27–8; *Cat.* 4. 10.

[15] Plut. *Ti. Gr.* 19. 3; *C. Gr.* 14. 3; Cic. *Rab. Perd.* 20.

declared to be bereft of citizen-rights. The puzzling language of a clause of C. Gracchus' *lex Sempronia*, passed as a reaction against the tribunal of Popillius Laenas, which condemned former supporters of Ti. Gracchus to death, does indeed imply that Laenas' tribunal was thought by its opponents to have deprived citizens of their rights without proper trial, but not that the senate had in some way formally enacted this.[16] The *hostis*-argument was part of the rhetoric of the situation when the 'last' decree was passed, part of the defence of supra-legal measures: it did not itself legalize anything.

If the significance of the 'last' decree from the constitutional point of view is, according to the standard explanation, simply that the magistrates were urged to save the *res publica* by ignoring strict legality, this does not entail any particular conception of the senate's place in the constitution. However, one scholar, U. von Lübtow, has held that the senate had a latent *imperium* which it handed over to the consuls in an emergency.[17] This view runs contrary to our ancient evidence, which understands *imperium* as something conferred by the people on magistrates, and finds no support among other scholars who would conceive the senate as something more than an advisory body.

More recently, T. N. Mitchell has argued that in a crisis the senate put into effect a latent supremacy of another kind, that of being a supreme deliberative body which the magistrates were bound to obey and the rest of the citizens were bound to support.[18] Mitchell's argument is chiefly based on two Ciceronian texts. In the *de Oratore* (2. 134) Cicero describes the issue in the Opimius case as 'whether a man should be punished for killing a citizen in accordance with a decree of the senate for the preservation of his fatherland, although this was not permitted by the laws'. On the usual view of the 'last' decree, Opimius is justified here in Cicero's eyes both because he had senatorial backing and because the preservation of the fatherland was an overriding consideration; for Mitchell it is the decree which Cicero wants to emphasize. However, this interpretation does not seem to be borne out by the word-order. Moreover, one would expect the preservation of the fatherland to be a major consideration for one who incorporated the sentence, 'ollis (sc. the consuls) salus populi suprema lex esto' ('let the safety of the people be their highest law') in his theoretical law-code[19]— a sentence which also stresses consular responsibility and initiative. Mitchell then takes the phrase from Cicero's speech in 63 for Rabirius, 'summum in consulibus imperium, summum in senatu consilium putare', not to mean simply that the consuls were the chief executives and the senate the supreme deliberative body, but rather to indicate a superiority of the *consilium* over the *imperium*.[20] Once again, this is not the most natural interpretation of the text, nor, as we have seen, is it an interpretation of the constitution which would have

[16] Cic. *Rab. Perd.* 12; Plut. *C. Gr.* 4. 1; *VRR* 163–4.
[17] Von Lübtow, 1955, 334 ff.
[18] Mitchell, 1971.
[19] Cic. *Leg.* 3. 8.
[20] Cic. *Rab. Perd.* 3.

been accepted without dispute. Yet the greatest argument against Mitchell's view is the text of the 'last' decree itself: how can a decree, which entrusts the *res publica* to the consuls and other magistrates and urges *them* to protect it, be a declaration by the senate that it has taken charge in a crisis?

Cicero himself in general believed in the subordination of the magistrates to senatorial authority both in his theoretical works and in practical politics;[21] the fourth Catilinarian speech shows what store he set on getting senatorial backing for his execution of the Catilinarians. This means that he is likely to over-emphasize the role of the senate in any discussion of the 'last' decree, as we can see in his dismissal of the notion that Marius could have given a guarantee of protection to Glaucia and Saturninus in 100 without a decree of the senate.[22] Yet even his language there does not justify the interpretation of Mitchell. For the Caesar portrayed by Sallust the stress is elsewhere: describing the precedent the execution of the Catilinarians would set, he says, 'once a consul has drawn his sword by virtue of a decree of the senate following this example, who will fix a limit for *him* or who will control *him*?'[23]

[21] Cic. *Rep.* 2. 56 and 61; *Leg.* 3. 6; *Sest.* 137 and 143.
[22] Cic. *Rab. Perd.* 28.
[23] Sall. *Cat.* 51. 36.

VII

The Higher Magistrates and the Pro-Magistrates

The Nature of the Magistrate's Power

Rome's wars were won and Rome's provinces governed by magistrates who, though they might receive special instructions and were subject in the later Republic to rules defined in law or *senatus consultum*, had full discretion to take major decisions without consultation of the senate or people—'as they judge to be in accordance with the public interest and their own good faith', to use a standard phrase found in legal texts.[1] They were expected to do their best for the *res publica* and, if this was afterwards considered inadequate, they were liable to prosecution on their return to Rome.

At home the deliberative functions undertaken by the higher magistrates and their part in legislation were performed in conjunction with the senate and assemblies, but magistrates carrying out administration had similar discretion to those outside Rome. The chief restriction within the city was the use of *provocatio* and appeal to the tribunes by those over whom magistrates might be exercising power.[2] Lower magistrates could also be overruled by their superiors, but the hierarchy of power was usually more latent than apparent: consuls did not normally intervene in the jurisdiction of praetors, and neither they nor the praetors concerned themselves with the majority of functions which made up the *cura urbis* exercised by the aediles.[3] The censors' power was notoriously arbitrary and it was only at the end of the Republic that attempts were made to establish a legitimate route to challenge it (see below with nn. 116 and 121).

If one follows Mommsen and regards the powers of magistrates as the

---

[1] e.g. in *lex agr.* 35, 78; *RDGE*, nos. 2, lines 39–40, 44–5; 6, line 9; 7, lines 50–1; 9, lines 71–2; 10, A11, B14; 12, line 19.

[2] See Chap. VII below with nn. 16 ff.; Chap. VIII with nn. 14 ff.

[3] Chap. VIII with nn. 23 ff.

original unique authority of the king redistributed in small parcels, then the multiplication of magistracies may appear as the dilution of authority, rather than its reinforcement.[4] It is preferable, in my view, to treat the increase in magistracies at its face value—an indication that, as the Republic went on, the Romans became subject to more government. It remains true, however, that this increase in government did not add to the authority of the supreme magistrates in the city. Moreover, the growth of Roman military power and empire, which ultimately allowed a single Roman commander discretion over territory which in the present day forms more than one nation-state, made the powers of a consul in Rome seem insignificant compared with those of a consul or proconsul abroad.

Before any consideration of the nature of the individual offices there are some fundamental concepts relating to the magistracy which need to be considered. One is *potestas*, the magistrate's power, in particular that supreme form of it entitled *imperium*; then there are two notions, unconnected in themselves, which both bear on the way these powers were either allowed to collide or prevented from colliding—those of *collega* and *provincia*; finally there is the religious aspect of magisterial power, the right to consult divine will through taking *auspicia*.

Power and Coercion

Every magistrate had *potestas*—in its institutional sense a capability legitimized by statute or custom.[5] The right to confer this capability rested generally with the Roman people. Cicero, though his ideal was a *res publica* governed by an aristocracy (*optimates*), makes his protagonist Scipio argue that it was intolerable for such men to claim this status without popular confirmation.[6] In practice not only the highest regular magistrates, the consuls and praetors, were elected, but also minor magistrates such as the *triumviri capitales*, the *triumviri* for the founding of colonies or distribution of lands, and the tribunes of the soldiers of the first four legions.[7] Exceptions to the rule were, first, the other tribunes of the soldiers and holders of military posts conferred by the commander, secondly, the dictator and master of the horse, whose emergency offices

---

[4] *Staatsr.* i. 24.

[5] In *Res Gestae* 34. 1 *potestas* appears first in a generalized sense, referring to Augustus' power before 27 BC, and then in 34. 3 in this more precise sense—the power he (allegedly) shared with other magistrates. For the phrase which links capability and legitimization, *ius potestasque esto*, see e.g. Fiesole frag. (*RS* i. 32); *lex Gen. Urs.* (*RS* i. 25), capp. 62, 65, 66, 99, 100, 103, 125–6, 128–33; *lex imp. Vesp.* (*RS* i. 39), line 19; *lex Falcidia* (*RS* ii. 59 = *Dig.* 35. 2. 1. pr.); *lex Quinctia* (*RS* ii. 63), lines 22, 39.   [6] Cic. *Rep.* 1. 50.

[7] Chap. VIII with nn. 70 ff.

normally derived from simple nomination (see below with nn. 73 ff.), and thirdly, for the most part, pro-magistrates (see below with nn. 89 ff.), in so far as their office might be held not to derive from their original magistracy (there were a few who actually received extraordinary pro-consular command from the people).

Potestas in its strongest form, that granted to consuls, praetors, pro-consuls, propraetors—and to the dictator and his master of horse—was termed *imperium*. This noun means generally 'command', either a specific command or the power to give commands, and is frequently used in this restricted constitutional sense, which Cicero characterized as *regium imperium*.[8] It is obviously related to the exercise of military command, but it seems that holders of *imperium* were not thought to have the right automatically to be military commanders, since the ratification of a *lex curiata* concerning military *imperium* was required first.[9] The insignia and apparatus associated with *imperium*, the rods and axes in bundles (*fasces*) carried by lictors, the folding chair (*sella curulis*), and the bordered toga were apparently an inheritance from the kings. Moreover, the ceremony of a triumph, which seems also to have been a legacy from this period, could only be performed by a victorious commander if he possessed *imperium*.[10]

Magistrates with *imperium* could act in a judicial capacity, whether this was *iuris dictio*—the definition and ratification of a civil lawsuit performed in the city by the *praetor urbanus* or *peregrinus* before the actual hearing of the case (see below with nn. 59 ff.)—or the actual investigation (*quaerere, cognoscere*) of a crime or a delict against administrative law. In practice, in Rome and Italy consuls only undertook criminal trials of special cases, while in civil matters we only know of them being assigned jurisdiction over lawsuits concerning the possession of land—a product of the controversies arising from the legislation of the Gracchi.[11] Abroad it seems that a magistrate might either judge cases himself or conduct a preliminary investigation before assigning the trial to a judge or panel of judges.[12] A development of the late Republic was the establishment of

[8] Cic. *Leg.* 3. 8. Examples of this sense of '*imperium*' in *lex. agr.* 87; *frag. Tar.* (*RS* i. 8), 7; *lex Rubr. Gall.* (*RS* i. 28), XX. 50; *lex Gen. Urs.* cap. 94; *Res Gestae* 1; Cic. *Fam.* 1. 1. 3; *Att.* 4. 1. 7; 7. 7. 6.   [9] *Staatsr.* i. 610–14; Chap. V with nn. 47–8.
[10] For the king having 12 *fasces* see Cic. *Rep.* 2. 31. See in general Marshall, 1984, with earlier bibliography, and, on the origin of the triumph, Versnel, 1970; Warren, 1970.
[11] See below, Chap. IX, and on special criminal investigations see also Chap. III with n. 13; for civil jurisdiction App. *BCiv.* 1. 19. 80; *lex agr.* 24, 33–6.
[12] *Lex prov. praet.* (*RS* i. 12), Cnidos IV. 34–7; Cic. *2Verr.* 2. 32–3; *Flacc.* 71; *QF* 1. 2. 10; *Att.* 6. 1. 15; *tabula Contrebiensis* (Richardson, 1983), and see in general *Imp. Rom.* 55–8; 224 n. 29.

permanent criminal tribunals, which originally were all presided over by praetors, but ultimately were in part placed in the hands of former aediles, who had not been granted *imperium*, with the title of *iudex quaestionis* (investigation judge) or *quaesitor* (investigator).[13]

On the other hand, a magistrate might proceed more directly against those he believed to be lawbreakers and those who obstructed him in the exercise of his functions. Cicero in his proposed set of laws laid down that 'a magistrate shall coerce a disobedient and a criminal citizen with a fine or bonds or blows, unless an equal or greater *potestas* prevents him, to whom there shall be *provocatio*'. This clearly does not represent the situation in the late Republic after the *leges Porciae* had banned the flogging of citizens, except when on military service.[14] More importantly, it may mislead us about the extent to which a magistrate in the civil sphere got his way by using force. It might be imagined that, inasmuch as the Romans were a people devoted to war, their civil life was like that of a military camp, subject to military discipline and the force of arms. In fact the opposite is the case under the Republic: within the area of the city the actions of magistrates were strictly subject to public law; normally they could not command troops and had only a few civilian minions. Moreover, people in general were not expected to go about their business carrying weapons.

Mommsen indeed elevated *coercitio* (coercion) into a fundamental characteristic of Roman magistrates, in so far as they had a right and duty to maintain public order. *Provocatio*, in his view, was created as an antithesis to this and the conflict between these two forces, in which the victory largely went to the latter, was a highly significant part of the constitutional development of the Republic.[15] We may agree with him in seeing the conflict between *imperium* on the one hand and *provocatio*, especially when associated with appeal to the tribunes, as a fundamental matrix of Roman society. However, while it is clear that a magistrate who was obstructed would resort to force through his lictors or other attendants, if he could see no other means to get his way, any notion that a consul or praetor went about the city maintaining public order and repressing crime seems far removed from reality. Those functions, in so

---

[13] For examples of *iudices quaestionis* see *ILS* 45, 47; Cic. *Clu.* 126, 147; *Brut.* 264; Suet. *Jul.* 11. Mommsen (*Strafr.* 205–8) believed, on the basis of some dubious passages in *Schol. Bob.* 149–50St. that these were simply chosen from the jury. Against this see *VRR* 121–2.

[14] Cic. *Leg.* 3. 6, with Lintott, 1972, 258. On the *leges Porciae* see Cato, *ORF*, no. 8, fr. 117; Cic. *Rep.* 2. 54; *Rab. Perd.* 12; 2 *Verr.* 1. 14; 5. 151, 163, 173; Sall. *Cat.* 51. 21.

[15] *Staatsr.* i. 136 ff., esp. 136, 141, 151.

far as they were exercised, fell to minor magistrates.[16] Nor is it likely that in the earliest days of the Republic the consul exercised quasi-regal power, as Mommsen believed. This would not only conflict with one element in the tradition about the invention of the office of dictator, that it was to furnish a stronger authority to repress sedition, but also with the portrayal of Valerius Poplicola, the founding father of the Republic, who is said not only to have enacted the outlawry of suspected tyrants but also to have gone to great lengths to avoid the imputation of tyranny himself. As for the *lex de provocatione* attributed to him, I continue to believe it to be an anachronism, in so far as it is held to have anticipated the recognition of appeals made to the plebs and their tribunes during the social conflicts of the early Republic and the subsequent fortification of these appeals by legal sanction.[17] However, an enactment that limited the power of a magistrate to proceed summarily against citizens, as if he was an autocrat, would have been a suitable codicil to the outlawry of *reges*.[18]

The *provocatio* laws eventually in theory protected citizens from summary execution and flogging even outside Rome, but it was hard to control a Roman magistrate with *imperium* in the field.[19] The fact that in practice it was abnormal to find Roman magistrates using force on free citizens in the city or its neighbourhood is surely a reflection not only of the restraints placed on them by the laws, but also of the power of the tribunes both within the *pomerium*—the religious boundary which from the fourth century seems to have largely coincided with the line of the so-called 'Servian' wall—and (by the late Republic) in the built-up area immediately outside it as far as the first milestone.[20] On occasions when coercion by magistrates with *imperium* led to executions, either there had been a reference to an assembly, or, usually following some mass unrest, an inquiry (*quaestio*) occurred, which would have entailed at

[16] *VRR*, ch. 7; Nippel, 1995, ch. 1. The rule that the axes were only incorporated in the *fasces* outside the *pomerium* (Livy, 24. 9. 2) was a sign that within the *pomerium* a magistrate with *imperium* was not expected to inflict capital punishment on his own authority, a principle which, in my view, antedated the development of *provocatio*.

[17] On the dictatorship see Chap. III with n. 9, Chap. VII with nn. 70 ff.; on Poplicola Chap. IV with n. 19; on *provocatio* Lintott, 1972.

[18] *Dig.* 1. 2. 2. 16 can be read in this sense, if we delete the reference to *provocatio* and the phrase *iniussu populi* as anticipations of later developments.

[19] See e.g. *Imp. Rom.* 44–6.

[20] See Livy, 3. 20. 7; Dio, 51. 19. 6, with Lintott, *CR* 21 (1971), 5–6; *tab. Heracl.* (*RS* i. 24), 20; Gai. *Inst.* 4. 104; and on the *pomerium* Varro, *LL* 5. 143, cf. 46–54; Gell. 13. 14. 4–7 (based on Messala's work on augury). The Servian wall actually crosses the Aventine, said by Messala (Gell. 13. 14. 4) to have been outside the *pomerium*, but Messala may have been simply referring to that part of the hill outside the wall.

least some delay and deliberation, even if it did not amount to the elaborate hearing which the Romans considered appropriate in formal capital cases. This illustrates both the power that magistrates with *imperium* might exercise as a last resort and also the restraints surrounding it. It was not an everyday weapon and, as the controversies over the *quaestiones* held by Popilius Laenas and Opimius over the supporters of the Gracchi show, it required some sort of consensus, if it was to be undertaken without subsequent reprisals against the *imperium*-holder.[21]

Nervertheless, other varied, and in some cases ingenious, forms of coercion remained open—flogging (until this was forbidden by the *leges Porciae*), imprisonment (normally only temporary),[22] fines, the taking of pledges, selling into slavery for failing to obey a levy, relegation from the city, even the destruction of a house. Associated with this was the right of summons (*vocatio*), which even applied to those in the country outside Rome.[23] A complex tradition arose concerning the limiting of fines which a magistrate could make at his discretion—the *multa maxima*—associated with the *leges Aterneia Tarpeia* (454), *Menenia Sestia* (452), and *Iulia Papiria* (430).[24] Even if the definition of the fine in number of animals is the product of later learned antiquarianism, the principle of a limit on summary fines need not be doubted. Later texts suggest that the maximum was half a man's property.[25] On the whole, the more drastic forms of coercion were a prerogative of the senior magistrates, though aediles, for example, could order a flogging and continued to have this power over actors even after the *leges Porciae*, while the *triumviri capitales* seem to have had powers of summary imprisonment over free men as well as slaves.[26]

Collegiality and Provinciae

Colleagues were not usually required to act in unison. Among the tribunes of the plebs the possibility of a member exercising *intercessio* against one or more of his colleagues would have frequently been a stimulus to consultation, but there was nothing abnormal in conflict *per*

---

[21] See below Chap. 9 with nn. 39 ff.

[22] Gell. 4. 10. 8; *VRR* 100, 102 f., 169; Nippel, 1995, 7, 52.

[23] *Staatsr.* i. 141–3, 151–61; Gell. 13. 12. 5–8 (Varro), cf. ibid. 1–4 (Capito); Tac. *Ann.* 13. 28 on *vocatio*. For house-destruction after an execution see Livy, 2. 41. 11; 4. 16. 1; 8. 20. 8; also 6. 20. 13 with Ovid, *Fasti* 6. 183–5.

[24] Cic. *Rep.* 2. 60; Livy, 4. 30. 3; Dion. Hal. *AR* 10. 50. 2; Festus, 220, 268–70L; Gell. 11. 1. 2.

[25] *Lex Silia* (Festus, 288L, *RS* ii. 46); *lex lat. Bant.* (*RS* i. 7), 12; Cato, *ORF*, no. 8, fr. 167; *JRLR* 131–2; Crawford, 1985, 19–20.

[26] Plaut. *Amph.* 155; *Miles* 211–12; *Trin.* 990; Val. Max. 6. 1. 10; Asc. 37C; Tac. *Ann.* 1. 77; Suet. *Aug.* 45. 3; Gell. 3. 3. 15; *VRR* 94–5, 102–3.

se. An exception was that the censors were required to act jointly in degrading a citizen in the census, but they could perform other functions individually, for example the final ceremony of the *lustrum* for which they drew lots.[27] Frequently in the mature Republic we find that the functions of colleagues are separated either in time or in space. In the early part of the Second Punic War, when two consular armies were joined in the Cannae campaign, we find that the supreme authority symbolized by the display of the *fasces* alternated between the consuls day by day—an unsatisfactory situation, which the Romans for the most part avoided in the future.[28] In the early and middle Republic consuls spent much of their time away from Rome campaigning, but, when they were both at Rome, it was the rule that they displayed the *fasces* and were responsible for political leadership in alternate months. The consul who undertook this in the first month of the year is generally held to have been the *consul prior* or *maior*. This honour might have been granted him through seniority in years, or in rank as a former consul, or because he achieved the necessary majority of votes earlier in the election than his colleague: we do not know the exact rules under the Republic. There is an important reference to 'the consul first elected' in the Greek texts of the law about the praetorian provinces of 101–100, but it is not certain that this is the equivalent of *consul prior*.[29] In a similar way we find the praetors and quaestors generally each having separate functions, although the treasury came to be entrusted to a pair of quaestors, and the aediles, curule and plebeian, worked in pairs in the administration of the games (see below, Chap. VIII).

The norm, then, seems to have been to avoid conflicts by separating the activities of magistrates. We would be wrong, therefore, to see collegiality in principle as a form of constitutional check: the multiplicity of magistrates was perhaps in origin intended rather as cover for a multiplicity of functions and insurance against the sudden death or dis-

[27] *Staatsr.* i. 42; ii. 1. 384 ff.; see below with nn. 105 ff.

[28] Pol. 3. 110. 4; 113. 1 ff.; Livy, 22. 41. 2–3, 44. 5; cf. 28. 9. 10 for the auspices being with Livius Salinator on the day of the battle of the Metaurus.

[29] Cic. *Rep.* 2. 55, Val. Max. 4. 1. 1, and Plut. *Popl.* 12. 5 all suggest that the 'prior consul' is the older; Festus, 154L, that the *maior consul* is the man elected *prior*; Gell. 2. 15. 4–8 that seniority in either age or status was the criterion under the Republic. See also *lex prov. praet.* Cnidos (*RS* i. 12), III. 28 = Delphi B. 5, for an instruction to the 'first consul', and the comments of Drummond, 1978, 81–3, and Ferrary, 1977, 647 ff. The latter argues—on the basis of the phrase, 'qui primus sit praetor factus, eum legem curiatam ferre, sin is ferre non possit, qui postremus sit' (*Cic. Leg. Agr.* 2. 28)—not only (rightly) that the phrase in the *lex prov. praet.* must refer to the first consul elected, but (less convincingly) that this was the meaning of *consul prior* at the time.

ability of a magistrate. Nevertheless, colleagues could obstruct one another, though the evidence for this is unsatisfactory for all magistracies except the tribunate. Whereas a more powerful magistrate, for example a consul in relation to a praetor, or a tribune, could actually forbid another from acting in a certain way, a man could only cancel his colleague's action, after it had occurred, by acting in a contrary sense. In this way the decrees of Verres as urban praetor were rescinded by another praetor taking different decisions later on the same questions. These are referred to as *intercessio*, the term for obstruction, but clearly consisted of corrections to the decrees of Verres.[30] Where we find magistrates, other than tribunes, actually obstructing their colleagues in the late Republic, it is by exploiting their power of consulting the auspices in order to detect unfavourable religious omens.

The Roman concept which lay at the root of the separation of magistrates in space was *provincia*. This has been interpreted etymologically as a space associated with planned conquest, that is, a theatre of war—a meaning which later evolved into that of a piece of territory to be administered rather than conquered.[31] It remains true that the use of the term for tasks within the civil sector, the jurisdiction of the praetors and the functions of the quaestors, for example, is well attested for the second century BC and, if we trust Livy, goes back to the third century.[32] The provinces of the consuls, normally actual or potential theatres of war before Sulla, were first chosen by the senate and then distributed by lot or arrangement; those of the praetors, whether jurisdiction in Rome or a governorship abroad earmarked by the senate, were allotted; similarly the administrative tasks of the quaestors.[33] The senate thus customarily selected the most urgent tasks to be performed and these were shared out as impartially as possible among the magistrates. The procedure clearly sought to control aristocratic rivalry and to save aristocratic pride. It was ironically a measure of the *popularis* tribune C. Gracchus

[30] *Staatsr.* i. 258–70; Val. Max. 7. 7. 6 for a consul overruling a praetor; Cic. *2 Verr.* 1. 119 for another praetor overruling Verres. Note also Caelius' promises of assistance (*auxilium*) against a fellow praetor, Trebonius, in 48, which also would have consisted of alternative decisions about the debts in question (Caes. *BCiv.* 3. 20. 1; cf. Dio, 42. 29. 3–4).

[31] Bertrand, 1989; *Staatsr.* i. 51 n. 2. The definition in Festus (253L)—'what the Romans had conquered (*vincia*) before (*pro*)'—is not convincing.

[32] See e.g. *lex rep.*, lines 69, 72, 79–80; *lex agr.* 46; and Livy, 24. 9. 5, 43. 11. 8, for the jurisdiction of the urban praetor.

[33] On consuls and praetors see e.g. Livy, 30. 1. 1–2; 32. 1. 1–2 and 8. 4–5; 42. 4. 1–2; 43. 12. 1; Sall. *Cat.* 26. 4; on quaestors, Cic. *Verr.* 1. 34; *Sest.* 8; *Mur.* 18; *Phil.* 2. 50, with *Staatsr.* ii. 1. 532–3 for allotment, Cic. *Att.* 6. 6. 4; Livy, 30. 33. 2 for exceptions made to allotment. Our texts also suggest that Saturninus was specially appointed to his post at Ostia (Cic. *Har. Resp.* 43; Diod. 36. 12).

which first entrenched the senate's selection of consular provinces in statute.[34]

The provincial system to a large extent substituted separation of magistracies for a hierarchy of command. Boundaries, however, rarely were strictly defined, and it was not always easy to prevent a magistrate intervening outside his allocated area, as the senate found when dealing with the consul of 171 BC, C. Cassius Longinus, who suddenly decided when in Cisalpine Gaul to join in the Third Macedonian War.[35] Thanks to the Cnidos text of the *lex de provinciis praetoriis* we now know that it was first enacted about 100 BC that magistrates abroad should not travel or make an expedition outside their provinces without good reason. However, the exception allowed for expeditions *rei publicae causa* still gave a provincial commander great scope.[36] Where two commanders were in the same province, awkward questions of seniority could arise. In 177 the consul C. Claudius, hearing that the consuls of the previous year, who were now proconsuls, had defeated a tribal rising in the province of Illyricum allotted him, rushed out to the province and denounced the proconsuls for acting without this authority. He ordered them to leave the province forthwith, but they refused until he had gone through the proper rituals required of a commander before he set out. In their view, although as consul of that year he was their superior, he had not yet the right to be in the province. He threatened to send them to Rome in chains, but eventually returned to Rome for three days in order to legitimize his departure—by making vows to Jupiter and taking new auspices—before finally being able to assert his authority.[37] It is, moreover, hard to find in the Republic concrete evidence for a consul possessing an overarching authority in any way similar to that of the emperors later, although theoretical statements were made to this effect (see Chap. III with n. 7).

Auspices

The Romans did not normally consult oracles before taking public decisions. They possessed oracular documents, the Sibylline books, but

[34] Cic. *Dom.* 24; *Prov. Cos.* 3; *Fam.* 1. 7. 10; Sall. *Jug.* 27. 3; *Staatsr.* i. 54.

[35] Livy, 43. 1. 4–10.

[36] *Lex prov. praet.* Cnidos III. 4 ff.; *Imp. Rom.* 22–7.

[37] Livy, 41. 10. There was also a fatal conflict between a consul, Cn. Mallius, and a proconsul, Q. Caepio, in 105 about the time of the battle of Arausio, where apparently they had joint command as colleagues, but Caepio refused to co-operate with Mallius in spite of the latter's greater status (*axioma*) as consul in that year and the holder of the auspices (Dio 27, fr. 91, cf. 37. 39. 2 for a consul having a greater *axioma* than a praetor).

these were only to be consulted after prodigies, that is, prior events believed to be signs from the gods. Moreover, they were usually cautious about adding to their stock of written prophesy.[38] Instead they expected magistrates to obtain indications of future success or failure from the gods through seeking signs—from the heavens, the flight of birds, the attitude of birds to food, the entrails of sacrificed animals, and indeed from any event which might be judged to have prophetic value. These were called *auspicia*, literally 'the watchings of birds', and the experts, who were the authorities on their interpretation, *augures*. Magistrates had the right and duty to seek omens actively, *auspicia impetrativa* (as opposed to remarking when omens were thrust upon them, *auspicia oblativa*).[39] We hear of the auspices largely in connection with the senior curule magistrates—consuls, praetors, and censors—and the tribunes. Varro tells us of a quaestor seeking auspices from a consul, but this must have been because he was summoning a meeting of the *comitia centuriata* which he did not normally have the authority to do, not because he had no capacity to seek auspices himself. Indeed, this general capacity is implied by the consuls' edict for that assembly, which included a ban on minor magistrates looking at the sky for omens.[40] This consultation of omens by magistrates was essential before voting-assemblies, senate-meetings, and the departure of a magistrate to war.[41] However, it may have been undertaken on a number of other occasions.

The right to take the auspices seems to have been a consequence of popular election (it has been suggested that it was a particular consequence of the *lex curiata*, but this is not directly attested in our sources and the supposition creates problems).[42] It followed from this that it was not possessed by pro-magistrates.[43] So a proconsul, even if he found himself fighting a major battle which might decide the fate of the Roman empire—as he might well in the later Roman Republic—could not officially avail himself of an insight into divine providence. This does not seem to have worried the Romans, which in turn suggests that consultation of the auspices was undertaken less for enlightenment than for

[38] Livy, 25. 12. 2–12 for the acceptance of the *carmina Marciana*, which were believed to have predicted the battle of Cannae and recommended the building of a temple to Apollo as a means of expelling the Carthaginians from Italian soil.

[39] *Staatsr.* i. 76–115, esp. 77, 96 ff., 106 ff.; Wissowa, 1912, 523 ff.; North in Beard and North, 1990, ch. 2.

[40] Varro, *LL* 6. 91; Gell. 13. 15. 1; *Staatsr.* i. 92–3; see also Cic. *Leg.* 3. 10 and 27.

[41] *Staatsr.* i. 96 ff.; Chap. V with n. 23; Chap. VI with n. 31.

[42] Varro, *Rer. Hum.* 20 in Non. Marc. 131L, for the right being confined to magistrates. On the *lex curiata* see above Chap. V, n. 48.

[43] Cic. *Div.* 2. 76; *ND* 2. 9. On the problem this poses see Rich, 1996, 101–5.

reassurance, especially the soothing of emotions through the solemnity of ritual. It is also clear that they were only trusted as a prerogative of the most senior members of the élite and as a contribution to their political control.[44]

The rituals of the auspices, whose successful performance was thought to be necessary for the rightness, and the perceived rightness, of the public act that followed also provided opportunities for obstruction. Although it seems in principle that anyone could tell a presiding magistrate of a sudden omen, like a flash of lightning, he was not bound to take notice of it.[45] However, a report (*nuntiatio*) by another magistrate or an augur carried more weight, and might form the basis of a future declaration that the act was invalid by the college of augurs and the senate. The obstructive reporting of omens (*obnuntiatio*) became a political tactic in the late Republic after its status was reinforced by the *leges Aelia et Fufia* (mid-second century BC) and the *lex Caecilia Didia* (98 BC). In Cicero's ideal law-code his purpose in conferring the *auspicia* on all magistrates was to maximize the possibility of obstruction to undesirable measures.[46]

The Functions of Magistrates

(a) *Consul, Praetor*

The original title of the chief annual magistrates of the Republic is said to have been *praetor*, interpreted by Varro as the man who would give the lead in jurisdiction and the army. The title *praetor maximus*—preserved in an ancient law providing for the fixing of a nail in the temple of Jupiter Optimus Maximus—has been taken to show that originally one consul was superior to the other, but the isolation of this text makes any conclusion speculative.[47] Another text puts the change of title from praetor to consul in 449 BC, and this may indicate that the Twelve Tables referred to praetors only, not consuls. It is certain at least that the title consul was established by about 300 BC thanks to the earliest funerary inscription of the Cornelii.[48] According to tradition the first plebeian

[44] R. Gordon in Beard and North, 1990, ch. 7.

[45] Cato in Festus, 268L; Pliny, *HN* 28. 17; Serv. *ad Aen.* 12. 260.

[46] Cic. *Phil.* 2. 80 ff.; *Leg.* 3. 27; Wissowa, 1912, 529 ff.; *VRR* 132 ff.; de Libero, 1992, 53 ff., and see Chap. V, n. 95.

[47] Varro, *LL* 5. 80; Livy, 7. 3. 5–8—on this occasion '*praetor maximus*' was apparently interpreted as '*dictator*', but it was claimed that the consul of 509, M. Horatius, had been the first to perform the ritual. See Cornell, 1995, 227 ff.

[48] Zon. 7. 19. 1; *ILLRP* 309; *Staatsr.* ii. 1. 74 ff.

consul had been elected in 367 and from 342 one consul had to be plebeian. In theory there was nothing to prevent two plebeians being elected, but such was the influence and prestige of the patricians that this did not occur before 172.

We have earlier considered Polybius' picture of the breadth of the consul's power (Chap. III with nn. 4ff.) and have seen how the Roman year shaped his political activities (Chap. II). It seems that his chief function, down to the time of Sulla's reforms of 81 BC, was to be a military commander. Even after the experiment of proroguing the *imperium* of magistrates for long periods during the Second Punic War (see below with n. 92), the Romans returned for the most part to the practice of having major wars fought by consuls during their year of magistracy in the second century—for example M'. Acilius Glabrio in 191, L. Cornelius Scipio in 190, L. Aemilius Paulus in 168, P. Cornelius Scipio Aemilianus in 147.[49] This in the end led to C. Marius' five consecutive consulships in 104–100, an expedient which was not repeated under the Republic. Before they both left Rome, one or both of the consuls were responsible for performing the *feriae Latinae*, the major spring festival held by the Latin communities on the Mons Albanus—an occasion when the magistrates in general left the city and it was entrusted to a *praefectus*.[50] Before they left office, one of the consuls was required to hold the consular elections (if affairs outside Rome made that impossible, one of the consuls would normally nominate a dictator to perform this function (see below with n. 72)). In the periods when they were at Rome, usually at the beginning or end of the Roman political year, a consul would conduct discussions of foreign policy in the senate, he might find himself proposing legislation[51] (though most legislation took the form of plebiscites introduced by tribunes) or—every five years—conducting an election of censors. As we have seen, in the middle and late Republic—that is, once praetors became free to undertake civil duties throughout the year—he rarely undertook jurisdiction and only presided over extraordinary criminal investigations (see above with n. 11). He could, however, preside over formal procedures of private law, such as adoption, manumission, and emancipation.[52]

---

[49] *Staatsr.* ii. 1. 93–4; Giovannini, 1983, 66.

[50] Strabo 5. 3. 2 (229); Tac. *Ann.* 6. 11; *Staatsr.* i. 663–74. For the departure of the consuls and praetors see Livy, 25. 12. 1–2, but contrast Dio, 41. 14. 4.

[51] Examples are the *lex Servilia de repetundis* (106 BC); *lex Caecilia Didia* (98), *lex Lutatia de vi* (78), the *leges Calpurnia* (67) and *Tullia Antonia* (63) *de ambitu*, *lex Gabinia Calpurnia de Delo* (58), *lex Licinia de sodaliciis* (56), Caesar's *leges Iuliae* of 59, and the *leges Pompeiae* of 55 and 52. See *MRR, sub annis*.   [52] *Staatsr.* ii. 1. 102; i. 189–90.

After Sulla's dictatorship, the balance of the consul's activities changed. But there is no evidence that this was the result of legislation by Sulla, and Mommsen's suggestion that consuls actually lost their military *imperium* is in conflict with the evidence.[53] Italy did not cease to be a military problem: the insurrection of Lepidus, the slave-revolt led by Spartacus, the Catilinarian revolt and consequential unrest in south Italy can be cited, apart from the episodes belonging to the civil wars before and after Caesar's dictatorship. However, more campaigning and provincial government was entrusted to pro-magistrates over long periods with the result that a number of consuls never undertook command abroad. Moreover, the consular and praetorian elections now tended to be held in midsummer and this altered the shape of the consular year. The presence of one or both consuls in Rome most of the year also meant that they had more influence over political decison-making. The sort of judgements Cicero regularly expressed about the quality of consuls[54]— whose yardstick was the attachment to the principles he himself espoused—reflected the new importance attached to their political views.

The superiority of the consul in both middle and late Republic lay in his possession of the initiative both at home and abroad, if he was prepared to exploit it. He was the man a foreign embassy could not neglect to cultivate. His was the authority to which recourse was made in a crisis: as we have seen (appendix to Chap. VI), the 'last' decree of the senate was in form a request to the consuls to perform one of their major functions—to defend the *respublica*. Consuls were also hard to restrain. Tribunes on occasion undertook obstruction in protest against their behaviour: C. Curiatius tried to block the departure of D. Iunius Brutus to Spain in 138 after conflict over the levy; C. Ateius Capito tried to prevent Crassus' departure to Syria and Parthia in 55 on what was held to be an ill-omened and unjustified expedition. Both were unsuccessful.[55]

When a consul was abroad, restraint was even more difficult. The scandalous conduct of Scipio's officer Pleminius at Locri, combined with rumours about Scipio's own neglect of his duties, led in 205 to a special commission being sent under a praetor to investigate the matter. In view of the possibility that Scipio might be asked to return to Rome to answer about his conduct, the commission was reinforced with two tribunes

---

[53] *Staatsr.* ii. 1. 94–5; *contra* Balsdon, 1939, 58–65; Giovannini, 1983, 73 ff. See esp. Cic. *Prov. Cos.* 36 and *Fam.* 12. 14. 4–5 for consuls having provinces from the beginning of the year.

[54] Cic. *Att.* 1. 14. 6, 19. 4; *QF* 2. 5. 2 (4. 4).

[55] Cic. *Leg.* 3. 20; *Div.* 1. 29–30; Livy, *Per.* 55; *Oxy Per.* 55; Plut. *Crass.* 16.

and one aedile of the plebs, who were, if necessary, expected to exploit the sacrosanctity of their persons in order to constrain him physically—remarkably, inasmuch as this power was normally only exercised within the city.[56] In 172, the senate wished to prevent M. Popilius Laenas, the consul of 173, from continuing the unjustified and bloodthirsty war he had been conducting against the Ligurian Statellates, whom he had been reducing to slavery. It was compelled to enlist the co-operation of two tribunes, who threatened with a fine the current consuls (one of whom was M. Popilius' brother), if they did not go out to the province as his successors, and threatened M. Popilius himself with a tribunal of inquiry, if he did not release the remnants of the Statellates from slavery.[57] In short, though Polybius was to an extent misleading about the scope of consular power (Chap. III with nn. 4ff.), he was not misleading about its importance as an element in the constitution.

If consuls at Rome were not confined by routine administration and jurisdiction, this was because they had junior magistrates as their colleagues, who were designated by their own original title, *praetor*. Originally (in 367 BC) a single praetor was elected; the number was increased to two about 242, perhaps originally to provide an extra military commander at the end of the first Punic War.[58] Later the presence of two praetors at Rome enabled the distinction between the 'urban' and 'peregrine' jurisdictions to be created, though on occasion these might be combined to free a praetor for other duties: the urban praetor peformed jurisdiction between citizens, the peregrine praetor did so when one party at least was a foreigner. Two more praetors were created to deal with the provinces of Sicily and Sardinia with Corsica in about 228, a further two in 198/7 to provide governors for Spain, then in 81 Sulla seems to have brought the number up to eight.[59]

As a military commander, a praetor might either be an adjunct to the consul or have a separate *provincia*. In the first half of the third century

---

[56] Livy, 29. 20. 4–9.

[57] Livy, 42. 21–2. Popilius was actually put on trial on his return but escaped on a technicality, thanks to the favour of the praetor investigating.

[58] Gell. 13. 15. 4, discussing *minus imperium*; Livy, *Per.* 19; Lydus, *de mag.* 1. 38; Richard, 1982.

[59] Livy, *Per.* 20; 31. 50. 10–11; 32. 27. 6; Cic. *Fam.* 8. 8. 8; *Staatsr.* ii. 1. 201–2. *SC Bacch* (*FIRA* i. 30), lines 4 and 8 (186 BC), is the earliest indisputable evidence for the term *praetor urbanus*. 'Praetor quei inter ceives ious deicet' first appears in *lex agr.* 73 (111 BC), 'praetor quei inter peregrinos ious deicet' in *lex rep.* 12 and 89 (122 BC) (the variant, 'p. q. i. cives et peregrinos i. d.' in *lex Quinctia*, 9 BC—*RS* ii. 63, 18–19). On the 'urban' and 'peregrine' jurisdictions and an instance of their being combined see Chap. II with n. 7. A later example of combination occurred in 78 BC (*SC Ascl.* (*RDGE* 22), Gk. 2).

we have a number of examples of former consuls becoming praetors, sometimes in the year following their consulship (Ap. Claudius Caecus in 295, L. Papirius Cursor in 292, L. Caecilius Denter in 283, Q. Marcius Philippus in 280, A. Atilius Calatinus in 257).[60] This suggests a prestige not far short of that of the consul. Later the status of the praetor became especially dependent on his function as a judicial magistrate. For Cicero the primary element in this was civil jurisdiction. This was not the actual judgement (judication) of private lawsuits—which was left to *iudices* who were private citizens at the time—but the original assessment of whether the plaintiff's suit could be properly made the subject of a legal action, the determination of the nature of this legal action, and the assignation of a single *iudex* or a panel of *recuperatores* to hear the case.

From the early second century onwards we find praetors assigned to special criminal jurisdiction before they went out to a military province—for example, those who pursued the bandits (*sicarii*) in Apulia in 185 or the poisoners in 184.[61] Later, investigations of *sicarii* came to occupy a praetor throughout his term of office.[62] The praetor who was appointed to supervise a special form of civil procedure in 171, when Spaniards complained of extortion by Roman governors, provided another important precedent. When a permanent tribunal (*quaestio perpetua*) was set up *de repetundis*, to provide a means of recovery of money extorted by Roman magistrates and officials, its presidency came to be entrusted each year to one of the praetors.[63]

Sulla seems to have increased the number of praetors to eight, and his reorganization of the courts necessitated that all should either perform civil jurisdiction or preside over one of the *quaestiones perpetuae* during their year of office.[64] By the late Republic these civil duties had become very important. Apart from their significance in principle as a means of repressing malfeasance or corruption, the criminal courts might be used as an instrument of political attack or reprisal—for example in the aftermath of C. Gracchus' death.[65] They were also regularly exploited for the pursuit of personal feuds. Though the praetor neither voted in a

---

[60] See *MRR, sub annis.*

[61] Livy, 39. 29. 8–9, 38. 3, 41. 5; see also 40. 19. 9 and 37. 4 for the investigation of the Bacchanals in Apulia and the poisoners at Rome.

[62] This emerges from the case of L. Hostilius Tubulus (*pr.* 142)—Cic. *Fin.* 2. 54; *ND* 1. 63, 3. 74; Lucilius, 1312M.

[63] Livy, 43. 2. 3 ff.; *lex rep.* 15–16 and 19, with *ILS* 45 and *JRLR*, p. 118.

[64] See Cic. *Fam.* 8. 8. 8 for a *s. c.* of 51 BC referring to the eight provinces for ex-praetors; for the allocation of these provinces after the end of the urban magistracy *Att.* 1. 13. 5; 14. 5; 15. 1.; for the occasional combination of the urban and peregrine magistracy, above n. 59.

[65] See Badian, 1956, and in general Gruen, 1968.

quaestio perpetua, nor, as it appears, conducted any form of summing up, he was responsible for the management of proceedings before, during, and after the trial and even had some right of asking questions.[66] In private law the edicts of the praetors were in the last two centuries of the Republic a major source of innovation—to a great extent replacing legislation before the assembly in this field. These not only replaced the oral rituals prescribed for the introduction of lawsuits by the Twelve Tables and other early laws with new procedures, in which the praetor himself provided a written *formula* according to which the case would be judged, but actually introduced new actions, either depending on the concept of *bona fides* (good faith, akin to our notion of equity) or as a remedy for a particular unjust state of affairs.[67]

Apart from their judicial duties we find praetors introducing legislation, especially in the late Republic (M. Porcius Cato in 101 or 100 BC; L. Aurelius Cotta in 70; Q. Metellus Nepos in 60; Q. Fufius Calenus in 59).[68] They also had the right to convene the senate, more regularly exercised in the period before Sulla than later, when consuls tended to remain at Rome during their magistracy, but important in a crisis.[69] Finally, they had specific sacral duties, apart from any that might devolve upon a praetor through being the senior magistrate in Rome at the time: they presided over the *ludi Apollinares* on July 13 and the *ludi piscatorii* across the Tiber in June; they also had the duty of making the public sacrifice of a cow to Hercules at the *ara maxima*.[70] Under the Principate they came to take over the games that formerly were handled by the aediles.

(b) *Dictator, Magister Equitum*

The tradition about the invention of the dictatorship is confused. It was ascribed by the annalists to the earliest years of the Republic (perhaps on the basis of existing entries in the *Fasti*, perhaps from the stories about famous episodes in the early Republic). It is explained by Cicero and Livy as a response to the need to have a unified command in war, but

---

[66] *Lex rep.* 4, cf. 3, 5–6 for the difference in function between praetor and *iudices*; *lex rep.* 35 for the rubric of a chapter almost entirely lost, referring to the asking of questions.

[67] See e.g. Jolowicz and Nicholas, 1972, 199–232; Watson, 1974, 31–62; Lintott, 1977.

[68] *Lex prov. praet.* (*RS* i. 12), Cnidos, III, 4ff. (Cato); Livy, *Per.* 97, Asc. 17C (Cotta); Dio, 37. 51. 3 (Nepos) and 38. 8. 1 (Calenus). See also Chap. III with nn. 5–6.

[69] On convening the senate see Chap. III with n. 5, Chap. VI with nn. 45 and 47; Cic. *Fam.* 10. 12. 3 for an example in 43 BC. Praetors may well have presided over the senate for Caesar in 49. On sacral duties see Livy, 25. 12. 10; Varro, *LL* 6. 54; Festus, 274L; Macr. *Sat.* 1. 17. 28; *Staatsr.* ii. 1. 236.

[70] Livy, 25. 12. 10; Macr. *Sat.* 1. 17. 28; Varro, *LL* 6. 54; Festus, 274L; *Staatsr.* ii. 1. 236.

Livy also mentions its value as a means of cowing the plebs. Dionysius of Halicarnassus on the other hand describes the dictator as the answer to civil unrest.[71] That it was in origin a military office is shown by the title of the dictator's subordinate, 'master of the horse' (*magister equitum*), and by the original title of the dictator, *magister populi*, that is, master of the citizen army. The identification of the dictator with the infantry in particular is illustrated by the fact that he had to seek approval before he could mount a horse.[72] The military function was primary in the middle Republic (officially described as *rei gerundae causa*); dictators were, however, also nominated to hold elections in the absence of the consuls, to fix a commemorative nail in the temple of Jupiter Optimus Maximus, to hold elections, to deal with a sedition or to establish a festival.[73]

The dictatorship seems to have been conceived as a short-term magistracy with special powers, which could be created with the minimum of delay, since the man was simply nominated, not elected. Nomination lay normally with one of the consuls, not with a praetor nor with another dictator nor an *interrex* (a special law was passed for L. Valerius Flaccus to nominate Sulla, and in 49 Caesar was nominated by M. Lepidus after a similar law).[74] A popular vote might be held, but it was unusual.[75] The term of office was in principle supposed to be brief and we find some dictators abdicating as quickly as they can. However, we also hear of a six-month term.[76] Mommsen held that the dictator's *imperium* ceased simultaneously with that of a magistrate who had nominated him, but this belief was based more on theory than evidence: indeed, if we read without prejudice one of the texts he cites, it appears that a dictator

---

[71] Zon. 7. 13. 12 ff.; Chap. III with n. 9, Chap. IV with n. 23; *Staatsr.* ii. 1. 141–72.

[72] *Magister populi*—Cic. *Rep.* 1. 63, referring to the augural books; *Leg.* 3. 9; Festus, 216L; cf. Diod. 12. 64. 1; 19. 72. 6; *Staatsr.* ii. 1. 156–9; horse—Livy, 23. 14. 2; Plut. *Fab. Max.* 4. 1; Zon. 7. 13. 13.

[73] *Staatsr.* ii. 1. 155–9. For *rei gerundae* see e.g. *fasti Capitolini* (*Inscr. It.* xiii. 1. 32 ff.) on 367, 362–60, and 316–12 BC; Livy, 8. 29. 9; 23. 23. 2 (the last military dictator was Iunius Pera in 216–22. 57. 9); for elections see e.g. *fasti Cap.* on 349–8 BC; for nail-fixing (*clavi figendi*) *fasti Cap.* on 363, 331, and 263 BC; Livy, 8. 18. 12–13; 9. 28. 6; for quelling sedition see *fasti Cap.* on 368 BC; Livy, *Per.* 11; for founding a festival Livy, 7. 28. 7–8.

[74] *Staatsr.* ii. 1. 147–8; Plut. *Marcell.* 24. 11–12 for the dictator not being elected by senate or people but nominated; Cic. *Att.* 9. 15. 2; Caes. *BCiv.* 2. 21. 5; App. *BCiv.* 1. 98. 459; 2. 48. 196; Dio, 41. 36. 1; Lucan, 5. 382–4. A variant tradition about 458 BC (Dion. Hal. *AR.* 10. 24. 1) has a nomination by a *praefectus urbi*, not by the consul.

[75] *Staatsr.* ii. 1. 149; Festus, 216L; Dion. Hal. *AR* 5. 70. A vote was perhaps customary when the nominator was not a consul, see Livy, 22. 31. 7–11 (217 BC), thought by Coelius Antipater to be the first example; 27. 5. 16–17 (210 BC); also 5. 46. 10–11 on Camillus.

[76] For quick abdication see Livy, 3. 29. 7; 9. 34. 12; 23. 22. 11 and 23. 3; for a six-month term Cic. *Leg.* 3. 9; Livy, 3. 29. 7; 23. 22. 2–11 and 23. 2; App. *BCiv.* 1. 3. 9.

may have continued his magistracy after the end of the civil year in 202/1.[77]

The supremacy of the dictator was manifested by 24 *fasces*—though perhaps only 12 were normally displayed in the city. The existing magistrates continued with their regular term of office—Cicero's belief that no other magistrates should hold office simultaneously with the dictator or his master of the horse does not correspond with Republican practice, as we know it, but may reflect an earlier writer's view of the original nature of the office. However, magistrates with the right to be accompanied by *fasces* did not appear with them before the dictator.[78] It is maintained in a number of our sources that there was no right of *provocatio* against a dictator.[79] However, it is also suggested that this was not explicit in the dictator's appointment: it did not abolish the *provocatio* law. One story indeed about the quarrel between L. Papirius Cursor and his master of horse Q. Fabius Maximus Rullianus seems to designed to illustrate that the dictator's supreme power did not necessarily extend into the city, the realm of *provocatio*. This story also sought to show that the power of a dictator did not override that of the tribunes—a point attested also by the tradition about appeals against the dictator C. Maenius, and by the threat of a tribune to veto an election held by a dictator.[80] Moreover, when Caesar as dictator in 44, perhaps already *dictator perpetuo*, deprived the tribunes Caesetius Flavus and Epidius Marullus of their magistracy, this gave rise to disquiet because of the infringement of the sacrosanctity of the office.[81] We have one example of a dictator being prosecuted after leaving office, whose authenticity may be contested but which may still

[77] *Staatsr.* ii. 1. 160–1, followed by *MRR* i. 318 n. 1. Livy, 6. 1, only shows that Camillus *chose* to abdicate at the end of the year, while in 30. 39. 4–5 and 40. 4 the dictator appears to have been performing his duties and even celebrating the Cerealia on 10 April in the following consular year.

[78] *Staatsr.* i. 383 (reinterpreting Livy, *Per.* 89, which suggests that Sulla was the first to have 24), ii. 1. 155–6. For 24 *fasces* see Pol. 3. 87; Dion. Hal. *AR* 10. 24. 2; Plut. *Fab.* 4. 3; App. *BCiv.* 1. 100. 465; Dio, 54. 1. 3; for the alleged suspension of other magistrates, apart from the tribunes, Pol. 3. 87. 8; Cic. *Leg.* 3. 9; Dion. Hal. *AR* 11. 20. 3; Plut. *Ant.* 8. 5; *Mor.* 283b; App. *Hann.* 12. 50; for relinquishing *fasces* when meeting a dictator, Livy, 22. 11. 5; Plut. *Fab.* 4. 3; *Staatsr.* i. 378 n. 3.

[79] Livy, 2. 18. 8; 3. 20. 8; Dion. Hal. *AR* 6. 58. 2; Plut. *Fab.* 9. 1; *Dig.* 1. 2. 2. 18 (Pomponius); Zon. 7. 13. 13. See also Plut. *C. Gr.* 18. 1, where it is said that L. Opimius was using dictatorial powers.

[80] Livy, 2. 30. 5; Papirius Cursor—8. 32–3, esp. 33. 8; Maenius—9. 26. 7ff., esp. 10 and 16 (placed in 314 BC, though in the *fasti Capitolini* Maenius holds this office in 320); election —27. 6. 2–11, esp. 3–5. See also Livy, 7. 3. 9, Cic. *Off.* 3. 112; Val. Max. 5. 4. 3 for resistance to a dictator in 363.

[81] Plut. *Caes.* 61. 10; Suet. *Jul.* 79. 1; App. *BCiv.* 2. 108. 452. A tradition which stressed the superiority of the dictator is found in Livy 6. 16. 3 and 38. 13.

be regarded as illustrating a general principle. Moreover, the text of the *lex repetundarum* implies that, although immune when in office, like other senior magistrates, both he and his *magister equitum* could be charged after demitting.[82] How absolute the power of the dictator was, seems to have been an issue which was determined not by statute or by any clear rule, but by casuistry, and it remained debatable at the time when the annalistic tradition was being developed in the last two centuries of the Republic. As with many uncertain constitutional issues, the different positions that could be taken reflected either an aristocratic, authoritarian ideology or one that was popular and libertarian.

The dictator normally nominated a *magister equitum* as his deputy and lieutenant both in the field and in civil administration. This man had only six lictors with *fasces*. In the city he could, like the dictator, summon the senate and perhaps also an assembly. Once chosen, he could not be deposed, but his office ceased with that of his superior. In many respects he might function in parallel to the dictator, like a second consul, rather than as a direct subordinate.[83] However, the more spectacular stories about the office show that his subordination was a major issue. We have already considered the quarrel between Papirius Cursor and Fabius Rullianus which allegedly stemmed from disobedience of the dictator's instructions in his absence. This sort of drama was re-enacted on a grander scale during the Second Punic War between the dictator Fabius Maximus and his master of the horse Minucius Rufus, to the extent that Minucius is actually alleged to have engineered the promulgation of a law which would have put his powers on a level with that of the dictator.[84]

After the Second Punic War the office of dictator fell into disuse, partly because this short-term office was inappropriate for the new needs in campaigning, partly because there was for a long time no sedition to quell. It was not revived to deal with the Gracchi—something which caused Appian surprise.[85] In 133, the consul Scaevola refused to take any public action, which thus excluded the nomination of a dictator, whereas in 121 the consul Opimius seems to have been only too keen to undertake any repressive action himself.[86] Subsequently the decree of the senate which encouraged Opimius to use force against C. Gracchus and

[82] Livy, 9. 26. 17 ff.; *lex rep.* 8–9 (*JRLR* 90, 114).
[83] *Staatsr.* II. 1. 159, 173–8. On lictors see Cic. *Leg.* 3. 9; Dio, 42. 27. 2. Dictators specifically created without a master of the horse were exceptional (*fasti Cap.* 249 BC; Livy, 23. 12. 11).
[84] Livy, 22. 24–30, esp. 25–6; Plut. *Fab.* 9. 2–3.
[85] *BCiv.* 1. 16. 67.
[86] Val. Max. 3. 2. 17; Plut. *Ti. Gr.* 19. 4; *C. Gr.* 13. 5–14. 3.

M. Fulvius Flaccus became institutionalized—the so-called ultimate decree (Appendix to Chap. VI).

The dictatorships, however, granted to Sulla and Caesar in the late Republic revived the institution in a stronger and more authoritarian form. In the first place the old restriction on the length of the office was abandoned: Sulla was made dictator without time-limit, according to Appian, even though in fact he surrendered his office after about a year, while Caesar, after renewing his dictatorship four times was in the end appointed *dictator perpetuo*.[87] Moreover, a new grander function and justification was introduced, that of bringing stability to the political order, *rei publicae constituendae*.[88]

(c) *Proconsul, Propraetor*

In the early Republic the need for extra military commanders was satisfied either by the creation of a dictator and master of horse or, allegedly for a long period at the end of the fifth and beginning of the fourth centuries, by the creation of military tribunes with consular powers. (Since nothing certain is known about this office except that consular tribunes in varying numbers were recorded in the annals, with the result that a proposal could be made to revive the office in 53, it does not receive further discussion here.[89]) In the middle and late Republic it became established practice to prorogue (*prorogare*) the *imperium* of consuls and praetors beyond the annual term of their magistracies, in order that they might continue as military commanders. There were also examples of the direct grant of *imperium* to a private citizen so that he might function as a pro-magistrate without being elected to a magistracy.

In the first attested example the extension of *imperium* was granted to Q. Publilius Philo in 326 in order that he could complete the capture of Naples.[90] We hear of similar short extensions in the early third century and during the First Punic War in cases of military need, which had the further consequence that a commander might hold a triumph as a proconsul.[91] The military emergency of the Second Punic War led both to

[87] App. *BCiv.* 1. 3. 10 and 98. 459; Cic. *Phil.* 2. 87; *RRC* i, no. 480, pp. 488 ff.

[88] App. *BCiv.* 1. 98. 459 and 99. 462 on Sulla. For Caesar see the inscription from Taranto, Gasperini, 1968 and 1971 (refuting M. Sordi's attribution to Octavian in *Epigraphica* 31 (1969)).

[89] *Staatsr.* ii. 1. 180–92; Cornell, 1995, 334–7; Ridley, 1986. For the proposed revival Dio, 40. 45. 4.

[90] Livy, 8. 23. 11–12, 26. 7; *Staatsr.* ii. 1. 646–7; Jashemski, 1950, 1 ff.

[91] Jashemski, 1950, 9 ff. See e.g. Livy, 10. 22. 9; *Fasti Triumph.* 280 BC (*Inscr. It.* xiii. 1, p. 73).

the extension of the commands of magistrates for a year or more and to the appointment of private citizens—in particular the vote to P. Scipio by the assembly of a long-term command *pro consule* in Spain with a *pro praetore* as his second-in-command. Proconsuls continued to be appointed specially for Spain after Scipio returned to Rome in 206, until the number of praetors was increased in 197.[92] In the second century prorogation was still needed, although it required unusual political influence to extend it over more than one year.[93] Nor were there in this period direct grants of proconsular *imperium* by an assembly: military emergencies instead provided the justification for the extraordinary elections of Scipio Aemilianus and Marius to consulships. A major development was the practice of retaining praetors in Rome during their term of office—something necessitated by the increase of criminal courts which required a president—and then sending them after their magistracy to a province as a proconsul or propraetor. The first clear example of this occurs in the career of Marius.[94] In the late Republic the increased military commitments were not matched by an increase of magistrates willing and competent to command, and praetors continued to spend their magistracies normally in jurisdiction at Rome. Prorogation thus became the norm, frequently for three years.

We also find men being granted *imperium pro praetore* by the senate or by delegation from a senior magistrate. This is first attested in 295. In the last two centuries of the Republic it commonly occurred when a commander demitted his command or left his province before a successor arrived: in such circumstances he would appoint a deputy who would have his full powers in the mean time (the *lex de provinciis praetoriis* of 101/100 is known to have regulated this procedure).[95] Such men were entitled *pro praetore*.[96] These magistrates were of a different rank to the *legati* whom a magistrate with a command abroad had as his assistants while he was exercising *imperium* himself. The latter were

---

[92] Livy, 26. 18; 26. 19. 10 for Scipio's propraetor M. Iunius Silanus; 29. 13. 7; 31. 50. 10–11; 32. 27. 6 and 28. 11. Cf. 23. 30. 19 for the grant to M. Marcellus in 215, and see Jashemski, 1950, 20 ff.; Kloft, 1977, 28 ff.; Giovannini, 1983, 42.

[93] A notorious example is the command of T. Flamininus in Greece (Pol. 18. 11–12; Livy, 32. 32. 7–8 and 37; Walbank, 1967, 359 ff.; Badian, 1970, 40 ff.).

[94] Kloft, 1977, 35 ff., with Badian's review, *Gnomon*, 1979, 792–4.

[95] Livy, 10. 25. 11, 26. 12, 29. 3 for appointments by commanders (contrast 10. 26. 15 for appointment by the senate); 21. 32. 3; Pol. 3. 49. 4, 56. 5, 76. 1 (with Jashemski, 1950, 22–4, on Cn. Scipio); *lex prov. praet.* (*RS*, i. 12), Cnidos IV, 31–39, cf. Cic. *Att.* 6. 3. 1 and 4. 1.

[96] *Staatsr.* ii. 1. 656–7; Balsdon, 1962, 134–5—including examples of *pro quaestore pro praetore*—ILS 8775, OGIS 448, IGRR iv. 401; Badian, 1965, 110–13; *Staatsr.* ii. 1. 674–5, 679–80.

usually selected by the magistrate himself, but owed their appointment to action in the senate.[97] In the late Republic Pompey was granted *imperium pro consule* without holding a magistracy on more than one occasion, first by the senate alone, then by the people.[98] This became a precedent for a number of other appointments, especially in the brief revival of republican government after Caesar's murder.[99] Furthermore, some subordinates of those granted great proconsular commands by the assembly in the late Republic were granted the status *pro praetore*. Cn. Cornelius Lentulus Marcellinus is attested as a *legatus pro praetore* of Pompey in Cyrenaica and this is presumably true of Pompey's other *legati* under the provisions of Gabinius' law of 67 repressing piracy; Caesar also calls his *legatus* Labienus *pro praetore*.[100] Such magistrates were forerunners of the *legati Augusti* who were the emperor's deputies in the provinces specially assigned to him.

(d) *Censor*

The two censors were the magistrates appointed specifically to conduct the census, that is, to count the Roman people, register their property, and thus review the membership of the citizen body and its various ranks. The annalistic tradition placed the first election of censors in the latter half of the fifth century, but the function that they performed would have been required from the time of the creation of the *comitia centuriata*.[101] It may well have been initially undertaken by the consuls or another supreme magistrate (in the late Republic consuls deputized for censors in their financial functions).[102] However, no substitute could perform for the censor the ritual purification, the *lustrum*, which was the culmination of the census itself.[103] We cannot tell for sure that this was a

[97] *Staatsr.* ii. 1. 677–8; Schleussner, 1978, 101 ff.; Linderski, 1990. For examples of the ordinary post of *legatus* see e.g. Pol. 35. 4. 5 and 9; Livy, 36. 2. 11 and 17. 1; 39. 31. 4; *Per.* 48; Cic. *Att.* 1. 1. 2; 2. 18. 3; 19. 4; 4. 1. 7, 15. 9; 5. 11. 4, 21. 5; 6. 3. 1, 5. 3, 6. 3; *Sest.* 33; *Vat.* 35 ff.; *Mur.* 32.

[98] Cic. *Phil.* 11. 18; *Imp. Cn. Pomp.* 62; Livy, *Per.* 91; Val. Max. 8. 15. 8; *MRR* on 67 and 66 BC.

[99] See *MRR*, *sub annis*, on Pompey's corn-supply post in 57 BC and those of M. Brutus, C. Cassius, Sex. Pompeius, and Octavian in 43.

[100] Reynolds, 1962; *Syll.*³ 750; Caes. *BG* 1. 21. 2; Balsdon, 1962, 138, arguing that the title was probably held by Pompey's *legati* in Spain from 54 BC onwards.

[101] Livy, 4. 8. 2–7; Festus, *s. v. rituales*, 358–9L; Dion. Hal. *AR* 11. 63. 1–3; Zon. 7. 19. 6; *Dig.* 1. 2. 2. 17. See on the censorship *Staatsr.* ii. 1. 331–464; Pieri, 1968, esp. 60 ff. on the military function; Suolahti, 1963.

[102] *Lex agr.* 89; *lex portorii Asiae* (Engelmann and Knibbe, 1989), 72 ff.; cf. 88 f., 101 ff., and *passim* for the Principate; Cic. 2 *Verr.* 3. 18; *Staatsr.* ii. 1. 426, n2.

[103] Varro, *LL* 6. 93, cf. 11 with a false derivation from *luere* = to pay; Cic. *Leg.* 3. 7; *de Or.* 2. 268; Pieri, 1968, 77 ff. and 99 ff. *Staatsr.* ii. 1. 352–3 (showing that this took place the year

duty of the censors when first they were elected, but it seems likely that the performance of the ritual was a major reason for the creation of the magistracy. In any case it must be regarded as central to the concept of the magistracy as we find it in the middle Republic, and it shows that more was at stake than the mechanical tasks of counting and assessment of property: the ranking of citizens and the assessment of their moral worth has a particular point as a preliminary to a purification.

Although regarded as senior magistrates and elected in the *comitia centuriata* under the presidency of a consul, the censors were in no wise colleagues of the consuls or praetors.[104] Though they occasionally exercised civil jurisdiction in matters with which they were specially concerned, they had neither *imperium* nor lictors, nor had they any right to convene either the senate or an electoral, legislative, or judicial assembly.[105] On the other hand, they had curule chairs and the other appurtenances of senior magistrates, such as a *toga praetexta* and *apparitores*; they had the right to fine (through selling a man's property); they were not subject to a veto by a consul or praetor (nor could a praetor summon them). They could, however, obstruct each other and were liable to religious obstruction and to *intercessio* by the tribunes, though this could not be used against the census itself. We also find examples of a tribune exploiting his sacrosanctity to imprison a censor and even prosecuting him while he was still in office.[106]

In the last two centuries of the Republic they were normally elected every five years,[107] though there were no censors between those of 86 and 70 (see below) and there were a number of small deviations from the norm. They were unusual among Roman city magistrates in having no fixed date for demitting office. Tradition maintained that their office had originally lasted five years, but was then cut down by a *lex Aemilia* to eighteen months, because it seemed too tyrannical. This limit was exceeded by Appius Claudius, censor from 312 to 310, allegedly after a threat by a tribune to imprison him had been frustrated by the promise of protection from three other tribunes. By the late third century, the

after the censors' election in the middle and late Republic). See also Pieri, 56–7, following Dumézil, 1943, for the root *cens* meaning 'solemn declaration'.

104 Gell. 13. 15. 4 (Messala); Livy, 24. 10. 1–2; 40. 45. 6–8; *Staatsr.* ii. 1. 352 ff.
105 Zon. 7. 19. 8; *Staatsr.* ii. 1. 354; and see *lex agr.* 35 for civil jurisdiction.
106 Zon. 7. 19. 8; *Staatsr.* ii. 1. 354–7; on obstruction see Cic. *Clu.* 122; Livy, 40. 51. 1; 42. 10. 4; 45. 15. 8; App. *BCiv.* 1. 28. 126; on imprisonment of censors Livy, 9. 34. 24; Plut. *QR* 50 (*Mor.* 276 e–f). Attempted prosecution of censors, while in office, is deferred (Livy, 24. 43. 2–3; 29. 37. 17), but is permitted (43. 16. 10–16).
107 Varro *LL* 6. 11 and 93; Ps. Asc. 189St.; Censorinus, 18. 13.

lustrum regularly took place the year after the censors entered office. In 168 a request by the censors, made presumably to the senate, for the prorogation of their term, in order that they might see to the execution of the repair of buildings and check the performance of the contracts they had let, was vetoed by a tribune.[108] A five-year magistracy would have been exceptional in the Roman republic: on the contrary it seems to have been the practice that magistrates elected to perform special functions— from the dictator down to the commissioners who distributed land, founded colonies, or dedicated temples—only held office as long as their appointed task required. It is thus more likely that the censors' term of office grew from small beginnings, instead of being curtailed. Moreover, if we trust the evidence of the *fasti* of the early Republic, the first century and a quarter of the censorship was marked by considerable irregularity in its intervals, which were in any case longer than five years. In these periods, therefore, a five-year term would have had no relationship to the date of the next census. By contrast, in the fifty years preceding the outbreak of the First Punic War, the average interval between censorships was less than five years.[109] However, there may well have been an occasion in this last period, when a pair of censors argued that they had the right to stay in office until the next election of censors, which led to accusations of tyranny and hence legislation that the office should not last more than eighteen months. There was held to be a religious objection against replacing a censor who died in office because the Gauls had captured Rome during the *lustrum* of M. Cornelius, who was a suffect censor. The only solution was for the remaining censor to resign and a new pair to be elected. This too may have been motivated by a reluctance to see any one man in the censorial office too long.[110]

The censors carried out their primary function of counting the Roman people and registering their property in the Campus, where the *villa publica* had been constructed as their base, with the aid of *iuratores* (to take the oath from the citizens) and, according to Varro, of *curatores privati* from the tribes, who may have represented certain of those absent.[111] Those citizens in the *potestas* of their fathers or grandfathers

---

[108] Livy, 4. 24. 4–7 (434 BC); 9. 33. 4—34. 26 (Appius Claudius); 45. 15. 9; Zon. 7. 19. 6; *Staatsr.* ii. 1. 351–3, suggesting *inter alia* that Appius Claudius' term was specially extended so that he could complete his public works.

[109] On the frequency of the censorship in the early Republic see Astin, 1982.

[110] Livy, 5. 31. 7.

[111] Cic. *Leg.* 3. 7; Varro *LL* 6. 86 (for the censors' summons to the infantry army and *curatores*); Festus, 51, 358–9L; *Staatsr.* ii. 1. 359 ff. For *iuratores* see Plaut. *Trin.* 872;

did not have to appear in person anyhow; others might be registered in their absence (Scipio Aemilianus complained about this in his censorship of 142), and in the late Republic this seems to have been common.[112] We are told that censors might sell a person's property, perhaps as a penalty for evading the census or fraudulent registration. More commonly they degraded people by depriving them of their existing tribal registration and allocating them to the *aerarii*, an obscure category whose title seems to mean taxpayers and which is associated with a heavier rate of tax. In view of the importance of the tribe in the identity of a Roman citizen (Chap. V with nn. 49 ff.) this may not mean that they had no tribe at all, but that they were relegated to one of the urban tribes, particularly one of the pair held inferior, the Esquilina and Suburana.[113] In the middle Republic this is the penalty associated with the censorial *nota*, which was the mark placed against a man's name on the register. However, in the late Republic we have no evidence that this penalty was inflicted in consequence of the censorial *nota*. Our sources are discussing those of high rank, and it is conceivable that the loss of senatorial or equestrian status was considered then a sufficient punishment. The one reference to creating *aerarii*, in Varro, seems to be an indication that the procedure was in disuse. Allegedly, censorial condemnation was originally inflicted for poor cultivation of land, but our examples from the middle Republic relate to cowardice and disobedience in the army, dereliction of civil duties and a wide range of offences in exercising them, corruption, and debt.[114] The completion of this review of the people was the purificatory ceremony of the *lustrum* (see above), which involved prayers for the coming five years.[115] The censors also conducted a review

---

Poen. 55–8; Livy, 39. 44. 2 (though there is an alternative reading *viatores*); for oaths *Tab. Heracl.* (*RS* i. 24), 148; Gell. 4. 20. 3; for the *villa publica* Livy, 4. 22. 7 (the censors' base within the *pomerium* was the *atrium Libertatis*—Livy, 43. 16. 13, 45. 15. 5).

[112] Livy, 43. 14. 8; Gell. 5. 19. 16 = *ORF*, no. 21, fr. 14; Cic. *Att.* 1. 18. 8 for Cicero preventing Atticus being counted in his absence; *Tab. Heracl.* (*RS* i. 24), 142 ff., for registers being sent from colonies and *municipia*, which may have begun before Caesar's legislation.

[113] Zon. 7. 19. 8; Livy, 4. 24. 7; 9. 34. 9; 24. 18. 6, 43. 3; 27. 11. 15; 44. 16. 8; 45. 15. 8; *ORF*, no. 21, fr. 13 = Gell. 4. 20. 3–6, fr. 22 = Cic. *de Or.* 2. 268; Varro, *Gerontodidaskalos* 196 Astbury = Non. Marc. 190. 28; Dion. Hal. *AR* 20. 13; PsAsc. 189St.; Pieri, 1968, 113 ff.; Botsford, 1909, 62; Fraccaro, 1933. On ignominious tribes see Dion. Hal. *AR* 19. 18. 1; Pliny, *HN* 18. 13; and note Livy, 45. 15. 3–7, on the impossibility of the censors' depriving a citizen of a tribe altogether.

[114] *ORF*, no. 8, fr. 124 = Gell. 4. 12. 1; Pliny, *HN* 18. 11; *Staatsr.* ii. 1. 375 ff.; and see n. 117 below.

[115] Varro, *LL* 6. 93; Livy, 1. 44. 2; Dion. Hal. *AR* 4. 22. 1–2 with references to the *suovetaurilia*; Val. Max. 4. 1. 10; Suet. *Aug.* 97. 1; *ORF*, no. 21, fr. 22 = Cic. *de Or.* 2. 268; *Staatsr.* ii. 1. 412–3.

(*recensus* or *recognitio*) of the *equites* in the forum, which seems not to have been regarded as an integral part of the census, since it could take place after the *lustrum*.[116] The basic definition of the equestrian centuries in the *comitia centuriata* would have already taken place in the Campus; in the forum censors might decide a person was unfit for cavalry service and order him to 'sell his horse', or they might recognize that he had served his required term.[117] The selection (*lectio*) of the senate by the censors has been examined earlier (Chap. VI with nn. 13–30). It need only be noticed here that this, like the *recognitio equitum*, was not related to the *lustrum*, since it might take effect before this ceremony and its validity was independent of the performance of the ceremony.[118]

The moral censure exercised by the censors appears to be an extraordinary, and arbitrary, supplement to the jurisdiction of the courts. In view of the interval between censorships, it was unlikely to take place until after any trial and so would never have applied to those found guilty of a capital crime. It was, however, a secondary threat to those acquitted on capital charges and to those who had been condemned, been acquitted, or indeed escaped prosecution for less serious offences. Even if financial penalties had fallen into disuse in the late Republic, the loss of status involved in *infamia* of any kind was a serious matter in a society where ambition was focused on glory and a good name. We do not know the origin of this censorial power—whether it arose from deliberations within the élite or from a tribune appealing to popular feeling in a plebiscite. Although the nature of the office of censor suggests that the activities of these magistrates were a piece of élite self-regulation, it may be that this particular function was added as a result of public outrage in some crisis.

Apart from their strictly censorial functions, the censors also had the task of letting out public contracts, not only for the expense of public money on works and the management of public property but also for the receipt of revenue through taxes and rents. They auctioned the collection of taxes to the highest bidder, after specifying the terms of taxation in a *lex*. In assigning public works contracts they also presumably made themselves open to bids. The importance of this function was noted by

[116] Varro, *Sesquiulixes* 478–80 Astbury; Livy, 29. 37. 8, cf. 5; Festus, 47L; Plut. *Pomp.* 22. 5–9; *Staatsr.* ii. 1. 398ff.

[117] Livy, 24. 18. 6–7; 27. 11. 13–14; 29. 37. 12; 34. 44. 5; 45. 15. 8; *ORF*, no. 8, frr. 78–80 (= Gell. 6. 22. 1), 124 (= Gell. 4. 12. 1); no. 21, fr. 18 (= Gell. 3. 4. 1), fr. 21 (= Cic. *de Or.* 2. 258). See also Cic. *Rep.* 4. 2, for the *plebiscitum reddendorum equorum*, which in Cicero's view implied the equation of cavalry with infantry.

[118] Livy, 9. 30. 1–2, on 311 BC; Dio, 37. 46. 4 on 61; *Staatsr.* ii. 1. 419.

Polybius.[119] The censors' concern for the revenues from public land and water also extended to the definition of boundaries and the prevention of improper exploitation.[120]

The duty of these magistrates was to perform a number of essential and time-consuming tasks, which annual magistrates would have had difficulty in completing. These functions had serious consequences for the status and prosperity of the citizen-body as individuals both in their public and private life: in this respect the censors touched the citizen-body more nearly than any other magistrate, even than the chief dispensers of civil jurisdiction, the *praetor urbanus* and *peregrinus*. It was thus appropriate that the censors were men of the highest prestige: even after the office was opened to plebeians in 339, they were mainly patricians, and from 209 onwards they were, with one exception, drawn from among the former consuls. The censors, moreover, like the two main praetors, were the most part autonomous in their decisions. The only restraints were tribunician obstruction and prosecution—until the *lex Clodia* provided formally for appeal against the *nota*.[121] It is thus not surprising that the tradition about the development of the censorship stressed its autocratic nature and the desirability of keeping this in check by limiting the length of the office.

[119] Pol. 6. 17. 1–6; *Staatsr.* ii. 1. 426–64; Nicolet, 1975, ch. 1; *Imp. Rom.* 76–7, 86–91.

[120] *Lex agr.* 35; *Tab. Heracl.* (*RS* i. 24), 73 ff., 82; Livy, 39. 44. 4; 43. 16. 4; Front. *aq.* 94–5, 97 (*RS* ii, 43); Pliny, *HN* 8. 11; Tac. *Ann.* 13. 51; *CIL* vi. 919.

[121] See Livy, 8. 12. 16, for the opening of the magistracy to plebeians, *Per.* 59 for the first pair of plebeian censors in 131. On the original rank of men elected censor see Suolahti, 1963, esp. 23–4; on the *lex Clodia* Asc. 8C; Dio, 38. 13. 2 (Plut. *C. Gr.* 2. 8 provides evidence for a hearing in relation to a *nota* before the *lex Clodia*, but this presumably was at the discretion of the censors).

VIII

Tribunes, Aediles, and Minor Magistrates

Tribunus Plebis

The origin of the tribunes of the plebs is the cornerstone of the story of the Conflict of the Orders, which was the chief domestic theme in the annals of the early Republic. In the course of their first secession in 494 the plebs elected tribunes as their spokesmen in negotiations with the patricians and swore an oath to take vengeance on anyone who did violence to the persons of the tribunes, declaring them sacrosanct (Chap. IV above with nn. 24–5). At first, according to our sources, there were only either two or five. The college of ten was established in the year 457 or at least when the tribunate was restored after the downfall of the decemvirate. Their unusual date for entry into office, 10 Dec. may be a survival from their early history.[1] It follows from the nature of their office that the earliest tribunes came from outside the aristocracy. Throughout the Republic the tribunate remained an office only open to plebeians, but in the last two centuries of that epoch it was regularly held by those who would go on to higher magistracies, and some of the most distinguished holders were from the plebeian nobility, like the Sempronii Gracchi (not to mention a man like Publius Clodius who had been adopted from the patriciate into the plebs). Yet men were also elected who seemingly had no distinguished forebears, and many tribunes appear to have made no further progress in their public careers, for example, C. Cornelius, the tribune of 67 (mentioned below).

The tribunes presided over meetings of the plebs (*concilia plebis*), in which resolutions were passed. At first, these seem to have been only

---

[1] For their number see Piso, fr. 23P; Cic. *Corn.* 1. fr. 49 Puccioni (where the manuscripts of Asconius' lemma give the number eventually elected in 493/2 as ten, a reading usually deleted; Asconius thought that a passage in his own text of Cicero was corrupt); Asc. 76–7C; Livy, 2. 33. 2; 58. 1 (five tribunes first in 471); 3. 30. 7 (ten in 457); 54. 11–13; Dion. Hal. *AR* 6. 89. 1–2 (five); 10. 30. 2 (ten in 449); a further variant tradition, that four were first elected in 471, is in Diod. 11. 68. 8. On 10 Dec. see Livy, 39. 52. 4; Dion. Hal. *AR* 6. 89. 2; *Fasti Praenestini* (*Inscr. It.* xiii. 2, pp. 136–7) sub *die*. In general see *Staatsr.* ii. 1. 274–330; Niccolini, 1932; Bleicken, 1955; Thommen, 1989.

binding on the plebeians themselves, but the *lex Publilia* of 339 seems to have made it possible for them to be validated for the whole *populus Romanus*, through ratification either by the senate or by another assembly. The *lex Hortensia* of 287 made *plebiscita* equivalent to *leges* passed in the *comitia centuriata* or *tributa* (Chap. IV with nn. 42 and 50). One particular feature of such assemblies was the protection of the tribune, when speaking, from interruption, treated by Cicero as an element of the sacrosanctity of the tribunate.[2] Plebeian assemblies were also used to conduct political prosecutions. Initially these cannot have been accepted as legally valid procedures by the opponents of the plebs, even if they were effective in exacting a fine or driving the accused into exile. Indeed, they may well have been specifically outlawed by the Twelve Tables. (Chap. IV with n. 31, Chap. IX with n. 13) Later, in the annals of the middle and late Republic, we find that the tribune is the only magistrate to prosecute in capital trials for *perduellio* before the assembly and a frequent prosecutor in matters involving a fine. This may have been a development encouraged by the aristocracy, in order that the delicate and often invidious task of prosecuting eminent men should be entrusted to a representative of the people as a whole.[3] In this way the leaders of what Mommsen termed 'a revolution in permanent existence',[4] were not only accepted as a part of the constitution but assigned an important function within it.

A similar process of absorption transformed their relationship to the senate. Originally, we are told, the tribunes watched proceedings in the senate from the door and sought to block measures unwelcome to the plebs by obstructing the exit. Later they were permitted to sit and speak in the senate, and to introduce subjects for discussion.[5] The first certain instance of tribunician participation is in 216, but their rights in this respect are likely to go back to the time of the *lex Hortensia* or earlier.[6] Nevertheless, they retained the substance of their revolutionary power, in so far as they could veto the outcome of any debate, as Polybius

[2] Cic. *Sest.* 79; Val. Max. 9. 5. 2; Dion. Hal. *AR* 7. 16. 4–17. 5. On legislation in the *concilium plebis* see Chap. V with nn. 15 and 62–71.

[3] See e.g. Livy, 25. 3. 13 ff.; 26. 2. 7–3. 12; 43. 8. 2–3; *Staatsr.* ii. 1. 300–3; 318–25; Brecht, 1939; Hardy, 1912, i. 152–69; Lintott, 1987, 44–5, 47–8; also Chap. IX with nn. 19 ff.

[4] *Staatsr.* ii. 1. 281.

[5] Val. Max. 2. 2. 7; Zon. 7. 15. 8. Some doubts about the tradition in Badian, 1996, 191–2. However, the idea that the tribunes gained admission to the senate through pressure caused by obstruction is in keeping with the general tradition about the growth of the office. Badian also rightly points out that the annalists sometimes depicted tribunes as members of the senate in the early Republic, see n. 6 below.

[6] Livy, 22. 61. 7. Livy, 4. 6. 6, 48. 15 f., and Dion. Hal. *AR* 10. 31. 2 are surely anachronistic.

(6. 16. 4) remarked (see Chap. VI with nn. 15, 45, 84–7). Polybius states further that tribunes could prevent the senate convening. Presumably they could in theory have used their sacrosanctity to block the entrance of the building designated for a meeting, but we have no evidence of this being actually attempted.

The obstruction exercised on senatorial proceedings is but one instance of the tribune's exploitation of his sacrosanctity.[7] This had many facets. Sacrosanctity was on occasion used aggressively, enabling a tribune to preclude resistance when he was physically manhandling opponents in order to throw them into prison or even to precipitate them from the Tarpeian rock. However, there is only one reliably attested instance of precipitation by a tribune under the Republic and a single reliably attested attempt or threat. As for imprisonment, we have seen that this was a weapon of the tribunes against the censors, and one dramatic conflict in the late Republic actually led to a consul being incarcerated—an episode which ended more in farce than tragedy.[8] Sacrosanctity was also the basis of the tribune's power of arrest, which he either exercised directly himself or through the aedile of the plebs, who was in origin his subordinate (see below, with nn. 28–9). Under the Principate tribunes sought to extend this into a general power of summons—improperly, as certain jurisconsults pointed out, and summons from the country to the city was formally forbidden by a *senatus consultum* of AD 56.[9] A tribune could propose a fine in an assembly, and this was the most common modality of prosecution (see above). He could, moreover, inflict a fine prescribed by a statute, which that statute permitted any magistrate to inflict.[10] However, the original form of coercion by means of a financial penalty available to a tribune was the consecration of property (*consecratio bonorum*), attested on a few

---

[7] On the principle see Cic. *Sest.* 79; *Tull.* 47; *Leg.* 3. 9; Festus, 422L; Livy, 2. 33. 1; 3. 55. 6–7 (stating that the person of the violator was *sacer* to Jupiter, while his property was due to Ceres, Liber, and Libera). See also Dion. Hal. *AR* 6. 89. 2–4; Plut. *Ti. Gr.* 14. 5–8; 15. 1–2; 21. 5; *C. Gr.* 3. 5–7; App. *BCiv.* 1. 13. 57; 2. 108. 453; 4. 17. 65, with Niccolini, 1932, 68 ff.

[8] Vell. 2. 24. 2; Livy, *Per.* 59; Pliny, *HN* 7. 143, for precipitation (under the XII Tables it was a regular penalty for false witness—Gell. 20. 1. 53 = XII Tab. VIII. 12 (23), *RS* ii. 40, p. 692); questionable instances ascribed to the early Republic in Dion. Hal. 7. 35. 4; 10. 31. 3–4; Gell. 17. 21. 24–5; for imprisonment see Cic. *Leg. Agr.* 2. 101; *Att.* 2. 1. 8; Dio 37. 50. 1–2; 38. 6. 6. See also Chap. VII with n. 106.

[9] Livy, 29. 20. 11; Dion. Hal. *AR* 7. 26. 2–3, 35. 3; Gell. 13. 12. 6–9, citing Antistius Labeo and Ateius Capito to the effect that it did not extend to summoning persons through an intermediary; Tac. *Ann.* 13. 28.

[10] *Lex Silia* (*RS* ii. 46), 11–14; *lex lat. Bant.* (*RS* i. 7), 11–12; *lex osca Bant.* (*RS* i. 13), 35–7; Adamesteanu fr. 4–5.

occasions in the later Republic.[11] No explanation has been transmitted to us of the source of this power, but it may have been related to the belief that, in so far as the tribune himself was *sacer*, he could transfer that condition to objects, if he wished.

More commonly, sacrosanctity was used defensively in the form of *intercessio*, the interposing of a tribune's person in order to block the actions of other magistrates in their public capacity. Apart from the veto of a decree of the senate, this obstruction might affect legislation (Chap. V with nn. 28, 92–3) and the exercise of *imperium* against private individuals. *Intercessio* in this last context was termed *auxilium* ('help'), and was usually in response to a formal appeal. For Gellius, writing in the second century AD when the tribune's political power was nugatory, this was the chief function of the tribunate and explained why the tribunes could not normally spend a night away from the city. (Tribunes left the city for the Latin festival and were occasionally sent at other times on special business.) It was, too, to ensure that *auxilium* was always available, that the door of a tribune's house was always open day and night during his year of office, while during the day, under the Republic, the tribunes had a station by the Basilica Porcia near the *comitium* and senate house.[12]

There were some spectacular examples of *intercessio* against legislation—sometimes effective, sometimes not—in the late Republic. This had to be effected before the voters separated into their various units—perhaps because up to that point it was the obstruction of another magistrate, whereas afterwards it would have been the obstruction of the *populus Romanus* itself.[13] In 100, Servilius Caepio backed the veto of Saturninus' grain law by some of his colleagues by breaking up the *pontes* and throwing down the voting baskets (they had, it should be noted, intervened at the last possible point). In 67, when Servilius Globulus attempted to prevent the herald reading the bill of C. Cornelius which sought to restrict the grant of *privilegia*, Cornelius read it himself. In 62, after Cato and Minucius Thermus had tried to veto Metellus Nepos' proposal to recall Pompey to Italy, Nepos attempted

---

[11] Livy, 43. 16. 10; Cic. *Dom.* 123; Pliny, *HN* 7. 144; *Staatsr.* i. 157–8; Niccolini, 1932, 135–6.

[12] Cic. *Leg.* 3. 9 and 16; *ILS* 212, l. 30 (Claudius); Gell. 13. 12. 9; Plut. *Cato mi.* 5. 1; *QR* 81 (283 B–D); *Staatsr.* i. 269 ff., esp. 278 n. 4; ii. 1. 292–3. See also on leaving Rome Dion. Hal. *AR* 8. 87. 6; Livy, 9. 36. 14; 29. 20. 9–11; App. *BCiv.* 1. 24. 102; Plut. *C. Gr.* 10. 2; 11. 3; and, on the tribune's station being by the *tabula Valeria*, Coarelli, 1985, 53–62.

[13] Asc. 71C; Chap. V with n. 28. On the proper times for the veto see Rilinger, 1989. There is no example known to me of an election actually being vetoed by a tribune. For a threat so to do see Livy, 27. 6. 2–11. See also Cic. *Leg. Agr.* 2. 30 for vetoes on a formal *lex curiata* and for Rullus forbidding such a veto on the election of his agrarian commissioners, with Kunkel and Wittmann, 1995, 217.

likewise to read the bill himself, but Cato seized the text and, when Nepos proceeded to recite the bill by heart, Thermus stopped his mouth.[14] The physical element in the use of sacrosanctity to effect obstruction is patent. It is also remarkable that tribunes were prepared directly to defy vetoes. In Cornelius' case Cicero based his defence of that action on the ground that it was wrong to frustrate popular will—an argument which reached back to Tiberius Gracchus' tribunate and to Polybius' comment on the duties of tribunes.[15] If a bill actually was voted through after a veto was ignored, this argument was very powerful. If my earlier suggestion was right, the point about the timing of the veto was that it was one thing to obstruct a magistrate, another directly to frustrate the Roman people. In desperation a tribune might resort to a blanket form of obstruction: faced with opposition to his agrarian bill, Tiberius Gracchus proclaimed in an edict a cessation of public business, presumably threatening to veto any activity which did occur, and placed seals on the public treasury. Whether this should be termed technically a *iustitium* or not, it had a similar effect to the more usual suspension of business by a curule magistrate.[16]

The origin of the tribune's *auxilium* is also illustrated for us by a series of dramatic episodes from the annals of Rome. A starting-point is the apocryphal story concerning Volero Publilius resisting a levy, in which an annalist has tried to illustrate the nature of *provocatio* and appeal to the tribunes in its basic form. Publilius called first on the tribunes; then, when they demurred and a lictor began to strip him of his clothing preparatory to a flogging, he cried 'Provoco ad populum' and, after supporters had driven the lictor back, found shelter in a crowd of plebeians.[17] A later episode, which may well have been founded on fact, even if the story has been presented in the most dramatic form possible as an *exemplum* illustrating the nature of appeal, relates to the dictator L. Papirius Cursor and his master of horse Q. Fabius Maximus Rullianus in 325. Fabius, after escaping execution for disobedience in Samnium by appealing directly to the soldiers, flees to Rome in order to exploit the protection of tribunes, pursued by the dictator. Once at Rome, the dictator orders Fabius' arrest and the tribunes are in doubt about whether to offer *auxilium* or not. However, while the tribunes

---

[14] *Ad Herenn.* 1. 21; Asc. 58C; Plut. *Cato mi.* 28. 1.

[15] Cic. *Corn.* 1, fr. 31 Puccioni = Asc. 71–2C; App. *BCiv.* 1. 12. 51–53; Plut. *Ti. Gr.* 15. 3–4, 7 (*ORF*, no. 34, fr. 16); Pol. 6. 16. 5.

[16] Plut. *Ti. Gr.* 10. 8; cf. App. *BCiv.* 1. 55. 244, Plut. *Sulla* 8. 6, *Mar.* 35. 4 for a *iustitium* proclaimed by a consul; Niccolini, 1932, 111.

[17] Livy, 2. 55. 4–9; *VRR* 12–13; Lintott, 1972, 229–30.

waver, the opinion of the assembled crowd is on Fabius' side and
this induces the reluctant dictator to desist from seeking to execute
him.[18] The tribunes' protection here is founded on their being the representatives of the plebs as a whole and, where they are reluctant to act, the
assembled crowd lends its weight.

This aspect of appeal seems to have become less important as the
tribune became integrated into the workings of the law. However, the
duty of the tribune to act as the representative of the plebs as a whole,
when affording *auxilium*, may be seen on occasions where the execution
of a capital sentence was the issue. In 270 the three hundred survivors of
a Roman and Campanian garrison of Rhegium, who had defected from
the Roman cause and been defeated, were sent to Rome. A tribune
attempted to obstruct their execution, but a popular vote was held and
with the people's approval the execution was carried out. In 210, a
similar execution of three hundred Campanian traitors was preceded by
a popular vote.[19] Later during the Second Punic War, after Q. Pleminius
and some thirty other Romans condemned to death for crimes at Locri
had been brought to Rome, the tribunes seem to have impeded the
executions and instead sought to obtain a pardon for the condemned
men by bringing them before the people. They were unsuccessful, however, and Pleminius either died of natural causes in prison or was
executed after subsequently stirring up a riot.[20] We also find appeals to
the tribunes after the imposition of a fine, which led to a decision by the
assembly. In these cases the fines had been imposed by the *pontifex
maximus*. In 189 P. Licinius Crassus had taken pledges and inflicted a fine
on Q. Fabius Pictor the *flamen Quirinalis*. He appealed to the tribunes
and there was *provocatio* to the people. A subsequent assembly voted for
a compromise, whereby the *flamen* submitted to the *pontifex maximus'*
command, but the fine was revoked. This was not a judicial verdict, but
a political solution, and it is likely that the proposal emanated from the
tribunes in their capacity as mediators. Similar cases occurred in 180, 159,
131, and at some later date during the Republic.[21]

[18] Livy, 8. 32–35; Lintott, 1972, 236–7. On the relative powers of the dictator and tribune
see Chap. VII with nn. 80–81.
[19] Val. Max. 2. 7. 15; Dion. Hal. *AR* 20. 16. 1–2; Oros. 4. 3. 5; Livy, 26. 33. 10–14, stating that
there had been a precedent for this after the capture of Satricum in 319, contrary to Livy's
narrative in 9. 16. 1–10; Lintott, 1972, 240–3.
[20] Livy, 29. 21–2; 34. 44. 6–8; Lintott, 1972, 241–2.
[21] Livy, 37. 51. 1 ff.; 40. 42. 8 ff.; *Per.* 47; Cic. *Phil.* 11. 18; Festus, 462–4L; Lintott, 1972,
244–5; Bleicken, 1959, 341 ff.; Martin, 1970, 79 ff.; *Staatsr.* ii. 1. 57 ff.; *Strafr.* 40, 559–60.
Mommsen believed that the *pontifex maximus* himself presided over these tribal
assemblies, but, although this view may seem to have gained in plausibility with the

One interesting consequence of appeals to the tribunes was that on occasion they found it necessary to deliberate as a committee. The divergent accounts of the trial of L. Scipio Asiaticus in 187 have as a common feature an appeal by his brother Africanus to the tribunes. This was directed against the attempt to imprison Asiaticus for failing either to pay over the sum for which he had been condemned or to provide sureties for its payment. In effect this was an appeal against the verdict of either the assembly (according to Cornelius Nepos) or an investigating praetor (according to Valerius Antias). After consultation the majority of the tribunes, not surprisingly, were only prepared to oppose imprisonment, if Scipio co-operated by giving security. Tiberius Gracchus, however, one of the tribunes of 187, declared that he would not permit Asiaticus' imprisonment but he would not obstruct the extraction of public money from his estate. Gellius actually quotes a decree of the tribunes, taken by Cornelius Nepos from the records of the annals. Even if this derived from the *annales maximi*, it need not be an authentic text. However, it is testimony that the college of tribunes delivered resolutions formally in writing.[22] We find these deliberations taking place after appeals against a levy. In particular we are told of a certain C. Matienus who during a turbulent levy in 138 was 'accused before the tribunes on the charge of having deserted the army in Spain and after condemnation was flogged for a long time with rods under the yoke (*furca*) and sold for a single sesterce'. This quasi-trial must have arisen from an appeal by the victim, which in the event was turned down.[23]

Consultation might also have taken place when appeal was made to the tribunes in the course of private proceedings. In the two-part process characteristic of Roman private law this was only made in the first part, against the decision of the praetor. The clauses permitting appeal in the *lex agraria*, for example, can only refer to action by magistrates. One reason for the regular location of the tribunes by the *basilica Porcia* was their proximity to the original position of the praetor in the *comitium*.[24] The representative (*procurator*) of Cicero's client P. Quinctius obtained, in 83, tribunician support against what he thought was an improper

revelation that a priest proposed the *lex Fonteia* (*RS* i, no. 36), since the object of the assemblies was not so much the ratification of a penalty but an instruction to compromise, the presidency of one or more of the tribunes still seems to me more likely.

[22] Gell. 6. 19. 1–7 (Cornelius Nepos), ibid. 8 (Valerius Antias); Livy, 38. 54–5, cf. 52–3 (alleging, less plausibly, that the tribunes blocked a trial of Scipio Africanus in his absence); Fraccaro, 1911, 286 ff., 303 ff.; Gruen, 1995; Lintott, 1972, 254–5.

[23] Livy, *Per.* 55; for an investigation of soldiers' cases during a levy Livy, 42. 32. 7–8; Lintott, 1972, 243. [24] *Lex agr.* 34, 36; Coarelli, 1985, 53 ff.

concession by the praetor to the plaintiff Naevius, to wit, that security should be immediately provided for the sum claimed. An appeal to the tribunes by L. Quinctius, Cicero's opponent in the case of M. Tullius, over the formula provided by the praetor for the action in question was, on the other hand, ineffective, perhaps because it was actually rejected by the tribunes.[25] Nevertheless, the principle of appeal against jurisdiction by magistrates seems well established. Intervention in criminal *quaestiones*, however, seems normally not to have been permitted, because it was specifically forbidden by the laws which established them. The chapter in the *lex repetundarum* which forbids delay or interference with the trial is directed against any magistrate and thus *a fortiori* against tribunes. A similar provision is to be found in the Latin law from Bantia, and in the law about the praetorian provinces of 101–100 there is one forbidding obstruction by a magistrate to the proceedings before *recuperatores* established by the law.[26] It is, however, clear that the tribunes were expected to offer protection against unfairness in jurisdiction as well as against the misuse of force by a magistrate and in this respect made an important contribution to the practice of law.

Criminal *quaestiones* aside, the range and limits of *intercessio* seem to have been established casuistically and by experiment. For example, the justification of opposing the triumph of C. Pomptinus in 54 was that the vote which had legitimized it had been underhand; similar obstruction had been anticipated by Appius Claudius in 143, because the people were opposed to it, which he was able to deter by the protection of the sacred person of his sister, a Vestal Virgin.[27] The one guiding principle would have been that it was legitimate to oppose the senate or individual magistrates, but not to oppose the will of the Roman people as a whole. On this account Polybius' comment after his reference to the veto (6. 16. 4–5), that the tribune must set his sights on the will of the people, is particularly well judged.

---

[25] Cic. *Quinct.* 29, 63, 65; *Tull.* 38–9. For other appeals against praetorian decisions see Asc. 47, 84C (cf. Plut. *Caes.* 4. 2); *Staatsr.* i, 274; Niccolini, 1932, 118 ff.

[26] *Lex rep.* 70–72; *lex lat. Bant.* (*RS* i. 7), 7 ff. (cf. the oath in lines 14 ff.); *lex prov. praet.* (*RS* i. 12), Delphi, C24 ff. Contrast Cic. *Vat.* 33–4 for one known exception, where Vatinius seems to have exploited a loophole in the law under which he was being tried, the *lex Licinia Iunia* of 62. See Lintott, 1978.

[27] Dio, 39. 65. 2; Cic. *Cael.* 34; Val. Max. 5. 4. 6; Suet. *Tib.* 2. 4.

Aedilis

The office of aedile is one whose origins are in some respects at variance
with its later functions. The name suggests a connection with buildings
or more specifically temples (*aedes*). However, tradition maintained that
the two aediles of the plebs were first created after the first secession of
the plebs as general assistants of the tribunes, in particular receiving
from them a delegated judicial power.[28] This account would have been
the more credible, in that in the middle Republic the aedile of the plebs
was regarded as sacrosanct and it was envisaged that by virtue of this
quality he could even arrest a magistrate. However, by the time that Livy
wrote, jurists had interpreted the law ascribed to Valerius and Horatius
in 449, which had enacted legal penalties against those who did harm to
tribunes and aediles (and to *decemviri stlitibus iudicandis*), as carrying no
implications about sacrosanctity: the very fact that aediles were coerced
by higher magistrates, it was argued, showed that they were not sacrosanct like tribunes.[29] In effect, the sacrosanctity had become a wasting
asset. The other specifically plebeian features of the *aediles plebis* were
their duties as presidents of the *ludi plebeii* and as keepers of plebeian
records—probably based on the temple of Ceres on the Aventine.[30]

According to the annalists, the creation of the curule aediles was part
of the patrician response to the political agitation by Licinius and Sextius
in the period 376–367 BC. The restoration of the consulship and the
admission of plebeians to this office was followed by the creation of both
the praetorship and the office of curule aedile. A pair of curule aediles
were to match the plebeian aediles. This office was open to patricians
(perhaps the original intention was that it should be theirs exclusively),
but it appears that plebeians were not in fact excluded. We are told of a
compromise whereby a pair of patricians and a pair of plebeians held
office in alternate years, though this seems to have been obsolete by the

---

[28] Dion. Hal. *AR* 6. 90. 2–3; Gell. 17. 21. 11 (in a section which uses Cornelius Nepos);
Festus, 258–9L; Zon. 7. 15. 10; *Staatsr.* ii. 1. 470–522; Sabbatucci, 1954; Garofalo, 1989, 28 ff.

[29] Livy, 3. 55. 7–9; 29. 20. 11; Festus, 422L (Cato); Dion. Hal. *AR* 7. 26. 3, 35. 3–4; Plut. *Cor.*
18. 3–4. Badian (1996, 195–6) argues that the story of the mission to Scipio is a fiction and
that the aediles of the plebs were never sacrosanct. I prefer to see the apparent absurdities
of the tradition as arising from the lack of legal definition of sacrosanctity in the middle
Republic. See also Gell. 13. 13. 4 (Varro) for the theoretical liability of all aediles to respond
to a private prosecution; Garofalo, 1989, 33 ff.

[30] See e.g. Livy, 23. 30. 17; 27. 6. 19 and 36. 9; 28. 10. 7; 29. 38. 8 (games); *Dig.* 1. 2. 2. 21;
Livy, 3. 55. 7; Dion. Hal. *AR* 6. 94. 3; *Staatsr.* ii. 1. 476 (on the temple of Ceres). Sabbatucci,
1954, sees plebeian aediles as in origin priests of Ceres, but this seems to press the evidence
too far.

late Republic.[31] The curule aediles were elected in a tribal assembly under the presidency of a 'greater' magistrate. Their office in the late Republic seems to have begun on the same date as that of the consuls and praetors, and it is likely that this was always so.[32] The plebeian aediles, on the other hand, continued to be elected in the plebeian assembly under the presidency of a tribune.[33] Curule aediles had, as their name implies, a curule chair, but they had not the general rights of coercion available to magistrates with lictors. Indeed Varro deduced from the prosecution of a curule aedile in what was probably a civil suit that, unlike 'greater' magistrates, aediles could properly be summonsed to answer a suit brought by a private citizen.[34] They published edicts relating to their various spheres of duties, such as the markets, the games, and the sale of slaves, infringement of which would have made the perpetrator liable to the destruction of his wares, perhaps a fine or seizure of a pledge, even (in the case of actors) a flogging, or, regarding the sale of slaves, a civil action.[35] A reference in a document from the early Principate to the regulation of the sale of slaves includes the phrase 'ex imperio aedilium curulium de mancipis emundis vendundis', but this cannot be taken as evidence for the curule aedile possessing *imperium* in the special sense we have discussed earlier (Chap. VIII with n. 8). *Ex imperio* means simply 'in accordance with the order' and refers to the aediles' edict in this matter.[36]

Nevertheless, in spite of the differences in origin and status between the two pairs of aediles, by the middle Republic their functions and powers had to a great extent become assimilated. Their *provincia* was above all the city of Rome and its people. Here they were concerned

---

[31] *Staatsr.* ii. 1. 482; Livy 6. 42. 14; 7. 1. 1 and 6). See also 9. 46. 1ff. and Piso fr. 27P (Gell. 7. 9. 2–6) on Cn. Flavius, and Festus, 436L, on 366 BC, when the *ludi Romani* first became scenic (Livy 7. 2)—here *curules* is a supplement, but the context requires in any case that a plebeian was a curule aedile. By contrast, it is stated in Pol. 10. 4. 1–2 (on 211 BC) that it was customary for two patricians to be elected.

[32] Gell. 7. 9. 2 (Piso 27P); 13. 15. 4 (Messala, fr. 1a Bremer); Livy, 25. 2. 7; Varro, *RR* 3. 2. 1, 17. 1 and 10; Cic. *Planc.* 49; *Att.* 4. 3. 3–4; *Staatsr.* ii. 1. 483.   [33] Plut. *Cato mi.* 46. 3.

[34] Piso 27P (Gell. 7. 9. 6); Dion. Hal. 6. 95. 4; Varro *Rer. Hum.* XXI in Gell. 13. 13. 4.

[35] Edicts—Plaut. *Capt.* 791ff.; Macr. *Sat.* 2. 6. 1; Gell. 4. 2. 1–4; duties—Cic. *Verr.* 5. 36, on which see Taylor, 1939, for arguments that Cicero was plebeian, not curule aedile (*Qui primi ludi Romani appellati sunt* suggests not what were commonly called *ludi Romani*, but other games, i.e. the *ludi plebeii*, which claimed to be older, and these are linked with the Floralia and Cerealia, normally managed by plebeian aediles); destruction of wares—Plaut. *Rud.* 372–3, cf. Pers. 1. 129–30 and Juv. 10. 100–2 on aediles in Italian towns; taking of pledges—Tac. *Ann.* 13. 28; flogging—Plaut. *Trin.* 990; Suet. *Aug.* 45. 3.

[36] *Tabulae Herculanenses* no. 60 (Arangio-Ruiz and Pugliese-Carratelli, 1954, 55); Serrao, 1956, 198–9.

with temples, with markets—in particular with the corn-supply—with
the streets, ensuring that these were kept in good repair and free from
obstruction, and with aspects of hygiene, the water-supply and
funerals.[37] Apart from the *ludi Apollinares*, entrusted to the praetors, the
two pairs of aediles shared responsibility for the rest of the major games
at Rome: the *ludi Romani* fell to the curule magistrates, the *plebeii* to the
plebeian, while of those instituted later the *Megalensia* normally were
held by the curule aediles and the *Floralia* and *Cerealia* probably by the
plebeian.[38] Although watching for fires was the particular function of the
triumviri capitales or *nocturni*, the aediles here seem to have had a supervisory role, to judge from their prosecutions of incompetent *triumviri*.[39]
They had a responsibility for keeping order at the games and in the
markets, inasmuch as they were the magistrates directly responsible.
However, as Mommsen pointed out, police work as such was not their
function. Only on one occasion do we find them involved in the arrest
and coercion of those believed to be criminals, when during the suppression of the Bacchanals in 186 the curule aediles were instructed to
find and keep under open arrest all priests of the cult, while the plebeian
aediles' task was to ensure that the rites were not performed in secret.[40]

Both pairs of aediles, however, appear as prosecuting magistrates,
dealing with a range of offences in criminal and administrative law. These
trials were conducted before the people, like the prosecutions by tribunes, with the vote being taken in a tribal assembly (since in no case was
the offence capital). Mommsen assumed that the aediles' jurisdiction
arose simply because they were acting on the basis of laws which
instructed any magistrate who had the power to fine, to enforce the law.[41]
Such clauses certainly existed, but they do not explain the variety of
prosecutions undertaken or threatened. The aediles' activity here may
also be seen as descending from the original function of the plebeian
aedile as an assistant to the tribune and protector of the plebs, but it
should be stressed that in the middle and late Republic these prosecutions
are not the exclusive province of the plebeian aediles. Nor should we take

---

[37] Plaut. *Rud.* 372–3; *Stich.* 352–3; *Capt.* 791ff. (with Fraenkel, 1960, 37, 126); *tab. Heracl.*
(*RS* i. 24), 20–52; Cic. *Verr.* 5. 36; *Leg.* 3. 7; *Fam.* 8. 6. 4–5; *Phil.* 9. 17; Livy, 23. 41. 7;
30. 26. 6; 31. 4. 6 and 50. 1; Dion. Hal. *AR* 6. 90. 2–3; Sen. *Ep.* 86. 10; Dio 49. 43. 3.
[38] Cic. *Verr.* 5. 36; *Har. Resp.* 27; Livy, 34. 54. 3; cf. Dion. Hal. *AR* 6. 95. 4 on the Latin
festival; *Staatsr.* ii. 1. 517–21.
[39] Val. Max. 8. 1. *Damn.* 5–6; see also Dio, 53. 24. 4–5, on Egnatius Rufus.
[40] Livy, 39. 14. 9; *Staatsr.* ii. 1. 512; *VRR* 94–6, 99–101; Nippel, 1995, 16–22.
[41] *Staatsr.* ii. 1. 495–6, criticized by Greenidge, 1901, 340–41. For examples see n. 10
above.

Cicero's rhetoric too seriously and believe that the repression of political corruption was the centrepiece of the aedile's job-description.[42]

Some prosecutions were made for offences against specific laws. We hear of trials and condemnations for infringement of the *lex Licinia agraria* through possessing an excess of *ager publicus* and for less defined offences by stockbreeders, perhaps exceeding the maximum of beasts permitted on public land or failing to pay tax (*scriptura*). Also attested is a trial before the *comitia tributa* for the use of magic (*veneficia*) to move crops, a crime defined by the Twelve Tables.[43] It is interesting that here the aediles were dealing with matters outside the city. Prosecutions for usury resulted from Roman legislation on this topic and so perhaps did the charge of profiteering from corn-shortages.[44] There were, on the other hand, trials for rape or seduction (*stuprum*), at a time when this offence was not apparently covered by legislation.[45] Occasionally, we find charges which were political and seem to recall the original character of the plebeian aedile as defender of the plebs. Claudia, the sister of P. Claudius Pulcher the consul of 249, was actually indicted in 246 for insulting the plebs by publicly wishing them dead. In the late Republic, when Clodius prosecuted Milo for his use of gladiators for violence during and after his tribunate, the accuser's object seems to have been to present himself as a champion of the people.[46] This seems to have been Cicero's vision too, when he threatened, if his *repetundae* action against Verres failed, to prosecute him for offences against the *provocatio* laws, by exploiting his position as aedile the following year. He similarly threatened to bring charges against the promoters and agents of judicial bribery.[47] It is unlikely that Cicero would have been able to cite any exact

---

[42] *VRR* 96 n. 2; Garofalo, 1989, 108–13.

[43] Dion. Hal. *AR* 14. 12; Val. Max. 8. 6. 3; Livy, 7. 16. 9; 10. 13. 14—*lex Licinia*; Livy, 10. 23. 13 and 47. 4; 33. 42. 10; 34. 53. 4; 35. 10. 11–12; Ovid, *Fasti* 5. 285 ff.—stockbreeders; Pliny *HN* 18. 41–43—*veneficia*.

[44] Prosecutions—Livy, 7. 28. 9; 10. 23. 11–12; 35. 41. 9–10; 38. 35. 5–6; laws against usury—Livy, 7, 16. 1 and 42. 1; Tac. *Ann.* 6. 16; Gai. *Inst.* 4. 23; App. *BCiv.* 1. 54. 232–3; law on corn-profiteering—Plaut. *Capt.* 492 ff.

[45] Livy, 8. 22. 2–3, with Val. Max. 8. 1. *abs.* 7; Livy, 25. 2. 9; Plut. *Marcell.* 2. 5–7 with Val. Max. 6. 1. 7–8; perhaps Livy, 10. 31. 9.

[46] Claudia—Gell. 10. 6. 1–4 (Capito); Livy, *Per.* 19; Val. Max. 8. 1. *damn.* 4; Suet. *Tib.* 2. 3; Milo—Cic. *QF* 2. 3. 1–2, 6. 4; *Sest.* 95; *Vat.* 40–42; *Mil.* 40; Asc. 48C; Dio, 39. 18. 1 (mentioning the charge). The view of Gruen (1974, 298 n. 139) that what Cicero described was three *contiones* simply preparing the way for a prosecution in the *quaestio de vi*, accepted by Garofalo (1989, 107) runs counter to Cicero's vocabulary—*diem dicere, prodicere, ad populum accusare.* Of course Clodius might have changed modes of prosecution, but this did not detract from the formality of the procedure in the *contiones.*

[47] Cic. *Verr.* 1. 36; 2*Verr.* 1. 14, 5. 151, 173; *VRR* 96–7; Garofalo, 1989, 109–15.

precedent for acting as he promised. Nor would Clodius have been able to justify his accusation of Milo with examples. Nevertheless, their behaviour presupposes a strong tradition of aedilician prosecutions over the years. Moreover, the range of prosecutions undertaken in the middle Republic show that the aedile was not simply concerned with the fabric of the city of Rome. *Tota urbs* for Cicero involved the *populus Romanus* in many of its civil activities.

We cannot document the process by which the two pairs of aediles became assimilated and their functions became elaborated. However, one factor in particular will have stimulated the process—the preoccupation of the consuls and to some extent even of the praetors with war and foreign affairs in the period of Rome's rise to predominance in the Mediterranean. As Rome became a larger and more complex city from the Gallic sack onwards there was a need for a magistracy whose focus was the city itself and the citizens in their everyday life. The tribunes moved beyond their role as defenders of the plebs and became in addition magistrates with a constructive, as well as an obstructive, role in the politics of the community as a whole. But arguably their role as protectors and mediators, in addition to their political functions, did not leave room for an additional administrative role. Hence it was that the plebeian aediles, the former assistants of the tribunes, and their curule counterparts found a role which expanded with the city they served.

Quaestor

In the late Republic the *quaestores* were junior magistrates, who either supervised the treasury at Rome, the *aerarium Saturni*, or held independent administrative posts in Italy, or—and this was true of the majority—were assistants to consuls or to pro-magistrates abroad. There were also judicial magistrates sometimes called *quaesitores*, normally former aediles, who presided over permanent criminal courts, *quaestiones perpetuae*, for which there were no praetors available.[48] The terms *quaestor* and *quaesitor* are evidently different forms of the same noun, meaning investigator, which by the late Republic had completely different connotations (in Greek 'quaestor' is regularly translated as 'tamias', that is, treasurer or quartermaster). As far as we can tell, the two late Republican posts had nothing to do with one another. However, the early tradition about the quaestorship. which in any case is obscure,

---

[48] On the quaestor see *Staatsr.* ii. 1. 523–90, though the treatment of *quaesitores* (582 ff.) is not very satisfactory (*VRR* 122 n. 3).

is further bedevilled by what may be a confusion between a judicial magistrate, the *quaestor parricidii*, and those quaestors who either looked after the treasury at Rome or assisted the consuls.[49]

According to Pomponius in the *Digest* the *quaestor parricidii* was mentioned in the Twelve Tables—a notice which there is no reason to reject. The tradition that Sp. Cassius was accused of treason by a quaestor in 486 is not the only version of the story, and we cannot in any case put too much faith in the annalistic stories about this or about the later prosecution of M. Volscius Fictor.[50] However, it is still a reasonable conjecture that the *quaestores parricidii* actually antedated the Twelve Tables and may even have originated in the regal period. It was certainly held as early as the second century BC that the kings had *quaestores* of some kind, though there was dispute over whether these were simply chosen by the monarch or actually elected.[51] Quaestors of any kind play no part in the Livian tradition (apart from the two stories about accusations mentioned) until we hear of the addition of the two consular quaestors to the existing urban quaestors in 421. This implies the existence of the latter from some unspecified time earlier in Rome's history. Tacitus, however, sees the consular quaestors as the natural successors to those appointed by the kings and prior to the other Republican quaestors: the original quaestors were first elected by the people (as opposed to being chosen by the consuls themselves) in 443 and the urban quaestors added to them.[52]

Whenever, and in whatever order, the consular and urban quaestors were first created, it seems best to keep them distinct from the *quaestores parricidii*, as Pomponius did. The quaestor who is depicted initiating an assembly-trial by the *commentarium vetus anquisitionis*, preserved for us

[49] See Lydus, *de mag.* 1. 25, on the difference between *quaestor* and *quaesitor*, with Cloud, 1971, 18–26. Contrast Varro *LL* 5. 81, which states that the investigating quaestors were in charge of capital crimes, with Livy, 4. 43. 4, where, in spite of a corrupt text, it is clear that only two types of quaestor are envisaged—the *urbani* and those *qui consulibus ad ministeria belli praesto essent*. Pomponius (*Dig.* 1. 2. 2. 22–3) sets the *quaestores parricidii* and the administrative quaestors side by side without further comment, while Zonaras (7. 13. 3) conflates these two magistracies.

[50] *Dig.* 1. 2. 2. 22–3; Cic. *Rep.* 2. 60; Livy, 2. 41. 11; 3. 24. 3. For further bibliography see the works cited in Chap. IV n. 37.

[51] See Iunius Gracchanus, frr. 1–2 (p. 37 Bremer) in Ulp. *Dig.* 1. 13. pr. and 1 for election under Romulus; contrast Tac. *Ann.* 11. 22 (election first in 447 BC), Zon. 7. 13. 3 (election first at the beginnning of the Republic).

[52] Livy, 4. 43. 4; see also the speech ascribed to Canuleius (4. 4. 3), where the creation of the quaestorship is one of the innovations of the Republic; Tac. *Ann.* 11. 22. Their date of entry into office (5 Dec.—*lex Corn. XX quaest.* (*RS* i. 14), 10, 18, 22, 26, 30, cf. Cic. *Verr.* 1. 30) is presumably of ancient origin, but remains mysterious.

by Varro, is probably a consular or urban quaestor.[53] The title, *quaestor urbanus*, is associated in legal texts with supervision of the *aerarium* from the late second century BC.[54] This is likely to have been the chief function of the urban quaestors from the beginning. The consular quaestors, on the other hand, would have been expected to deal with financial and other administrative matters relating to the army when it was away from Rome. According to Tacitus, the number of quaestors was raised to eight 'with Italy paying tribute and the taxes of the provinces accruing', while a late source, John the Lydian, talks of the creation in 267 of twelve quaestors called *classici*, of which there is no further trace in our sources.[55]

We find specific posts in Italy in the late Republic and Principate in addition to the quaestors at the treasury, the consular quaestors, and those assigned to provinces. One was the quaestorship at Ostia, which had a responsibility for the import of corn and whose authority for this reason might be exercised elsewhere on the Tyrrhenian coast: hence it was sometimes referred to as the *provincia aquaria*. Another was the supervision of the drove-roads reaching from Apulia to the central Appennines. We also hear of a *provincia Gallica*, perhaps connected with the public land in the *ager Gallicus*.[56] Among the provinces Sicily was unusual in the late Republic in having two quaestors, one at Syracuse and one at Lilybaeum (we do not know when this practice began). These seem to have had special concern for the corn-supply.[57] It may be that the number of quaestorian posts was raised more than once before Sulla's dictatorship, as more quaestors were required to support provincial governors, though, in so far as a quaestor might remain through more than one governorship, a new quaestor would not have been automatically allocated to each province every year.[58] However, when Sulla

---

[53] Varro, *LL* 6. 90–91, perhaps deriving from the early third century, after the creation of the *rostra* and the *tabernae argentariorum*. On this problem see Latte, 1936; Kunkel, 1962, 35 ff. For a possible example of a quaestor prosecuting in an assembly-trial in the late Republic see Lintott, 1971a.

[54] *Lex rep.* 72, 79; *lex agr.* 46; *lex Corn. XX quaest.* (*RS* i. 14) I, 1–3; *tab. Heracl.* (*RS* i. 24) 37 ff. See also Cic. *2Verr.* 1. 37; *Flacc.* 30; *Att.* 2. 6. 2; *Phil.* 9. 16.

[55] Tac. *Ann.* 11. 22; Lydus, *de mag.* 1. 27, with the incomplete text of Livy, *Per.* 15. See also Mattingly, 1969, 509 ff. for doubts about Lydus' accuracy and an ingenious attempt to emend the text, which seems to misinterpret the word *hoionei*.

[56] Italian quaestors—Cic. *Sest.* 39; *Har. Resp.* 43; *Mur.* 18; *Vat.* 12; *Att.* 2. 9. 1; Tac. *Ann.* 4. 27. 2; Suet. *Claud.* 24. 2; Dio, 55. 4. 4; 60. 24. 3; *Staatsr.* ii. 1. 570 ff.; Mattingly, 1969, arguing at 506–9 that the *Gallica provincia*, only attested by Suetonius, results from textual corruption of *callium provincia*.

[57] Cic. *Div. Caec.* 39, 55–6; *2Verr.* 2. 44, 3. 168, 5. 114; *Planc.* 65.

[58] C. Gracchus stated that he stayed in Sardinia three years, though it was legal to leave

increased the number to twenty and made the quaestorship the qualification for entry to the senate,[59] this ensured that there was a sufficient number of quaestors to fill provincial posts each year, in addition to the two posts at the treasury, the two to three Italian quaestorships, and those assigned to the consuls. Quaestors continued to be assigned to the consuls during their year of office, although many of the latter did not leave Rome.[60] Indeed, in 38 BC, after Caesar had raised the number of quaestors to forty, we find two quaestors being assigned to each consul. [61]

The allocation of quaestors was supervised by the senate. The specific administrative posts at Rome and in Italy seem to have been settled by lot. However, magistrates seem to have had some discretion in selecting quaestors as their subordinates.[62] We do not know within what limits this operated, nor can we elucidate the obscure references to a *lex Titia* and a *senatus consultum* of perhaps 137 BC which in some way regulated the sortition.[63] The quaestors attached to major magistrates were their assistants in all kinds of activity. Those of the consuls seem in effect to have held the post of private secretary or aide-de-camp at home and abroad with particular responsibility for money, including army pay.[64] The same was true of those appointed to serve a magistrate or pro-magistrate abroad, though these quaestors had a wider remit, being deputy to the commander or governor and usually his temporary replacement, if he left his post for any reason.[65] We have already seen how they might in certain circumstances be given an independent command with *imperium pro praetore* (Chap. VII with n. 96). However, their financial concerns were as pre-eminent abroad as they were in the city.[66]

The quaestors at the treasury at Rome in general supervised ingoings and outgoings under the direction of the senate and the consuls, but also

---

after one (Plut. *C. Gr.* 2. 9 = *ORF*, no. 48, fr. 23), cf. Sall. *Jug.* 95. 1, 103. 4; Diod. 34/5. 39 on Sulla in Africa.

[59] Tac. *Ann.* 11. 22; *lex Corn. XX quaest.* (*RS* i. 14), prescr.

[60] Consular quaestors—Cic. 2*Verr.* 1. 34–7 (in the eighties BC); *Clu.* 99; *Red. Sen.* 21; *Sest.* 8 (after Sulla).   [61] Dio, 43. 47. 2; 48. 43. 1.

[62] Cic. *Sest.* 8; *Vat.* 12; *Mur.* 18; *Phil.* 2. 50; *Att.* 6. 6. 4; Livy, 30. 33. 2; *Staatsr.* ii. 1. 532.

[63] Cic. *Mur.* 18; *Dig.* 1. 13. 2.

[64] Pol. 6. 12. 8; Cic. 2*Verr.* 1. 34–40.

[65] Cic. 2*Verr.* 1. 40; 2*Verr.* 2. 44 (quaestor allots judges); *Att.* 6. 3. 1, 4. 1, 5. 3, 6. 3. See also *Syll.*³ 700 for M. Annius' military exploits, and Sall. *Jug.* 95 ff. on Sulla in Numidia.

[66] Pol. 10. 19. 1–2; Livy, 26. 47. 7–8; *lex prov. praet.* (*RS* i. 12), Cnidos IV, 40 ff. = Delphi C, 3 ff.; Sall. *Jug.* 104. 3; Cic. *Fam.* 12. 14. 1 and 5; 15. 1 and 6. Note also *EJ*² 191 for a quaestor being honoured by tax-contractors in the early Principate.

had a number of special duties. We find them *inter alia* pursuing arrears of taxation (*stipendium*) from priests and, on the other hand, paying back to the taxpayers recompense in proportion to their contributions from the proceeds of Manlius Vulso's triumph.[67] They were also responsible for paying out expenses for those going out on official business, for the entertainment of distinguished foreigners in Italy, for the letting of certain public works contracts, and the payment of sums due to contractors. They might even speak publicly about the balances available in the treasury.[68] The surviving texts of statutes, in particular, show them receiving the money or security for the money due to the treasury through criminal condemnations and through the sale of public land. They also pay out money due to plaintiffs.[69] Furthermore, booty or pledged security was turned into cash by sales conducted by the quaestors.[70] The *aerarium* was a repository not only of money, but of documents. Apart from records relating to money, the texts of statutes, proposed statutes (*rogationes*) and *senatus consulta* were deposited here.[71] Moreover, it was with the quaestor at the *aerarium* that magistrates had to register the oaths they had taken to obey certain late-Republican statutes.[72] The quaestors at the treasury may have had less discretion than other quaestors, but they still had considerable responsibilities. In the late Republic this was emphasized in Cato's quaestorship, when he took the trouble to expose the fraud and inaccuracy of the scribes. The actual accounting of Rome's money lay in the scribes' hands and they had tended to exploit the inexperience of the quaestors to whom they were responsible.[73]

Minor Magistrates

There were a number of magistracies which the Romans held to be of lower status than the quaestors, which were for the most part elected by the people each year. There were also minor magistracies which were elected occasionally, when they were needed. The former under the

---

[67] Livy, 23. 41. 7; 33. 42. 4; 39. 7. 4–5; 42. 6. 11.

[68] Livy, 45. 13. 12, 44. 7; *Ad Herenn.* 1. 21; Cic. *Att.* 2. 6. 2, 16. 4; *Phil.* 9. 16; *tab. Heracl.* (*RS* i. 24) 37–49; Val. Max. 5. 1. 1e; Plut. *QR* 43 (275b–c); *Staatsr.* ii. 1. 553–6. For the entertainment of foreign embassies see also *RDGE*, nos. 9. 67 ff.; 10. B 12 ff.; 15. 64–5; 16. 9 ff.; 22. Latin 13, Greek 25–6; 26. 24 ff.; Reynolds, 1987, no. 8. 74 ff.

[69] *Lex rep.* 57–69; *lex agr.* 46–7. See also Livy, 38. 60. 8.

[70] Plaut. *Capt.* 111, 453; *lex agr.* 46, 74; Livy, 7. 27. 8–9; Gell. 13. 25. 26–7.

[71] Sisenna, fr. 117P; Suet. *Jul.* 28. 3; Schol. Bob. 140St; Tac. *Ann.* 3. 51.

[72] *Lex lat. Bant.* (*RS* i. 7), 24, cf. the restored text in *frag. Tar.* (*RS* i, 8), 20 and 22.

[73] Plut. *Cato mi.* 16–17.

Principate were held by men who had only recently come of age, and were regarded as the first steps in a career; under the Republic they were probably also held by young men, but we know so little about some of them that we cannot be sure. When the legislator of the *lex repetundarum* was listing magistrates who might be prosecuted for taking money improperly, and also those who were to be excluded during and after their magistracies from membership of the juries, the three lowest designated were the *triumvir capitalis*, the *triumvir agris dandis adsignandis*, and the *tribunus militum* of any one of the first four legions.[74] Of these the first and third were elected annually, the second, the commissioner for distributing lands, was elected *ad hoc*, but in the Gracchan period there had been a commission in existence continually since 133. These three magistracies were perhaps selected on account of the authority they conferred and because their incumbents had higher status than those in other minor magistracies.

Other magistracies are listed in Pomponius' summary preserved in the *Digest*—the 'ten for judging lawsuits'(*decemviri stlitibus iudicandis*), the 'four for cleaning roads in the city' (*quattuorviri viis in urbem purgandis*), the 'three masters of the mint' (*tresviri monetales*). He also mentions a further group, who acted for magistrates in the evening, presumably as a kind of watch, the 'five on either side of the Tiber' (*quinqueviri cis et ultis Tiberim*).[75] Cicero in his theoretical version of the Republic talks generally of the function of minor magistrates—in commanding the troops which they have been ordered to command, looking after public money, watching over the imprisonment of condemned men, inflicting capital punishment, minting bronze, silver or gold, judging law suits, and doing whatever the senate has decreed. His formula is deliberately laconic, but it may well be that he envisaged one college whose members shared and performed as required the tasks of the tribunes of the soldiers, the quaestors, the *tresviri capitales*, the *monetales*, and the *decemviri stlitibus iudicandis*.[76] The existence of a single college of certain

---

[74] *Lex rep.* 2, 16, 22; cf. *lex lat. Bant.* 15. Cicero (*Clu.* 148) mentions only the *tribunus militum* below the quaestor in the list of those ex-magistrates liable for judicial corruption under the *lex Cornelia de sicariis et veneficis*, but this may be the result of compression.

[75] *Dig.* 1. 2. 2. 29–31. The title of the road-commissioners has been taken in my text from *tab. Heracl.* (*RS* i. 24), 50–1. The text of Livy, 39. 14. 10 (following Heusinger's emendation), has *quinque viri uls cis Tiberum*.

[76] Cic. *Leg.* 3. 6. The passage begins: 'minores magistratus partiti iuris ploeres in ploera sunto' ('there shall be a number of minor magistrates sharing legal authority for a number of tasks'). On this see Rawson, 1991, 142, who argued that this showed that in Cicero's constitution quaestors were not to be members of the senate.

minor magistrates, if not of the sharing of tasks, is attested in Cassius Dio's account of Augustus' reform of the vigintivirate. Dio says that the twenty men had originally been twenty-six, but the two men who looked after roads outside Rome had been disbanded, as had the four men sent to Campania. This left the three *capitales*, three *monetales*, four in charge of roads inside Rome, and the ten for judging lawsuits. The two men concerned with roads outside Rome are attested in the *lex agraria* of 111 BC and also on the *Tabula Heracleensis*: thus they may have been still in existence under Caesar's dictatorship. The four sent to Campania are the *praefecti* sent to Capua, Cumae, and eight other Campanian towns to perform jurisdiction in place of the praetor at Rome, who became redundant in the period after the Social War—perhaps with the founding of the colony of Capua after Caesar's legislation of 59, perhaps with the further change to Capua's status in the triumviral period. These were elected officials, by contrast with the *praefecti* with a similar function sent by the praetor to towns with Roman citizenship (originally without the vote), such as Fundi, Formiae, and Caere.[77] Hence there were under the Republic some fifty regularly elected minor magistrates—twenty-four military tribunes and twenty-six civil functionaries. Apart from these, there were colonial and land-commissioners elected *ad hoc* and certain other occasional magistrates such as the *duoviri* appointed for the dedication of a temple or altar, or the *tresviri mensarii* created to provide funding for the Second Punic War.[78]

Paucity of information means that for most of these magistrates a brief survey must suffice. The tribunes of the soldiers of the first four legions are portrayed by Polybius as the most significant subordinates of the consuls in military matters. They not only commanded in the field, but played an important part in the levy each year and the exaction of the military oath from the recruits. Even if the procedures described by Polybius had become to some extent antiquated through the multiplication of legions and their maintenance for long periods overseas from the Second Punic War onwards, the significance of the tribunes remains considerable.[79] There were originally, we are told, 6 *tribuni militum* elected by the people, then 16, and finally 24. Further tribunes for legions

---

[77] Dio, 54. 26. 5–7; *lex agr.* 28; *tab. Heracl.* 50–1; Festus, 262L; *ILLRP* 441 (it is not clear whether this man held his prefecture before or after his quaestorship, his only other magistracy); *Staatsr.* ii. 1. 592 ff. esp. 609 ff. on the *praefecti*. On the latter see now Pobjoy, 1996, 11–21, 158–9.

[78] *Staatsr.* ii. 1. 619 ff., 641; Livy, 7. 28. 5; 22. 33. 7–8; 23. 21. 6–7 and 30. 13–14; 24. 18. 12–13; 26. 36. 8; 40. 44. 10; *ILLRP* 121, 281.

[79] Pol. 6. 19–26, esp. 19. 1–2, 6–9; 21. 1–10.

above four were nominated by the consuls.[80] In the late Republic such positions overseas were granted at the discretion of the commander, and this led to their being given as sinecures to unmilitary men.[81] The elected military tribunate was still an office of considerable prestige for which there was much competition in the late Republic. In Polybius' time 14 of the places went to those with five years military service, 10 to those who had completed ten. The elections were held at some point after those for the consulship and praetorship in the assembly of tribes, and the magistracy lasted, coterminously with the higher magistracies, for a year from 1 January.[82] It may have seemed eventually a curious survival, but it did maintain to some extent the principle that the Roman people selected its own military leaders.

In spite of the great number of their products which we possess, little is known of the *monetales*. The magistracy seems to have been undertaken by those below the rank of quaestor. It was an elected office, to judge from its later incorporation into the 'twenty-six men', and presumably one elected by a tribal assembly. Although the moneyers were a college of three, coins were frequently struck in the name of only one or two. Hence it has been argued, especially on the basis of the legend *L. Flaminius Chilo pri(mus) fl(avit)*, that the three divided up the year among themselves. It is not clear who took the decisions to mint. Probably, as expenditure was in the hands of the consuls and senate, so was minting policy in a particular year. Denominations and weight-standards were the subject of legislation, although it has been argued that the moneyers or quaestors were responsible for restoring on occasion a weight-standard that had been neglected over a number of years.[83]

We have a glimpse of the supervisory operations of the two colleges of commissioners for roads—for those inside and those immediately outside the city—on the *Tabula Heracleensis*. As to the *decemviri stlitibus iudicandis*, we know that under the Republic they judged actions initiated by *sacramentum* (that is, by one of the ancient *legis actiones*) in dispute over *libertas*, the status of being free. There is also an obscure reference in Livy to their persons being inviolate by law. The office seems to have been held, as later during the Principate, by young men before their quaestorship. Augustus was to make the *decemviri* presidents

---

[80] Livy, 7. 5. 9; 9. 30. 3; 27. 36. 14. Contrast Festus, 316–7L, on those nominated by the consuls, called 'rufuli', allegedly because their creation had been provided for in a law of a Rutilius Rufus. See *Staatsr.* ii. 1. 574 ff.

[81] See e.g. Caes. *BG* 1. 39. 2–4; Cic. *Fam.* 7. 5. 2, 13. 2.

[82] Pol. 6. 19. 1; Cic. *Verr.* 1. 30; *Att.* 13. 33. 3; Sall. *Jug.* 63. 4; Plut. *Cato mi.* 8. 4–5.

[83] *Staatsr.* ii. 1. 601–3; *RRC* i, no. 485; ii, chs. 3 and 5, esp. 619–20.

of the centumviral court.[84] The *praefecti* sent to Campania would have performed jurisdiction in place of the praetor and also more general administration, when in 211 this region of Roman citizens (originally possessing citizenship without the vote) had been once again subjected to Rome after its defection to Hannibal and been deprived of its own local government.[85]

The functions of the *tresviri capitales* are better attested in our sources, but difficult to define satisfactorily. They were first created *c.*290–87, according to Livy, though even before this there existed apparently the office of *triumvir nocturnus*, which clearly had one of the tasks of the later *triumvir capitalis*—that of acting as a night watch against fires and malefactors.[86] However, probably later in the third century (after the creation of the second praetor), a *lex Papiria* provided for the election of *tres viri capitales* by the *praetor urbanus* each year to exact judicial wagers used to initiate lawsuits (*sacramenta*) and to judge cases themselves. This election seems to have taken place after the entry of the praetor into office and so would have been completely separate from the elections of magistrates such as quaestors or *tribuni militum*: conceivably it was, or became, associated with that of the *decemviri stlitibus iudicandis* and the *praefecti*.[87] The judicial work to be undertaken according to this law was related to the ancient form of bringing a private action, the *legis actio sacramento*, but the *tresviri* may have in fact dealt with what we would consider criminal offences.[88]

In the middle and late Republic the *tresviri* are attested in their central function of supervising the prison and executions, for example in the case of the poet Naevius.[89] At night they kept watch not only for fires—they had at their disposition a *familia publica* (public gang of slaves) to act as a primitive fire-brigade[90]—but also for thieves and run-away slaves. The latter were apparently flogged at the *columna Maenia*, the station of the *triumviri* during the day on the north-west side of the *comitium* in the direction of the prison, before being returned to their masters. Similar treatment may have been meted out to thieves, perhaps

---

[84] *Tab. Heracl.* 50–1; Cic. *Caec.* 97; *Dom.* 78; Livy, 3. 55. 7; *ILLRP* 316 on the career of Cn. Scipio Hispanus; Dio, 54. 26. 6; Suet. *Aug.* 36.

[85] Livy, 26. 34; Frederiksen, 1984, 244 ff. See also n. 77 above.

[86] Livy, 9. 46. 3; *Per.* 11; *Staatsr.* ii. 1. 594 ff.; *VRR* 102–6; Nippel, 1995, 22–6.

[87] Festus, 468L = *RS* ii. 45.

[88] Kunkel, 1962, 97 ff.

[89] Plaut. *Miles* 211–12; Gell. 3. 3. 15 (on which see *VRR* 102 n. 7); Val. Max. 6. 1. 10; 8. 4. 2; and in general Cic. *Leg.* 3. 6; *Dig.* 1. 2. 2. 30.

[90] *Dig.* 1. 15. 1; Val. Max. 8. 1. *damn.* 5.

on the ground that they did not merit the protection of the *lex Porcia* because of their shameful status.[91] The function of the *tresviri* was in part to ensure the security of the citizens' lives and property, but they had normally neither the time nor the resources to act like a modern police force. However, in a crisis they were given a wide remit. At the time of the Bacchanalian conspiracy in 186 the *tresviri* were instructed to set watches throughout the city to prevent nocturnal gatherings and arson, assisted by the *quinque viri uls cis Tiberim* in their various regions. Similar orders were given in 63 to the 'minor magistrates'—the term would include the *tresviri* and *quinqueviri*—at the time when news broke of the Catilinarian conspiracy.[92]

We also find evidence of judicial activity, though this seems to be of a different kind to that attested by the *lex Papiria*, in that it was not based on a formal civil action by wager, *legis actio sacramento*, but proceeded by the simple laying of information or arrest. Varro tells us that the *tresviri* in his day investigated the crimes previously dealt with by the *quaestores* (*parricidii*). In Plautus denunciations are made to the *triumvir* for theft and for the possession of an offensive weapon (in fact a cook's knife). There are further references to seizure (*manus iniectio*) as the beginning of an action before the *triumvir*. A glimpse of this in action is provided by Cicero's defence of Cluentius: when Asuvius had been murdered, his friends seized Oppianicus' friend Avillius as the suspect and 'placed him before the feet of the *triumvir* Q. Manlius'. This may have been how on another occasion C. Cornelius came to be imprisoned for homosexual intercourse.[93]

The nature of Roman criminal procedure against members of the plebs is a matter for a subsequent chapter. It is sufficient here to observe that the *triumvir* seems to have investigated or judged a number of matters, some of them resulting from formal civil actions, some resulting from arrest or the laying of information about an alleged crime. These crimes were on the whole not the kind of cases which were normally prosecuted before an assembly by a tribune or aedile. The *triumvir* on occasion went on to punish those he held guilty. In so doing,

---

[91] Plaut. *Amph.* 155; Hor. *Epod.* 4. 11; Asc. 37C; PsAsc. 201St on Cic. *Div. Caec.* 50; Coarelli, 1985, 47–53, on the location of the *columna*. For actors lacking the protection of the *lex Porcia* see Suet. *Aug.* 45. 3.

[92] Livy, 39. 14. 9–10; Sall. *Cat.* 30. 7.

[93] Varro *LL* 5. 81; Plaut. *Asin.* 130–3; *Aulul.* 416–17; *Bacch.* 688; *Capt.* 1019; *Rud.* 778, 857; on *manus iniectio*, *Persa* 62 ff.; *Truc.* 759 ff. (not necessarily the *manus iniectio quadrupli* prescribed for certain delicts, on which see *VRR* 104 n. 3); on Avillius Cic. *Clu.* 38; on Cornelius Val. Max. 6. 1. 10.

like any other magistrate, he was subject to the *provocatio* laws and liable to intervention by a tribune. On one occasion we are specifically told that tribunes refused to intervene over a free man imprisoned.[94] In general, if the *triumvir's* freedom of action was strictly limited *de iure*, it would have been in fact much greater inasmuch as he was punishing those whom the plebs regarded as alien to them or their enemies. Hence any resort by the accused to *provocatio* would have been unlikely to secure backing from tribunes.

Finally, mention should be made of an occasional magistrate of great importance and the subject of controversy in the late Republic, the land-commissioner—most commonly one of three, a *triumvir a(gris) d(andis) a(dsignandis)*, as he is assumed to be in the epigraphic texts discussed above, but also one of five, seven, ten, fifteen, or twenty.[95] Whether we hear of a law authorizing the land-distribution or not (in some instances Livy's account may be compressed; it is also possible that the reinforcement of a colony was not thought to require a law), these commissioners were elected.[96] Servilius Rullus proposed a five-year term for his land-commission. However, normally such men had no fixed term of office: they were expected to continue their task until it was finished. Tiberius Gracchus' law seems to have provided for the rotation of the chairmanship of his commission, though its members were to continue in office year after year: only the death of incumbents led to substitutions.[97] The office, moreover, could be combined with other magistracies. Tiberius and Gaius Gracchus, M. Fulvius Flaccus and M. Livius Drusus (*tr. pl.* 91), for example, were simultaneously tribunes and land-commissioners.[98] Servilius Rullus' prospective *decemviri* were to be granted praetorian *potestas*, whatever that precisely meant. It is not clear that this was as uncommon as Cicero implies. However, commissioners must in any case have had the power necessary to organise the citizens they were settling on the land and to provide any colony with a constitution: they would have also had the right to take the

---

[94] Val. Max. 6. 1. 10.

[95] See above, n. 74, cf. e.g. *ILLRP* 467–75; *ILS* 49; Cic. *Leg. Agr.* 2. 17; *Att.* 2. 6. 2; *Phil.* 5. 21 and 33; Pliny, *HN* 7. 139.

[96] See e.g. Cic. *Leg. Agr.* 2. 17 ff.; Livy, 34. 53. 1; 37. 46. 10; *Staatsr.* ii. 1. 626–7; Badian, 1996, 188; and see below.

[97] Cic. *Leg. Agr.* 2. 31; App. *BCiv.* 1. 9. 37 and 18. 73, with Gabba's (1958) commentary and Carcopino, 1928, 149 ff.

[98] App. *BCiv.* 1. 13. 55 and 24. 102–5; Plut. *C. Gr.* 10. 3–4 and 11. 3; *ILS* 49. Pompey would still have been a land-commissioner under Caesar's legislation (Cic. *Att.* 2. 12. 1 and 19. 3), when he was given charge of the corn-supply in 57, see *MRR*, *sub annis*.

auspices when they were founding a colony.[99] It was one thing to settle newly conquered or newly exploited territory; it was another to review and adjust existing holdings of public land, as the Gracchan commission was expected to do. For this purpose the Gracchan *tresviri* were granted judicial powers, apparently by a separate law, and appear on their boundary-stones as '*A(gris) I(udicandis) A(dsignandis)*'.[100] After a protest by some Italians to Scipio Aemilianus, the judicial powers in cases involving them were transferred to the jurisdiction of the consul. Later, it seems likely that C. Gracchus was prepared to concede that the commissioners under his law should have no judicial powers (hence the *triumvir* is merely '*A(gris) D(andis) A(dsignandis)*' in the *lex repetundarum*), and in the agrarian law of 111 jurisdiction in Italy is confined to praetors, consuls, and censors.[101] However, later in the Republic we find other examples of agrarian commissioners with judicial powers.[102]

The *Cursus Honorum*

It is obviously sensible that men should have experience in junior civil posts before they proceed to higher magistracies, just as military officers are expected to gain experience as subordinates before they become generals. The principle was recognized in Greece, in the fourth century BC if not earlier, as has been shown by the publication of the 'Vatican Fragments of Greek Political Theory', usually identified as part of Theophrastus' work on laws.[103] We know nothing about Roman practice in this regard in the early Republic. It seems likely that in principle that a magistracy which was conceived as assisting one higher than itself, such as the quaestorship, was held before that higher magistracy. However, the praetorship, which was subordinate to the consulship, though one of the higher magistracies, was frequently held after the consulship in the early third century.[104] One regulation mentioned by Polybius may go back to

---

[99] Cic. *Leg. Agr.* 2. 31 on the *auspicia* proposed by Rullus, following the precedent of a *lex Sempronia*—probably a law of Gaius, since he was concerned with founding colonies, not of Tiberius Gracchus, as Cicero supposes. The *potestas* is conceivably a power of jurisdiction and not *imperium* (Cicero makes no allusion to the *decemviri* having lictors and *fasces*).

[100] Livy, *Per.* 58; Macr. *Sat.* 3. 14. 6; *ILLRP* 467–74; *AE* 1973, 222; *JRLR* 44.

[101] App. *BCiv.* 1. 19. 79–80; *lex rep.* 2, 13, 16, 22; *lex agr.* 15, 24, 33–6; *JRLR* 46. The commissions of which M. Drusus was a member were *a. d. a.* (*ILS* 49).

[102] *Inscr. Ital.* xiii. 3, no. 6; *ILLRP* 474—on a Gracchan terminus restored after Sulla.

[103] See Aly, 1943, fol. B, 172 ff., ; Oliver, 1977.

[104] Examples are P. Sempronius Sophus (*cos.* 304, *pr.* 296), Ap. Claudius Caecus (*cos.* II 296, *pr.* II 295), L. Papirius Cursor (*cos.* 293, *pr.* 292), L. Caecilius Metellus Denter (*cos.* 284,

the third century—that requiring ten years military service before the holding of any political magistracy. It is generally assumed by scholars that the lowest magistracy affected by this rule would normally have been the quaestorship. As we have seen, some of the posts of tribune of the soldiers were available to those who had not completed ten years service.[105] It is possible that certain other minor magistracies, such as the post of *monetalis*, were available to those who had not completed their military service. On the other hand, it may have been common originally to go straight to the praetorship or even the consulship after the completion of military service. We also hear of an old law forbidding the holding of the same magistracy twice within ten years.[106]

In 180 BC—in a period in which the competition for office (*ambitio*) had become immensely vigorous, and immediately following a law against *ambitus* (electoral bribery)—the first 'lex annalis' was passed by L. Villius, which according to Livy, prescribed the minimum age for seeking and attaining the various magistracies.[107] Livy's account is elliptic and his main statement has been doubted. However, powerful arguments have been produced to show that the *lex Villia* introduced first the succession of quaestorship, praetorship, and consulship, secondly the compulsory two-year interval (*biennium*) between the holding of magistracies, and thirdly the requirement of a minimum age for the two main offices, if not the quaestorship (the timing of the latter being in any case determined by the need for the completion of ten years military service).[108] The rules were repeated with some modifications in Sulla's *lex annalis* of 81, of which we have little detail, but it appears from the evidence of Cicero that by virtue of this law the minimum age for the quaestorship was 30, for the praetorship 39, and for the consulship 42.[109] The aedileship was not a compulsory element in a career, nor was the

pr. 283), Q. Marcius Philippus (*cos.* 281, *pr.* 280), L. Postumius Megellus (*cos.* 262, *pr.* 253—and, apparently, simultaneously censor). See *MRR*, *sub annis*.

[105] Pol. 6. 19. 1 and 4. Mommsen (*Staatsr.* i. 505, n. 1) argued that the case of P. Scipio (Livy, 25. 2. 6–8; 26. 18. 6–9) proves that the ten-year requirement was not absolutely compulsory before the *lex Villia* of 180. What the first story shows is that the tribunes thought Scipio too young for the aedileship, but that there was no definite legal bar, only the possibility of tribunician obstruction to the candidacy. However, it is likely in any case that rules were stretched by the exigencies of the Second Punic War.

[106] Livy, 7. 42. 2; 10. 13. 8; Plut. *Mar.* 12. 1; Astin, 1958, 19–20.

[107] Livy, 40. 44. 1; *Staatsr.* i. 505ff.; Astin, 1958, 1ff., criticizing some arguments of Mommsen. On *ambitus* see Lintott, 1990.

[108] Astin, 1958—with statistical evidence and discussions of Cic. *Att.* 13. 32. 3; *Fam.* 10. 25. 1–2. On the *cursus* and exceptions to it see Asc. 25C; Cic. *Har. Resp.* 43, with Lintott, 1971b, 448 nn. 5–6, 451 n. 1; Badian, 1959.

[109] App. *BCiv.* 1. 100. 466; Cic. *Phil.* 5. 48; *Leg. Agr.* 2. 3–4.

tribunate of the plebs, which in any case was not open to patricians nor bound by the same rules as the other major magistracies.[110] By these rules the Romans sought to restrict the scramble for office which was at its most intense in the late Republic.

[110] So Servilius Glaucia could move straight from the tribunate to the praetorship with only the interval between 9 Dec. 101 and 1 Jan. 100 separating the two magistracies (App. *BCiv.* 1. 28. 127, with Gabba's (1958) commentary—Appian wrongly believed that Glaucia was praetor when he presided over Saturninus' election to his second tribunate). As to re-election to the tribunate, see Cic. *Amic.* 96 and Livy, *Per.* 59, on Carbo's proposal that tribunes could be re-elected *ad infinitum*, and App. *BCiv.* 1. 21. 90–22. 91; Plut. *C. Gr.* 8. 2 on C. Gracchus' re-election, with Jones, 1960*b*; Hall, 1972

IX

Criminal Justice

Some indications of the nature of Roman judicial procedure have emerged in preceding chapters, when the subject of discusssion has been the functions of assemblies and those of certain magistrates—in particular the praetors, tribunes of the plebs, aediles, and *tresviri capitales*. It is not within the scope of this book to investigate the intricate web of actions comprised in Roman private law, which sought to resolve disputes between individual citizens and indeed aliens under Roman jurisdiction: what is germane is the procedure where the individual came face to face with public authority because of an alleged offence against the community.

There is an immediate problem of definition. Modern legal systems differentiate clearly between civil and criminal law through distinctions in procedure, in the source of the prosecution, and in the nature of the judgement. Criminal cases are for the most part defined by the fact that the state prepares the charge, a particular form of procedure is used, and judgement is given in favour of the public authority rather than those who were in fact wronged. Under the Roman Republic, as Polybius pointed out, in criminal matters we find both trials before an assembly and investigations by a magistrate, which might be authorized by the senate or the people.[1] In the late Republic a procedure known as the *quaestio perpetua* was developed through a series of statutes, whereby in each case a magistrate was instructed to investigate with the help of a panel of judges, offences touching the public interest.[2] On the other hand, private actions were marked out by the two-part procedure, which we have noticed when discussing the office of praetor. The plaintiff went to the *praetor urbanus* (or *peregrinus*, if a non-Roman was concerned) and asked for an action, explaining his grievance. The praetor produced a *formula*, which laid down the conditions to be satisfied if the action was to succeed: that is, it said 'If such and such be proved, let the judge

---

[1] Pol. 6. 14. 6–8, 13. 4–5 and 16. 2
[2] See Kunkel, 1962, and *RE quaestio*, 24 (1963), 720–68; *JRLR* 11 ff.

condemn, if not, absolve'. The *formula*, also named a judge (at the choice of the parties, if they had someone in mind) or a panel of judges and handed over the case to be tried. This judge, or judges—the latter sometimes a board of *recuperatores*, sometimes the *decemviri stlitibus iudicandis* or the centumviral court—heard the evidence and pleas and delivered the verdict, which was supported by the praetor's authority detailed in the formula. A bronze tablet has shown that this procedure was adapted by a provincial governor to settle a dispute between two Spanish communes over land and water rights.[3]

However, the boundary between civil and criminal prosecutions and the distinguishing criteria were not the same as those normally found nowadays in English law. Theft, for example, under the Republic was treated as a private wrong to be pursued by civil action. Assault, battery, and personal affront were a matter of private prosecution until Sulla's *lex de iniuriis*. There was in any case no public prosecutor at Rome: the gap was filled in varying ways according to the procedure used—by magistrates such as the tribune or aedile in an assembly, by wronged parties or their relatives, or, in the majority of *quaestiones perpetuae* and certain trials before *recuperatores*, where it was permitted to bring actions on behalf of the Roman people or of other injured individuals, by private citizens for a variety of motives. These included public spirit, the promotion of a public career, and the pursuit of a private feud.[4] This is a key factor in the understanding of Roman criminal law. As for penalties, that under the *lex de iniuriis* seems to have been paid to the person harmed. The *quaestio de repetundis* was established to compensate people—especially, if not invariably, non-citizens—for unjust exactions by Roman magistrates and pro-magistrates, and the original penalty was the transfer of money back from the guilty man to those he had wronged. In this court for a period after C. Gracchus' legislation not only the introduction of a prosecution but its conduct in court essentially belonged to the wronged individual himself; later, cases were entrusted to a prosecutor by the court—in practice, it seems to a Roman *patronus*. The monetary penalty was doubled to create a penal element, and ultimately a further penalty to the people, in the form of exile, was paid for particularly heinous offences. Nevertheless, in the Principate actions according to the shortened process introduced by the *SC Calvisianum*

---

[3] Richardson, 1983.
[4] On actions before *recuperatores* see Schmidlin, 1963; Lintott, 1990, and *JRLR* 13–14; 29–30.

under Augustus had resemblances to a civil suit about property.[5] If we look at the development of criminal law under the Republic, we can see the private pursuit of revenge or compensation in parallel with, or sometimes overlapping, the pursuit of crimes by public authority. With the passage of time the importance of public authority increases without eclipsing the private pursuit of wrongs, and in any case those who are entrusted by public authority with the conduct of a prosecution are often not magistrates, nor some kind of professional official, but private citizens.

Not surprisingly, in view of what has just been said, there was never an organized corpus of Roman criminal law. In the Twelve Tables, to judge from the surviving fragments, there could be found a series of penal actions,[6] which were inadequate to deal with the complexity of possible offences, especially political ones, which the growth of the city entailed. In the last two centuries of the Republic there was a flood of legislation about criminal matters, but these dealt with only single crimes or groups of crimes. Indeed some crimes were the subject of a succession of laws, for example the *leges de repetundis*. As Tacitus flippantly remarked (*Ann.* 3. 27), when public affairs were at their worst, there were most laws. These were principally concerned with crimes committed by magistrates and senators in their public capacities, but also extended to matters like murder, violence, and forgery perpetrated by any person.

The Early Republican Background

While the surviving fragments of legal texts are in many ways the most solid literary evidence we possess from early Rome, any detailed account of the development of the criminal law of that period will largely be speculation. The account here will be a brief one, intended both to furnish the necessary background to the law of Polybius' lifetime and of the late Republic and, like the preceding survey of the tradition about the early stages of the constitution (Chap. III), to shed light on the Romans' own understanding of their past. The evidence suggests that there was at Rome a progression from the regulation of private revenge and retaliation, especially that performed by kinship groups, to the conduct of public investigation and the enforcement of publicly sanctioned

---

[5] See Lintott, 1981, and *JRLR* 12–32, with the bibliography cited there, and for the *SC Calvisianum SEG* ix. 8 = *FIRA* i. 410 ff.

[6] *RS* ii. 40, *Tab.* I. 13–21, VIII. 8–10, 13, 23–24a, IX. 1–6 (= *Tab.* VIII, 1–24 in *FIRA* i).

procedure and penalties. The laws attributed to king Numa show a distinction being made between deliberate murder, which is probably declared to be the same as the killing of one's kin, and unintentional or involuntary homicide: compensation was to be made for the latter to the dead person's blood-relations by the formal sacrifice of a ram.[7] The Twelve Tables permitted a thief who came by night or one who defended himself with a weapon to be killed on the spot, while recommending that neighbours should be summoned to witness this act. For other forms of theft, where guilt was established before a public authority, a range of penalties was instituted, including subjection to the injured party as a bondsman (*addici*).[8] In matters of personal injury, the Twelve Tables prescribed exact retaliation (*talio*) for the maiming of a limb unless an agreement for compensation was made, and a range of financial penalties for lesser injuries.[9] All these provisions presuppose actions brought by injured parties probably according to a procedure similar to those used for civil actions of that time (*legis actiones*), which would have been the equivalent then of the civil actions provided by the praetor in the late Republic to deal with such offences. Regarding murder, arson, and other capital offences there survive from the Twelve Tables regulations for execution of the guilty in a manner fitting the crime, with no indication of the preceding form of trial. It has been recently plausibly suggested that these too were prosecuted by a form of civil law procedure.[10] However, the traditional view has been that these capital crimes were prosecuted by magistrates before the assembly, in the same way that offenders against the community as a whole were.[11]

Now there can be little doubt that trials of those held to be guilty of treason (*perduellio*) were held in an assembly at the time of the Twelve Tables, as later in the Republic. The question is whether this procedure was required by statute or customary law for all capital charges. The passage of Polybius concerning his own time, in which it is stated that 'the people judges alone on a capital charge', has been shown to be inconsistent with what he says elsewhere (and indeed with the practice

---

[7] Festus, 247L; Serv. *Ecl.* 4. 43; *Tab.* IX. 4 (*RS* ii. 40, p. 702) = *FIRA* i, *Tab.* VIII. 24. On these texts see Cloud, 1971. The assimilation of murder to kin-murder is denied by Thomas, 1981, 676–9.

[8] *RS* ii. 40, *Tab.* I. 17–21 = *FIRA* i, *Tab.* VIII. 12–16.

[9] *RS* ii. 40, *Tab.* I. 13–15 = *FIRA* i, *Tab.* VIII. 2–4.

[10] *RS* ii. 40, *Tab.* VIII. 4–6, 12 = *FIRA* i, *Tab.* VIII. 8–10, 23; Kunkel, 1962, 97 ff.

[11] *Staatsr.* i. 162 ff.; ii. 1. 301 ff.; 538 ff.; 615 ff.; iii. 351 ff.; *Strafr.* 151 ff.; Strachan-Davidson, 1912, i. 152 ff.; Greenidge, 1901, 319 ff.

of that period), unless we understand it to refer to 'those who have held the highest offices' mentioned at the end of the preceding sentence.[12] More important is the provision of the Twelve Tables that '*privilegia*' should not be proposed to the assembly and that no proposal should be made concerning the *caput* of a citizen (in Roman law *caput* means not merely the life of a citizen but his existence as a citizen), except in 'the greatest' or 'very great assembly'. The last phrase was taken by Cicero to mean the *comitia centuriata*, though originally it may have meant no more than a fully attended assembly. The *privilegia* clause, however it was precisely formulated, was understood by Cicero to forbid condemnation by legislation without the full procedure of a trial.[13] Mommsen believed that this clause required that any capital trial should take place in the *comitia centuriata*. But it has been powerfully argued against his view that, although this clause prevented any decision by an assembly other than the *comitia centuriata* on the application of a capital penalty to a citizen, it carried no implications for other forms of judgement.[14] Moreover, if no reference had in fact been intended to the *comitia centuriata* specifically, the original law would have regulated assembly procedure only. It should be stressed that the clause was still regarded as valid by Cicero in the heyday of the capital judgements made by the *quaestiones perpetuae*.

As we have seen, in the early Republic there were magistrates called *quaestores parricidii* who were said to have investigated crimes (the term '*parricidium*' seems originally to have meant the murder of a member of one's kinship group and was then extended to the murder of any free man).[15] Livy portrays quaestors actually prosecuting before the assembly, but in one case the tradition is a variant, in the other no trial actually occurred, and on neither occasion was the charge murder. It is doubtful whether these accounts have any value, nor would they, even if true, warrant the conclusion that this was the only method of trial

---

[12] Pol. 6. 14. 6, cf. 13. 4, 16. 1–2, and see above, Chap. III with n. 18; Lintott, 1972, 257–8.

[13] *RS* ii. 40, *Tab.* IX. 1–2 (pp. 696 ff.); Cic. *Leg.* 3. 11 and 44; *Rep.* 2. 61; *Dom.* 45; *Sest.* 65. On *maximus comitiatus* see now Gabba, 1987, arguing that *comitiatus* seems to mean the gathering of the people for an assembly, while *comitia* means the assembly so formed. A possible parallel to this phrase is *dēmos plēthuōn*, a fully attended assembly, found frequently in an archaic Athenian law about the powers of the Council, re-engraved in the fifth century (*IGi.*³ 105, 25, 39–43). Bleicken (1959, 352 ff.) first suggested that the *privilegia* clause was directed specifically against trials held in the *concilium plebis*.

[14] Heuss, 1944, 115 ff.; Bleicken, 1959, 352 ff.; Kunkel, 1962, 31 ff.; cf. Lintott, 1972, 227.

[15] Varro, *LL* 5. 81, and see Chap. VIII with nn. 49 ff. On the meaning of *parricidium* I follow the view of Cloud, 1971.

available to these magistrates.[16] They were perhaps regularly appointed 'investigators', as their name suggests, who acted as criminal judges, rather than prosecutors.

There was also a pair of magistrates appointed to indict men with treason (*perduellio*). The evidence about these is equally tenuous and enigmatic. In Livy's story of the unification of Rome and Alba Longa under king Tullus Hostilius, in which the duel between the Horatii and the Curiatii is critical, one outcome of the Roman victory is the murder of his sister by Publius Horatius and his subsequent indictment, not for murder, but for *perduellio*. The king creates 'according to the law' *duumviri*. In the '*lex horrendi carminis*' that follows they are instructed to indict, or perhaps condemn (the Latin term is *iudico*) Horatius; if he uses *provocatio* from the *duumviri*, there is to be a contest by, or with, *provocatio*. If the *duumviri* prevail, his head is to be covered, he is to be hanged from an unlucky tree and beaten either inside or outside the *pomerium*. In the story Horatius actually pleads to the people through *provocatio* and obtains acquittal.[17] The only certain historical example of a trial by *duumviri* is an oddity, being the accusation of C. Rabirius engineered by Caesar and Labienus in 63 on the charge of having participated in the lynching of the tribune Saturninus in 100. On this occasion the *lex horrendi carminis* was revived by plebiscite, except that no opportunity seems to have been given for the accused to defend himself, and Rabirius was only saved by *provocatio* resulting in some sort of obstruction to the process, perhaps by a friendly tribune.[18] It seems likely that in the early Republic accusations of *perduellio* were entrusted to *duumviri*, who were probably not a standing magistracy but chosen for the occasion. However, when their function was taken over by the tribunes of the plebs, only a (possibly garbled) version of the *lex horrendi carminis* survived as testimony to the early procedure. In this the *duumviri* were permitted to condemn a defendant out of hand, but, if he used *provocatio*, they had to justify their decision before the people.

From the third century century BC onwards—to judge from the

---

[16] Livy, 2. 41. 11; 3. 24. 3. In Pliny *HN* 34. 13, where a quaestor is said to have charged Camillus with embezzlement, it seems to be a quaestor of the treasury who is believed to have acted.

[17] Livy, 1. 26. esp. 5–8; *Staatsr.* ii. 1. 615 ff.

[18] Cic. *Rab. Perd.* esp. 10, 12, 17, 32; Suet. *Jul.* 12; Dio, 37. 26–27; Gelzer, *RE* 7 A. 1 (1939), 870 ff; Strachan-Davidson, 1912, 188 ff.; Santalucia, 1984—arguing that the procedure was summary and an exception to the regular jurisdiction in capital cases exercised by the *quaestores parricidii*. See Lintott, 1972, 261–2, and Chap. IV above, with nn. 26–30, for the view of *provocatio* taken here. For an overview of these problems see Santalucia, 1998, 29 ff.

stories in Livy and the text of the Oscan law on the Bantine tablet—if not earlier, crimes against the people, both capital and non-capital, were prosecuted in assemblies by tribunes, aediles, and quaestors (capital charges being for the most part reserved for tribunes).[19] The procedure involved was elaborate and initiated by a magistrate. He formally announced to the defendant (*diem dicere*) a date for a first hearing, after obtaining auspices for the assembly from the praetor.[20] Apart from ensuring the religious rectitude of the proceedings, this would have enabled the praetor to ensure that the trial did not clash with anything else of importance in the forum. The trial began with a *contio* devoted to *anquisitio* (investigation) in which speeches for the prosecution and defence were made; two similar *contiones* followed (each separated from the preceding one by at least one clear day), in which further speeches were made and evidence was given; then, after the interval of a *trinundinum* (at least three market-days), a vote was held in a formal assembly. Any fault or interruption in this formal assembly through inauspicious omens vitiated the whole process and entailed that it could only be revived from the beginning. A description of similar procedure in the Oscan law, perhaps taken by Bantia from the constitution of the Latin colony of Venusia, refers to five parts of the action, that is four *contiones* before the final assembly, which was held after a thirty-day interval. This is evidently a variant of the procedure used at Rome. Whether the procedure at Rome had been so elaborate always, and in every type of assembly trial, we do not know.[21]

Mommsen believed that this form of legal process evolved from that described in the Horatius story, and that in principle the processes were identical: they were two-part trials, linked by *provocatio*, in the first part of which (the three *contiones*) the magistrate arrived at a verdict, while in

---

[19] See e.g. Livy, 25. 2. 11–3. 7; 26. 3; 37. 57. 7–58. 12; *lex osca Bant.* (*RS* i. 13), 12ff. The '*commentarium vetus anquisitionis*' portrays a capital accusation by a quaestor (Varro, *LL* 6. 90–1); Cn. Pompeius may have conducted his accusation of Q. Fabius as a quaestor (Oros. 5. 16. 8, whose use of *diem dicere* is, however, not Cicero's and thus a reliable guide to the nature of the process); for a possible later example see Lintott, 1971a.

[20] Varro, *LL* 6. 91; Livy, 26. 3. 9; 43. 16 11.

[21] Cic. *Dom.* 45; *Sest.* 65; QF 2. 3. 1–2, 6. 4; App. *B Civ.* 1. 74. 342; *lex osca Bant.* (*RS* i. 13), 12–18. *RS* i takes 'quarta sit actio trinundinum prodicta die' (Cic. *Dom.* 45) to mean 'there should be a fourth accusation and at that time a day should be fixed in advance for the vote', not '. . . after a day has been fixed in advance'—a forced effort to reconcile the Cicero text and the *lex osca*. In fact it is clear from Livy, 26. 3, that at Rome there were only three *actiones* before the final legal action and vote (Appian, loc. cit., talks of four summonses). Cic. *QF* 2. 3. 1 shows a defence speech at the first *actio* (*contio*). For witnesses see Livy, 25. 3. 16; 26. 3. 5; 37. 57. 13–14; Val. Max. 6. 1. 7. On *trinundinum* see Lintott, 1965. Livy, 25. 2, however, suggests a vote after only a single day's trial.

the second part this judgement was referred to the people.[22] However, later scholars pointed out correctly that there is no trace of this sort of division, nor any evidence for the use of *provocatio*, in assembly-trials as we find them in the middle and late Republic.[23] The explanation offered by some scholars for this,[24] that *provocatio* was in principle illegal against a judicial verdict, conflicts with a statement by Cicero about the Twelve Tables—that they allowed *provocatio* from every judgement and penalty—and also with the proposals in the late Republic to allow *provocatio* against the verdicts of *quaestiones perpetuae*.[25] *Provocatio*, together with tribunician obstruction, seems to have been in fact illegal in such courts, not through some unwritten fundamental principle, but through specific clauses in the laws that established them.[26] On the other hand, the absence of *provocatio* in the course of assembly-trials may be explained by practical considerations, inasmuch as the procedure itself guaranteed a popular verdict and it would have been pointless to contest this by *provocatio*, nor would tribunes uninvolved in the prosecution have supported an appeal against the verdict.[27]

By the beginning of the second century trials before the assembly were the community's sanction against cowardice, imcompetence, and corrupt behaviour by its former magistrates, as Polybius pointed out. There were also a number of less grave offences, in some cases against specific laws, prosecuted by the aediles.[28] A number of crimes against the individual, such as theft and bodily injury, would still be prosecuted by civil procedure, as at the time of the Twelve Tables, and the penalty was paid to the injured party.[29] How were capital crimes, such as murder, arson, and witchcraft, treated?

The traditional view has been that these were prosecuted in an assembly, since other forms of procedure would have been violations of the *provocatio* laws. This view has continued to be held by scholars who believed that *provocatio* was not an integral part of an assembly trial. However, Kunkel developed a series of arguments of varying merit to

    [22] *Staatsr.* i, 162 ff.; ii. 1. 301 ff.; iii. 351 ff.; *Strafr.* 161 ff.
    [23] Brecht, 1939, 300 ff.; Heuss, 1944, 106 ff.; Bleicken, 1959, 332 ff.; Kunkel, 1962, 21 ff.; Lintott, 1972, 226–7.
    [24] Heuss, 1944, 119 ff.; Bleicken, 1959, 348 ff.; Kunkel, 1962, 27 ff.
    [25] Cic. *Rep.* 2. 54; Plut. *Ti. Gr.* 16. 1; Cic. *Phil.* 1. 21; Martin, 1970; Lintott, 1972, 228, 238 ff.
    [26] *Lex rep.* 70–72 with *JRLR* 149; *lex lat. Bant.* (*RS* i. 7), 7 ff. See Chap. VIII n. 26 above.
    [27] Lintott, 1972, 237 ff.
    [28] Pol. 6. 14. 6, on which see above with n. 12; Chap. VIII with nn. 41 ff.
    [29] For the usual penalty being *addictio* of the criminal as a bondsman of the injured party see Livy, 23. 14. 2–3; *ORF*, no. 8, fr. 224 = Gell. 11. 18. 18; Plaut. *Rud.* 888–91; Plut. *Cato mi.* 2. 6; Kunkel, 1962, 97 ff.

suggest that matters like murder were usually handled by a magistrate acting with a *consilium* of advisers as a jury.[30] First, it is clear that trial by magistrate and jury in the *quaestio perpetua* of the late Republic, where *provocatio* was forbidden, was not regarded as a fundamental breach of the Roman constitution. Secondly, during a period preceding and concurrent with the *quaestio perpetua* we find a number of other *quaestiones*—special tribunals under magistrates set up by law or *senatus consultum* to deal with mass lawbreaking or some other unusual crime (see below). It seems that *provocatio* did not take place, but no one objected to the tribunals on that ground. Thirdly, there is evidence that cases of murder and carrying an offensive weapon were denounced to the *tresviri capitales*, who we know had some sort of judicial powers.[31] Fourthly, given the cumbersome nature of trial before the assembly, only a few cases of this sort could be handled each year, which would mean that there were inadequate sanctions against some of the most serious crimes against the individual.

Kunkel's view that trials by a magistrate with the aid of a panel of assessors (*consilium*), which he had selected himself, were transformed by the mere presence of the *consilium* into a procedure not subject to *provocatio* (on the ground that *provocatio* was only possible against *coercitio*, the unmediated exercise of a magistrate's power against a person) is in conflict with the evidence (see above, with n. 25) and has been shown to misrepresent the relationship between the magistrate and such a panel. Kunkel's *consilium* has the authority of a judge or jury, but when a magistrate delivered a verdict, 'having consulted his *consilium*', the *consilium* was not a jury: it was the magistrate's decision: the views of the panel would normally influence that decision and provide him with moral support, if he followed them, but if the verdict was subsequently contested, it was the magistrate who took the blame—for example Popillius Laenas, Opimius, and, by analogy, Cicero.[32] It does not, however, follow that prosecution of a capital crime by a magistrate with a panel of assessors was illegal. This was only true if he disregarded *provocatio*, and there might be no appeal or it might fall on unsympathetic ears, so that neither the tribunes or the people themselves offered support. This was the likely outcome when common criminals were convicted.[33]

[30] Kunkel, 1962, 59 ff.; expanded in Kunkel, 1967 and 1968.

[31] Chap. VIII with nn. 87–8, 93–4. *Iudicare* is specifically mentioned as a function of the *triumviri* in the *lex Papiria* (*RS* ii. 45).

[32] Brunt, 1964; Garnsey, 1966; Lintott, 1972, 228, 259–62; *VRR* 165 ff.

[33] Lintott, 1972, esp. 238 ff.

Hence there is no objection in principle to holding that, just as the Bacchanals were tried on capital charges by specially appointed magistrates,[34] so too in the normal course of events murderers, arsonists, and witches were tried by magistrates as part of their regular duties after prosecutions by private individuals. These in the early Republic may have been the *quaestores parricidii*; later the task fell to the *triumviri capitales* (though it remains a problem whether these could on their own authority condemn a free citizen to death) or conceivably one of the praetors, as has been most recently suggested.[35] This does not exclude the possibility that some capital crimes against individual citizens were indeed tried in an assembly, as has been traditionally held. We are told that Cn. Pompeius Strabo, quaestor in 104 or 103, prosecuted Q. Fabius Maximus for killing his own young son. This appears to be a prosecution before an assembly, though we cannot put too much trust in the language of our one late source.[36] However, there cannot have been many trials before an assembly in any year and, in spite of criticism by Nippel and Jones,[37] there still seems to be force in Kunkel's argument that it would have made the repression of crime difficult, if this was the only way of proceeding against those charged with capital crimes. Nippel is right to point out that we should not seek to impute our current standards of law-enforcement and concern for criminality to the Romans. He assumes that the only opinion that mattered at that time was that of the élite, who were able to protect themselves with their slaves and clients. However, in fact the members of the plebs themselves would have suffered from violent criminal behaviour and had a greater influence on Roman politics then than the English common people in the eighteenth century. The ordinary Roman had to be his own policeman,[38] but he would have needed a reasonably accessible procedure to deal with capital crimes.

Finally, we should notice that in some political cases, where a capital trial of a group of offenders was carried out by a magistrate outside the city without reference to an assembly, the matter was referred to an assembly before the sentence was carried out. Such was the fate of the

---

[34] Livy, 39. 14 ff.; 40. 37. 4 and 43. 2–3.

[35] On the *quaestores* and *tresviri* see Varro, *LL* 5. 81; Val. Max. 5. 4. 7; Chap. VIII with nn. 87–8, 93–4; Kunkel, 1962, 70 ff.; Brunt, 1964; for the praetor as a criminal judge Mantovani, 1990, criticized as excessively speculative by Garofalo, 1990, but Mantovani's hypothesis cannot be confidently excluded.

[36] Oros. 5. 16. 8.

[37] Nippel, 1995, 25 ff.; Jones, 1972, 19.

[38] Nippel, 1995, 16 ff.; Lintott, 1968, 11 ff.

rebellious garrison of Rhegium in 270, the Campanian rebels in 210, and Q. Pleminius and the others involved in the Locri scandal in 205. We have no direct evidence of *provocatio*, but in two of the instances there was tribunician intervention. This illustrates how a capital sentence could be inflicted without recourse to a four-part assembly trial even in a matter of treason, but also how some respect could be accorded to the rights of the accused.[39]

The Development of the Law in the Later Republic

The change in the nature of Roman criminal law in the second century BC hinges on the growth of the *quaestio*. The term means originally 'inquiry', but it acquired in this period, in addition to its abstract sense, the concrete meaning of 'investigating tribunal' or 'court'. In the first place we find *quaestiones* set up by the senate, in which a magistrate or magistrates 'investigate', i.e. try, a capital crime of special importance.[40] Such were the inquiries into the Bacchanalian conspiracies, the women poisoners, and the murders in the Silva Sila.[41] These trials took place in public, but there is no evidence of any of the condemned using *provocatio*.

We also find *quaestiones* set up by plebiscite, sometimes on the advice of the senate, sometimes not, to 'investigate' misconduct by magistrates.[42] Again, we hear nothing of *provocatio* by defendants against the verdicts in these trials, but in one version of the trial of L. Scipio, there was an appeal to the tribunes against the execution of the verdict.[43] It is possible that the enabling laws forbade *provocatio*, but in any case the fact that the procedure had in each case been established by plebiscite would have made it more difficult for a defendant to claim that an injustice had been done. However, this was not the only experiment in bringing delinquent magistrates to book in the period preceding the first *quaestio perpetua*. On one occasion, in 171, when a Spanish embassy denounced three former governors of Spain in the senate for illegal exactions and humiliating treatment, a special form of civil procedure

[39] Val. Max. 2. 7. 15; Dion. Hal. *AR* 20. 16. 1–2; Livy, 26. 33; 29. 20–22; 34. 44. 6–8; cf. Pol. 6. 16. 1. See Lintott, 1972, 240–3.

[40] *Strafr.* 186 ff.; Strachan-Davidson, 1912, i. 225 ff.; Siber, 1942, 376–80; Kunkel, 1962, 45 ff., and *RE* 24 (1963), 720 ff.; Lintott, 1972, 253 ff.

[41] *FIRA* i, no. 30; Livy, 39. 14 ff.; 40. 37. 4 and 43. 2–3; *Per.* 48; Cic. *Brut.* 85 ff.

[42] Livy, 38. 54. 2–55. 8 (on which see Fraccaro, 1911; Gruen, 1995); 42. 21. 8–22. 8; Cic. *Fin.* 2. 54; 4. 77; *ND* 3. 74; *Brut.* 127–8, 160; Sall. *Jug.* 40; Asc. 45–6C; Val. Max. 2. 5. 3; 3. 7. 9.

[43] See Chap. VIII with n. 22; Scullard, 1973, Appendix 4.

before a panel of five *recuperatores* was provided for them; a similar procedure may have been used against provincial governors condemned in the 150s.[44]

The *quaestiones* so far considered have all been *ad hoc* creations, intended to remedy specific instances of criminal behaviour. However, there is good evidence (beginning in 142) of *quaestiones* dealing with bandits (*sicarii*) or with poisoners or witches (*venefici*) on a regular basis before Sulla's *lex Cornelia* reformed these courts;[45] similar *quaestiones* seem to have existed to deal with electoral bribery (*ambitus*) and embezzlement (*peculatus*).[46] These early regular *quaestiones* seem to have followed the traditional form of a magistrate investigating with the aid of a *consilium* of advisers. The magistrate controlled the trial and delivered the verdict himself. Nor was he restricted by the elaborate rules controlling the whole conduct of the trial, which characterized the *quaestiones perpetuae* that were to be created by C. Gracchus and later legislators. [47]

It was the development of the *quaestio de repetundis*, the court which dealt with the recovery of money illicitly obtained by Romans in authority, that provided the model for other permanent criminal tribunals. According to Cicero, the *lex Calpurnia de repetundis* in 149 established the first *quaestio perpetua* (that is, a tribunal permanently established by statute, which had to be automatically called into being by the appropriate magistrate each year).[48] What little we know about this and a subsequent law, the *lex Iunia*, derives from the text of the *lex repetundarum* which superseded them, that preserved on the bronze fragments from Urbino. It appears that the penalty was simple restitution and the form of procedure was the ancient civil process called *legis actio sacramento*.[49] This form of action was transformed by the *lex repetundarum* engraved on the bronze tablet, which powerful arguments require us to identify as part of C. Gracchus' legislation.[50] The new pro-

---

[44] Livy, 43. 2; *Per.* 47. Note also the prosecution of L. Lentulus Lupus 'under the Caecilian Law' in the same period (Val. Max. 6. 9. 10—emended by Mommsen, *Strafr.* 708, to refer to the 'Calpurnian Law', but this can be no more than a possibility). On the prehistory of the *quaestio de repetundis* see Venturini, 1969; Lintott, 1981, 164–76; *JRLR* 11–16.

[45] Cic. *Fin.* 2. 54; 4. 77; *ND* 3. 74; Asc. 45C on Cic. *Mil.* 32; *ILS* 45; *Ad Herenn.* 4. 47 and 53; Cic. *Inv.* 2. 60; *Rosc Am.* 11, 64–5, 90.

[46] Plut. *Mar.* 5. 3–10; Cic. *de Or.* 2. 274; Plut. *Pomp.* 4. 1–6.

[47] Kunkel, 1962, 45 ff.; *RE* 24 (1963), 720 ff.

[48] *Brut.* 106; *Off.* 2. 75; *Verr.* 3. 195; 4. 56.

[49] *Lex rep.* 23, 74, 81, with *JRLR* 14 ff. and the commentary ad locc.

[50] A summary of the arguments in *JRLR* 166 ff.

cedure marks an epoch in the growth of criminal law; its chief features are as follows.

Each year a praetor was instructed to select an album of jurors, 450 strong, from which a panel of 50 were to be created for each case by a mixture of selection and rejection by the parties concerned. These jurors were to be drawn from the equestrian order, and they were not to have held minor magistracies or have any close kinship with any senator. The praetor presided over the court and was required to ensure that the procedure laid down in the statute (in minute detail) was correctly followed, but the verdict both in the main trial and in the subsequent assessment of damages was delivered by the jury, a simple majority being decisive. Summons was a matter for the injured parties or their representatives: in particular it was open to non-citizens. It did not involve the ritual formulae associated with *legis actiones*, but was carried out by denunciation to the praetor (*nominis delatio*). Once the charge was accepted, any plaintiff could be assigned a *patronus* by the court, if he so wished, but he continued to play an important part in the proceedings himself. It was understood that a particular prosecution could cover wrongs to a number of different people. If a verdict of guilty was returned, a further investigation was carried out to assess the damages owed to the various parties with complaints (*litis aestimatio*). Damages were assessed at double the loss, thus introducing a penal element. Moreover, successful prosecutors were offered rewards, full Roman citizenship for those who did not possess it or, alternatively, *provocatio* and freedom from military service and compulsory public duties in their communities.[51]

It is not the place here to discuss the political implications of the law and its effectiveness in bringing redress to the injured. In practice, even before Sulla's reforms, further statutes changed the procedure for bringing charges, with the effective result that prosecution before the jury was undertaken by a Roman orator on behalf of the injured party or parties, and the scope of the court was extended to the receipt of bribes, so that from then on not all actions were suits to recover money lost.[52] Nevertheless, the structure of the court remained essentially the same and it seems to have been imitated by L. Saturninus when he created the '*quaestio de maiestate*' in 103 (or 100)—concerning the diminution of the majesty of the Roman people either by military failure or misconduct in relation to political institutions at home, that is, treason against the

---

[51] See the summary in *JRLR* 16 ff.; Lintott, 1981, 178 ff.; Sherwin-White, 1982.

[52] *JRLR* 25 ff. and Lintott, 1981, deal with this in greater detail.

Roman people.[53] It is possible that this procedure may have been extended to the *quaestiones de ambitu* and *de peculatu* (n. 46 above) before Sulla's reforms. The important difference between these other courts and the *quaestio de repetundis* lay in the fact that in them there was no resemblance to civil procedure, since a penalty was pursued, not the recovery of money, and the prosecution was probably from the start open to any Roman citizen (the injured party was of course the people as a whole).

The reforms carried out by Sulla as dictator in 81 reorganized the existing criminal *quaestiones* on the model provided by the *quaestio de repetundis*, and in addition created new tribunals to deal with forgery and *iniuriae*.[54] Sulla's policy of entrenching the power of the senate led to smaller juries drawn from this body alone, but this element in the reforms was overthrown by the *lex Aurelia* of 70, and the last years of the Republic saw juries of over fifty in number—senators, *equites*, and *tribuni aerarii*—selected by a mixture of allotment and rejection by the parties.[55] A new court was established to deal with violence in a public context by the *lex Lutatia* of 78 and reformed by a *lex Plautia*, probably of 70.[56] Two further *leges de ambitu* were passed in the sixties (the second by Cicero and his consular colleague Antonius); these were followed in 55 by Crassus' law *de sodaliciis*, concerning the exploitation of associations and political clubs for bribery and violence, and in 52 by Pompey's *lex de ambitu*.[57] Pompey meanwhile had passed a law about *parricidium*.[58] In 65 a *lex Papia* established a *quaestio* to deal with the improper acquisition of citizenship: it possibly introduced penalties other than the loss of the citizenship illegally assumed.[59] Nor should we forget Caesar's massive *lex Iulia de repetundis* of 59.[60] Some modifications were made to the jurors and procedure in *quaestiones* under Caesar's dictatorship, while Augustus, apart from revising procedure in *quaestiones*, created

    [53] Ferrary, 1983.

    [54] Cloud, *CAH* ix, 2nd edn., 1994, 514–28. On the *lex de iniuriis* see Just. *Inst.* 4. 4. 8; *Dig.* 3. 3. 42. 1; 47. 10. 5–6; 48. 2. 12. 4; on the *lex de falsis (testamentaria)* Cic. 2*Verr.* 1. 108; Just. *Inst.* 4. 18. 7.

    [55] On senatorial juries see Cic. *Verr.* 1. 30; *Clu.* 74 (jury of 32); on the *lex Aurelia* Asc. 17C with *MRR* on 70 BC; on later juries Cic. *Att.* 1. 16. 3 and 5; Asc. 28, 39, 55C (Cic. *Planc.* 45 may refer to the pre-Sullan period); on *tribuni aerarii* Nicolet, 1966, i. 598 ff.; *Staatsr.* iii. 192, 533.   [56] Cic. *Cael.* 70–1; *Sest.* 89, 95; Sall. *Cat.* 31. 4; Asc. 55C; *VRR* 107 ff.

    [57] Lintott, 1990, 8–10.

    [58] *Dig.* 48. 9. 1; Cloud, 1971.

    [59] On the *lex Papia* see Cic. *Arch.* 10; *Balb.* 52; *Att.* 4. 18. 4; *Off.* 3. 47; Val. Max. 3. 4. 5 (impossible chronologically); Dio, 37. 9. 5. It is not clear whether the *lex Fabia de plagiariis* (Cic. *Rab. Perd.* 8; *Dig.* 48. 15; *RS* ii. 51) introduced a new *quaestio* for kidnapping.

    [60] *RS* ii. 55; *Dig.* 48. 11; Lintott, 1981, at 202–7; Venturini, 1987.

new courts. Under the Principate, although the use of these tribunals eventually declined in favour of investigation by a magistrate (called *cognitio*)—in effect a return to the earliest *quaestio* procedure—the cumulation of the substantive provisions of these statutes provided the closest approximation to a criminal code that Rome achieved.

At the same time as this there were important developments in trials before *recuperatores*. This term originally designated the jury in a civil action for recovery employed in circumstances where speed was important; later, trial before *recuperatores* came to be used as a sanction to enforce statutes. Prosecution was usually open to anyone who wished, as in most *quaestiones*, and there was a resemblance between the two procedures, although that before *recuperatores* was much more simple. The panel of *recuperatores* was formed by selection and rejection from a previously created album; there were rules about the summoning of witnesses and even in some instances rewards for accusers. The most remarkable example of this is in the Cnidos text of the law about praetorian provinces of 101–100 BC, where the full panoply of the procedure is merely deployed to ensure obedience to the wide variety of administrative measures contained in the statute.[61] Hence government was not only backed by the sanctions of the criminal law but by these administrative remedies.

Because our Ciceronian evidence tends to suggest that it was normal for a skilled orator or massive bribery to secure the acquittal of a guilty man, it is easy to think that the criminal law of the late Republic was ineffective. But that would be to underestimate the system of *quaestiones perpetuae*. About 50 per cent of those accused in the *quaestio de repetundis* on our evidence were in fact condemned,[62] which suggests a reasonable degree of severity, if we take into account lay juries and a system of prosecution which was not professional, however experienced certain orators were. This certainly contrasts with our evidence about the middle Republic, where there is no known instance of a man being condemned in a trial before an assembly on a capital charge. One feature of the system which contributed to severity was the absence of any form of appeal from *quaestiones perpetuae* (as indeed there was no appeal from a judge in a civil case)—something which Marcus Antonius was proposing to reform in 44 BC[63] and which would in due course be changed under

---

[61] *RS* i. 12, Cnidos V, 9 ff.; cf. *lex lat. Bant,* (*RS* i. 7) 9–11; *lex agr.* 37–9; *lex Iulia agraria (Mamilia)* (*RS* ii. 54), ch. 55; Schmidlin, 1963; Lintott, 1990*b*; Mantovani, 1989, 121 ff.

[62] See the table at the end of Lintott, 1981.

[63] Cic. *Phil.* 1. 21.

the Principate. This helps to explain why defendants from among the élite resorted to a battery of impressive defence counsel and other illegitimate means in order to secure acquittal at their trials. If all else failed, the worst effects of condemnation on a non-capital charge, the loss of property and reputation, could be mitigated by a timely retirement into voluntary exile.

X

The Influence of Society and Religion

Polybius understood that there was more to a *politeia* than political institutions. In his comparison of the Roman constitution with those of other peoples in their military aspects, he points to the importance of Roman funerals in inspiring courage and patriotism, while in relation to political life he stresses, first, Roman disapproval of profiteering through political corruption and, secondly, their serious attitude to religion.[1] Modern commentators have gone much further along this road, often being more interested in the sociology of the Roman republic than in its laws or constitutional norms. Since the groundbreaking work of M. Gelzer and Fr. Münzer[2] interest has been focused in particular on the relations between members of the aristocracy—on their modes of competition and the nature of their political alliances—and on the vertical links between the aristocracy and the plebs. The resulting studies have highlighted the governing class and within this the influence of the group, rather than the individual. It has been hard to accord to the plebs an investigation on the same scale, since our evidence makes only very generalized conclusions possible. Hence the overall trend has been to underline the aristocratic element in politics, to the extent that the democratic and monarchic elements that Polybius analysed are treated as something formal and mechanical, which could be manipulated by the dominant forces in the aristocracy.[3] It is true, as will appear, that Roman republican society was centred on the aristocracy; it is also true that in certain periods a circle of aristocrats did dominate Roman society politically. But the first proposition does not necessarily entail the second: it merely helps to explain how in certain circumstances it might be realized.

---

[1] Pol. 6. 53–54. 4; 56.

[2] Gelzer, 1912; Münzer, 1920.

[3] For discussions of this trend and the growing reaction against it see e.g. Lintott, *CAH* ix, 2nd edn., ch. 1; North, 1990*a* and 1990*b*; id., review of Brunt, 1988, *JRS* 79 (1989), 151–6. Useful comments on North's paper (1990*b*) may be found in Harris, 1990. For a restatement of Gelzer's views against in particular the criticisms of Millar (1984 and 1986) see Burckhardt, 1990.

Aristocratic Families and their Values

Sallust, in a well-known passage of a speech put on the lips of Gaius Marius, claimed that the majority of those elected consuls who subsequently performed badly had been supported by 'ancient nobility, the gallant exploits of their ancestors, the resources springing from their maternal connections and their marriages, and their numerous *clientelae*'. In the same vein Cicero refers to 'those born of noble family, on whom all the benefits of the Roman people are conferred while they sleep.'[4] It appears from their reconstruction of the early Republic (Chap. IV), that the Romans believed the patriciate to have formed a closed aristocracy, which was eventually forced to yield its virtual monopoly of the supreme offices of the city in the fourth century BC. After this surrender, a new aristocracy developed which was no longer closed. Descent from a family already renowned was always a great advantage, a certain amount of wealth was a *sine qua non*. Yet the ascent to the highest magistracy proceeded through popular elections, and success there required at least some evidence of personal excellence and achievement, *virtus* and *facta*. This success could in turn be transmitted to future generations of a family as a support in their careers and an example. Here there was a potential source of corruption, to which Sallust and Cicero allude: ancestral achievements and status were no guarantee of the *virtus* of the man currently seeking election.

The patrician families were an important, but not a particularly privileged group within this aristocracy. From 342 they had access to only one of the consulships available each year (Chap. IV with n. 42). By contrast, the *lex Ogulnia*, which divided the major priesthoods between patricians and plebeians (Chap. IV, with n. 46), although it originally had diminished the influence of patricians, by the later Republic must have had the opposite effect of entrenching their influence in an important sector of political life. The institution of the *interregnum* (Chap. IV, with n. 20, Chap. VI with n. 11) was the one occasion when the patricians functioned collectively: if by chance no consul, praetor, or dictator was alive in office, the patricians met to select from among their number an *interrex*, or rather a series of *interreges*, who each held office for five days and were responsible for maintaining and transmitting *imperium* and the auspices to properly elected magistrates as soon as possible. Although the priesthood of the Salii was reserved for patricians and there

---

[4] Sall. *Jug.* 85. 4; Cic. *Verr.* 5. 180; *Leg. Agr.* 2. 100.

may have been other religious *sodalitates* of a similar kind, we have no evidence from the middle and late Republic of political associations which were exclusively patrician. Nor did patrician families in this period attempt to maintain *de facto* the rule rescinded by the *lex Canuleia* by intermarrying only with other families of their kind.[5]

We must now consider how far the exclusive aristocracy of the patricians, which Romans held to have dominated the early Republic, was supplanted by another drawn from both patrician and plebeian families, whose members monopolized access to high office and authority in the senate. Sallust portrays the later aristocracy, the *nobilitas* of the Republic, exercising the same dominance of the consulship as the early patricians. They passed it from hand to hand, thinking it polluted if a new man, however excellent, obtained it; the plebs were confined to other magistracies. Moreover, in the period of the Jugurthine War they are said 'to have prevailed through *factio*', 'so that matters at home and abroad were decided by a few, and the same men had in their power the treasury, provinces, magistracies, glory, and triumphs'.[6]

Factio is not a simple equivalent to the modern word 'faction'. In Roman comedy it means the power that derives from wealth and social status.[7] In this last passage from Sallust's *Jugurtha*, it is contrasted with the dispersed power of the mass of the plebs and seems to indicate the concentration of individual influence in a narrow group through personal connections and intrigue. In an earlier passage in a speech attributed to the tribune C. Memmius the unifying force which derives from sharing the same desires, hates, and fears is said to be friendship among good men, *factio* among bad.[8] *Factio* is thus an abstract notion here, embracing the various forces which contribute to the solidarity and dominance of a corrupt oligarchy, not a term for a particular dominant group. Cicero in the *de Re Publica* gives the term the more specific sense

---

[5] On the *interregnum* see Jahn, 1970; on the Salii see Cic. *Dom.* 38; on the *lex Canuleia* Chap. IV with n. 36. Classic examples of patrician–plebeian intermarriages were those of Cornelia, daughter of Scipio Africanus, to Ti. Sempronius Gracchus (*cos.* 177)—famous as a good marriage (Livy, 38. 57. 2–8)—and of Scipio's grandson by adoption, Aemilianus, to Sempronia, the daughter of the marriage just mentioned. The earliest example recorded is in Livy 6. 34. 5.

[6] Sall. *Cat.* 23. 5; *Jug.* 63. 6–7, cf. *Cat.* 31. 7 (Catiline's jibe at Cicero); *Jug.* 41. 6–7.

[7] Plaut. *Aul.* 167, cf. 227; *Cist.* 493–4; *Trin.* 466–7, 491–9; Statius, *Plocium* 172Rib; Titinius, 108Rib; Turpilius, 208Rib.

[8] *Jug.* 31. 14–15, cf. 27. 2 for *factiosi*; *Cat.* 51. 40. See also Nonius, 304M; *Ad Herenn.* 1. 8; Caes. *BG* 8. 50. 2 and *BCiv.* 1. 22. 5 for *factio paucorum* (where *factio* means 'collective power'), and for other references and discussion Seager, 1972a.

of a narrow oligarchy which is the corrupt equivalent of an aristocracy, into which, on his (Platonic) theory, an aristocracy has a natural tendency to decline. However, in the cynical account of political justice Cicero puts in the mouth of Furius Philus, it is said that any rule by a small aristocratic group 'is *factio*, but they are called *optimates*'.[9] It should be emphasized that the discussion in *de Re Publica* is in a context where the Roman constitution is not identified with narrow oligarchic rule, but a mixed constitution (see below, Chap. XII). *Factio* can also mean a specific oligarchic group in the writings of Sallust and Caesar.[10] For Sallust the domination of a corrupt oligarchy is a sign of the Republic in decline in a particular period. He does not see several *factiones* in the aristocracy at one time, but a single *factio* against which individual popular leaders struggled with varying success. How far he was correct is a question which must be reserved for a final analysis of the Republic. Our present concern is with the effectiveness of the mechanics of aristocratic dominance, and it is clear that the mere deployment of the word *factio* by Roman writers is of limited value, because it is a vague and generalizing notion. We need to consider the alleged control of the consulship and the nature of aristocratic solidarity.

After the consulship was first regularly opened to plebeians in the fourth century (according to tradition, through the plebiscite of Licinius and Sextius, see Chap. IV with n. 41), and, later, one consulship was reserved for plebeians, a large number·of plebeian families were honoured by the election of their members to the consulate, some of which remained prominent till the end of the Republic. So we find the Fulvii, Atilii, and Claudii Marcelli making their first appearance in the *Fasti* already by 300 BC. In the third century, with a number of plebeian families by now established in the aristocracy, fewer new families reached the consulship, but among the latter were the Caecilii Metelli, the Domitii, Sempronii, Aurelii, Lutatii, and Licinii. There were also outstanding individuals like C. Fabricius Luscinus and M'. Curius Dentatus, whose families made no subsequent political impact. Nevertheless, new names form only about eight per cent of the total in the consular lists in the period between the Pyrrhic War and the the Second Punic War. How far these men had held office prior to the consulship is not known. Indeed their earlier tenure of the praetorship is the more questionable, in that down to the period of the First Punic War that office was

---

9 Cic. *Rep.* 1. 44 and 69; 3. 23 (Philus); 3. 44.
10 Caes. *BG* 1. 31. 3; 5. 56. 3; 6. 11. 5, 12. 1; Sall. *Jug.* 31. 4; *Hist.* 3. 48. 3 and 8.

frequently held after the consulship (Chap. VIII with n. 104). There was a similar percentage of new names in the consular *fasti* in the first half of the second century. Here our knowledge of the holders of the praetor-ship permits us to narrow the number of new holders of curule office to three.

A well-known analysis of the period from 232 to 133 BC shows that the 200 consulships were shared between 58 *gentes*, 26 of which accounted for 159 consulships, and ten of which accounted for 99, effectively half the total.[11] The use of the *gens* as an indicator of exclusivity is somewhat misleading, as by this time leading patrician and plebeian *gentes* had multiplied into a number of branches (*stirpes*). Nor in some cases can we be sure that those whom we take to be kin shared anything more than their *nomen*. Nevertheless, the analysis seems at first sight to confirm the statements we find in Sallust about the monopoly of the consulship by the men that the Romans termed *nobiles*, men with an ancestral connec-tion with that office. These were the men whose funerals Polybius found so impressive—though it is not clear whether it was only consular families that had the right to display their *imagines* (wax masks) both in their *atrium* at home and at funerals, or this privilege was accorded to all men who attained curule office and to their descendants: the latter seems more probable.[12] Gelzer argued for a definition of nobility as the possession of consular ascendants and this remains generally accepted. However, A. Afzelius ultimately only accepted this definition for the late Republic, believing that earlier it was coextensive with the possession of *ius imaginum* through curule office, while P. A. Brunt has argued for a somewhat less restrictive definition, including collaterals of former consuls, members of old patrician families and holders of priesthoods.[13] On any of these views the elective aristocracy of the Republic was self-perpetuating to a significant extent.

On the other hand, it was not an aristocracy which was formally closed and bounded by descent, and, in so far as it depended on popular election, it was competitive. If the figures just cited for the middle Republic suggest a fairly stable ruling group, this picture needs

---

[11] Scullard, 1973, 10–12.

[12] On *ius imaginum* see *Staatsr.* i. 442–7; Pol. 6. 53. 4–6; Pliny, *HN* 35, 6; Sen. *Ben.* 3. 28. 2; *Ep.* 44. 5. Cic. *Leg. Agr.* 2. 3 suggests that it was a reward for election to the consulship, but *Verr.* 5. 36 and *Rab. Post.* 16 imply that any curule office, even the aedileship, would do. The *elogium* of Scipio Hispanus (*ILLRP* 316) states that he obtained his nobility after office no higher than the praetorship. On *imagines* in general see now Flower, 1996 (*testimonia* collected at 281 ff.).

[13] Gelzer, 1912; Afzelius, 1938, modified in Afzelius, 1945; Brunt, 1982.

modifying. It was pointed out long ago that one quarter of the consuls elected between 178 and 82 came from families which had never produced a consul before (that is, from either branches of previously known *gentes* or completely new *gentes*). Recently K. Hopkins and G. P. Burton have shown that the number of *gentes* represented in the consular lists was considerably higher in the century from 132 to 33 BC than it was in the previous one hundred years.[14] Furthermore, this last study has demonstrated how far the Roman Republic was from possessing *de facto* an hereditary aristocracy. Of the consuls from 249 to 50 BC only 62 per cent were direct descendants in the male line from a consul, while another 7 per cent had consular collaterals. In fact, if the analysis is confined to the last century or so of the Republic the proportion is higher, but that is an unsurprising consequence of the multiplication of families which had reached the consulship previously. This is to look on the positive side, but the negative corollaries are just as important, though difficult to evaluate because of the lack of direct information about the rate of reproduction of Roman aristocrats. Only about 40 per cent of consular families showed three or more consuls in six generations, with another 20 per cent showing two consuls in succeeding generations. If we move outside what is termed the 'inner élite', that is, those consuls with consular fathers and grandfathers, it is likely that about a third of the sons of other consuls, who would have survived to age 40 in the period 249–195, did not become praetor or consul, and the same would have been true of 44 per cent of the sons of those who had not ascended beyond the praetorship, who would have survived to the same age.[15]

In other words, a considerable proportion of male members of consular families either chose not to pursue a political career as far as high office or failed in the attempt. Poor health, political incompetence or lack of electoral appeal are possible factors in either contingency; if a man chose to avoid a political career, it may have also been through lack of money or the need to concentrate on looking after the family's estates in order to avoid financial problems.[16] In any case, the result is an aristocracy in which there was both upward and downward mobility which, it is plausible to imagine, operated not only in the heart of the senatorial order but on its margins, so that there would have been frequent movement from equestrian to senatorial status and back.[17]

---

[14] Willems, 1878, i. 396; Hopkins and Burton, 1983, 53, tab. 2. 1.

[15] Hopkins and Burton, 1983, 57, 63–4 with tabs. 2: 3 and 2: 7.

[16] On the deliberate choice of a career different from those of one's ancestors see Cic. *Off.* 1. 116.   [17] Hopkins and Burton, 1983, 66 ff.

Thus, if we use the term self-perpetuation of the Roman aristocracy, this can only be understood in broad terms. Moreover, the implication of the mobility of families suggests that there was no very tight and rigid control over the electoral process by established families. Those which through accumulated success over the years had obtained great prestige were in a good position to secure future electoral success for their own members; the influence of those, whose hold on the consulship had lapsed or which had only recently attained this height, seems much more uncertain. Scholars who believe in the manipulation of elections in the interest of an oligarchy have been forced to postulate a wide ramification of connections between leading families and other families in the aristocracy. Moreover, in order to explain how the manipulation was successful, they have needed to assume strong vertical connections between the aristocracy and the plebs.

There can be little doubt that under the Republic powerful families supported their members who sought high office, with whatever resources they had available. A major function of the display of *imagines* at home was to stimulate the young to imitate their ancestors, and this was achieved even more forcefully on the occasion of funerals.[18] It was through *honores*, high office, and the display of *virtus* in these offices that a family achieved distinction in the public eye, termed *gloria* or *fama*. This is well illustrated in the epitaphs of the Scipiones, where the magistracies and the military victories are cited as testimony to the virtue of the really distinguished, whereas those who died too young for any great achievement are commemorated as having the *virtus* of their ancestors, which they unfortunately lacked the opportunity to translate into noble exploits.[19] In Plautus a young man is berated for destroying through vice the reputation handed down to him by his ancestors: '. . . that you should lend strength to the *honor* of your descendants, your father and grandfather made the road easy and open for you to obtain *honor*', where *honor* has the double meaning of 'reputation' and 'high office'. Similar sentiments are to be found in one of the Scipionic epitaphs, which claims that its subject through his good character added to the virtue of his clan and that his high office ennobled his family.[20]

One way that family influence could be translated into votes was

---

[18] Sall. *Jug.* 4. 5; Pol. 6. 54. 3.

[19] *ILLRP* 309 ff., esp. 311–12; Wiseman, 1985, 3 ff.; Flower, 1996, chs. 5 and 6, pp. 128 ff.; Earl, 1960 and 1967, 25 ff.

[20] Plaut. *Trin.* 644–6 (cf. 271–3, 651 ff. for other references to the aristocratic tradition); *ILLRP* 316.

through the presidency over the elections by a member of that family, especially before the *lex Gabinia* of 139 introduced secret ballot, since it was the job of the presiding magistrate to select the *rogatores*, who asked voters for their choice of candidate (Chap. V with n. 32). In 182/1 Cn. Baebius Tamphilus was allowed by his colleague to hold the consular elections in the interest of his brother M. Baebius, and the latter was duly elected. There are a number of occasions when a presiding magistrate can be seen to have declared the election of someone of his own *gens*, and indeed of his own *stirps*—for example, Sp. Postumius (cos. 174) seems to have presided over the election of A. Postumius as censor for 174 and of L. Postumius to be consul in 173. However, when M. Popilius Laenas (*cos.* 173) was followed to the consulship by his brother Gaius in 172, he did not preside over the relevant elections. In 192/1, it was expected that Scipio Nasica would be elected through the influence of two other Cornelii, his cousin Scipio Africanus who was escorting him to the elec-tion, and Cornelius Merula who was presiding, but Cornelian influence was overcome by T. Quinctius Flamininus. Again in 185/4, when Appius Claudius the consul was seeking to get his brother Gaius elected, it was not straightforward and the consul resorted to what was regarded as improper pressure, *vis Claudiana*, in order to succeed.[21] The conclusion of the most thorough study of the influence of the presiding magistrate on elections is that, in spite of all the opportunities he had for influencing the result, it cannot be argued that his influence was always decisive.[22] If a presiding magistrate could not be sure of managing an election in the interest of his family, it is hard to imagine that any other member of the nobility would be better placed to do so. However, it may be argued, a number of failures do not refute the view that nobles had the ability to control elections. We need to examine the resources which might have enabled them to do so.

Friendship and Obligation

Aulus Hirtius in the eighth book of Caesar's *Gallic War* records Caesar's indignation that in 50 BC his favoured candidate, Ser. Sulpicius Galba, was robbed of the consulship because of his close links with Caesar, although he had been superior in influence (*gratia*) and votes. Galba was a patrician and would have had useful family connections, but what Hirtius had in mind was connections beyond those of blood and marriage. The nature of these is well illustrated in a letter which Cicero

[21] Livy, 40. 17. 8; 42. 9. 7–8; 35. 10. 1–10; 39. 32. 12–13.
[22] Rilinger, 1976, esp. 143 ff.

wrote to Pompey in 62 BC.[23] In this Cicero alluded to the lack of good-will that Pompey had shown to him in his previous letter and said (dis-ingenuously) that this did not matter, since he himself was fully conscious of the services (*officia*) he had rendered Pompey: if no return was made for these, he would be happy to hold the balance of services rendered. He goes on to say that if his support for Pompey had not won him Pompey's favour, the public interest would create a rapprochement between them and bring them together. Cicero then refers to their relationship as *amicitia*, friendship, and claims that, when Pompey on his return recognizes the importance of Cicero's achievements, he will allow him to have the relationship to himself that Laelius was recorded as having to Scipio Africanus (Aemilianus). Three elements in a poten-tial political alliance are mentioned here: first, the mutual assistance arising from services rendered and repaid; secondly, a common approach to political issues; thirdly, the friendship that arises from mutual respect for the qualities of the other person. This corresponds well with the theoretical discussions of obligations and friendship in Cicero's *De Officiis* and *De Amicitia*. In the latter Cicero adopts the *persona* of the younger C. Laelius, consul in 140 BC, and friend of Scipio Aemilianus, in order to argue that friendship does not derive from human weakness and the need to remedy this by the exchange of services: it comes, rather, from men's natural affection for those whose good qualities they admire. Great advantages (*utilitates*) do in fact ensue, but the causes of affection do not proceed from the expectation of these, nor are men beneficent and generous in order to demand gratitude (*gratia*). Advantages may be gained by the mere appearance of friend-ship, but if friendships were glued together purely by advantage, they would be dissolved when this changed.[24] Above all, Cicero argues, friendships should not be used to justify the requesting, or the perfor-mance on request, of immoral actions, such as support for the sub-version of *res publica* or the raising of civil war against the fatherland.[25] In *De Officiis* Cicero considers the obligations that arise out of the various grades of human relationship (*societas*). The closest are those to fatherland and to parents, but none is more distinguished than the

[23] Caes. *BG* 8. 50. 4; Cic. *Fam.* 5. 7. 2–3; Brunt, 1988, 351–81.

[24] Cic. *Amic.* 26–32, cf. 51 on pretended friendship. See Griffin, 1997, 95–6, for the influence of Aristotle (*Eud. Eth.* 3 and *Nic. Eth.* 9) on Cicero's views on friendship. There is also a resemblance to Aristotle's arguments in *Politics* 3, that a *polis* is not a contract for mutual advantage, but an association (*koinônia*) for the exercise of virtue.

[25] *Amic.* 40–43; cf. *Fam.* 11. 27. 8 (to Matius) and Cicero's deliberations in 49 BC (e.g. *Att.* 9. 10. 2 ff.).

friendship (*familiaritas*) of good men of similar character—and this is also the most agreeable. Another social link (*communitas*) is created by the giving and receiving of services, which remains strong as long as the services are mutual and acceptable. In performing duties, a man needs to calculate the differing obligations arising out of the different kinds of relationship.[26]

Both Cicero's theoretical works and his letters are testimony to a broad spectrum of social and political links, variously motivated. Cicero seems to have tried to live by the ideals he was to enunciate in *De Amicitia*. Even when he sought to justify lapses, as when he explained to Lentulus Spinther his new political adherence to Pompey, Caesar, and Crassus after the conference of Luca, he did so not only in terms of personal obligation in response to former favours from Pompey, but in the light of his respect for Pompey's standing, the personal kindness of Caesar to his brother and himself and, especially the public interest.[27] For others, no doubt, friendship in politics was viewed more as a business relationship, in which services were exchanged, though one should not rule out the element of personal affection, plentifully attested in Matius' apologia for his loyalty to Caesar.[28] Regarding the importance of the *res publica*, as in eighteenth-century Britain, so in Republican Rome men did not normally seek election or manage their careers, in order to take sides on political questions.[29] Nevertheless, political divisions could have a catastrophic effect on personal relationships, as on that between Scipio Aemilianus and Tiberius Gracchus, his cousin and brother-in-law, or that between the former friends Publius Sulpicius and Quintus Pompeius, tribune and consul respectively in 88 BC—the example with which Cicero begins *De Amicitia*. Caesar's complaint about the election of 50 BC was that the connections on which Galba could normally have counted were ineffective. It is no coincidence that Caelius, when commenting on the election to the augurate which followed, and in which Caesar's candidate Marcus Antonius was successful, remarked: 'That was a big election and support was clearly determined by party

[26] Cic. *Off.* 1. 55–9. On the vocabulary of *amicitia* see Hellegouarc'h, 1972, 63 ff. *Familiaritas* means generally a close political connection (in which affection may have played little part), while *necessitudo* (71 ff.) means a a similarly close relationship, where obligation is the strongest factor.

[27] Cic. *Fam.* 1. 9. 9–12.

[28] Cic. *Fam.* 11. 28. 2, 4–6. On which see Griffin, 1997. For the importance of affection in aristocratic politics see also Pares, 1953, 74–5, citing the views of Edmund Burke and Charles Fox.

[29] See e.g. on British politics, Pares, 1953, 2; on Roman, de Sanctis, 1907, 484–5.

feeling; very few followed personal connections and performed their obligation.'[30] On the eve of civil war loyalty to the two contestants was more powerful than repayment of services rendered, the normal source of political influence.

In what sense were there 'party politics'?

The unusual nature of the political situation in 50 BC is reflected by the Latin term '*partes*' used by Caelius, translated above as 'party feeling'. *Partes* means a broad political grouping, not a small coterie of friends, thus something similar to a modern political party. However, the word is only used comparatively rarely, and nearly always to refer to the political parties created by civil war—those of Sulla, Marius, Cinna, Caesar, Pompey and the tyrannicides.[31] We should not therefore infer that there were broad aristocratic groupings which determined normal peaceful politics, similar to Whigs and Tories in nineteenth-century Britain. This was once a dominant interpretation of late Republican politics, reflecting the views of Mommsen in his *Römische Geschichte*, but it cannot stand up to analysis.

Cicero, it is true, talks in *pro Sestio* of two types of Roman politician— those who wished to be held, and were, '*optimates*', and alternatively the '*populares*': the former sought to please all the best men, the latter the masses. The *optimates* are sound men who seek to preserve the status quo and their leaders are the *principes publici consilii*, that is, the ex-consuls who are the senior members of the senate. Cicero's treatment of the theme seems to be original, in that he states that 'all the best men' include men in lower ranks of society, including freedmen, but the basic classification is not. The term *optimates* is first found in the eighties BC and may well go back earlier.[32] This élite is often referred to by Cicero simply as the 'good men', '*boni*', though the term is also used to cover 'all the best men', whose interests *optimates* are seeking to promote.[33] The phrase '*viri boni*' has probably a political sense in the rhetorical hand-book, *Ad Herennium*, of the eighties BC, where it describes the men who

---

[30] Vell. 2. 4. 4; Plut. *Ti. Gr.* 21. 7–8; Cic. *Rep.* 1. 31; *Amic.* 2; *Fam.* 8. 14. 1; Caes. *BG* 8. 50. 4; Meier, 1966, 7 ff.

[31] Hellegouarc'h, 1972, 110 ff. Exceptions are Sallust's use of the term to refer to the *nobilitas* and the *populus* in *Jug.* 40. 2–3 and 43. 1, and perhaps Cicero's use of *partes bonae* in *Att.* 1. 13. 2, which may there be translated as 'the good cause'.

[32] Cic. *Sest.* 96–8, cf. 103. We find '*optimates*' earlier in *Ad Herenn.* 4. 45 and Cic. *Inv.* 2. 52 (here referring to those who opposed Flaminius' land-bill of 232 BC). See in general H. Strasburger, *RE* xviii. 1. 773–98.

[33] e.g. *Att.* 1. 13. 3, 14. 1 and 6, 16. 3, 8, 9 and 11.

supported Q. Caepio against Saturninus, and *bonus* and *civis bonus* certainly mean 'sound conservative' in a fragment of L. Crassus' attack on the former Gracchan supporter, C. Carbo in 119.[34] Thus *optimates* and *boni* have a common cause, which may be roughly called conservatism, but it is only this which links them. They are too broad a group to be fairly described as a political party, since they might include the whole governing class of Rome. Cicero's terminology reflects that found earlier in the Greek world, where the upper class is usually given names such as the 'handsome and good men', 'best men', 'most virtuous' or 'most agreeable men': Thucydides by contrast bluntly talks of the 'powerful' (*dunatoi*) or 'most powerful'.[35]

As for *populares*, they are essentially a series of individuals, who took a stand in the interests of the people as a whole and were remembered for it, whether they advanced popular welfare through land-bills or grain-bills, or defended plebeian liberty and political rights through laws about *provocatio* or secret ballot. One feature they shared was the direct use of the assembly to legislate, without seeking, or at least without obtaining, prior senatorial approval. There was also an inherited ideo-logy, as we can see, for example, in the speeches Sallust places in the mouths of C. Memmius and C. Licinius or in Cicero's *Pro Cornelio*.[36] There was, however, no political organization of *populares* as such and indeed no necessary continuity between generations.[37] Cicero gives, as a comparison to the catalogues created of members of philosophical schools, a roll-call of *populares*, which deliberately omits some of the most obvious, like the Gracchi, Saturninus, and P. Sulpicius, and includes some doubtful examples. Different lists emerge when he recalls famous demagogues for rhetorical purposes.[38] Evidently, such lists of heroes or villains were made, but there could be debate as to who should be included, as in discussion of intellectual traditions.

In short, we would be wrong to posit the existence in the Roman Republic of firm political groupings on any scale larger than the devoted political adherents who sometimes clustered round a great man

[34] *Ad Herenn.* 1. 21; *ORF*, no. 66, fr. 14 = Cic. *de Or.* 2. 170. See also the fragment of Metellus Numidicus' speech of 107, *ORF*, no. 58. fr. 6.

[35] Lintott, 1982, 92–3, 121 n. 18.

[36] Sall. *Jug.* 31; *Hist.* 3. 48M; Cic. *Corn.* 1. frr. 48–51 Puccioni = Asc. 76–8C. See also Plut. *C. Gr.* 3. 5 = *ORF*, no. 48, fr. 31 and, on *provocatio*, Cic. *Verr.* 5. 163.

[37] See in general Meier, *RE* Supp. x. 549 ff.; Seager, 1972*b*; Perelli, 1982; Ferrary 1982; Mackie, 1992.

[38] Cic. *Acad.* 2. 13. Contrast *Har. Resp.* 43; *Sest.* 101 and 103; *Corn.* 2. fr. 5 Puccioni = Asc. 80C. The catalogue in *Acad.* 2 has items in common with the list in *Verr.* 5. 180–1 of new men who made their way despite their political enemies.

like Scipio Aemilianus or Pompey. The notion of mass political parties, such as have arisen in the last two centuries of world politics, is anachronistic. As for the relationships which sprang from *officia* and *gratia*, the point that Cicero makes in *De Amicitia* is crucial: these were likely to be dissolved as soon as interests diverged. As in politics nowadays, people were pulled in different directions by a variety of connections, interests, and beliefs, and in the Roman Republic there was no party discipline to keep them in line. But might not that be supplied by family loyalty? Here it must be remembered that a grouping based on close kinship would have been at best very small, and even here, as the story of Ti. Gracchus and Scipio Aemilianus showed, there could be divisions. Moreover, even if it is conceded that families and their connections by marriage regularly co-operated to ensure the election of their members, as is alleged by Marius in Sallust's *Jugurtha*, this does not entail that they co-operated when it came to taking a view in the senate or in an assembly. Münzer prefaced his famous work with the remark, 'every political party strives for power and dominance in the state'. If this seems self-evident to us, it is because the statement is not so much a generalization based on empirical evidence, but an analytic truth whose validity derives from the current notion of a political party: a political grouping which did not seek power would be more usually termed a pressure-group. We should not attribute, however, without direct evidence the motivation of a modern political party to an ancient aristocratic coterie.[39] When Sallust refers to the domination of a *factio* in the years of the Jugurthine problem and in the 70s BC, he means, not one particular political grouping among many, but in effect the political establishment of the period, those who would have called themselves *boni* or *optimates*.[40]

Those scholars who have held that the aristocracy of the Roman Republic monopolized political power through the manipulation of the electorate have believed both in the coherence and consistent co-operation of aristocratic factions and in strong links which bound members of the lower classes to them.[41] If groupings were generally small and flexible—apart from the consensus which tended to unite the aristocracy in defence of its own interests against the plebs and its leaders and to transcend friendship and personal obligation—then it must be very doubtful whether any rigid system of vertical links could

[39] Münzer, 1920, 1. More relevant is Thucydides' description (8. 54. 4) of the aristocratic *sunōmosiai* at Athens, that had as their object lawsuits and offices.

[40] Sall. *Jug.* 31. 4; *Hist.* 3. 48. 3 and 8M.

[41] Münzer, 1920; Syme, 1939; Rouland, 1979.

have been maintained. This is of course no argument against the existence of vertical links: it merely raises questions about their political effectiveness.

Plebeian Connections and Dependence

Our information about organization among the plebs and about its connections with the aristocracy is tantalisingly inadequate. The importance of the *tribus* has already been mentioned (Chap. V with n. 61). As the fundamental divisions of the *populus Romanus*, on which census enrolment was based, they included men from all ranks in society and had at least a rudimentary organization. *Curatores* assisted with the census, and there were also *divisores*, whose function seems to have been to distribute benefits from patrons to members of the tribe, and who in the late Republic were notorious as a channel for bribery.[42] One proposal in the late Republic, made by a tribune of 61, was that a candidate who promised money to a tribe should suffer no penalty if he failed to deliver, but, if he did pay, he was liable to pay 3,000 sesterces to every member of that tribe. A casual comment by Cicero on the elections that year is revealing: 'Favonius carried my tribe more respectably than he did his own, he lost that of Lucceius.'[43] Later, under Crassus' *lex Licinia de sodaliciis* of 55, it is an indication of the importance of the tribe in corrupt practices that the jury were selected on a tribal basis—presumably in order to select those tribes least likely to have been involved in the corruption alleged at the time. Since these jurors were senators, *equites,* and so-called *tribuni aerarii,* who seem to have had the same property-qualification as *equites,* this suggests that the corruption was conceived to link the richer and poorer members of the tribe.[44] These connections were not just a feature of the late Republic: they are plausibly retrojected by the annals into early Roman history and persisted after the Republic's fall. Camillus is portrayed by Livy summoning to his house his fellow tribesmen and clients, 'which formed a large part of the plebs', to see if he could raise from them the money to pay a judicial fine. Horace portrays the fellow-tribesman coming to dinner at a rich man's house with his felt cap and slippers under his arm. Augustus, apart from legislating against bribery, is said to have distributed 1,000 sesterces a man to his fellow-members of the Fabia and

[42] Varro, *LL* 6. 86 for *curatores;* for other references see Chap. V n. 61, and Lintott, 1990*a*, 7–8.

[43] Cic. *Att.* 1. 16. 13; 2. 1. 9.

[44] Cic. *Planc.* 36–8; *Schol. Bob.* 160St.

Scaptia tribes, in order that they should not feel the need to seek money elsewhere. This somewhat disingenuous explanation may not conceal so much an attempt by Augustus himself to corrupt the electorate as a manifestation of old-style aristocratic patronage. However, it fits neatly with Horace's picture of a professional *nomenclator* (election-agent) who will dig the candidate in the ribs and make him shake hands with electoral 'brokers': 'this man is very powerful in the Fabian tribe, the other in the Veline; this one will brusquely give and take away the *fasces* and the curule ivory from whom he pleases.'[45]

Crassus' law of 55 had been directed in particular against *sodalitates*, organizations even more obscure than the tribes. Those at work in late Republican elections were evidently not the religious brotherhoods, nor were they the warrior bands of early Rome, whose existence has been revealed to us by the inscription from Satricum.[46] They were, nevertheless, upper-class groups, who were also involved in law-suits, to judge from the reference in the *Commentariolum Petitionis* to the *sodalitates* of C. Fundanius, Q. Gallius, C. Cornelius, and C. Orchivius, whom Cicero had won over by defending the men concerned. The Gracchan *lex repetundarum* on the fragments from Urbino forbids the selection of *patroni* for the plaintiff, or of jurors, from among those who are in the same *collegium* or *sodalitas* as the defendant.[47] The function of the *sodalitas* as an instrument for mutual assistance in public life was thus already established by the latter half of the second century BC. The *senatus consultum* of 56, which paved the way for the *lex Licinia*, had required the dissolution of *sodalitates* and *decuriati*, recommending that members of groups that persisted should be made liable under the law against violence.[48] This suggests that, in the late Republic at least, *sodalitates* had developed connections with the plebs as a whole, and the same is implied by the fact that *sodalicia* was the term given to a particular form of bribery within the tribes.

Collegia were a form of association of particular importance among the plebs. Some—such as the scribes, smiths, carpenters, horn-players, and trumpet-players—were trade-guilds of great antiquity and accepted as an essential part of the Republic: the last four, because of their military importance, were allocated centuries in the *comitia centuriata*.[49]

[45] Livy, 5. 32. 8; Suet. *Aug.* 40. 2; Hor. *Ep.* 1. 6. 52ff., 13. 15.
[46] Stibbe, 1980.
[47] *Comm. Pet.* 16 and 19; *lex rep.* 10, 20, 22, and 25. There is a direct comparison with the *sunōmosiai* existing in Athens in 411 (Thuc. 8. 54. 4).
[48] Cic. *QF* 2. 3. 5.
[49] Plut. *Numa* 17. 1–4; Dion. Hal. *AR* 4. 17. 3–4, and see Chap. V with nn. 60 and 80.

Others, such as the Capitolini and the Mercuriales, were especially concerned with cult, though the former was the association of those living on the Capitol, while the latter was a guild of merchants.[50] Others seem to have grown out of the localities of the city, whether from the *vici* (the quarters linked to the streets of the inner city) or the *pagi* outside, such as the Aventine or Ianiculum.[51] By the late Republic many other professional associations had grown up, and associations of one kind or another seem to have multiplied among the freedmen and slaves who now filled the city: their particular focus was the Compitalia, the festival of the crossroads, celebrated by the masters of the *collegia* at the end of December or the beginning of January.[52] The variety of these associations gives point to the joke pseudo-*collegia* in Horace (including beggars, actresses, and cabaret-artistes) and in Pompeian graffiti (sleepers, petty-thieves, and late-drinkers). In fact, it is impossible to draw a clear line between *collegia* of different types: one can only see variations in emphasis. Professional associations and local associations both had unifying cults, while professions and trades would have been frequently based in a particular area, for example the goldsmiths from the *via Sacra*.[53] The author of the *Commentariolum Petitionis* advises Cicero to take into account all the *collegia*, *pagi*, and *vicinitates*, if he wants electoral success—their members, though resident at Rome permanently or temporarily, in the late Republic would not have been confined to the four urban tribes, but would have included men from the old rural tribes near Rome as well as migrants from further afield.[54] So here is another potential channel of electoral influence, perhaps one less controlled by aristocratic patronage. One common feature of tribes, *sodalitates*, and *collegia* should be stressed: all possessed a degree of organization, so that candidates for election, and indeed legislators, by approaching a few men could have influence on many more. It was for this reason that they were cultivated in the massive exercises in bribery in the late Republic and became the focus of repressive legislation.

We must finally consider what many historians seem to have regarded as the chief link between the aristocracy and the plebs, the relationship between the individual *patronus* and his *cliens*. The importance of this feature of Roman society is shown by the fact that its institution is ascribed to Romulus. Although the dependence of the poor on the rich

[50] Cic. *QF* 2. 6. 2; Livy, 2. 27. 5; 5. 50. 4; *ILLRP* 696; *ILS* 2676.
[51] Dion. Hal. *AR* 4. 14. 2–4; 15. 2–6; Cic. *Dom.* 74; *Comm. Pet.* 30.
[52] *VRR* 78 ff.; Ausbüttel, 1982, 87 ff.; Accame, 1942.
[53] Hor. *Sat.* 1. 2. 1 f.; *CIL* iv. 575–6, 581 = *ILS* 6418 d, e, f; *ILLRP* 110.
[54] *Comm. Pet.* 30; *VRR* 86–7; Taylor, 1960, 132 ff.

and powerful is a common feature of societies then and now (Dionysius of Halicarnassus cited specifically the *pelatai* of Athens and the *penestai* of Thessaly as parallels to Roman *clientes*), the rights and duties of a client were closely defined at Rome, and the status of clients *vis-à-vis* their patrons was allegedly protected by a clause of the Twelve Tables, which declared *sacer* the patron who caused unjust harm to a client, that is, liable to be killed on sight.[55] The client is said to have been expected to help his patron by various forms of financial assistance and support at elections.[56] The principle that a client and his patron would not accuse or bear witness against one another in court was embodied in statute in the Gracchan *lex repetundarum* and probably in other laws regulating *quaestiones perpetuae*.[57]

A client was expected to show respect for his patron by greeting him in the morning at home and accompanying him to the forum, thus manifesting his prestige and even affording him some physical protection.[58] It was traditional that a client would obtain legal advice and advocacy from his patron. Cicero suggests that originally great and eloquent men did not involve themselves in private cases, but were forced to intervene against injustice on behalf of their dependants, when clever and unscrupulous men started to exploit their experience in oratory to pervert the truth. Among these great and eloquent men were Cato the Censor, Laelius, Scipio Africanus, and the Gracchi who were Scipio's grandsons. Scipio Aemilianus, by contrast, is portrayed by Polybius as originally reluctant to involve himself on behalf of clients in this way.[59] Even if Cicero's reconstruction of the development of private advocacy is theoretical, it may be true that in the early Republic a patron did more work as a legal adviser (which is what the Latin term *advocatus* means) than as a speaker in court (which became an important meaning of the word *patronus*). Nevertheless, the importance of the patron's legal functions is clear. In the homily, discussed above, from Plautus'

---

[55] Dion. Hal. *AR* 2. 10. 1–3; *RS* ii. 40, *Tab*. VIII. 10 (pp. 689–90) = *FIRA, Tab*. VIII. 21. See Gelzer, 1912, in *Kleine Schriften* i, 1962, 68–75 (62 ff. in Seager's trans.) and Brunt, 1988, 382–422, for opposed views of the significance of *clientela*—in particular Brunt, 1988, 407 ff., for criticism of the ascription to patrons of considerable legal powers over their clients and some doubts over the genuineness of the clause of the Twelve Tables. Among the many who follow Gelzer are Badian, 1958, and Rouland, 1979.

[56] Dion. Hal. *AR* 2. 10. 2; Livy, 5. 32. 8. On the *lex Publicia*, perhaps of 209 BC, which limited gifts by clients at the Saturnalia to wax-tapers (*cerei*) see Macr. 1. 7. 33; on the *lex Cincia*, which restricted gifts generally see *MRR* i. 307; *RS* ii. 47.

[57] *Lex rep.* 10 and 33; Dion. Hal. *AR* 2. 10. 3; Plut. *Mar.* 5. 7; *JRLR* 126.

[58] Sen. *Ben.* 6. 34; Livy, 6. 18. 5; 38. 51. 6.

[59] Cic. *Inv.* 1. 4–5; Pol. 31. 23. 7–12; Dion. Hal. *AR* 2. 10. 1.

Trinummus, which reflects the pursuit of *gloria* by aristocratic families, the young man is encouraged to make efforts for his friends in the forum, not for his girl-friend in bed.[60]

It is on the basis of this sort of evidence that scholars have argued that strong links of dependence tied the poorer members of society to the wealthy and powerful and made them political pawns to be manipulated. We cannot exclude this as a possible picture of the early centuries of the Republic. Even the conflict of the orders could be seen as a struggle between bulk of the aristocracy and their dependants and a few powerful outsiders with theirs—it is, after all, the patron–client model of society which emerges in the stories of Sp. Maelius and M. Manlius Capitolinus (Chap. IV with nn. 38–9). It is evident, however, that by the second century ties between patrons and clients had not become unimportant but had become much more complex and confused. Moreover, they were becoming regularly overshadowed by other channels of political influence, through organizations such as tribes and *sodalitates*, and, on particular occasions, defeated by the deployment of money in cash-bribes and entertainment.

I have already mentioned the prohibition in the Gracchan *lex repetundarum* on patrons or clients of the accused being appointed as advocates (termed here *patroni*) of the plaintiff or giving testimony against the accused. It is interesting that this refers both to present patron–client relationships and to past ones, implying not only that these connections could be abandoned and changed for others, but also that a residue of personal loyalty might persist after a connection was abandoned. The competitive nature of patronage in the early second century is alluded to by Plautus: everyone wants as many clients as possible; they don't care whether these are good or bad, they want a reputation for having quantity rather than loyalty. The story of L. Philippus and Vulteius Mena in Horace shows how in the late Republic a client might be picked up off the street at a patron's fancy.[61] Scipio Africanus had gained his aedileship, according to Polybius, because he was a generous giver of gifts as well as an affable man ready to help people. Acilius Glabrio, the victor over Antiochus at Thermopylae, aroused a bitter reaction in his candidature for the censorship because of the bounties in cash (*congiaria*) he had distributed on his return.[62] In 182 the first sumptuary law against expenditure on dinners was passed; in 181 what

60 Plaut. *Trin.* 651.
61 *Lex rep.* 10 and 33; Plaut. *Men.* 571 ff.; see also *Trin.* 468 ff.; Hor. *Ep.* 1. 7. 46 ff.
62 Pol. 10. 5. 6; Livy, 37. 46. 2–6, 57. 9–58. 2.

was perhaps the first criminal statute specifically against electoral bribery.[63] Moreover, it is hardly a coincidence that we find in 180 the first *lex annalis*, a statute which regulated the timing and order in which offices were held, the *cursus honorum* (Chap. VIII with nn. 105 ff.). The initial effect of bribery would have been to liberate votes that were formely tied.[64] The laws which introduced secret ballot (Chap. V with n. 35) would have created further liberty for the voter, and this prepared the way for the politics of the late Republic, where both electoral competition and bribery reached new heights.

How far then should we consider the plebs of Rome under the control of the aristocracy when they voted? First, it must be emphasized that the evidence regarding patronage and bribery, whether exercised individually or through organizations such as the tribe, relates to elections, not to legislation or indeed to trials before an assembly. It is nowhere suggested that the plebs could be diverted from voting in their own interest by the demands of a superior on whom they were individually or collectively dependent. In practice, popular legislation or its prospect might create a new source of dependents for an aristocrat—for example, the 5,000 men who used to escort Tiberius Gracchus.[65] Secondly, although in the last two centuries of the Republic an elector was not left to make up his own mind in peace, but was subject to pressures, largely from above, the likelihood is that these were a variety of pressures which did not all point in the same direction. The very complexity of the ties by which he might be bound in fact created choice and a modicum of freedom. Similarly, the multiplicity of the connections between members of the élite which appear in the late Republic, the one period in which we have adequate information about the details of aristocratic relationships, is a powerful argument that in normal politics one or two powerful factions did not control the political process. When this did in fact happen, this was the result of civil war, as in the seventies, when the *Sullani* dominated, or the result of a political crisis, as in the aftermath of Gaius Gracchus' overthrow. In other words, it was created by political and ideological cohesion rather than the normal links of *amicitia* and *officium*.[66]

---

[63] *ORF*, no. 8, frr. 136, 139–40; Macr. 3. 17. 1–3; Livy, 40. 19. 11. On the political importance of dinners see Cic. *Mur.* 74–6; Tac. *Ann.* 3. 55; and on the development of electoral manipulation generally Lintott, 1990a, Nicolet, 1975, 407 ff.

[64] cf. Namier, 1968, 104.

[65] Sempronius Asellio, fr. 6P.

[66] This important theme is developed by Meier, 1966, ch. 1, esp. 14 ff., 29 ff.

Religion

When in 193 the praetor M. Valerius Messalla wrote a letter to the Asiatic city of Teos, in which he declared that the Romans recognized the right of that city to provide asylum, he remarked that the Romans ascribed their phenomenal success in building an empire to their piety to the gods.[67] Cicero's collection of ideal statutes in his dialogue *De Legibus* begins with laws about cult and other religious procedures. His justification for this is the need to impress on his citizens that the gods are in control of everything, not only because this view is correct, but on account of its utilitarian consequences—respect for treaties, oaths, and human society itself. At the end of the recitation of religious statutes, Cicero comments through the persona of Atticus that they are not very different from the laws of Numa and Roman tradition, and confirms this in his own persona by saying that he was trying to give laws appropriate to the ancient Roman republic, which he had proved in *De Re Publica* to have been the best of constitutions.[68]

Religion was a central part of the Romans' own concept of their city. It was something which conferred dignity and authority on those who took the lead in its ceremonies. Because it contained, and was recognized as containing, many ancient elements, it could be used to bolster a conservative ideology. However, it had an even more direct impact on Roman politics, inasmuch as its public, and many of its private, operations were not isolated in a sacred sector, but were intimately linked with the other civic activities of Romans. Rome's calendar was, like those of many other civilizations, a religious calendar. Yet, it was not simply measured out by festivals—some ancient, largely with agricultural connotations, some more recent, often connected with an imported deity: the complex designation of days in a month was traditionally proclaimed each month by priests—on the first (*kalendae*) they announced with appropriate sacrifices the day of the *nonae*, and on that day the *rex sacrorum* announced the rest of the monthly calendar of festivals.[69]

As we have seen, public actions were preceded by the taking of the auspices as an assurance of divine approval (Chap. VII with nn. 38–46). *Prodigia*, unusual and remarkable natural events, led to public religious holidays in which apotropaic ceremonies were held to appease the angry

[67] *RDGE* 34, 11 ff.

[68] Cic. *Leg.* 2. 15–23. On religion under the Republic generally see Wissowa, 1912; Latte, 1960; North, *CAH* vii. 2.², 573–624; Beard, 1990, and *CAH* ix², 729–68.

[69] Varro, *LL* 6. 27–8; Macr. 1. 15. 9–19.

gods. Formal entertainments in *ludi* took place under divine patronage and as a divine celebration.[70] However, the most striking feature is that the majority of the most important acts of public religion were performed, not by priests, but by the elected magistrates of the Roman people—indeed in one case by the wife of one. On the notorious occasion when a man dressed as a woman, supposedly P. Clodius, was alleged to have intruded on the ceremonies of the Bona Dea in 62, this was taking place in Julius Caesar's house, not because he was *pontifex maximus*, but because he was a magistrate with *imperium* (they were held in Cicero's house in 63).[71] In many ceremonies—sacrifices, vows, prayers, and festal celebrations—priests may have advised the officiating or presiding magistrate, but had no action to perform themselves. Their advisory role was also to be seen, when they were consulted by the senate over a religious problem. In this respect political and religious life interlocked, while each contributed its own focus and source of authority. Moreover, priesthoods, like magistracies, were filled by members of the aristocracy. Indeed, the majority of priesthoods, which were usually held for life, could be combined with tenure of a magistracy. The exceptions were the posts of *rex sacrorum*, for whom political or military office was specifically forbidden, and of *flamen Dialis*, who was surrounded by taboos which effectively ruled out military command or service away from Rome, and made tenure of any magistracy difficult.[72]

It was an essential difference between a priesthood and a magistracy that the former was, with a few exceptions, held for life, while the latter was annual. Moreover, under the Republic priesthoods might be assigned to those who had not yet taken the *toga virilis*.[73] The ancient priesthoods devoted to specific cults—such as the *rex sacrorum*, the *flamines*, and the Vestal virgins—were chosen by the *pontifex maximus*; appointment to the colleges of *pontifices* (who had general priestly functions), *augures*, and *decemviri sacris faciundis* (whose particular concern

[70] On the institution of the *ludi Romani* see especially Fabius Pictor, fr. 15–16P (= Cic. *Div.* 1. 55; Dion. Hal. *AR* 7. 71–3).

[71] Cic. *Att.* 1. 13. 3; Plut. *Cic.* 19. 4f.

[72] On the *rex* see Dion. Hal. *AR* 4. 74. 4; also Livy, 40. 42. 8 ff., where attempts are made to get a potential appointee to resign his post as *duumvir navalis*. On the *flamen Dialis* see Gell. 10. 15. 1–25, 31–2; also Livy, 31. 50. 7–9, where a *flamen Dialis* is elected aedile but cannot take the oath to obey the laws and this has to be performed by a substitute.

[73] On termination of priesthoods, largely through forced or voluntary abdication, see Beard, 1990, 24; for children as priests Livy, 40. 42. 7, and *ILLRP* 311, where the P. Cornelius P.f. Scipio who died young after being made *flamen Dialis* has been identified with Africanus' son, but this is hard to reconcile with the latter's augurate.

was the Sibylline books) was achieved during the middle Republic by co-option.[74] From some time in the third century, however, (the occasion is probably lost to us with the books of Livy which cover 292 to 219 BC) the *pontifex maximus* was chosen through popular election under the presidency of a *pontifex*, or rather through election by seventeen tribes—less than half the Roman people, so that it could not properly be described as popular election. A form of election that was probably similar was used for the *curio maximus*, the official whose task it was to collect religious contributions from the *curiae*.[75] This procedure was extended to all the *pontifices*, the augurs, probably the *decemviri sacrorum*, and perhaps the *epulones* by the plebiscite of Cn. Domitius Ahenobarbus in 104, after an earlier attempt by the tribune C. Licinius Crassus in 145 had failed.[76] The *lex Domitia* was apparently rescinded by Sulla, but its provisions were revived by T. Labienus in 63.[77] The use of election seems to be part of a wider pattern of popular involvement in the organization of public religion. The replacement of *duumviri* with *decemviri* (later *quindecimviri*) *sacris faciundis*, of whom half were to be plebeian, is said to have been enacted by one of the Licinian Sextian laws in the fourth century; the numbers of augurs and *pontifices* were increased, allowing for the admission of plebeians to these colleges, by the *lex Ogulnia* of 300; the *tresviri* (later *septemviri*) *epulones* were actually instituted by a plebiscite of 196.[78] However, popular election was not used for ancient priesthoods connected with a particular cult—such as the *flamines*, the Vestals and the *rex sacrorum*. This is not simply a matter of chronological stratification, as it is likely that the *pontifices* and augurs originated under the kings. Nevertheless, it seems that originally plebeian interest centred on the priesthoods that had the greatest political impact, and it was into those priesthoods that a form of popular election was introduced. In so far as this can be seen as a process which restricted the original patrician monopoly of religion, it may also be related to the fact that so many public religious acts were performed, not by priests, but by elected magistrates. For it is conceivable that this

[74] *Staatsr.* ii. 1. 18 ff.; Beard, 1990, 22 ff.

[75] Cic. *Leg. Agr.* 2. 17–18; Livy, 25. 5. 2–4; Dio, 37. 37. 1–2; *Res Gestae* 10. 2; cf. Livy, 39. 46. 1; 40. 42. 11, where the 'creation' of the *pontifex maximus* seems to be distinguished from the co-option of a *pontifex*. On the *curio maximus* see Livy, 27. 8. 1–3; Festus, 42L *s.v. curionium aes.*

[76] Cic. *Amic.* 96; *Leg. Agr.* 2. 18; Vell. 2. 12. 3; Asc. 21C; Suet. *Nero* 2. 1 (wrong Domitius).

[77] Dio, 37. 37. 1; *Staatsr.* ii. 1. 30–31; and see Cic. *ad Brut.* 13 (1. 5). 3; *Fam.* 8. 4. 1 and Caes. *BG* 8. 50. 1–4 for later elections of augurs and a *quindecimvir sacrorum.*

[78] Livy, 6. 37. 12 and 42. 2; 10. 6. 3–9; 33. 42. 1 (cf. Dio, 43. 51. 9 for the previous existence of seven *epulones* in 44 BC, when Caesar added three more *epulones* and one *quindecimvir*).

was not a tradition from the beginning of the Republic, but a change brought about at some time in its first two centuries as a concession to the plebs.[79]

We now know a unique example—in the Greek text of an inscription from Cos—of a law proposed to an assembly by a priest, C. Fonteius Capito, later consul in 33 BC. However, apart from any questions about the correct transmission of the Latin original (Fonteius may have also been recorded as a magistrate and this may have been ellipsed in the Greek text), the law dates from about 40 BC, when under the triumvirs traditional norms were neglected.[80] There was also a tradition, known to Cicero, that the *pontifex maximus* presided over the election of a college of tribunes on the Aventine after the *decemviri* who had drawn up the Twelve Tables resigned. This is without parallel and is perhaps an ingenious attempt by a Roman writer to explain how the tribunate was revived after it had lapsed during the decemvirate.[81] The *pontifex maximus* is certainly found doing business with an assembly in cases where a priest has appealed to the tribunes against his authority, but here it seems more likely that this is an assembly of the plebs convened by the tribunes themselves (Chap. VIII with n. 21). He did, however, have a regular function in presiding over the purely formal assembly of *curiae* in the *comitia calata*.[82] It does not follow from this evidence that the supreme priest should be reckoned among the magistrates, but it is clear that he was regarded as a source of political authority in parallel to the magistrates, nor would it be sensible to ask whether this authority was religious or secular: it was both.

Although many acts of cult were the responsibility of magistrates, certain priests had charge of rituals—not only the *flamines* dedicated to specific cults, the *rex sacrorum*, the Vestals, the Salii, the Luperci, but also the *pontifices* and the *epulones*. Moreover, the form of augury that was used to ensure divine acceptance over a period, *inauguratio*, as opposed to the taking of *auspicia*, was performed by an augur, not a magistrate.[83] Both the augurs and the *decemviri (quindecimviri)* might take action in their own field of divination. However, the three main colleges of *pontifices*, *augures*, and *decemviri (quindecimviri)* functioned as authoritative advisers in matters of religious policy. So also did the *haruspices*,

[79] North, *CAH* vii. 2², 588–90, 619–24.
[80] *RS* i. 36, pp. 497 ff.
[81] Cic. *Corn.* 1, fr. 50 Puccioni = Asc. 77C; Livy, 3. 54. 11.
[82] Chap. V with nn. 44–6; *Staatsr.* ii. 1. 37 ff.
[83] On the priests see the table in Beard, 1990, 20–21. An exhaustive discussion of the difference between *auspicia* and *augurium* is provided by Catalano, 1960.

the experts in divination from entrails, who, as imported Etruscans, remained outside the main organization of Roman religion. These groups of priests were called into action when some unusual or untoward event happened—a portent, a public disaster, or a religious problem.

We have in the annalist Cassius Hemina an early authority on the aftermath of the defeat at the Allia and the Gallic sack of Rome in 390 or 386. The senate consulted the *haruspex* L. Aquinius, who replied that the sacrifices on the day after the Ides had led to disaster. Then the *pontifices* were consulted and they decreed that all Kalends, Nones, and Ides should be 'black days' thereafter.[84] In 217, after the consul Flaminius left the city on the expedition which ended in the battle of Trasimene, there was a multitude of portents—affecting the heavens, water-supplies, statues, domestic animals, and fowls. The other consul, C. Servilius, reported these to the senate, bringing before it the witnesses to the prodigies. The senate immediately decreed special animal sacrifices and three days of prayer at all the couches of the gods. It further requested the *decemviri* to examine the Sibylline books, so that further action should be taken in accordance with the divine prophesies. The *decemviri* duly recommended a number of donations to the Capitoline triad, to Juno Regina on the Aventine, to Juno Sospita at Lanuvium, and to Feronia. When these had finally been completed, the *decemviri* themselves held a sacrifice at the town of Ardea. At Rome in December there was, in addition to a sacrifice, a banquet for the gods (*lectisternium*) and a public dinner in honour of Saturn. The cry 'Saturnalia' was kept up day and night, and the day was ordered to be a public festival in perpetuity.[85] Further expiation occurred after the defeat itself on the initiative of the dictator Fabius: although there were no new portents, the *decemviri* were required again to consult the Sibylline books. Their ensuing instructions were further sacrifice to Mars, games for Jupiter, temples for Venus of Eryx and Mens with a day of prayer and a *lectisternium*, and the vow of a *ver sacrum* (that is, all the animals born in that spring) to Jupiter, if in five years time the Roman people should have survived the conflict with Carthage and the Gauls.[86]

When the sacrilege at the Bona Dea ritual was announced to the

---

[84] Cassius Hemina, fr. 20P = Macr. 1. 16. 21–4; cf. Livy, 6. 1. 11–12. See also Gell. 5. 17. 12, stating that, according to Verrius Flaccus, the days after the Kalends, Nones, and Ides should also be black. In the event, according to the later calendars, many Kalends, Nones, and Ides were *fasti* and so were the days following them.

[85] Livy, 22. 1. 8–20.

[86] Livy, 22. 9. 7–10. 10; Plut. *Fab.* 4. 4–6.

senate in late 62, the sacrifice had already been performed a second time on the instructions of the Vestals and no further expiation was in fact undertaken. However, the matter was referred to the *pontifices* and Vestals and they pronounced that sacrilege had occurred. When the matter came back to the senate, it recommended to the consuls that a bill should be brought to the people providing for a special criminal investigation, an amended version of which was passed after considerable obstruction and conflict.[87]

Common features in these examples spread over three centuries are regular procedure, a concern to establish religious facts, and a readiness for controlled innovation. The senate acts as a co-ordinator and can initiate certain routine action itself, but the authority to decide on difficult religious problems remains with the colleges of priests. The element of political control is important. When in 199 there were a series of earthquakes, the *feriae*, holidays for sacrifice and expiation, which were decreed as a response, came to dominate public life to the detriment of necessary political administration. So, after consultation of the *decemviri*, three more days of prayer were decreed and it was ordered that no one should report a further earthquake during these *feriae*. The following year, however, the earthquakes returned and there were *feriae* for thirty-eight days, followed by three days of prayer, when they finally ended.[88] Ritual was an important resource in handling the fears and instability that may arise from disaster and uncanny occurrences. Ideas and initiative came from the élite, but, where appropriate, constitutional procedure involving the assembly was invoked, and in the treatment of portents we can see a concern for popular perceptions. Religion, then, was not merely a matter of aristocratic fiat, but could be a subject of dialogue with the people at large. This is well illustrated in the religious history of Rome at the time of her greatest military crises.

According to Livy, by 213 BC, under the stress of the Second Punic War, traditional religious rites and prayers had come to be replaced by new ones, not only in private cult but in public. The senate's first reaction was to order the confiscation of both prophetic books and manuals of prayer and to forbid sacrifice in public places or shrines according to a new or foreign rite. The following year the new *praetor urbanus et peregrinus* P. Sulla began to read the prophesies of a certain Marcius, which were among the books collected by his predecessor. One of these was a warning about Cannae, which was not surprisingly correct

---

[87] Cic. *Att.* 1. 12. 3, 13. 2–3, 14. 4–5, 16. 2.

[88] Livy, 34. 55. 1–5; 35. 40. 7.

(this sort of pseudoprophesy is better known in the surviving *Oracula Sibyllina* and prophetic books of the Bible); the other was a recommendation that annual *ludi* in honour of Apollo should be established, in which the *decemviri* should make sacrifice according to Greek rite, if the enemy was to be expelled from Italy. After consultation of the senate and inspection of the books by the *decemviri* this festival was duly established.[89] The importance of religion of some sort among the people of Rome at the time is immediately apparent. The senate's immediate instinct is to repress innovation and foreign rites as subversive. However, it later decides to follow one of the popular sacred books by creating a new festival.

This was not the first adoption of Greek ritual. It had been introduced into the cult of Ceres before the Hannibalic War with the aid of Greek priestesses from Neapolis and Velia, who had been given Roman citizenship.[90] There had been an exotic example of new ritual in 216 after Cannae, following the discovery of the unchastity of two Vestals and consultation of the Sibylline books, when a Greek man and woman and a Gallic man and woman were buried alive in a stone tomb in which human sacrifices had been made.[91] An even more spectacular example of the introduction of a new cult was the transportation of the stone representing the Mater Idaea from Phrygia. This was initiated in 205, the year of the consulship of Scipio (the later Africanus), when anxiety over what were hoped to be the final campaigns of the war was at its height. The stimulus was once again the Sibylline books, combined with an encouraging response from Delphi to the gifts from the spoils of Scipio's Spanish victory. When the embassy called in at Delphi on the way to Asia, it was instructed that the goddess should on her arrival at Rome be lodged with the best man. In Livy's version of the story, for the final stage of the Mother's journey from Ostia to Rome all the matrons of Rome were instructed to accompany the man selected to be her host—another P. Scipio, the consul's cousin—and carry the stone in relays. The journey to the Palatine became a great religious procession, and the day of the Mother's arrival was subsequently celebrated as the Megalensia.[92]

[89] Livy, 25. 1. 6–12, 12. 2–15.

[90] Cic. *Balb.* 55; Arnob. *adv. gentes* 2. 73.

[91] Livy, 22. 57. 5–6; Plut. *QR* 83. 283f–284c. The ritual was repeated in 114 after a similar discovery of Vestal unchastity, cf. Dio fr. 87. 5; Oros. 5. 15; Macr. 1. 10. 5.

[92] Main narrative in Livy, 29. 10. 4–11. 8, 14. 5–14; for Delphi see 28. 45. 12; 29. 10. 6, 11. 5–6; also 22. 57. 5; 23. 11. 1–6 for Fabius Pictor's consultation of the oracle in 216. Other references are in *MRR* on 205 BC. Other versions of the story depicted the 'Magdalen' figure Claudia Quinta pulling the ship by its cable single-handed.

In the story of the Mater Idaea the senate's policy is arguably not merely a response to popular aspirations, but a deliberate attempt to provide a distraction for popular tension and anxiety by focusing it on a new and extraordinary ritual. It is a classic justification of Polybius' judgement that the Romans had so dramatized religion and brought it into the centre of their private and public life that there was no possibility of surpassing their efforts, and that this was done for the sake of the masses.[93] In 200 BC, however, before the Second Macedonian War, it was a popular assembly that took the initiative. This voted for a tribune's proposal that the consul who was entrusted with the campaign should vow games and gifts to Jupiter. The *pontifex maximus* objected to the resolution on the ground that it was formally invalid, since it did not specify a certain sum of money, but the consul referred the matter to the *pontifices*, who approved the resolution, saying that the precise sum of money could be left to the senate to decide as with quinquennial vows.[94]

In the years that followed there are no spectacular examples of religious innovation. Indeed, when there is a religious problem, the senate is found acting in a conservative direction. When the alleged books of Numa, containing a mixture of texts on pontifical law and Pythagorean philosophy, were found buried in a stone sarcophagus on the Janiculum in 181, they were rejected *in toto* as dangerous and burnt.[95] Five years earlier, the reaction to the Bacchanalia seems in general an example of severe religious repression, even if the reports of the crimes associated with the cult at Rome were to some extent justified. It is clear both from Livy's own narrative and other indications that the cult had been developing over a period. At first it had been focused on public celebrations on three days a year conducted by women, but now it took place on five days a month and involved men as well. Apart from the crimes alleged to have been generated by the cult, particular features of it which disturbed the political and religious authorities were its frequency, the fact that it happened at night, and the use of initiation and secret rituals.[96] It may, nevertheless, be regarded as a concession to

[93] Pol. 6. 56. 8–9.

[94] Livy, 31. 9. 5 ff.

[95] Cassius Hemina fr. 37P in Pliny *HN* 13. 84–7 (the latter also cites variant traditions about the number and nature of the books in Sempronius Tuditanus, Varro and Valerius Antias); Livy, 40. 29. 3–14. See also Pailler, 1988, 623–67.

[96] Livy, 39. 8–19, esp. 14. 8–10; *SCBacch* (*FIRA* i, no. 30), esp. 7 ff.; 10 ff.; 15; cf. Cic. *Leg.* 2. 21 and 35–6 on nocturnal Bacchic rites. The cult was familiar to the early 2nd-cent. theatre audience (Plaut. *Amph.* 703–4; *Aul.* 408–11; *Bacch.* 53; *Cas.* 979–83; *Mil.* 1016). On Bacchanalia see Pailler, 1988, esp. 467–521; North, 1979; and for what is arguably a

popular religious feeling that the cult was not suppressed entirely at this time. It could in future be conducted with official permission as a private cult—in small numbers and without male priests or *magistri*. Moreover, it could involve men and women together—one of the new features of the cult which had been considered a source of corruption.[97]

Religion was a matter of genuine importance for the people as a whole, and the members of the élite, who for the most part were the source of its administration, had to take account of popular religious feeling. The use of popular election for certain priesthoods may have been introduced as a way of restricting intrigue and corruption in their transmission, but it was also conducive to giving priests the authority characteristic of a magistrate. How far the reaction to popular feeling by the senate and priestly colleges can be characterized as responsive, rather than repressive, is a different matter. On occasions it does seem to have been responsive. However, although the senate and the priests were forced to tolerate considerable changes in private religious behaviour, since the very nature of paganism was to be open-ended and in any case there did not exist the political apparatus or social structures which could control such behaviour, their attitude to public religion was generally conservative and proprietorial. In so far as we can talk of *popularis* measures promoted by members of the élite in religious matters, they concerned the use of election for priests and the regulation of the use of the auspices. In matters of cult the ideology praised by Polybius was paramount, that of controlling the passions of the plebs, or, if we take Cicero's point of view, ensuring that the people were dependent on the advice and authority of the *optimates*.[98]

contemporary Bacchic underground shrine at Bolsena see Massa-Pauvant and Pailler, 1979; Pailler, 1971, 384 ff.

[97] FIRA i, no. 30, 10–21.
[98] Pol. 6. 56. 11; Cic. *Leg.* 2. 30.

XI

The Balance of the Constitution

For, whenever we fixed our eyes on the power of the consuls, it appeared completely monarchic and royal, whenever on the senate, it appeared by contrast aristocratic: and indeed if one were contemplating the power of the many, it appeared to be clearly democratic.

(Polybius, 6. 11. 13)

We have already considered the nature of Polybius' account of the Roman constitution, the probable influences on it, and some of its more obvious peculiarities. It is appropriate, now that we have reviewed the three chief elements—assemblies, senate, and magistrates—and examined other factors contributing to its nature, to look again at the Polybian concept, to see how helpful it is in formulating a general concept of the constitution. It is an important feature of Polybius' analysis that, although as he proceeds, the monarchic, oligarchic, and democratic are treated as elements or parts which conflict or co-operate, at the beginning they are aspects or facets—not what the constitution was, but how it appeared to an observer from a certain angle. On this construction his view cannot easily be challenged, because, when the aspects are considered in isolation, they do produce varying, paradoxical conclusions.

Nevertheless, his theory of the progression of constitutions and the place of the Roman mixed constitution among them deals not with appearances but with a varying balance of real political power. So it is not unfair to question the validity of the theory, provided it is clear what sort of questions are being asked. Questions of the form, 'Is it really after all an oligarchy (or monarchy, or democracy)?', though fruitful in controversy, are liable to lead to the tendentious suppression of certain features of the constitution. It is more helpful to concede the existence of the three elements and ask about their relative effectiveness as a contribution to Roman political life.

A further preliminary point should be made. Polybius saw the balance of the elements changing through Rome's history. There can be little doubt that there were changes in the early Republic in the relationship between senate and people and in the relationship of the consuls to the senate and to the people or their representatives, the tribunes. It is worth considering how far this was true in the middle and late Republic, where we have better evidence, with the *caveat* that this need not be the simple, linear progression that Polybius postulated. This means that we are making constitutional analysis depend on political history. But there is nothing necessarily improper in that. It was observed about eighteenth-century England: 'In a mixed constitution, where the bounds of the respective powers are not precisely and effectively fixed, their actual relations at any time will be determined by the accident of personalities and the advantage which the need of surmounting emergencies, or the prestige of emergencies already surmounted, may give to one institution or another.'[1]

The Magistrates

For Mommsen, the magistracy, archetypically the consulship, was the central feature of the Roman Republic, and the most important changes were those which affected it. This theory allowed him to see Roman constitutional history as a cyclical process—a variation on that of Polybius—whereby first the power of the monarch was diluted by the institution of the consulship and the subsequent limitations placed on consular authority, and eventually it returned with its original strength in the dictatorships of Sulla and Caesar and ultimately in the Principate and Dominate. However, there were vital differences between the consul and the monarchs whose reigns bracketed the Republic. The consul was elected by the people and, in Mommsen's view, was their representative and mandatory.[2] As such, he had a right and duty to act as he thought their interests required. The Roman Republic was not a Greek democracy, where the assembly took an active part in administrative decisions; it was a constitution in which elected leaders were meant not only to give leadership but to chastise those who failed in their duty of obedience.[3] In practice, this authority became weakened, he thought, by collegiality and by the multiplication of magistracies. (Other scholars

---

[1] Pares, 1953, 61.
[2] *Staatsr.* i. 4–8; ii. 1. 11; iii. 1. 327.
[3] *Staatsr.* i. 43–4, 136 ff.; Mommsen, 1857, ii, ch. 1.

would want to add *provocatio* to the debilitating factors, but for Mommsen this was a process under the consul's control, and, if necessary, might be overridden.[4])

It is evident that this is a significantly different view from that of Polybius and arguably much more idiosyncratic. In Mommsen's eyes the monarchic element in the Republic is also the democratic element. There were of course consuls who set themselves up as charismatic leaders—for example, Scipio Aemilianus, Marius, and Caesar. However, Mommsen's concept, though it may suit the self-representation of a Caesar, is hardly how things were normally perceived during the Republic. We may be reminded of Cicero's claim, at the beginning of his speech to the people about Rullus' agrarian law, that he was a *popularis consul*, but that was a tendentious claim made to turn the plebs away from their own leaders, the tribunes, and cannot merit the status of a constitutional principle.[5]

It is better to return to our earlier criticism of Polybius (Chap. III with nn. 4 ff). On the positive side, the importance of the initiative of senior magistrates has been illustrated both at home and abroad. Mommsen's perception of the relationship of the magistrate to the senate may owe much to his own concept of the Republic, but finds confirmation in some ancient attitudes (Chap. VI with nn. 5–9). The dependence of the senate on the man who convened the meeting is clear. Even if he did not always set the agenda—and the debate might be hard for him to control—it was he who chose which motions were to be put to the vote. The drafting of the minutes which contained the resolutions of the senate was under his supervision. Although the pressure on magistrates to execute what had been decreed was considerable, many decrees contained discretionary clauses of the form, 'if he (they) shall so decide (*si ei videbitur*)', or 'as they shall judge to be in accordance with the public interest and their own good faith (*utei eis e re publica fideque sua videbitur*)'.[6]

On the other hand, the picture of a Rome dominated by the consuls' *fasces*, which is implicit in Mommsen's theory, is misleading. There is no evidence that consuls went about the city maintaining order by their *coercitio*. Where they exercised power was in the course of performing their own particular functions.[7] The consuls did have praetors as junior

---

[4] *Staatsr.* i. 24; 140 ff.; 150–1.

[5] Cic. *Leg. Agr.* 2. 6–7 and 102.

[6] Some examples in *senatus consulta* preserved in inscriptions are *RDGE*, nos. 2, lines 12–14; 7, 50–1; 9, 70–2; 10, A11, B15; 12, 16–20; 14, 73–4; 15, 63–4; 22, Latin 12, Greek 24 f. See also Livy, 22. 33. 9; 25. 7. 4 and 41. 9; 26. 16. 4; Cic. *Fam.* 8. 8. 5; *Staatsr.* iii. 2. 1027–8.

[7] Heuss, 1944; Nippel, 1995, 5 ff.; *VRR* 89–92.

colleagues, but in the third century the praetorship was often held by ex-consuls and, in spite of its importance for jurisdiction at Rome, until the growth of criminal *quaestiones* it developed as much in response to military and imperial needs as to those of Rome's domestic administration. Moreover, a praetor's activities at Rome were essentially autonomous, above all in the field of jurisdiction, but also on the occasions when he presided over the senate or legislated (Chap. III with nn. 5–6; Chap. VII with nn. 58 ff.)

It was as an army-commander, or the governor of a province, that a consul or praetor seemed most kingly—something which clearly influenced Polybius' perception of the consulate.[8] However, this had no constitutional effect on domestic politics, since the *imperium* lapsed on the commander's return within the city boundary, or, if he was triumphing, later that day at the conclusion of his triumph.[9] The ethos of the Republic in Polybius' day was, moreover, hostile to the tacking together of magistracies and the commands of pro-magistrates—*continuare magistratum* or *imperium*.[10] So Republican office lacked the permanence to be truly kingly. There were of course exceptions made to this principle during crises—for example in the Second Punic War, when M. Claudius Marcellus held magistracies or pro-magistracies almost continuously for about eight years and Scipio Africanus was effectively eleven years in office, or again when Marius was given a succession of consulships during the Cimbric Wars. Such precedents were cited by Cicero in order to justify the linking of the command against Mithridates to Pompey's existing command against the pirates.[11] But it may be too simple to ascribe such measures simply to the needs of a political emergency: some Romans in certain periods may well have preferred to be commanded regularly by the same man or men. Indeed, it would have been surprising if the plebs were proof against the attraction of charismatic leadership, and the careers of the Scipiones and Marius suggest that they were not.

It has been suggested recently that in the fourth and early third century, before a new patricio-plebeian aristocratic consensus had become established, the prevailing custom was one of the dominance of a few major political figures, who might have sought support for their

[8] Pol. 6. 12. 5–9; Richardson, 1991.

[9] *Lex prov. praet.* (*RS* i. 12), Cnidos IV. 38–9 and Delphi C. 3; Cic. *Fam.* 1. 9. 25; Livy, 26. 21. 5; 45. 35. 4; Dio, 53. 32. 5; *Staatsr.* i. 128 ff.

[10] *Staatsr.* i. 517 ff.; Astin, 1958, esp. 7 ff. For the vocabulary see Sall. *Jug.* 37. 2; Livy, 9. 15. 11, 41. 1 and 42. 2; 24. 9. 1; 27. 6. 4 and 8; Vell. 2. 91. 3.

[11] Cic. *Imp. Cn. Pomp.* 60 ff. See *MRR* on the years 215–201 BC and 107 BC onwards.

administration from the assemblies rather than the senate.[12] When once again we find a concentration of command during the Second Punic War, it is at a time when, as Polybius pointed out, the authority of the senate was at its height[13] and its position was reinforced by the need to co-ordinate strategy over a number of theatres of war and social and economic policy at home. Hence there was no great change to the balance of the constitution, and, when this war was over, political and military office was once again for the most part distributed in small parcels, as Rome's empire expanded in the east. Moreover, the legislation preventing the holding of the same office twice within ten years was probably re-enacted.[14]

The charismatic magistrate, influential with the assemblies, returns as a characteristic feature of the late Republic, beginning with Scipio Aemilianus and ending with Pompey and Caesar—or perhaps more accurately with Caesar's heir. Their power came to be the greater because of the long-term unbroken command of the same troops. This has been recognized as an important factor in the downfall of the Republic by historians and political scientists since Machiavelli.[15] Even if we do not ascribe to these commanders the desire to set themselves up as military dictators (as in my view we should not),[16] it remains true that they were able, first, to amass a great deal of influence over the plebs who served them and, secondly, to monopolize the skill and knowhow of managing large military forces. For all this, as long as the Republic lasted in some form, any attempt to seize a unique personal dominance was imperilled by the traditional hostility to tyranny. As the famous stories of the three would-be tyrants of the early Republic illustrated, this was an offence for which a man could be killed on mere suspicion.[17] It was not merely a matter of *invidia*; any behaviour which implied that the individual considered himself so privileged that he could disregard the norms which bound other members of the aristocracy was the mark of a *rex*. In Livy's narrative, this was how Scipio Africanus was perceived in his last years, even though he held no office at the time. It was certainly how their opponents felt about Caesar and Pompey in 59.[18]

---

[12] Cornell, 1995, 342–4, 370–7, pointing to, *inter alia*, the fact that according to the *fasti* 54 consulships between 366 and 291 BC were shared by only 14 individuals.

[13] Pol. 6. 51. 6–7—though one should not underestimate the part played by the assemblies in view of the important legislation of that period.

[14] See Chap. VII with nn. 90–93, on prorogation, and Livy, 7. 42. 2, Astin, 1958, 19–20 on repetition.   [15] *Discorsi*, 3. 24.

[16] See *VRR* 2–3, 205–7.   [17] Chap. IV with nn. 37–9; *VRR* 55–8.

[18] Livy, 38. 50. 9; Cic. *Att.* 2. 24. 3; *QF* 1. 2. 15. Of course, the same view could be held of dominant tribunes—Plut. *Ti. Gr.* 19. 3; *C. Gr.* 14. 3.

The Senate and the Aristocracy

The importance of the aristocratic element in the Republic and the importance of the senate as an institution, though obviously linked, are not completely parallel and coextensive. We have seen the centrality of the senate in administration in Polybius' account of its functions (6. 13) and in the narrative of a typical consular year (Chap. II). As the only deliberative council in the Republic, it was the chief locus of public policy-making. It is true that arguments and counter-arguments could be presented to an audience by selected speakers at a *contio*. This might have led to amendments to a proposed bill, as for example those proposed by Cicero to Flavius' bill in 60.[19] However, what took place in a *contio* was not so much a free discussion about the merits of the proposal as a staged debate that publicized the issues for the benefit of the audience of voters and enabled the bill's proposer to test public feeling. In the senate by contrast, in spite of the magistrate's control over the summoning of that body and over its final vote, there was considerable opportunity for free discussion and for the creation of a momentum in the debate which was autonomous and unpredictable (Chap. VI with nn. 67 ff.). Nor should one underestimate the effect of the informal conversations of senators, when they were waiting to undertake public business or on social occasions.

The senate was not a legislative organ under the Republic, nor did it strictly have executive functions. Although it might lay down rules which were intended as general norms and not simply as advice to the current magistrates (Chap. VI with n. 91), any change in the law which might be proposed in a debate had to be referred to an assembly and voted through with correct formal procedure. The structure of a senate debate was indeed not well suited to the drafting of complex legislation (there was no equivalent to the 'Committee' stage of a bill in the British parliament). As for executive powers, the senate did not have the authority to supervise officials and penalize delinquents at Rome that the Athenian democratic *boulē* possessed at Athens. That was a matter for the magistrates and those who brought prosecutions. At home the senate developed a *de facto* executive power over finance, in that magistrates

---

[19] Cic. *Att.* 1. 19. 4. See also 1. 14. 1–2, where Fufius Calenus seems to have been trying to elicit from Pompey a proposal for the amendment of the consular bill about the Bona Dea affair in 61; *Imp. Cn. Pomp.* 52 and 60 for objections, which may have been translated into amendments, to the *leges Gabinia* and *Manilia.*

were expected to refer certain financial matters to it every year: in particular, it decided the global sum of money to be allocated by the censors in contracts and it held a veto over outgoings from the treasury, except, according to Polybius, when the consul drew money.[20]

In foreign affairs it not only took strategic decisions about the selection of war-zones and commanders (decisions which otherwise would have had to be made by the consuls themselves), but it handled the reception of foreign deputations and the despatch of Roman embassies with appropriate instructions. Fundamental decisions about declaring war and making peace with major enemies were taken by the people down to Polybius' time, but it is not clear how far this practice was maintained in the late Republic (there is no evidence, for example, for an assembly vote in 74 before the Third Mithridatic War). Similarly, the ratification of treaties of peace or alliance, which were, in theory at least, the people's prerogative in Polybius' day, seem to have been monopolized by the senate in the late Republic, to judge from the inscriptions recording the conclusion of treaties.[21] The senate's interventions in the affairs of her Italian allies, emphasized by Polybius, were effected largely through instructions to magistrates, though there was also diplomatic contact with representatives of these communities. In method, this was no different from the management of foreign and military policy outside Italy. What was remarkable was the close involvement with the internal affairs of the communities in a time of peace, in particular the assumption of criminal jurisdiction by the Romans.[22] However, this cannot be said to have affected the constitutional position of the senate at Rome.

The senate, it may be said, without the magistrates' executive power would have been an impressive but ineffective torso. However, while this image reflects the importance of magistrates to the senate and the dependence of magistrates on the senate which Polybius described, it does not do justice to the fact that the functions of the senate were called into being by the power of the magistrates. The senate's influence resulted from the need to check and co-ordinate that power in the interest of the efficient administration of Rome's affairs and of the coherence of the aristocracy. The senate was the natural forum for common policies to be formed and differences between aristocrats to be brokered and reconciled. Its political weight fulfilled both a constitutional and a social need.

---

[20] Pol. 6. 13. 1–3; Chap. III with nn. 4 and 12.

[21] Pol. 6. 13. 6–9 and 14. 10; *Imp. Rom.* 39, with n. 78; and see on declarations of war Rich, 1976, 13–19.

[22] Chap. III with n. 14; Pailler, 1988.

So far the discussion of the senate has concerned its relation to the magistrates, which may be roughly equated with Polybius' monarchic element. It is interesting that when Polybius came to describe the power the senate had over the Roman people, he produced what seems a somewhat recherché and bizarre answer—the dependence of the plebs on the contracts let out by the censors under senatorial supervision, and on the decisions of individual senators as judges of civil lawsuits.[23] He cannot, it appears, cite a feature of the political organization of Rome whereby the plebs is dependent on the aristocracy: instead he points to economic and social dependence. Arguably, even if he overemphasized the importance of state-contracts for the livelihood of ordinary Romans, he was right in the area in which he sought to find the source of aristocratic dominance over what was constitutionally the sovereign element in Rome. In the foregoing chapter we considered aspects of the argument that the votes of the Roman *populus* or plebs, though in theory the expression of their own will, were in fact determined by various forms of social dependence on the aristocracy. It was evident that these votes were subject to all kinds of external influences, through patronage, group-membership, and bribery. But in the last two centuries of the Republic, at least, the picture is confused and it seems more appropriate to talk of competitive pressures than control. Nevertheless, this clearly was a channel of aristocratic power, even though it was not normally exercised in a coherent and rigid fashion. What did it amount to?

First, it appears that the Roman people accepted the principle of being led in peace and war by an aristocracy to a large extent hereditary—one whose composition did change over a period, in that it was open to outsiders, but changed slowly. This aristocracy collectively possessed an authority which tended to induce deference, though this was not proof against popular turbulence when passions ran high, especially in view of the tradition of plebeian resistance to the aristocracy which was an important part of Rome's annals. Aristocratic authority was reinforced by its management of public religion, whose rituals shaped the calendar and the conduct of public life in general. Here, although some concessions were made to popular sentiment, the interpretation of the requirements of the gods remained an aristocratic prerogative and the ensuing decisions took priority over, and could render void, even resolutions of the assemblies. Secondly, many plebeians would have been economically and socially dependent on aristocratic families, in particular those who were their former slaves or descendants of their

---

[23] Pol. 6. 17; Chap. III with nn. 20–21.

former slaves. Such men looked to their patrons for legal assistance, lived perhaps in property belonging to their patron, or operated a business for which their patron had provided the capital.

The political effect of this dependence was mitigated by the complexity of the relationships in which a plebeian might be involved. Nor could any such relationship necessarily outweigh the plebeian's pursuit of his own self-interest, when great matters were at stake, such as the vote on an agrarian bill. However, the prior existence of dependence made it more difficult for major political figures to get a permanent grip of plebeian support in order to carry through policies in defiance of aristocratic sentiment. Indeed it was one of the reasons why a genuine 'popular party' was not created, in spite of the existence in the *collegia* of the basis of a plebeian organization.[24]

When viewed strictly from the constitutional point of view, the aristocratic element in the Roman Republic appears in the senate's range of administrative powers in finance and foreign affairs, and its capacity to obstruct magistrates, as Polybius saw. However, this element was much more than the functions of the senate: the aristocratic ethos was a vital part of the context in which political action took place, a board on which the pieces moved in pursuit of *virtus* and *gloria*, but there were penalties for landing on certain squares—especially that marked 'tyrannical aspirations'. Viewed more broadly, the aristocratic element was the nature of Roman society itself, in which for much of the Republic the plebs were not only kept in awe by the wealth, the fame, and the ancestral religious and social privileges of the aristocracy, but might also be kept divided by personal allegiances to individual aristocrats.

The Power of the People

Aristotle might well have classified the Roman Republic as one of the more moderate forms of democracy. Neither rich nor poor had dominance over political life; offices were held according to a property-qualification, but were few and impermanent. There was general participation in politics, but socially the community was under the influence of farmers with moderate property or the free citizens with time to spare. However, he would have been worried by the fact that it was the

---

[24] For Clodius' efforts in that direction, which might also be regarded as an attempt by one patrician family to monopolize the patronage of the plebs, see *VRR* 80–83, 193–4; Lintott, 1967.

popular assemblies, not the law, which were sovereign, as in extreme democracies. For there were no 'entrenched clauses': the most fundamental principles of the Republic could be subverted by a single statute, provided that it was proposed and voted through with correct procedure.[25] In Polybius' account the powers of the assembly to elect, legislate, and decide on peace and war are recounted swiftly and almost casually—perhaps because he did not want to overstress the democratic element, since he clearly thought that Rome had at the time a constitution of a different shade to that of his own community, the Achaean league, whose democracy was characterized by *isēgoria* (political equality) and *parrēsia* (freedom of speech).[26] In fact, the powers of the Roman assembly, taken in isolation, would support an interpretation of Rome as some kind of democracy, and the institution of the tribunate would give this view a further dimension.

The range of decisions taken by the assemblies was considerable. They elected not only the magistrates whose offices formed part of the *cursus honorum*—from censor and consul down to quaestor—thus largely determining the membership of the senate in the middle and late Republic, but also a number of minor magistrates, such as the *tresviri capitales* and *monetales*. A restricted assembly of less than half the number of tribes was used to elect the *pontifex maximus* and for two periods in the late Republic members of the chief priestly colleges (Chap. X with nn. 75–7). Legislation dealt with many different topics. First and foremost were alterations to the constitution, such as the augmentation of the numbers holding a certain magistracy or the introduction of a new magistracy.[27] Similar to these were changes in public religious offices and procedure.[28] Alterations to the civil law were made by statutes passed in the assembly throughout the Republic, though from the second century BC onwards this was to a great extent supplanted by the exercise of the praetor's *ius honorarium* in adapting old actions and creating new ones.[29] Changes to the criminal law, in particular the introduction of new permanent tribunals (*quaestiones perpetuae*), were, however, usually matters for legislation (Chap. IX with nn. 48 ff.). Moreover, it was the assembly which ultimately controlled admission to Roman citizenship.[30]

[25] Ar. *Pol.* 4. 1291^{b}30–92^{a}15, 92^{b}25–30.

[26] Pol. 6. 13. 9–12; cf. 2. 38. 6; Nicolet, in Nicolet, 1983, 15 ff.; and see Chap. III with n. 22.

[27] See e.g. *lex Cornelia XX quaest.* (*RS* i. 14); *lex Papiria* (*RS* ii. 45).

[28] See e.g. Livy, 31. 9. 5 ff.; 33. 42. 1.

[29] Cic. *Leg.* 1. 17; Gai. *Inst.* 4. 30; see also the works cited in n. 67 to Chap. VII.

[30] Perhaps the most important example is the series of laws enfranchising the Italians, the *leges Iulia, Calpurnia* and *Plautia Papiria* (*MRR* on 90 and 89 BC), but for others see Livy, 27. 5. 7; 38. 36. 7–9; 41. 9. 9, and *Imp. Rom.* 161–2.

Apart from these constitutional and legal enactments, the founding of colonies and the distribution of public land were set in motion by statutes passed in the assembly. We also find a number of statutes passed on economic and social matters, including laws about moneylending, sumptuary laws restricting luxury, and the grain-laws of the late Republic.[31]

The assembly is attested as taking decisions about peace and war and ratifying treaties down to 171. After that, as we have seen earlier (n. 21), the senate may have taken over the ratification of treaties, and there is uncertainty about the declaration of major wars. However, on the whole in the middle Republic the assembly did not legislate about specific matters in foreign and military policy. In this respect it was quite unlike the Athenian *dēmos*, which passed decrees about the sending of expeditions and embassies. Nevertheless, *popularis* politics in the late Republic introduced something of the spirit of Athens. C. Gracchus legislated about the organization of the province of Asia—and there is another obscure *lex Sempronia* relating to Africa, distinct from the *lex Rubria* which sought to found a colony at Carthage.[32] Later, the law about the praetorian provinces of 101–100 BC, passed at the acme of the power of Saturninus and Glaucia, dealt with many aspects of eastern affairs of varying importance, which would have normally been resolved through *senatus consulta*—the reinforcement of troops and their grain-supply, the new duties of governors of Macedonia, the writing of letters about piracy.[33] In the post-Sullan period, the laws, such as the *leges Gabinia, Manilia,* and *Vatinia,* which established the great overseas commands, seem to have included detailed provisions, apart from the appointment of the commander himself, that made inroads into what had been the discretion of the senate at that time.[34]

If legislation through the assembly became more important in the late Republic, the people's control of punishment in political matters became more remote. There is a problem about Polybius' selection of popular sovereignty over honour and punishment as the most significant power of the assembly, in that, although in his day a number of trials before the assembly are attested, we know of no single capital trial of this kind ending in a condemnation, which calls into question their effectiveness as a

---

[31] Lintott, 1987, 42; *JRLR* 34–58; Virlouvet, 1985.

[32] Cic. *Verr.* 3. 12; *lex agr.* 82 with *JRLR* 269–70.

[33] *RS* i. 12 with Lintott, 1976, 70–2.

[34] e.g. the permission given to Pompey by the *lex Manilia* and to Crassus by the *lex Trebonia* to make peace or war with whom they chose (App. *Mith.* 97. 446–7; Plut. *Cato mi.* 43. 1; Dio, 39. 33. 2).

popular weapon against the aristocracy.[35] In any case, with the creation and development of the *quaestio perpetua*, the people delegated their powers of punishment to a jury, albeit one which might contain fifty men or more. In the procedure attested by the bronze fragments of the Gracchan *lex repetundarum*, the democratic aspect of the law can be seen in the effort to publicize every part of the procedure, and the jury, although it probably had a wealth-qualification, was deliberately purged of all those with senatorial connections.[36] However, this restriction of the jury was not maintained in subsequent legislation, and in any case, although there were occasional assembly-trials in the late Republic, the people had been persuaded effectively to relinquish a democratic prerogative in the interest of greater efficiency in political prosecutions.

Although Polybius introduces the tribunate almost as an afterthought, when discussing the restrictions on the senate (6. 16. 4–5), it could be argued that this magistracy constituted the major part of the democratic element of Rome. It was the *concilium plebis*, convened and presided over by the tribunes, that was the most effective medium of legislation. The tribunician *intercessio* was an almost indefeasible means of obstruction against both magistrates and senate. When deployed in defence of an individual Roman in the form of *auxilium*, it was an effective guarantee of the legal rights of any Roman confronting those more powerful than himself: indeed it was called into action even by members of the élite who were isolated and in danger, which attests its perceived effectiveness, even if this may be thought a perversion of its original purpose. Lower-class Romans were unable to take political initiatives themselves, but in the tribune they had, at least potentially, a dedicated spokesman, whose leadership might, at least in theory, allow them to make a significant impact in politics.

In spite of the apparent importance of the popular element in the constitution, modern scholars have tended to believe that appearances are deceptive. The argument runs on two tracks: first, the assemblies were not truly representative of the people; secondly, neither the assemblies nor the tribunes for the most part promoted the interests of the people, but tended to serve the ambitions of members of the élite.

It is already clear that the Roman assemblies were unlike the Athenian *ekklēsia*, in that ordinary Roman citizens, to all appearances, did not contribute actively to the debates. Private citizens did have a right to

---

[35] Pol. 6. 14. 6; Chap. IX with nn. 19 ff. Machiavelli, *Discorsi* 1. 28 and 31, regarded this leniency of the *popolo* as one of the republic's virtues.

[36] *Lex rep.* 12–23, 36–8, 53, 65–6, 79 with *JRLR* 20ff.; Sherwin White, 1982.

speak before a bill was vetoed or voted on, but in the middle and late Republic it was members of the élite that were likely to be called (Chap. V with n. 27). Moreover, the actual composition of the assembly would rarely constitute even a representative sample of the total population of Roman citizens after the expansion of territory and of the citizen body that took place from the mid-fourth century onwards. The elections of the late Republic, which were regularly held in July, would have given an opportunity for men to assemble from all parts of Italy and Cisalpine Gaul, though we have no idea how many in fact came. In the late Republic the citizens in the city and its environs seem to have numbered 200,000 plus, about a quarter of the total registered citizen population.[37] If we assume that the majority of these voted and a further 50,000 came in from outside for the elections, then the consuls, tribunes, and other magistrates would have been elected by about a quarter of the registered citizen population (910,000 in the census of 70/69). These assumptions are probably optimistic. Nevertheless, one may suggest that, even if by the late Republic the magistrates were elected by a minority of Roman citizens, they still would have owed their election to a great number of people. As for legislation, we are told that on certain occasions a considerable number of men came in from outside Rome to participate. According to Appian and Diodorus, Tiberius Gracchus' agrarian bill caused people to flock into Rome—colonists, Latins, and others—and range themselves on either side of the issue of the bill. Later, when Gracchus wanted support for re-election to the tribunate, he tried to summon the men from the countryside, but, since these were pre-occupied with the harvest, he resorted to the urban *dēmos* instead.[38] In the city he was regularly accompanied, according to a contemporary, by an entourage of 5,000 men,[39] and his total urban support is likely to have been considerably greater. We hear again of an influx of rural voters at the time of Saturninus' legislation of 100 BC and later that year at the time of his attempted re-election.[40] Even if this was a comparatively small proportion of the citizen population—at the time, over 300,000— we are dealing with a greater raw total of participants in politics than could be mustered by any Greek city.

At this point we must make allowance for the distortions produced by the Roman system of block voting in classes and centuries in the *comitia*

[37] See Frank, 1933, 329; Beloch, 1886, 392 ff.; Brunt, 1971, 376 ff.

[38] App. *BCiv.* 1. 10. 41, 13. 57, 14. 58; Diod. 34. 6. 1–2 (probably deriving from Poseidonius and showing the near-contemporary source of this tradition).

[39] Sempronius Asellio, fr. 6P.

[40] App. *BCiv.* 1. 29. 132, 30. 134, 32. 143.

centuriata and in tribes in the *comitia tributa*, alluded to earlier (Chap. V with nn. 51ff. and 79). The former assembly was weighted to disadvantage the masses, as Cicero pointed out. A disproportionate influence was given to wealth and also to age. However, although elections of consuls might be decided when the returns of the second class were counted—without the poorer citizens having had a chance to contribute to the result—in a close contest they might require the votes of all the centuries.[41]

In the tribal assembly there were two potential distorting factors: first, the possibility that certain rural tribes would be poorly represented; secondly, the fact that freedmen and, until the second century, their descendants tended to be confined to the four urban tribes through Roman reluctance to allow new citizens too great an influence. The evidence for this restriction, and for the attempts to overcome it, is so great that its importance cannot be disputed. But one motive for it, the desire to limit the influence of patrons over their former slaves (Chap. V with n. 52), may be regarded as in principle democratic. As for the under-representation of rural tribes, seventeen of them had territory within easy travelling distance of Rome, and there would have been little difficulty in their members participating in assemblies that they considered important. Cicero at one point suggests that Clodius packed badly supported rural tribes with a few of his supporters, but this allegation is isolated and, like all Cicero's charges against Clodius, must be viewed with some reserve.[42] What may be more significant is the influence of members of remote rural tribes who happened to have changed their domicile to Rome. Their importance may be deduced from the fact that, although there were only four urban tribes out of the thirty-five, members of the urban *dēmos* seem to have dominated the tribal assemblies, unless people from the countryside made a special effort to attend, both in the late second century and Cicero's day.[43] Nevertheless, on important occasions, men from the rural tribes who actually did live in the country did come to the city and affect the result.

We have considered in the last chapter some aspects of the argument that, whatever the composition of the assembly, its votes were controlled by the élite. There were certainly pressures on the voter—through

[41] Cic. *Rep.* 2. 39; *Phil.* 2. 82; *Leg. Agr.* 2. 4; Yakobson, 1992, esp. 44ff., though his argument from Cic. *Rep.* 2. 39–40 (pp. 48–9) is insecure, see above Chap. V, n. 77.

[42] Cic. *Sest.* 109; Taylor, 1966, 76.

[43] *VRR* 86, 179–81. Cicero's rhetorical tactics in *Leg. Agr.* 2. 71 imply that he is addressing an audience of city-dwellers, who can be expected to have the preponderant vote on an agrarian bill.

membership of tribes, *collegia*, and similar organizations and through individual connections with richer and more influential citizens. These would have been particularly powerful before the introduction of secret ballot (in the dialogue *de Legibus*, Q. Cicero is made to argue that it was oppression by the *principes* which led the people to demand the ballot laws). There was also electoral bribery (*ambitus*), which was understood by the Romans as something that cut across existing patron–client relationships (those gifts which reinforced existing ties were not *ambitus*), and indeed seems in fact to have developed in Rome precisely because it had this function.[44] However, such pressures are features of democratic societies in general, and the question is whether the voter has nevertheless the freedom to choose what he considers to be more in his interest. In the last two centuries of the Republic the pressures acting on the voter would have been frequently conflicting and weakened by their complexity, which would have given him some room for manoeuvre.

The example I have just cited of the ballot laws shows that the people were prepared not only to vote in their own interest but to demand legislation, as apparently in the same decade they demanded an agrarian law from Ti. Gracchus.[45] Cicero in his digression on optimate politics in the *pro Sestio* argued that the reason why at that time optimate politics were honourable and *popularis* politics were corrupt was that the people were happy with their lot and were not making demands; in his speech ten year earlier for Manilius' bill, he had argued that it was right to follow popular sentiment and give the Mithridatic command to Pompey, since in voting for Gabinius' bill the previous year, the people had been proved right and their optimate opponents wrong.[46] The plebs could not introduce legislation themselves; they had to wait on a magistrate who would work in their interest. However, they are portrayed in our sources as capable of agitating for measures and making rational choices. Popular agitation forms also the background to the attacks on senatorial policy over Jugurtha and to the subversion of Sulla's measures through the restoration of grain-distributions and of the full powers of the tribunes—to take some famous examples.[47]

It may be argued that this is a characteristic of the turbulent late

---

[44] See Lintott, 1990, with references to earlier literature; Bleicken, 1975, 278 ff. On the ballot-laws see Cic. *Leg.* 3. 34 ff. and Chap. V with nn. 34 ff.

[45] Cic. *Leg.* 3. 34; Plut. *Ti. Gr.* 8. 10.

[46] Cic. *Sest.* 104; *Imp. Cn. Pomp.* 53–6. See by contrast *Leg. Agr.* 101–2, where Cicero claims that he has popular support for his attack on Rullus' agrarian bill.

[47] Sall. *Jug.* 30. 1; 40. 3; *Hist.* 2. 45, 47; 3. 48. 23M; Cic. *Verr.* 1. 44–5.

Republic, which perhaps reproduced the struggles of the early Republic, not of the era of concord which in Sallust's view separated them.[48] However, even this middle period of the Republic saw the plebs vote through measures like the *lex Terentia* about the children of freedmen in 189 and the *lex Valeria* in 188 granting citizenship to Fundi, Formiae, and Arpinum—both measures unprompted by the senate. Nor do we know the circumstances under which Cato's *lex de provocatione* was passed.[49] Again, we find the *comitia centuriata* showing a mind of its own in its reluctance to support the declaration of the Second Macedonian War (as well as over a religious proposal which accompanied the eventual declaration).[50] It was a principle of *popularis* politicians that they legislated for the interests (*commodum* or *commoda*) of the people.[51] This implies that the people could be expected to support legislation in their own interest, even if upper-class patrons tried to suggest otherwise. Nor can one disregard the ideology which maintained that a law was an expression of popular will, even if the circumstances in which it was passed were dubious. This was what made it difficult to disregard legislation or declare it void in the last century of the Republic.[52]

If the Roman people were capable of bringing issues home to their politicians and persuading their leaders to promote certain policies, how should we conceive their leaders, in particular the tribunes? It has been argued that they too were manipulated in the era of Polybius, when the once revolutionary office had been absorbed into the constitution. This was the central argument of Bleicken in *Das Volkstribunat der klassischen Republik*, though he significantly nuanced his view in a much later article.[53] It is true that many tribunes co-operated with decisions of the

---

[48] *Hist.* 1. 11M.

[49] Plut. *Flaminin.* 18. 2; Livy, 38. 36. 7; *ORF*, no. 8, fr. 117.

[50] Livy, 31. 6. 3–4; 9. 5ff. It is evident that I cannot accept the view of Bleicken (1975, 288ff.) that legislation was generally a concordat between the magistrate representing the aristocracy, and the people. Although this is a fair description of a bill passed 'in accordance with the senate's decision', *de senatus sententia*, the very use of this special description implies that senatorial approval was not the essence of legislation generally. That legislation was a sort of concordat between the proposer and the voters is self-evident.

[51] Cic. *Sest.* 103; *Leg. Agr.* 2. 71, 76, 78, 81; *ORF*, no. 48, fr. 44 = Gell. 11. 10. 3; Ferrary, 1982, 748ff.; Perelli, 1982, 5–69.

[52] M. Antonius in a letter of 43 (*Phil.* 13. 31) could reproach the consuls, 'you have rescinded by a *senatus consultum* colonies of veterans which were founded by a law' ('veteranorum colonias, deductas lege, senatus consulto sustulistis'). Note also the elaborate nature of Cicero's arguments against the validity of Clodius' legislation (*Dom.* 43–61). On the annulment of statutes see Chap. V with nn. 97ff., *VRR* 132–48.

[53] Bleicken, 1955, repeated in Bleicken, 1972, and developed by Meier, 1966, esp. 117ff. By contrast see Bleicken, 1981, arguing that the tribunate was a base for innovation and opposition to majority opinion in the senate.

senate and helped to implement them—arguably, because they thought they were in the best interests of the Republic.[54] It seems also that the tribunate lost some of its cutting edge as a representative of popular interests in the middle Republic by virtue of the very fact that it was drawn into the mainstream of public business. Nevertheless, its co-operation was enlisted by consuls and senate precisely because it was the chief magistracy that represented the plebs and its function was to be external to the aristocracy in the senate. This was arguably why the most important political prosecutions were entrusted to it, so that the delicate and invidious business of seeking to ruin a member of the élite was put in the hands of a magistrate who, during his office, was expected to represent those outside the élite. Its externality in relation to the aristo-cracy and curule magistrates could also be exploited, when one of these magistrates was thought to be overstepping his office, or when a dispute within the aristocracy needed to be refereed.[55]

Polybius' statement that the tribunes were obliged always to carry out the people's decisions and set their sights on its wishes represented one attitude to the tribunate, which was contentious but perhaps not as extreme and radical as it has often been thought. It gains a special piquancy from the events of Ti. Gracchus' tribunate, when he brought about the deposition of his colleague Octavius on the ground that opposition to the people's wishes rendered him unfit to hold that office. He subsequently defended this action, when challenged, by arguing that a major crime against the republic, such as arson on the Capitol or in the dockyards, was not in itself a disqualification for the tribunate, but dis-obedience to the plebs was.[56] In fact, a veto on an agrarian bill, or indeed on any other bill dealing with public business which was a normal con-cern of the plebs, was at the time unprecedented.[57] So it was the extreme measure of Octavius which produced an extreme reaction.

The principle of a tribune's obedience to the plebs, however, can be viewed in a different way. It was a charter for the tribunes to perform their duties without fear or favour, in particular, for those from the plebeian nobility to subordinate their aristocratic connections to the

[54] Examples are in Livy, 30. 27. 3; 31. 50. 8; 39. 19. 4; 45. 35. 4. A late-Republican instance, preserved on bronze, is the *lex Antonia de Termessibus* (*RS* i, 19).

[55] Chap. VIII with nn. 117, 130ff.; Chap. VII with nn. 56–7.

[56] Pol. 6. 16. 5; Plut. *Ti. Gr.* 15. 2–4 and 7 = *ORF*, no. 34, fr. 16; cf. *Ti. Gr.* 14. 5–8 = *ORF*, no. 17, fr. 4. See also App. *BCiv.* 1. 12. 51–53; Cic. *Corn.* 1. fr. 31 Puccioni = Asc. 71–2C; Badian, 1972, 706ff.

[57] See Chap. II with n. 19 for the veto against the citizenship bill being withdrawn after it is made clear that this sort of bill is the assembly's prerogative, and Badian, 1972, 694ff.

interests of the plebs and the people as a whole. It was understood that, if such a man was elected tribune, he was entitled to associate himself with bills which might damage aristocratic interests and would not have got majority support from the senate, without being regarded as a traitor to his class. This was one of the foundations of *popularis* activity and ideology. So we find in the post-Gracchan period turbulent tribunes, such as Cn. Domitius Ahenobarbus and L. Marcius Philippus, both tribunes about 104 BC, who afterwards become 'pillars of the establishment'.[58] This may be regarded as a sort of legitimized opposition which tended to reinforce the senatorial regime.[59] However, much depended on what sort of men became tribunes. From the constitutional point of view, the defence of the interests of the plebs was entrenched and with it a potential source of political conflict.

Changes in the Balance

Polybius saw the balance of the Roman mixed constitution moving from the aristocratic towards the democratic, but it was not quite so simple. We have already referred to Cornell's argument (n. 12 above) that the constitution at the end of the fourth and the beginning of the third century combined charismatic leadership with popular participation to the disadvantage of the senate—in Polybius' terms combined the monarchic and democratic elements. The rest of the third century may be considered a period of senatorial domination, as the Second Punic War and the first half of the second century certainly were. But the examples of C. Flaminius and perhaps earlier of M'. Curius Dentatus show that the pattern of the fourth century could recur. It may be false periodization to write an end to the 'Conflict of the Orders' in 287 BC.[60] When the senate's dominance was challenged again about the middle of the second century, it was in part by traditional tribunician activity in support of the plebs—in this case over the military levy. But there was also a popular military leader, Scipio Aemilianus, who was a focus for plebeian expectations.[61] However, with the tribunate of Tiberius Gracchus the first step was taken towards a reinterpretation of the constitution.

[58] See *MRR* for their careers. Ahenobarbus reached the censorship before the social war. Philippus, after opposing Livius Drusus as consul, was censor under the Marians and later *princeps senatus* after Sulla's return.

[59] Meier, 1966, 40 ff., 117 ff.

[60] Pol. 2. 21. 7–8; Cic. *Inv.* 2. 52. See further Chap. III, n. 26; Chap. IV with nn. 49 ff.; Lintott, 1987, 52.

[61] Taylor, 1962; Astin, 1967, 98 ff., 175 ff.; Lintott, *CAH* ix². 59 ff.

It has been pointed out earlier that up to a point Tiberius Gracchus conducted his tribunate under traditional rules. Octavius' persistent veto was abnormal, and the consequent abrogation of his office by the assembly was controversial, as T. Annius sought to demonstrate by means of his legal challenge through wager (*sponsione provocare*). Yet if Tiberius' measure had been implemented and he himself had left office without further incident, Polybius' republic would still have been prevailing at Rome. What in fact followed was the first step towards turning the assembly into an alternative administration, that is, the bill which appropriated some of the proceeds of Rome's new possession in Asia for the agrarian programme, and Gracchus' own pursuit of a second tribunate—not certainly illegal, but with no apparent precedent more recent than the tribunates of Licinius and Sextius in the fourth century. Gracchus' candidature was accompanied by new and dramatic legislative proposals. It was merely, one might have argued, a matter of the assembly being encouraged to assert its own ultimate authority. But his crowd of supporters would have allowed him to swamp voting assemblies, and his continuation as tribune with the same popular backing threatened to create something approaching a political organization among the plebs—something unknown since the time of the *secessiones*—and one with a wealthy and noble popular hero at its head. So it is hardly surprising that his aristocratic opponents saw him as a tyrannical demagogue. It was not so much that the democratic element was being aggrandized constitutionally, but that the social power of the aristocracy as a whole was under threat, since the assembly was being educated into believing that it could vote itself what it wanted.

This story was repeated on a broader scale by C. Gracchus. The assembly was shown more ways of promoting its own welfare through laws about land, colonies, and grain. Gaius himself did get re-elected successfully for one year. Though the position of the senate was not challenged constitutionally, its members came under threat through new judicial procedures. Moreover, the assembly found itself passing more and more complex legislation (some idea of the complexity can be derived from the surviving parts of the texts of the Gracchan *lex repetundarum* and post-Gracchan *lex agraria*),[62] which included measures dealing with the administration of the empire and with finance. This too led in the end to a violent reaction and a period of aristocratic dominance. The last years of the century saw the popular leaders reverting to Gracchan principles with laws about land and grain and with inter-

[62] *JRLR*, esp. 59 ff.

vention in provincial matters. In order to make their position the more secure, they did not simply rely on the assembly's favour but enlisted the support of a great military leader, C. Marius, who was elected to a string of consulships (C. Gracchus too had sought the favour of a consul—C. Fannius—in 122). As I have suggested earlier, the law about the praetorian provinces is an indication of the democratic colouring of Roman politics at the time. The comparative triviality of many of the items which are incorporated into the law is significant, as is the enormously elaborate structure of oaths and penalties designed to enforce the performance of the law's provisions (see n. 32 above). Saturninus and Glaucia overplayed their hand, lost the support of Marius, and were destroyed like the Gracchi before them. However, *popularis* techniques were now well-established and a genuinely new political ideology had appeared.

The pendulum, however, swung back. The *lex Caecilia Didia* of 98 BC, passed in the aftermath of Saturninus' fall, provided for the first time a machinery for the annulment of bills, which *inter alia* could be used to back religious obstruction to legislation through the use of auspices.[63] Ironically, it was first deployed against an attempt to link *popularis* methods and bills providing popular welfare through land and grain with the interests of the senate and of the Italians—the legislation of Livius Drusus. After the Marsic War and the concession in principle of citizenship to Rome's Latin and Italian allies, it was the use by P. Sulpicius of legislation in the assembly to settle the outstanding issues of the year, which provoked Sulla's march on Rome.

The measures proposed by Sulla in 88, whose implementation only occurred over a short period, if it occurred at all, constituted a radical attempt to reinstate aristocratic authority. No measure was to be brought to the assembly without prior discussion in the senate, and all votes were to take place in the *comitia centuriata*, not in a tribal assembly (the *concilium plebis* being thereby rendered powerless).[64] When Sulla returned from the East and became dictator, he evidently did not revive the second measure (his own bill about the quaestorship was passed in a tribal assembly).[65] The requirement for prior senatorial discussion before any legislation in an assembly may have been brought back, but the need for it was drastically reduced by an equally radical measure—a ban on tribunician legislation and prosecution (we do not know what form it took). Tribunes were also prevented from seeking

---

[63] *VRR* 140 ff.   [64] App. *BCiv.* 1. 59. 266.   [65] *RS* i. 14.

higher office.[66] They only retained their obstructive powers, including the power to protect individuals, and the power to address the people. It could have been argued now that the large increase in the citizen body made assemblies at Rome so unrepresentative that legislation could not be entrusted to them alone: it was the newly enlarged senate that was a better representative of Italy.[67] Nevertheless, the balance of the constitution was upset, and the seventies became notorious for political corruption running unchecked. Moreover, as Cicero recognized, the plebs at Rome, deprived of its tribunes, resorted to the traditional method of riot in order to give vent to its grievances: the restoration to the tribunate of its full powers became desirable as a safety-valve.[68]

Meanwhile, constitutional developments at Rome were becoming eclipsed by the accumulation of power in the hands of commanders overseas. In spite of the precedent provided by the Second Punic War the Romans had on the whole bestowed military command for comparatively brief periods throughout the second century down to the last decade, when Marius achieved his first six consulships. This remained an isolated precedent in the earliest years of the first century (there was no attempt to imitate it in the Marsic War). However, civil war led *de facto* to a long proconsulship for Sulla in the East (which, when linked with his previous offices, meant that he was in continuous military command for almost a decade), while at Rome the leading Marians multiplied their tenure of annual magistracies.

Did Sulla, recognizing the dangers to the republic implicit in a career such as his, seek to eliminate them for the future? Following Mommsen, scholars have argued that it was Sulla's policy to separate civil magistracy from military command: the two consuls and the (now) eight praetors were to remain at Rome during their year of office and then all take over provinces, which conveniently at this point added up to ten (provided that Gallia Cisalpina was combined with either Transalpina or Illyricum). So there would be no need for extended commands.[69] Moreover, Sulla's *lex Cornelia de maiestate* had made it an offence to leave a province with an army or wage war without senatorial approval. It might be thought that Sulla was not so naïve as to think that a man such as

---

[66] App. *BCiv.* 1. 100. 467; Livy, *Per.* 89; Caes. *BCiv.* 1. 5. 1 and 7. 3; Cic. *Leg.* 3. 22; Asc. 81C; Sall. *Hist.* 3. 48. 8.

[67] On Italian representation see Wiseman, 1971, esp. chs. 3–4.

[68] Cic. *Leg.* 3. 23–4.

[69] *Staatsr.* i. 57–9; ii. 214 ff.; iii. 1104–5; Mommsen, 1857, ii. 353–6, criticized by Giovannini, 1983, 73 ff.

himself, who had decided to start a civil war by leading his army on Rome, would be deterred by the knowledge that, if he failed, he would be prosecuted under a law specially designed for the purpose. However that may be, we know now that the law was not designed for that purpose. The clauses in Sulla's law are taken over from those in a *lex Porcia* (probably of 101–100 BC), which are repeated in the *lex de provinciis praetoriis*.[70] It is true that praetors in the late Republic were not allotted provincial commands until their city magistracy was over.[71] However, consuls were still allocated provinces (until 52 BC determined before their election under C. Gracchus' *lex Sempronia*) early in their consulship and on a number of occasions left for them before the year was out.[72] The notion that Sulla sought to defuse the danger of long-term military commands by legislation is a chimera. Nor did his supporters, who controlled politics in the following decade, appear to recognize the problem. Metellus Pius was about nine years in Spain fighting Sertorius, Pompey about six; Lucullus was ultimately about seven years in the East, and there were many commands of about three years. The lack of sufficient competent commanders for the large number of battle-zones was one reason; intrigue and personal ambition another. The precedent had already been set in the seventies for the long-term commands that dominated the last years of the Republic.

The restoration of full powers to the tribunate by Pompey and Crassus in 70 BC led to vigorous tribunician activity, often linked with the voting of special proconsular commands. The association of Glaucia and Saturninus with Marius was re-enacted by Gabinius and Manilius with Pompey, by Vatinius with Caesar, by Clodius with Piso and Gabinius, and by Trebonius with Pompey and Crassus. The effect of these was to remove for considerable periods large sections of Rome's overseas activities from the supervision of any authority at Rome, and in Pompey's case this even included decisions on expenditure and the imposition of taxes.[73] Thus in the last decades of the Republic the senate was caught in a pincer movement between tribunes who, following the example of the Gracchi, were reasserting the theoretical sovereignty of the assemblies in order to take the lead in political decision-making at Rome, and pro-

---

[70] Cic. *Pis.* 50; *lex prov. praet.* (*RS* i. 12), Cnidos III, 3 ff.; Giovannini, 1983, 91 ff.

[71] Cic. *Att.* 1. 13. 5, 14. 5, 15. 1.

[72] 43 BC (Cic. *Fam.* 12. 14. 5) may be discounted as a peculiar year, but for other evidence see Cic. *Att.* 1. 16. 8, 19. 2; 4. 13. 2; *Sest.* 71–2; *Prov. Cos.* 36–7. See also *MRR* on 78, 74, and 63 BC and for discussion Balsdon, 1939.

[73] See e.g. Plut. *Pomp.* 25. 6; Cic. *Att.* 2. 16. 2; cf. 4. 1. 7 for Messius' proposal in 57 BC and see n. 34 above.

consuls who were exploiting the discretion granted them to manage affairs in the empire.

There is no need to elaborate here on the violence and corruption which characterized politics in the city at this time, but it should be stressed that this stemmed not so much from the domination of any particular man or group but from conflict and near-anarchy. This in turn was aggravated by a loss of credibility in institutions traditionally regarded as authoritative—the senate and the higher magistracies in the city. The senate itself, which since Sulla numbered over 500 members, would have lacked the coherence of the pre-Sullan body, and its junior echelons would have been powerfully influenced by the handful of great political figures. To treat this as the nadir of a Platonic (or Polybian) rake's progress is too simplistic. For all Clodius' activities, the city plebs was not allowed to create a tyrannical position for its own leader: instead, the traditional authority of the magistrate was asserted (albeit, in the form of a sole consul, not a dictator). It was not so much that Rome's mixed constitution evolved into monarchic demagogy, but that the conflicts of institution and ideology which were built into it created an impasse which led to civil war. The victorious commander could then exploit the sovereignty of the assembly to create for himself a magistracy which went beyond Republican bounds.

Polybius' analysis, therefore, though ultimately it cannot do justice to the progress of the Republic after his time of writing, is nonetheless a valuable pointer to the way in which we should interpret the changes in the Roman republic. It was in his day and remained subsequently a constitution in which different elements were in conflict. In the end the democratic and monarchic elements had the advantage. What Polybius does not bring out, at least explicitly, is the fact that there was not only a conflict between elements in the constitution but also between ideologies and between interpretations of the constitution. These changed over the centuries, as much as, if not more than, the institutions themselves.

XII

The Mixed Constitution and Republican Ideology

The varying beliefs of those who participated in Republican politics have already become apparent in the foregoing chapters. From the third century onwards at least, perhaps the majority of the élite supported senatorial authority in the interests of maintaining the status quo, others believed in the superiority of the elected magistrate, while plebeian leaders laid stress on the rights of the plebs—*provocatio*, the inviolability of tribunes, and the freedom of the plebeian assembly.[1] These ideologies can for the most part be only understood by us in general terms. However, in Cicero's *De Re Publica* we possess a work in which the theory of the mixed constitution is discussed in the light of the Roman Republic, and in his *De Legibus* a pendant to this, constructing a detailed constitution for the ideal republic on the basis of the elements of the Roman constitution. These not only reveal Cicero's political ideology but are important examples of the theory of the mixed constitution. It will become clear that, in spite of Cicero's knowledge of Polybius, his vision of the republic is significantly different, owing as much, if not more, to Aristotle. In order, therefore, to provide his work with a context, this chapter commences with a brief discussion of the origins of the theory of the mixed constitution in Greek political thought.

The Mixed Constitution in Classical Greece and in Polybius

Although the beginnings of the theory of the mixed constitution have been sought as far back as Solon and then in Pythagorean cosmological theory of the early fifth century,[2] it seems imprudent to postulate an origin before we have the first clear evidence for the theoretical discussion of politics and of the distinction between the three simple types of

---

[1] See e.g. Ferrary, 1982, esp. 755 ff.; Perelli, 1982, 5 ff.; Mackie, 1992.

[2] Alkmaion DK24, B4; Aalders, 1968; Nippel, 1980, 43 ff. The following discussion is to some extent a reprise of Lintott, 1997.

constitution in Pindar and Herodotus later on in that century.[3] It is more probable that the theory in fact originated with the first reference known to us—Thucydides' description of the constitution of the 5,000, established at Athens in autumn 411, as a blend which was moderate in the direction both of the many and of the few. The fact that the constitution was moderate was as important for Thucydides as that it was mixed, and in this respect his commendation is indeed part of an older tradition. Belief in moderation goes back to Solon and to Phokylides.[4] Viewed more concretely, the 5,000 was a democracy based on those who served in the Greek heavily armed phalanx, the hoplites: they constituted its primary assembly. Other examples could be found of this in the Greek world, and that contributed to the continued life of the theory in the fourth century.

It is to Aristotle that we owe the first proper discussion of the mixed constitution that we possess, but it is evident that he had a number of predecessors. One was Plato who had claimed that he was creating in the *Laws* an ideal mean point between democracy and monarchy.[5] Commenting on this constitution, Aristotle argues that 'it aims to be neither democracy nor oligarchy, but a mean between them, which they call *politeia*, for it is of the hoplite-soldiers'. However, he then refers to the Spartan constitution as possibly better, stating that there were people who believed that the best constitution of all was that mixed from all the constitutions—oligarchy, monarchy, and democracy—and praises the Spartan constitution as an example, because the kingship supplied monarchy, the *gerousia* oligarchy, and the ephors democracy.[6] In another passage Aristotle pointed out that there were people who praised Solon as lawgiver, on the ground that he had made a good mixture of the Athenian constitution, with oligarchic, aristocratic, and democratic elements.[7] We can only speculate on possible contexts for such discussions (for example, posthumous evaluation of Theramenes or debates on Phormisios' proposal to limit Athenian citizenship to

---

[3] Pindar, *Pyth.* 2. 86 ff. (*c.* 470 BC); Hdt. 3. 80–82, written, at the earliest, about the middle of that century.

[4] Thuc. 8. 97. 1; Solon, frr. 5 and 36 West; Ar. *Pol.* 4. 1295^{b}33–4.

[5] Plato, *Laws* 6. 756e–757a, cf. 3. 691e–692a and 693d ff. for earlier discussion of moderation and blending.

[6] Ar. *Pol.* 2. 1265^b–66^a. Others (1265^{b}40) had treated the ephorate as a tyranny and the Spartan way of life as a democratic feature.

[7] Ar. *Pol.* 2. 1273^b–74^a. Aristotle would have considered this too a *politeia*, cf. 4. 1297^b 12–15, where he points out that what were called *politeiai* in his own day were called *dēmokratiai* in the archaic period. See also Isoc. *Panath.* 153, where a *politeia* is democracy mixed with aristocracy.

those possessing land).[8] What is evident, however, is that a constitution based on hoplites had already been given the name *politeia* before Aristotle, and that the formulation of such constitutions had involved the blending of the simple constitutions and the concept of the mean.

The *politeia* finds its place in Aristotle's taxonomy of three correct and three deviant constitutions as the third correct constitution (following monarchy and aristocracy)—one in which the many manage their city in the common interest. For, in his view, although it is difficult for a greater number to be perfect in every virtue, this is most likely with military virtue. Hence the *politeia* wins its place among the constitutions based on virtue through being a hoplite democracy.[9] There is no mention here of mixing, but in the review of constitutions in Book 4, *politeia* is defined as a mixture of oligarchy and democracy, tending towards democracy (those mixtures tending towards oligarchy are, according to Aristotle here, called aristocracies). 'Only the mixture aims at the rich and the poor, wealth and freedom.'[10] Aristotle then discusses techniques of mixing oligarchy and democracy. One requires mixing the positive features of the two types of constitution regarding one of their component institutions (for example, fining the wealthy for non-attendance at assemblies, while paying the poor to attend), another is to take a mean-point between their provisions, a third is to combine provisions.[11] This in turn leads to a discussion of the mean, since a good mixture leads to a mean in which both the extremes are visible. However, Aristotle believes in a mean and moderation for its own sake, since the excellence requisite for a happy life is a mean and this applies to constitutions as much as to individuals. Hence societies based on those with moderate property holdings are best, because their members are more likely to obey reason, and more stable, since they are unlikely to be the prey of oligarchy, tyranny, or faction.[12] He later argues that a *politeia* must be constituted from the hoplites but with as broad a qualification as possible, in order to ensure that more people are members of the *politeia* than not.[13]

The impression given by Aristotle's arguments on this topic is somewhat confused. He recognizes the importance of earlier discussions of the mixed constitution, but for him the fundamental feature of the *politeia* is that it is a hoplite democracy. He discusses mixing in a precise

---

[8] According to the speech ascribed to him in Xen. *Hell.* 2. 3. 48, Theramenes believed in a constitution based on hoplites; for Phormisios' proposal see Lys. 34.

[9] Ar. *Pol.* 3. 1279ᵃ⁻ᵇ.   [10] Ar. *Pol.* 4. 1293ᵇ–94ᵃ, esp. 94ᵃ15–16.

[11] Ar. *Pol.* 4. 1294ᵃ⁻ᵇ.   [12] Ar. *Pol.* 4. 1295ᵃ–96ᵃ.   [13] Ar. *Pol.* 4. 1297ᵇ1–12.

and technical fashion, but he is more concerned with the mean and moderation as a characteristic feature of a community. Indeed, perhaps the most interesting reference to mixing is the passage where he says that only the mixed constitution can aim both at rich and poor, wealth or freedom—that is, combine the ideologies of oligarchy and democracy. His prime concern is the establishment of moderate men at the core of his city with their natural propensity to virtue; he also seeks to promote simultaneously the democratic ideal of shared liberty and the oligarchic ideal of granting privilege to wealth.[14] Above all, he is thinking of fusion, not of balancing conflicting forces, as Polybius was to do later.

We are largely in the dark about the development of the theory in the interval between Aristotle and Polybius. A writer whose works Cicero sought to obtain—though after the composition of *De Re Publica* and *De Legibus*—was Aristotle's pupil Dicaearchus of Messana. One of his books was entitled *Tripolitikos* (or *Tripolitikon*) and, if we trust a Byzantine reference to the *Dikaiarchikon*, recommended a constitution blended from the best features of the three unmixed constitutions. The author also had a particular interest in Sparta.[15] He probably developed Aristotelian theory to embrace the three constitutions, using Sparta as an example. Although Diogenes Laertius claimed that the Stoics approved of the mixed constitution, this statement is a suspiciously bold generalization: he may have only been referring to some Stoics contemporary with, or subsequent to, Polybius.[16] However, the fact that Cato the Censor is said to have referred to the mixed constitution in his *Origines*, describing Carthage as a mixture of monarchy, oligarchy, and democracy, is more probably evidence that this was a topic in circulation among his contemporaries, than that Cato had early knowledge of the contents of Polybius Book 6.[17]

We have already considered the overall character and detail of Polybius' account of the Roman constitution (Chap. III). The present chapter will confine itself to the place of this in relation to other accounts of the mixed constitution. The nature and indeed function of Polybius' treatment is quite different to that of Aristotle. Aristotle was writing a theoretical analysis (albeit with reference to existing political systems),

---

[14] Ar. *Pol.* 4. 1294^{a}15–17; 1295^{b}25 ff.; 1296^{b}22 ff. On the two partisan ideologies see also 5. 1301^{a}25 ff.

[15] Cic. *Att.* 13. 32. 2; Athen. 4. 141a; Photius, *Bibl.* 37 Bekker.

[16] Diog. Laert. 7. 131. A hypothetical example of such a Stoic would be Sphairos of Borysthenes, who was involved with the reforming kings of Sparta in the late third century (Plut. *Cleom.* 2. 2–3; 11), on whom see Erskine, 1990, 97–9, 134–8; Vatai, 1984, 124–6.

[17] Cato, fr. 80P.

which, in so far as it was practically oriented, was intended to help a lawgiver. Polybius was seeking as a historian to explain a major cause of Rome's rise to world power for statesmen who might well have to deal with the Romans themselves, but who in any case would derive educational benefit from studying how their political system worked. Aristotle was interested in analysing patterns of institutions that he hoped would remain static and thus create political stability. Polybius accepted that the balance between institutions would change, however slowly, and sought explanations which were dynamic and reflected the historical process.

In the *Politics* Aristotle had abandoned Plato's vision of a one-way progress through constitutions from a just monarchy to a tyranny springing from ill-disciplined democracy, in favour of a much more complex picture of possible constitutional changes which reflected the variety which could be discovered empirically in the Greek world. Polybius basically adopted Aristotle's taxonomy of the three correct and three deviant constitutions but for Aristotle's *politeia* substituted 'democracy'. This is a praiseworthy constitution in which people respect the laws, their parents, their leaders, liberty, and freedom of speech; its corrupt counterpart is *ochlokratia* or *cheirokratia*, where the mob or force rules.[18] Hence there is no primary constitution in Polybius which can be regarded as involving mixture. Moreover, he returned to Plato's view that each of the good primary constitutions became corrupt in turn naturally (*kata phusin*). The new element he introduced was a cyclic process (there is no evidence for this earlier in constitutional thought), in which a society moved from being a monarchy based on physical strength to being a monarchy based on justice, then tyranny, aristocracy, oligarchy, democracy, until finally it returned to the brutal form of monarchy.[19]

Growth and decay according to nature (*kata phusin*) were for Polybius the key to understanding the Roman constitution. However, the notion of the mixed constitution was also essential. Characteristically, Polybius introduced this by a reference not to a theoretician like Aristotle, but to a practical statesman and lawgiver—Lycurgus. The latter had sought to

[18] Pol. 6. 3. 7–4. 6.

[19] Pol. 6. 4. 7–9. 9, with Walbank, 1957, i. 643–7. The attempt by von Scala, 1890, 180 ff.—followed by Pöschl 1936, 100 ff.; and Ryffel 1949, 189 ff.—to link Polybius with fragments of neo-Pythagorean philosophy ascribed to Hippodamus, *Peri Politeias*, and Ocellus Lucanus in Stobaeus (*Flor.* 98. 71 and *Ecl. Phys. et Eth.* 1. 13. 2 and 20. 3) is unconvincing. The fragments cannot be securely dated before Polybius and in any case are accounts of nature with no relation to politics.

check the natural decay implicit in the simple constitutions by combining them all in the one he gave to Sparta, where there were three elements, the kings, the aristocratic element in the *gerousia*, and the *dēmos*. These balanced one another and prevented each other from toppling into disaster, the *gerousia* being in particular the element which supported the weaker of the other two. What Lycurgus achieved by calculation and foresight, the Romans achieved naturally, not through theory but through action and conflict.[20] In the evolution from monarchy towards democracy, they retained elements of the political organizations that they had discarded. Hence they too had a monarchic, aristocratic, and democratic element in their constitution which created balance by their opposition to and co-operation with one another. A similar process had taken place at Carthage, though the latter at the time of the Second Punic War had moved further on the evolutionary path towards democracy.[21]

When a reader of Polybius, versed in Plato and Aristotle, finds discussion of the corruption of simple constitutions and the use of blending as an antidote, he may feel himself on familiar ground. But this would be deceptive. The general character and details of the analysis of the Roman constitution have already been discussed in Chapter III. It was argued there that Polybius employed a novel approach, diverging from what had been the norm in classical Greek political thought. He focused on the real power of the various organs of the constitution rather than their formal function, which allowed him to bring into his calculations the effect of individuals and groups pursuing their sectional interests rather than those of the community. His vision of Rome's mixed constitution was of a political system that was already to a certain extent corrupt, but in which corruption could be held in check. It was not one that had attained to an ideal mean because moderate men were dominant and had transmitted to it their own character, but one where not only checks, but active opposition and conflict, played an essential role in keeping the balance. *Stasis* (civil strife), the bogey of Greek political thinkers, was not outlawed, but, as it were, domesticated and given a role in normal politics. Hence Rome attained the freedom from revolution for which Sparta had been praised. However, the natural process which created the constitution—thus conferring on it the status of being a product of history, rather than a philosopher's blue-print—was also a source of its weakness and ultimate demise.

[20] Pol. 6. 9. 10–10. 14.
[21] Pol. 6. 18; 51.

Cicero's *De Re Publica*

We are fortunate to possess as much of the *De Re Publica* as we do, thanks to the discovery of the Vatican palimpsest. This provides us with an adequate, if incomplete, knowledge of Books 1 to 3, in the first two of which much of Cicero's constitutional doctrine is expounded, as well as a scattering of fragments from Books 4 and 5, to supplement our knowledge of this part of the work from other authors.

Cicero began to write it in the year following the conference of Luca and the second consulships of Pompey and Crassus. The book went into circulation in 51. It is tempting to see it as a substitute for political action. Yet, although Cicero himself believed in 56 that he had been constrained to abandon honourable politics and to surrender his independence to the demands of the three dynasts, one should not regard this as a period of political retirement. In fact he was as much involved in public affairs as ever.[22] As I hope to suggest in the following analysis, it may be fairer to see the *De Re Publica* not as a piece of escapism but a contribution, albeit theoretical, to the current political debate.

The impression of escapism is produced by the literary imitation of Plato's *Republic* and by the fact that the dialogue is set in the past—not far distant, but over twenty years before Cicero's birth. Cicero himself is our witness that this is deliberate artifice in letters to Atticus and his brother Quintus of 54 BC. He was urged by Sallustius to change the setting to his own time, so that he could participate in person, thus being able to deal directly with topics which preoccupied him and avoiding the impression of an obvious fiction (the preceding dialogue *De Oratore* was set in Cicero's lifetime). His reason for retaining the displacement in time in spite of these objections was to avoid giving offence.[23] It follows from this that the dialogue had in fact a contemporary agenda and embodied Cicero's own views: as an imaginative re-creation of history, it was not bound by the requirements of authenticity.

In Cicero's dialogue the character Laelius refers to Scipio Aemilianus' frequent discussions about politics with Panaetius in Polybius' presence and claims that Scipio had argued that the ancestral Roman constitution was by far the best of all: Scipio is then asked to expand on this theme for the benefit of the other characters in the dialogue. We need not doubt that these discussions actually had occurred: indeed it is possible that

[22] See Cic. *QF* 2. 13. 1; *Att*. 4. 14. 1; 5. 12. 2; *Fam*. 8. 1. 4, together with the modern works cited in the following note, and, on his political commitments at the time, Lintott, 1974.
[23] Cic. *Att*. 4. 16. 2; *QF* 3. 5. 1. See Ferrary, 1984; Strasburger, 1960.

Scipio had influenced the presentation of the Roman constitution in Polybius.[24] However, there is no reason to think that Cicero had good information about the discussions, and in any case he was not trying to give a faithful reproduction of them. Equally, we cannot regard the dialogue as a reflection of Stoic views on constitutions, even if there is a Stoic flavour to some of the comments in the dialogue. For it purports to be primarily an expression of Scipio's views; we have no idea what Panaetius' opinions on constitutions were, nor does Cicero mention Stoic doctrine as one of his sources for the *De Re Publica*. What is evident is the influence of Aristotelian doctrine—something which Cicero himself stressed.[25]

Cicero takes over the classification of three good unmixed constitutions, paired with three corrupt ones. He holds that the good, even though they have no particular failings, may degenerate into their corresponding corrupt counterparts. However, following Aristotle rather than Plato and Polybius, he does not think that this is inevitable or, more specifically, that a single natural one-way process determines such changes. There are instead a number of cycles, which allow a tyranny or oligarchy, for example, to be followed by any of the other simple constitutions.[26] Like Aristotle again, Cicero believes that human society does not only derive from weakness and a need for protection but from a natural social instinct, leading to a pursuit of common interests and an acceptance of law.[27] In the light of this he sees the advantage of the mixed constitution to be in what he calls *aequabilitas*, evenhandedness, which allows privilege to the aristocracy and liberty and participation to the common people.[28]

Cicero's ideal, then, is a society held together by just organization, and this is how he envisages the constitution of the Roman Republic, not as something produced by evolution and conflict and relying on mutual threats for survival, as portrayed by Polybius. In Cicero's account of the

[24] For a possible instance see Chap. III, n. 4.

[25] Cic. *Div.* 2. 3 on Peripatetic influence. In *Leg.* 3. 13–14 he says that the topic of magistrates was discussed, after Theophrastus, by Diogenes the Stoic (if we accept Turnebus' emendation) and by Panaetius, but by no other Stoics. We do not know on what type of constitution these two last treatments were based. For Stoic ideas in non-constitutional sections see *Rep.* 1. 19 and 56; 3. 33. For recent arguments that Cicero must have based his work on Dicaearchus, rather than Aristotle himself, see Frede, 1989. However, without knowing what was in Dicaearchus' work, one cannot reach any safe conclusions based on the absence of certain Aristotelian ideas in Cicero. See also Taiphakos, 1995, ch. 5.

[26] Cic. *Rep.* 1. 44–5 and 68; 2. 45 and 65; cf. Ar. *Pol.* 5. 1304^b–6^a; 1316^a.

[27] *Rep.* 1. 39; Ar. *Pol.* 1. 1252^b; 3. 1279^a, 1280^a.

[28] *Rep.* 1. 69, but see 1. 53 for a hostile optimate view of *aequabilitas*. Cf. Ar. *Pol.* 4. 1293^b–94^a, esp. 94^{a}15–25.

development of Rome, the kings themselves make a large contribution to the creation of Rome's mixed constitution. Romulus imitates Lycurgus in creating the senate. Numa Pompilius institutes the popular election of the monarch (and the passing of the *lex curiata*), since the people would not accept a *res publica* without a king, and the consultation of the people continues until the accession of Servius Tullius—who seizes the kingship without the approval of the people but subsequently does pass a *lex curiata* about his own *imperium*. Moreover, Servius Tullius enhances the mixture by creating the *comitia centuriata*, which allows the semblance of participation to every citizen, but ensures that the votes of the rich are dominant.[29]

The kingship was thus in many ways admirable in Cicero's view; its failing was the lack of liberty. Hence, when Tarquinius Superbus succumbed to his insolence, and the natural metamorphosis of king into tyrant took place, this produced a powerful popular reaction against kingship.[30] Cicero regards it as inevitable that liberation from tyranny should lead to the acquisition by the people of a modest increment of liberty. The leaders of the new republic made concessions to public opinion in the form of restrictions on consular power and the legal entrenchment of *provocatio*. Then, in response to the debt crisis the tribunes were first created. This development is for Cicero an example of the triumph of the nature of public affairs (we might say, political necessity) over pure reason. Nevertheless it was paralleled by the creation of the ephors in Sparta and *kosmoi* in Crete, and could be justified by the principle of evenhandedness, whereby power was accorded to the magistrates, authority to the deliberations of the leading men (*principes*), and liberty to the people. Only in this way could a stable constitution be achieved.[31] This was balanced by an assertion of authority from above through the invention of the dictatorship and the requirement of the approval by the *patres* of assembly resolutions.[32]

The end of Scipio's main discourse on the development of the constitution is largely lost through gaps in the palimpsest, but little can have been mentioned after the Twelve Tables and the *lex Canuleia* (the law

[29] *Rep.* 2. 15–17, 23–5, 37–41. Cicero was in part dependent on Polybius for facts (*Rep.* 2. 27), but this does not entail that he followed Polybius in his interpretation of the mixed constitution, as argued for example by How, 1930. See Pöschl, 1976, esp. 72 ff.; Ferrary, 1984.

[30] *Rep.* 2. 45 ff. At 2. 51 Cicero notes that the change from king to tyrant is not according to Plato's model (it was in fact discussed by Aristotle, *Pol.* 5. 1310^b); Cicero also contrasts the king with his '*rector et gubernator civitatis* (pilot and steersman of the community)', of whom he has more to say later (5. 5–6 and 8).

[31] *Rep.* 2. 52–5 and 57–8.

[32] *Rep.* 2. 56.

about intermarriage between patricians and plebeians).[33] Hence there can have been at most a brief summary of the constitutional changes of the fourth and early third century BC—the opening to plebeians of curule offices, membership of the senate and of priesthoods, the integration of the tribunate into political operations as a regular magistracy, and the recognition of plebiscites as laws binding the whole community. This might have been justified on the ground that the elements of the constitution had been created in the early years of the Republic and later developments were secondary. Polybius, similarly seems to have ended his sketch of ancient Roman political history with the Twelve Tables and the Valerio-Horatian laws.[34] However, whereas Polybius believed in a constitution that was in a state of continuous evolution through conflict, and, on his own premisses, would not have wished to deny the importance of the developments from that time onwards, Cicero wished to portray the achievement of a constitution that was stable, balanced, and harmonious because it was under the control of its leaders. The mixture of which he approved would have been by Aristotelian standards aristocratic.[35] This picture would have been marred by the introduction of later conflicts and changes, such as the last secession of the plebs and the *lex Hortensia.* Moreover, it suited his political purpose to underestimate the importance of the achievements of popular agitation and the popular leaders. Plebeian rights are seen as concessions by their betters in the interests of liberty, justice, and political stability. They are not the reward of popular self-assertion and victory in a social conflict. Scipio's republic after the Twelve Tables is in this respect like Cicero's in the *Pro Sestio*—one in which the people have all they want and do not need to ask for more.

Cicero's attempt to paint the *popularis* leaders into the background of Republican history is an obvious reaction to the contemporary turmoil in Rome and his own traumatic experiences earlier in the fifties. It may also reflect the influence of Sullan ideology long after the man himself was dead and detested and his mutilation of the tribunate had been repaired. Cicero, as he makes clear in the *De Legibus* (see below), thought Sulla went too far in tilting the balance of the republic. Nevertheless, he

---

[33] *Rep.* 2. 63–4: one item whose text is not preserved was the story of the publishing of the list of *dies fasti* (days on which legal acts were proper in the eyes of the priesthood) by Cn. Flavius in 304 (*Att.* 6. 1. 8).

[34] Pol. 6. 11. 1; Chap. III with n. 26.

[35] *Rep.* 2. 57, 67 and 69; cf. Ar. *Pol.* 4. 1293b (elections according to excellence and wealth) and 1298b (all citizens control matters like peace, war and the holding of magistrates to account, but elected magistrates control other matters).

hankers after a constitution in which power and authority are the prerogative of the curule magistrates and the senate respectively, as they were in the seventies BC. This is represented most forcefully in the image of the mahout directing the elephant, the control of wild and powerful forces by a single, apparently weak, intelligent being.[36]

In another matter he has for a long time appeared to scholars to be reflecting the primacy of Pompey in the late fifties and expectations that he might be allowed a guiding hand over the direction of public affairs.[37] This is his treatment of the man he calls a '*rector et gubernator civitatis*' or '*moderator rei publicae*'. This man is introduced as an ideal type, diametrically opposed to the monarch who becomes a tyrant, like Tarquinius Superbus. Later, he apparently forms the centre of the discussion in Book 5, where he is visualized as a sort of Platonic sage who is prepared to spend some time in the Cave—a man learned in the law and Greek literature, who is prepared to put his wisdom to practical use and whose opinions will provide moral guidance for the Republic and direct its affairs.[38] It is hard to be sure how Cicero imagined that this could be realized in practice: the obvious assumption is that the *rector* would be the senior senator, but the part assigned him seems to involve greater political power, like that of a Greek lawgiver.[39] Hence we might think of Pompey in what Cicero at one time called his 'divine third consulship'. Of course, Cicero roundly states in a letter of 49 BC that the ideals of the *moderator* had never come into Pompey's head, but here there is a suggestion of disappointment.[40] It may also be that Cicero thought that he himself was the obvious candidate for this position and that his political works were in some way a lawgiver's response to the problems posed by the declining republic (see below).

However that may be, the presentation of the '*moderator*' is also interesting in that it may be related to other features of the work—the positive approach to monarchy to be found both in the theoretical

[36] *Rep.* 2. 56–8; *Leg.* 3. 23–5; on the mahout, *Rep.* 2. 67. Other more traditional images are those of the charioteer (*Rep.* 2. 68) and the steersman (see n. 37).

[37] The bibliography on this topic is enormous. See Schmidt, 1973, esp. 326–32 and for a new interpretation Powell, 1994. In particular, Eduard Meyer (1922, 180 ff.) thought that Cicero was advocating a form of principate for Pompey, even though the latter fell short of his ideal statesman—an idea which would be a guiding light for Augustus. Examples of critics of this view are How, 1930, 36 ff.; Powell, 1994, arguing that *rector* is simply a term for an ideal republican statesman with no exceptional powers.

[38] *Rep.* 2. 51; 5. 5–6 and 8. Cf. *de Or.* 1. 211 for a vision of a number of *principes* being *rei publicae rectores*.

[39] In *Rep.* 5. 6 the *rector* is the source of *instituta* and *disciplina*; in 5. 3 Numa is compared to the Greek kings as a source of law.

[40] Cic. *Att.* 7. 1. 4; cf. *Leg.* 1. 8; *Att.* 8. 11. 1–2.

discussions of Book I and in the historical sketch of Book II, and Scipio's dream that he might be called to set Rome to rights as dictator.[41] In this respect Cicero's vision is now somewhat different from that which he expounded a few years earlier in the *Pro Sestio*, in the rallying call to the young men of the upper classes to sustain the authority of the senate.[42] Here aristocratic dominance is not enough without the intermittent intervention of a single man. He cannot be a monarch, since monarchy is potentially corrupt and at Rome has been superseded by the republic, but he must fulfil the function, formerly performed by Rome's monarchs, of being an authoritative source of wise institutions.

Cicero's *De Legibus*

The manuscript tradition of the *De Legibus* is in its own way as unsatisfactory as that of the *De Re Publica*. The first introductory book, on natural law, is almost complete; so is the second book on religious law, although one lacuna must have been considerable; the third book on constitutional law has two important lacunas within the text and then breaks off—apparently near its end, since Cicero has discussed all his proposed statutes; of the remaining books, however many were written, we have only a few fragments. The work declares itself to be a pendant to the *De Re Publica*, as Plato's *Laws* was a pendant to the *Republic*,[43] though it is given a contemporary setting with Marcus himself, his brother Quintus, and Atticus, holding a discussion by the banks of the Liris in the territory of Arpinum. The friendly reference to Pompey in the introduction suggests both an imagined date and a real time of writing not long after his third consulship of 52.[44] The civil war does not even appear on the horizon. Hence the work is in time close to the first circulation of *De Re Publica* in 51.

The change of setting does, however, cause a displacement from that work and so does the agenda. In *De Re Publica* the Roman Republic in its early form is given as an illustration of the ideal mixed constitution. In *De Legibus*, although Cicero uses Roman institutions as the basis for his laws and even takes over chapters of the Twelve Tables, he is professedly deriving a code of ideal statutes from first principles.[45] This allows

---

[41] *Rep.* 1. 52, 54–63; 2. 4–43; 3. 47; 6. 12—on which see Pöschl, 1976, 24 ff., with references to earlier discussions.

[42] *Sest.* 96 ff.

[43] *Leg.* 1. 15 and 20; 2. 23; 3. 4 and 12.

[44] *Leg.* 1. 1–2 and 8; 2. 1–3. See in general Rawson, 1973, with references to earlier work.

[45] *Leg.* 2. 8–14; 3. 2–5; cf. 2. 23; 3. 44.

him scope for innovation, and, even though at one point he claims that he is only reproducing in statute what had been *mos*, unwritten norms, in his ideal early Republic, in practice there are important alterations to the constitution which change its balance.[46] One original element in the *De Re Publica*, however, is totally absent from the *De Legibus*—the *rector civitatis* or *moderator rei publicae*. It has been argued rightly that this shows that this man cannot have been conceived by Cicero as a semi-monarchic *princeps*, since there is no room for a magistrate of this type in the *De Legibus*.[47] Nevertheless, if such a man can be seen as a lawgiver and source of morals, then he is present in the *De Legibus* as the central figure in the dialogue, Marcus Cicero himself. One may compare *Rep.* 5. 5–6 (the discussion of the *moderator*) with *Leg.* 1. 14–20 where Marcus' task in that dialogue is explained: in each passage the person's function is to pronounce on the principles of the *res publica*, not the minutiae of civil law.[48]

The core of Cicero's constitutional rules in Book III is *imperium*. Cicero justifies this in a theoretical introduction, where, following the precedent of *De Re Publica*, complimentary reference is made to the justice and wisdom of ancient kings. The magistrates are the essential middle link in the chain of command which runs from the laws to the people. A magistrate is a talking law, while a law is a dumb magistrate. The desire of those who disapproved of regal power was not to obey no one, but not always to obey the same man. Therefore, in the republican mixed constitution *imperium* must be retained but limits must be placed on the magistrates' commands and the citizens' obedience.[49] The monarchic element in Cicero's republic is thus even more important than in Polybius'. We can see here too one source of Mommsen's belief in the centrality of the power of the Roman magistrate.[50]

In the code that follows Cicero begins by expressly requiring obedience to magistrates' commands (*imperia*) and requiring the magistrates to enforce their commands by coercion—through fines, bonds, and blows—unless this were blocked by intercession from a magistrate of equal or greater power, to whom the citizen concerned had the right of

---

[46] *Leg.* 2. 23; Rawson, 1973 = 1991, 141 ff.; Keyes, 1921.

[47] Rawson, 1973 = 1991, 141–2 with further references; How, 1930, 39 and 41.

[48] *Serendae mores*, the sowing of morals (*Leg.* 1. 20), corresponds well with the promotion of a moral conscience (*verecundia*) by the *rector* in *Rep.* 5. 6. Note also the rare word *responsitare* ('to give regularly legal opinions'), which appears both in *Rep.* 5. 5 and *Leg.* 1. 14. For legislators instilling morals see also Cicero's advice to Caesar (*Marc.* 23), including 'comprimendae libidines'.

[49] *Leg.* 3. 2–5.

[50] Chaps. VII with nn. 15–16, XI with nn. 2–4.

appeal (*provocatio*): such appeals were not to be valid against a military commander. This encapsulates the principles of the Roman republic, while being somewhat at variance with normal practice in implying that magistrates should be general law-enforcers, when in fact they had neither the time nor the resources so to be. Cicero has also effectively repealed the *lex Porcia* which banned the flogging of citizens.[51]

Cicero provides for the contesting of a fine or a penalty, 'when the magistrate has judged or proposed it', through the popular assembly—thus a form of assembly trial. It is just possible that 'has judged' means, or includes in its meaning, a decision by a magistrate in the early form of *quaestio*, such as that used for the Bacchanals (Chap. IX with nn. 40 ff.). In this case Cicero's clause may provide for automatic review of such decisions by the assembly. It clearly does not apply to all occasions where *coercitio* has been attempted and resisted by *provocatio*, but only those where the magistrate chose himself to resort to judicial procedure.[52] These clauses should be considered in conjunction with a later piece of exegesis, where Cicero explains why all magistrates are given the right to take the auspices and the right to hold trials. The former is to allow them to impede undesirable assemblies; the latter, 'in order that they might have power to summon an assembly, to which appeal might be made'.[53] Cicero is apparently proposing an innovation, whereby any magistrate can refer appeals to the assembly for decision, if he so wishes. He might have argued that this was a useful short-cut, but it also had the effect of making an inroad into the traditional competence of the tribune. In this respect it would have been consistent with the ideology of the *De Re Publica*.

Cicero also makes some alteration to the status and function of the magistrates, at least as they were understood in the late Republic. The consuls, who are given *regium imperium*, are designated the supreme military commanders and are specifically instructed that the safety of the people is the supreme law. This seems to be an exhortation to them to undertake on their own authority, where necessary, the kind of measures that were taken in the late Republic after the *senatus consultum ultimum*. In one respect this is a return to the status of the consulship in the

[51] *Leg.* 3. 6; Chap. VII with nn. 16 and 19.

[52] *Leg.* 3. 6 'cum magistratus iudicassit inrogassitve, per populum multae poenae certatio esto'. See on this section Lintott, 1972, 258–9.

[53] *Leg.* 3. 27, cf. 10 'Deinceps igitur omnibus magistratibus auspicia et iudicia dantur: iudicia [a] ut esset populi potestas ad quam provocaretur, auspicia ut multos inutiles comitiatus inpedirent morae.' I reject here Ziegler's expansion of the redundant 'a' into *ita*, which destroys the symmetry of the sentence structure.

pre-Sullan period, when major wars were fought by consuls, not proconsuls with long-term commands. However, the emphasis on the
consuls' responsibility for taking drastic action in an emergency is
closely connected with Cicero's own vision of the use of *coercitio*.[54] The
praetors, by contrast, are essentially magistrates to perform civil jurisdiction. Cicero does not assign them military duties. Nor is there
any mention of their function as presidents of *quaestiones*. Indeed, the
quaestio perpetua, which bulked so large in Cicero's own career, is conspicuous by its absence. It should be stressed that he is not seeking to
reproduce the historical constitution of the early Republic, but to create
an ideal set of laws which embody the principles of the uncorrupted
Republic. So he is not prevented from including the *quaestio perpetua*
merely by considerations of chronology.[55]

The censors are given their traditional duties in counting and classify-
ing the people, letting contracts for public works and taxes, and supervising morality. Cicero goes beyond tradition, however, in specifically
instructing them to prevent celibacy (it is not explained how)—something which had been the concern of Metellus Macedonicus in his
censorship of 131, whose speech was later recalled by Augustus.[56] The
effective power of the office is, moreover, extended by making the
magistracy last a full five years, by contrast to the other annual magistracies—as it had at its inception according to a tradition found in Livy
(Chap. VII with nn. 103–4). In a further clause, Cicero forbids the dis-
continuation of the office, such as had occurred during and after Sulla's
dictatorship. He returns to the censors at the end of his schedule, giving
them the task of conserving the texts of the laws, which was undertaken
in the Greek world by *nomophulakes*, and further, following the same
precedent, that of receiving from retiring magistrates accounts of their
performance in office—the procedure known in Greece as *euthunai*.[57]

The traditional function of the aediles as curators of the city, the corn-

---

[54] *Leg.* 3. 8 and 15–16; Keyes, 1921, 317. I take the consuls first for the convenience of my
argument; Cicero himself mentions the magistrates in ascending order of importance with
the dictator last in the series and the censors ranked below the praetors.

[55] *Leg.* 3. 8; Rawson, 1991, 147–8. We need not conclude, however, that Cicero disapproved of the *quaestiones perpetuae* in their late-Republican context, merely that he considered them inappropriate for his ideal state.

[56] *Leg.* 3. 7; Livy, *Per.* 59; Suet. *Aug.* 89. 2; *ORF*, no. 18, frr. 4–7.

[57] *Leg.* 3. 11 and 46–7. The censors are not to conduct prosecutions themselves. As to the
conservation of the laws, Cicero clearly does not mean that the Romans were not accustomed to preserve the texts of statutes, but that there was no one to look after these texts
properly, once they had been entrusted to the quaestors at the treasury (Rawson, 1991,
145–6; *JRLR* 7–9).

supply, and the games is briefly stated, and it is added that this office should be the first step to higher office: in other words Cicero is drafting a new *lex annalis*, in which the aedileship is the necessary first stage in the *cursus*. By contrast, the quaestors, not mentioned by name but by function, are relegated among the minor magistrates, and it seems to follow that they would not have seats in the senate.[58] The dictatorship is maintained as an extraordinary military and civil office (its remit including repression of civil strife), with a time-limit of six months, but nomination is to be subject to a decree of the senate. Not surprisingly, Cicero also retains the system of the *auspicia* returning to the patricians and their nomination of an *interrex*, if it happens that there are neither consuls nor dictator in office. After the regular magistrates, there is an item on pro-magistrates and *legati*, who can be created either by the senate or people.[59]

At this point—almost, it seems, as an afterthought—Cicero introduces the tribunes, who are granted their traditional sacrosanctity and powers of legislation and intercession (including the power to veto decrees of the senate). In the discussion that follows, he puts in the mouth of Quintus a diatribe against the vices of the tribunate, with special reference to Clodius' attacks on the Cicero family, ending with commendation of Sulla for his elimination of the tribune's offensive powers and reproof of Pompey for their restoration. Cicero's answer is fourfold. First, one cannot blame the tribunate for bad tribunes without taking into account the advantage deriving from good tribunes. Secondly, the power of the tribunes is a surrogate for the much greater force of the people, which is much more difficult to repress. Historically, recognition had been granted to the tribunes in order to quell sedition, and this had secured for the plebs the real liberty that was the aim behind the expulsion of the kings and the justification for it. The concession was made in the expectation that the tribunes would follow the authority of the leading senators. Finally, as for Cicero's own misfortunes, they did not arise from a conflict with the tribunate or with the masses (in which case, Cicero claims, he would have retired into exile with a good grace)

---

[58] *Leg.* 3. 6–7, cf. 10; Rawson, 1991, 142–3. *Pace* Keyes, 1921, 313–14, I cannot believe that 'omnes magistratus' in 3. 10, who are to have 'auspicium iudiciumque' and to form the recruiting ground of the senate, include these minor magistrates. See also Chap. VIII with n. 76 for my suggestion that Cicero may be envisaging a single college of minor magistrates, whose members would be assigned to a variety of functions.

[59] *Leg.* 3. 9 and 18. In the spirit of his attempt, while consul, to abolish *liberae legationes*, Cicero includes a ban on *legationes* undertaken for private business (cf. Chap. V with n. 40). He also appears to suggest that commanders should not bring back booty.

but from one against slaves and the threat of military force. The two central arguments here are a reprise of the exposition of the origin of the tribunate in Book II of *De Re Publica*.[60] The tribunate is necessary in principle for liberty and for the stability of the constitution. Moreover, good tribunes will follow the authority of the leading statesmen.

The senate is to be drawn from those who have obtained magistracies through election (see n. 58): there is to be no co-option by the censors. This popular feature is a form of balancing against the primacy in policy-making which Cicero assigns to the senate. He has already laid down that minor magistrates should follow its instructions; now he states that its decrees are to be binding (*rata*), unless vetoed. This seems to mean that they should be obeyed by magistrates without fail. The clause has been interpreted to mean that all *senatus consulta* should have the force of laws, but there is the difficulty that many of the former were normally addressed to specific magistrates and, when these went out of office, the decrees would in any case lose their effect. The senate is also to be a moral example, and this will help to justify the authority given to its decrees.[61]

There follows a long section about procedure in assemblies and the senate, largely about the former. First, in a pregnant and ambiguous phrase voting by ballot in assemblies is retained, but it is not to be secret from the aristocrats conducting it. In the following discussion a criticism of this provision is assigned to Quintus Cicero, who denounces it for weakening the authority of the optimates and hiding flawed votes—a view for which Cicero himself has sympathy, arguing nevertheless that it is a necessary concession of an appearance of liberty, which will still allow the authority of good men to have effect.[62] The usual rights to hold assemblies and meetings of the senate are conferred on the consul, praetor, dictator, and tribune. Senators are required to attend the senate and speak briefly and to the point. A chapter about observance of the auspices and the modalities of legislation includes provisions of the late Republican laws, the *leges Caecilia Didia* and *Licinia Iunia*. Cicero reproduces clauses from the Twelve Tables relating to *privilegia*, legislation about individuals, and the passing of capital sentences only by the centuriate assembly.[63] Within the section there are two further innova-

---

[60] *Leg.* 3. 9 and 19–26; *Rep.* 2. 45 ff.

[61] *Leg.* 3. 6, 10 and 27; Keyes, 1921, 312, arguing that Cicero advocated an assimilation of *senatus consulta* to laws.

[62] *Leg.* 3. 10 and 33–9. On the *leges tabellariae* see above, Chap. V with nn. 33–6. For similar arguments in nineteenth-century Britain see Lintott, 1990, 13 with n. 88.

[63] *Leg.* 3. 10–11 and 40–5. On the *leges Caecilia Didia* and *Licinia Iunia* see VRR 132–48, Chap. V with n. 95; on the Twelve Tables clauses see Chap. IX with nn. 13–14.

tions of interest. One is a requirement that moderation and calm should be observed in speaking in the assemblies and the senate. Cicero's explanation of this is partially lost in a lacuna, but his reason is likely to have followed Aristotelian principles, that observance of the mean is the essence of a mixed constitution.[64] The other innovation is to place responsibility for violence in a legislative or judicial assembly on the man who has convened it and is seeking approval for a proposal. This is linked with a confirmation of the right of veto and support for its use against undesirable measures. Cicero claims that here he is following a view expressed by his mentor L. Crassus in the senate in 92 BC, that, if violence occurs, it is the duty of the convenor to dismiss the assembly.[65] From one point of view this is obviously a measure in the interest of peace and moderation. But it is also, especially in the context of Cicero's encouragement of the use of the veto, an invitation to obstruction. The regulations end with a general ban on bribery and peculation and, linked with this, the conferral on the censors of the function of recording laws and political activities, which has been already mentioned.

Cicero's code of constitutional practice covers a wide spectrum between generalized moral advice and detailed technical provisions. It is not difficult to criticize it as naïve and idealized because of its pious optimism that moderation and good sense will prevail, and this criticism is reinforced by the paucity of the provisions for criminal justice in the code. Cicero's defence against the charge seems to be that he is not talking about the aristocracy of the corrupt late Republic but of men of the future, who may be ready to obey his laws, especially if they have had the benefit of the education and discipline that he hopes to have the chance to discuss elsewhere.[66] There is also a serious problem in his approach to the mixed constitution. Aristotle, though he was perhaps primarily concerned with the pursuit of the mean, gave some thought to the question of mixing. Cicero does so at one point—over voting, where he seeks to blend the popular liberty of the written ballot with the aristocratic authority of open voting.[67] However, on the whole his approach to the monarchic, aristocratic, and democratic elements in the constitution is to give to each its full power, even if the exercise of this power is not compatible with its simultaneous exercise by the other two elements.

As far as the full powers of the tribunate are concerned, Cicero follows

---

[64] *Leg.* 3. 10 and 40; Ar. *Pol.* 4. 1295ᵃ–96ᵇ.
[65] *Leg.* 3. 11 and 42; Rawson, 1991, 31.
[66] *Leg.* 3. 29.
[67] *Leg.* 3. 10 and 38–9; cf. Ar. *Pol.* 4. 1294ᵃ–ᵇ.

what he regards as the original principle of the aristocracy, that they must be conceded, but in the hope that the tribunes will voluntarily submit to the authority of the *principes*.[68] On the other hand, he does not consider the problem of resolving the potential conflict between the preeminence of *imperium*, especially in the 'kingly' *imperium* of the consuls, and the universal authority of the senate. It is not clear, for example, whose judgement is to be preferred in the interpretation of the laws which he himself is laying down. This would not matter, if his constitutional model was one of regularized conflict, like that of Polybius. However, the essence of Cicero's republic is harmony, moderation and stability, resulting from the acceptance by the people at large of the wise decisions of those they have set in authority over them.

Viewed as political documents of the late fifties, the *De Re Publica* and the *De Legibus* provide few, if any, political solutions to current problems. It is striking that they make no attempt to take into account the unification of Italy and the exponential growth of the empire as a whole. The corruption of the aristocracy in the late Republic is noted, but the only new measure offered is an increase in the term of office and powers of the censors. What Cicero does seem to be advocating is in fact a compression of the aristocratic stratum at the apex of society, with a narrower group of people qualifying for the senate, and the creation of close unity within this élite, which will allow it to overawe outsiders. The importance of his works was perhaps that they were a restatement of the legitimacy of optimate principles after a period in which their value had been drastically eroded. Sullan methods were disowned, but what we can take to be Sulla's vision of a republic, in which the authority of the élite determined the political process, was revived. If the works were in many ways anachronistic, it was because it was only in this way that the vision could be made convincing.

[68] *Leg.* 3. 25.

XIII

The Republic Remembered

In 28–7 BC Augustus restored the *res publica* to the senate and Roman people and brought back constitutional rule after twenty years of civil war and dictatorship. But under the name of *princeps*, his *imperium* was dominant. Within a few years the powers conferred first on him and later on Agrippa by the assembly (Chap. V, n. 2) made any return to a republican balance unthinkable. By the time Augustus died in AD 14, even the memory had faded: in Tacitus' words, 'the magistrates had the same names, the younger generation had been born after the victory at Actium, even the old had mostly been born amid the civil wars: how few were left who had seen a republic?'[1] In so far as the Republic was remembered under the Principate, it was as a regime that had been the vehicle of Rome's rise to world power, but had degenerated into corruption, civil conflict, and ultimately full-scale civil war.[2] Tacitus dismissed the mixed constitution as something 'more easily praised than realized, that cannot last, even if it has been realized'. This is of course a criticism of the theory that had been used to interpret the constitution of the Republic, not of that constitution itself, and perhaps more directed against Cicero's *De Re Publica* than against Polybius. Tacitus' own vision was one of power oscillating between the senate and the plebs, which to some extent reflects the Polybian picture of elements in conflict, even if it rejects any sort of linear progression. Tacitus saw these political conflicts escalating in the late Republic into civil war, as the liberty that had emerged from them became licence.[3] He had lived through one serious bout of civil war, when still a boy, and in his maturity had seen Rome narrowly escape a repetition of this after the downfall of the Flavian dynasty. Like those who accepted Augustus, he knew the sweetness of peace.

[1] Tac. *Ann.* 1. 1. and 3; 3. 28.
[2] Livy, *Praef.* 9–12; Tac. *Ann.* 1. 1; 3. 28; *Hist.* 2. 38; *Dial.* 40. 2–4; App. *BCiv.* 1. 2–3; Syme, 1986, ch. 30.
[3] Tac. *Ann.* 4. 33 ('*ut olim plebe valida, vel cum patres pollerent*'); cf. *Hist.* 2. 38, ('*modo turbulenti tribuni, modo consules praevalidi, et in urbe ac foro temptamenta civilium bellorum*').

A century later Cassius Dio, before he came to write his history of Rome, had lived through the most serious civil wars since Actium, those that had ultimately led to the establishment of the Severan dynasty. In Book 52, as a preliminary to his account of Augustus' principate, he staged a debate between Maecenas and Agrippa over the relative merits of monarchy and what he calls *dēmokratia*, that is, a republican system. Their common ground is the prevention of civil strife and an effective military policy abroad. For Agrippa, the spokesman for the Republic, these objects will be achieved by the combination of senatorial deliberation and popular ratification, by competition among the élite in wealth and valour, and by impartial justice. This may produce conflict (*stasis*), but there would be more of this under a monarchy. In reply, Maecenas appeals to the efficiency of monarchy, suggesting various devices whereby it may be made more acceptable and effective. Under it each group will perform their proper function. Moreover, monarchy is true *dēmokratia* and secure freedom, while the freedom of the masses is the slavery of the best men. In his view, *dēmokratia* is also to be avoided because of the ambitions of the élite, who seek primacy and have the wealth to hire the poor as their followers. This leads to dangerous foreign wars and abominable civil wars. The ultimate cause of these perils is the vast population and power of Rome.[4]

Thus the Republic became under the Principate a precedent to be dismissed, even if theoretical arguments could be adduced in favour of it. It was only in the Middle Ages that it came to be revived as a good example, although the majority of educated people still held views more akin to Maecenas' in Cassius Dio's debate. The influence exercised by classical literature and history on political thought from the time of Dante to the period of the American and French revolutions is an enormous subject, on which a great deal has been written in the last forty years. Much of this influence from the Renaissance onwards arose through discussion of the theory of the mixed constitution, whether this was derived from Aristotle and Polybius or from the examples of Rome and Sparta—these states being frequently compared with the contemporary example of Venice. Appeal was also made, however, to particular features of the Spartan, Roman, and Athenian constitutions.[5] It would be

---

[4] Dio, 52. esp. 7. 5; 9. 1–5; 13. 5–6; 14. 3–5; 15. 4 ff.; Millar, 1964, 102 ff.

[5] See e.g. Baron, 1966; Pocock, 1975; Skinner, 1978; Nippel, 1980—a work that deals with both the ancient and early modern worlds; Burns, 1991; Bock, Skinner, and Viroli, 1990; Rahe, 1994. Rahe chooses to pass over Rome, Polybius, and Cicero in his treatment of the ancient world, but frequently has occasion to refer to Rome when discussing early modern writers.

misleading to claim that what follows here amounts even to an outline
of the results of this recent research into the impact of ancient examples
on Renaissance and early modern political theory. It is an attempt to
select writings which seem to show a genuine understanding of the
nature of the Roman Republic, as opposed to a casual display of learning or a superficial gesture of respect. I also touch on the growth of antiquarian learning, whose development was largely, but not entirely,
separate from political discussions of the Republic. A series of humanist
scholars studied all aspects of ancient Rome for their own sake, and part
of their work was devoted to recovering the details of the Republican
constitution. This was to be the foundation of the historical scholarship
with which we have been familiar in the last two centuries.

The Middle Ages

Rome originally affected the political thought of the Middle Ages
through the teachers of rhetoric, called (somewhat confusingly for
students of the Roman Republic) *dictatores*, and through the lawyers.
The teachers of rhetoric not only provided model letters and speeches,
but came to write treatises on civil government, where they applied the
Latin texts with which they were familiar, especially Cicero's *De Officiis*
and Sallust's *Catiline*. The ideal to be pursued in their view was 'greatness', which could be achieved by the exercise of civic virtue, liberty, and
concord. Meanwhile men learned in the law, from Marsiglio of Padua
and Bartolo of Saxoferrato onwards, influenced by study of the Digest
and Aristotelian philosophy, made their contribution in commentaries
and treatises. Their primary themes were liberty, the avoidance of
tyranny, and civil concord. These required the rule of law and a ruling
power that set its face against arbitrary and self-interested government,
together with a citizen body which pursued virtue. Marsiglio (*Defensor
Pacis* I. 8–18) interpreted the Aristotelian *politeia* as a kind of *principatus
temperatus*—an elected ruler acting within a framework of law and with
intermittent intervention by a legislator. Bartolo on the other hand (*De
Regimine Civitatis* 20 ff., 284 ff.) after listing the Aristotelian constitutions
argued that different constitutions suited communities of different sizes:
for the small a *politeia* was appropriate, for the larger an aristocracy (as
at Venice, Florence, and ancient Rome) and for the largest a monarchy.
Moreover, it came to be held that the best guarantee of a ruling power
acting in a proper fashion was that he or they should hold office by

consent and indeed through some form of election.[6] There is no sign yet of any close analysis of how the Roman republic worked. However, ideological support for republican liberty, deriving from Latin texts and Roman examples, could be seen in those politically active in Florence at the end of the fourteenth and beginning of the fifteenth centuries, in particular in Coluccio Salutati and Leonardo Bruni. Bruni actually went so far as to write in classical Greek a description of the Florentine constitution as a mixed constitution blended from aristocratic and democratic elements, one which avoided the dangers of outright democracy. He carefully pointed out that in spite of democratic features such as short-term magistracies and the use of the lot, the *dēmos* and its council could only agree or disagree with what was put before them by the magistrates and higher councils: thus there was a strong aristocratic element and this contrasted with the earlier period in Florentine history when the army was not mercenary, but recruited from the people, and the masses were more powerful.[7]

Machiavelli

The consistency with which these ideas were held and the extent of their political impact are still a matter of debate.[8] From the philosophical point of view, much of the thought of the thirteenth to the fifteenth centuries may be fairly termed proto-republican. It is, however, beyond dispute that in the early sixteenth century Machiavelli, even if he did not create an ideological tradition *de novo*, transformed political thought both by his often ruthless pragmatism born of his own political experiences, and by the way he applied classical republican theory and examples to the problems of his time.[9] His two major works, *The Prince (Il Principe)* and *The Discourses (Discorsi sopra la prima deca di Tito Livio)* appeared in the period of his retirement after he was dismissed from his position as one of the chancellors to the Florentine republic in

---

[6] Skinner, 1978, i. 9 ff. (summarized by him in Bock, 1990, ch. 6, pp. 121–41), and 49 ff.; Baron, 1966, 57 ff. On the development of legal studies see D. R. Kelley, 'Law', in Burns, 1991, ch. 3, pp. 66–94. On Bartolo see especially Quaglioni, 1983, including editions of *De Tyranno* and *Tractatus de Regimine Civitatis*. Note also on Baldo degli Ubaldi Quaglioni, 1980.

[7] See e.g. Coluccio Salutati, *Epistolarium* (ed. F. Novati, Rome, 1891) i. 90, 197; ii. 25, 389; Skinner, 1978, i. 69 ff.; Baron, 1966, 47 ff.; 98 ff.; 124 ff.; but contrast 146 ff. on Salutati's reversion to favouring Caesar against Cicero. Bruni's *Peri tēs tōn Phlōrentinōn Politeias* can be found in the edition of C. F. Neumann, Frankfurt-on-Main, 1822.

[8] A. Grafton, 'Humanism and Political Theory', in Burns, 1991, ch. 1, pp. 19–29.

[9] Recent treatments include Pocock, 1975; Sasso, 1958; Bock, Skinner, and Viroli, 1990.

1513, and reflected both opinions formed during his period of service and modifications to those opinions resulting from his present condition. *The Prince* is primarily about the acquisition, maintenance, and exploitation of *principati*: so it is not surprising that the Roman Republic is scarcely mentioned. Nevertheless, in chapter 9 Machiavelli emphasizes the importance for a prince of popular support, even if he also warns of the dangers of a man putting excessive trust in it, when he has no other support, in confrontations with the magistrates or his political enemies—the examples of the Gracchi proved this. Later, in chapter 18, contrasting Hannibal and Scipio as commanders, he argues that Hannibal's cruelty in imposing discipline on his troops was a truly princely quality compared with Scipio's laxness, which was only tolerable because he 'lived under the government of the senate'.

The Prince is not concerned with republicanism as such; the *Discourses on the first Decad of Livy* is a different matter. It is of course not confined to those ten books in the material it adduces. Other Livian material appears; so do references to, and quotations from, Tacitus, whose *Annals* 1–6 first appeared in a printed edition in 1515, exploiting the recent discovery of the unique manuscript in a monastery near the Weser.[10] Most important for our present purpose, we also find Machiavelli using Polybius, whose history was already well-known in Florence. In the words of A. Momigliano, 'Polybius arrived twice in Italy, the first time in 167 BC, the second time at an uncertain date about AD 1415'. The books that survived as full texts (1–5) were translated into Latin by the middle of the century; those that survived as excerpts, including Book 6 containing the treatment of the Roman constitution, were in a manuscript in the Urbino library by 1482, but had not been translated into Latin by the early years of the next century. However, it is clear from a digression endorsing Polybius' judgement on the Roman Republic in Bernardo Rucellai's book *de urbe Roma* (written before 1505) that Polybius' constitutional theory was known and discussed in intellectual circles in Florence before the writing of the *Discorsi*, albeit among Machiavelli's political opponents.[11]

In *Discorsi* 1. 2 Machiavelli sets out his view of classical constitutional theory: first, the division of all regimes (*stati*) into three types—

[10] See e.g. Momigliano, 1977, 205 ff.

[11] Sasso, 1978, 391; Momigliano, 1977, 79–98, 'Polybius' Reappearance in Western Europe', esp. 87, following Dionisotti, 1971, 252 ff. B. Rucellai's *Liber de urbe Roma* may be found in J. M. Tartini's Appendix vol. 2 to A. L. Muratori, *Rerum Italiae Scriptores* (Florence, 1770), 785–803. The discussion of Polybius is at 947–9. Note also the argument, used later by Machiavelli, that vices cannot be easily separated from virtues in human nature.

principato, ottimati, popolare; then the sixfold division, where each type has its sound and corrupt form, and the cyclical progression; finally, the superiority of the mixed constitution. Machiavelli accepts the cycle of constitutions in theory, but comments that it can only rarely occur, since a republic that suffers these mutations is unlikely to remain on its feet but will become subject to a neighbour which is better ordered. On the other hand, he is not as pessimistic as Polybius, believing that the mixed constitution can put an end to the cycle. He also modifies Polybius in thinking that the licence of the democratic state does not degenerate into the brutal tyranny of some individual, but rather inspires the choice of a prince who will put an end to the licence. Here he follows the idea put forward by the spokesman for monarchy, Darius, in the debate staged by Herodotus among the Persian nobility.[12] Machiavelli then compliments Lycurgus and criticizes Solon. The latter in his view created a *stato popolare*, not only because his constitution was quickly replaced by a tyranny, but because he left it to subsequent constitution-makers in Athens to repress 'the insolence of the great men and the licence of the universal'. At Rome which lacked a legislator like Lycurgus, his part was played by chance (*caso*): even if the institutions (*ordini*) were initially defective, they did not deviate so far from a good constitution that they could not be put right. The kings created some good laws, but not sufficient for a free city. Hence the republic which replaced them mixed the regal power of the consuls with the optimate power of the senate. The insolence of the nobles then provoked an uprising by the people and the creation of the tribunes of the plebs, which stabilized the regime of the republic.[13]

The influence of the Livian narrative is clear, but so also is the Polybian vision of stability through conflict, and this becomes clearer in the following chapter, when Machiavelli discusses the 'accidents' which led to the creation of the tribunes. He exploits here one of his fundamental tenets, that men are at heart criminals and never do good except through necessity: it is hunger and poverty that make them industrious and laws that make them good. In his view, as soon as the nobles had ceased to fear the Tarquins, they revealed their insolence and venom against the plebs.[14] Machiavelli then turns to rebut the many who

[12] See esp. *Disc.* 1. 2. 23–4 (I use the paragraphing of the Rizzoli edition of G. Inglese and G. Sasso, Milan, 1984); Hdt. 1. 82. 4; Sasso, 1958, 310 ff.; 1978, 345 ff.

[13] *Disc.* 1. 2. 28–36.

[14] *Disc.* 1. 3. This view of man's essential corruption and the accompanying belief in the need to balance the selfish desires of groups in order to create political stability was to reappear in the thought of James Madison, *The Federalist* 51, cf. Rahe, 1994, iii. 45 ff.

dismissed Rome as a 'republica tumultuaria'. It is a good question, who these 'many' were. Among ancient writers strong candidates are Augustine and Sallust, from whom Augustine derived quotations on the corruption of Rome; one might also suggest Appian, whose *Civil Wars* was now available in a Latin translation. However, it is likely that Machiavelli has also in mind some of his contemporaries who took their cue from these classical sources.[15] He argues that the conflict between nobles and plebs was the cause of the laws that favoured liberty and that the cost was small—a very few killed, eight to ten exiled, and not many fined. It seems likely that this is his own conclusion from the Livian narrative, reinforced by Livy's comments on the moderation of the violence.[16] He goes on to say that, if the vision of the people rushing riotously through the streets, closing the shops, and leaving Rome is frightening to some, they must realize that in every city there must be ways for the people to give vent to their 'ambition'. In fact this had brought about the creation of proper plebeian leaders and the protection of liberty.

This leads to a discussion of two further questions of principle; first, whether the *grandi* or the *popolo* are the better guardians of liberty; secondly, whether Rome could have had a republic which eliminated the hostilities between senate and people. In answer to the first, Machiavelli contrasts Rome with Sparta and Venice. In principle, he argues, it seems better to place the guardianship of liberty in the hands of those who seek to avoid being dominated, the people, rather than those who seek to dominate and usurp the liberty of others, the aristocracy. However, the partisans of Sparta and Venice argue that by making the *potenti* constitutionally dominant, the ambitions of these men are satisfied while the revolutionary desires of the plebs lose their legitimacy. Thus, in their view, the nobles do not seek to overturn the republic in desperation, while the plebs are not inspired to seek further high office for their protagonists in the conflict with the nobility and eventually to turn them into charismatic leaders like Marius. Machiavelli's principal reply to this argument is to say that, although it is difficult to decide which *umore* (class attitude) is more dangerous, that which desires to maintain the *onore* it has already acquired , or that which desires to acquire that which it has not, in his opinion those who possess have the same desires as they

[15] Aug. *Civ. Dei* 2. 18; 3. 17; Sall. *Hist.* 1. 11–12M; App. *BCiv.* 1. 1–6; Sasso, 1978, esp. 356 ff., arguing finally that Machiavelli's target was those who compared Rome unfavourably with Venice.

[16] *Disc.* 1. 4, esp. 4–6; cf. Livy, 2. 29. 4. Machiavelli is, however, less dismissive of the violence than Dionysius of Halicarnassus was (*AR* 7. 66).

who do not, because of their fear of losing what they have unless they acquire new possessions—and the powerful possessors have the means to change the balance of the republic. Moreover, their corrupt ambition inspires corresponding desires among the have-nots either to rob the powerful of their gains or to achieve the riches and honours which the latter have abused.[17]

There is, however, a second answer to the supporters of Sparta and Venice, which is also Machiavelli's chief argument that the conflicts within the Roman republic were inevitable—that is, that the Roman example is to be preferred by those who seek a republic that can obtain an empire. The historical accuracy of his picture of Sparta and Venice is not our concern here. He portrays them as small republics concerned only to keep themselves in being rather than to expand, republics, moreover, whose size allowed them to be governed by a few men. They maintained this position by being closed societies—Sparta more rigorously so than Venice, but the effect was similar. In addition, at Sparta economic equality and the protection of the plebs by the kings removed a cause of conflict with the nobility. For Rome to have achieved this sort of tranquillity, he argued, it would have been necessary either not to employ the plebs in war, following the Venetian example, or to exclude foreigners, following that of the Spartans. If you want to create a citizen body which is armed and numerous, in order to create an empire, you cannot expect to manage this body simply to suit yourself. Constitutional manipulations, such as creating a prince for life or reducing the size of the senate will make no difference to this. A small city may be made stable by the methods Lycurgus applied to Sparta, but the nature of things is such that it is hard to keep a republic both small and secure: things either grow or diminish and one is forced to a policy of expansion in order to avoid decline. Hence the Roman policy is to be preferred, which makes an honourable goal out of what is necessary, and the conflicts are a necessary evil on the way to greatness. Furthermore, the tribunes are both important as guardians of liberty and as the medium of accusations.[18]

In the chapters that follow Machiavelli touches on various features of the Republic to illustrate his political doctrines. Like Polybius, he highlights the importance of rewards and penalties, however small the former were. The Romans were less ungrateful to their great men than the Athenians, but their Republic had not fallen under a tyrant like Peisistratus. Moreover, they were mild in their punishment of those who failed in their duties through ignorance or poor decisions. On the other

---

[17] *Disc.* 1. 5. 1–12, 15–20.   [18] *Disc.* 1. 5. 13–14; 6; cf. Pol. 6. 50.

hand, in his eyes, the story of Coriolanus showed how the capacity to accuse people on political charges allowed the citizens to discharge their wrath without the violence which produces hostility, fear, and factions (*parti*).[19] The importance of religion for the Romans (and for the Samnites) is illustrated from the reigns of Romulus and Numa and from republican history. The retention of the *rex sacrorum* in particular was a good example of the maintenance of an ancient tradition in order to minimize the appearance of change when a major reform was being undertaken.[20] The activities of the decemvirate and the mistakes made by the senate and people in creating and sustaining it are discussed at some length. It is compared unfavourably with the dictatorship, in so far as it brought with it the abolition of the existing magistracies.[21]

More generally, the problem of maintaining liberty after the expulsion of a tyrant is discussed in the light of the early Republic, this being contrasted with the aftermaths of the deaths of Caesar, Caligula, and Nero and the overthrows of certain Greek tyrants. In Machiavelli's view, the Roman people of the early Republic was like an animal released from captivity, liable to fall prey to whoever wanted to imprison it again. This is the reason for his well-known sentiment, that in such situations it is necessary to kill the sons of Brutus, the aristocratic enemies of the Republic who had lost the influence they had under the kings. On the other hand, by the time of Caesar and the emperors, the *popolo* had become so corrupt that it could not be maintained in liberty, and the same would have been true in early Rome if the rule of the kings had been maintained longer.[22] Machiavelli stresses the interdependence of good laws and good customs. This, he thinks, is what makes it difficult to overcome corruption. Moreover, legislation is ineffective if the political structure (*ordini*) of the republic remains the same. Under the Republic neither the authority of the people, the senate, the tribunes, or the consuls nor the forms of election and legislation underwent, he thought, major changes, and this made it impossible to check the corruption. For the system of election ceased to privilege *virtù* but depended on *grazia*, and legislation became a means to private power rather than the public good. Gradual reforms require a good and far-sighted man, and even he will find it difficult to persuade his fellow-

---

[19] *Disc.* 1. 25; cf. Pol. 6. 14. 4; *Disc.* 1. 29; 31; contrast 7. 1–11.

[20] *Disc.* 1. 11–15; 25.

[21] *Disc.* 1. 34–5; 40–5.

[22] *Disc.* 1. 16. 2–3, 11; 17. 4–8. Interestingly, Machiavelli attributes the later corruption, which Caesar exploited, to the Marian faction. He returns to the killing of the sons of Brutus in *Disc.* 3. 3.

citizens to make the necessary changes; wholesale reforms, on the other hand, require violence and the power of a tyrant. Indeed, if one has to create or maintain a republic in a corrupt city, it must be drawn more in the direction of a royal regime than a popular one.[23]

A particular source of corruption was 'the agrarian law'. It need not concern us here that Machiavelli's understanding of agrarian legislation is in some respects defective: although he rightly distinguished between the laws which redistributed conquered lands and those that limited land-holdings (the influence of Appian's *Civil Wars* Book 1, by then available in Latin translation, can be detected), he did not realize that the second type of law only affected public land. Nor is it clear how he thought that his principle of keeping the public rich and individual citizens poor was undermined by Roman agrarian legislation. What is important in the present context is the effect of agrarian legislation on the stability of the Republic. Machiavelli initially maintains that the desire of the plebs for agrarian legislation was a disease, resulting from the ambition that follows when necessities have been satisfied. The nobles, by contrast, threatened with the loss of either land or new possibilities of enrichment, were hard-working and patient in seeking to delay legislation or to satisfy partially plebeian demands by sending out colonies. However, after the issue had been put to sleep because the lands available for distribution were remote from Rome, it was revived by the Gracchi with disastrous consequences, since the strength of the opposition had been redoubled, and the mutual hatred of senate and plebs led to civil war, first between Marius and Sulla, then between Caesar and Pompey. At this point, after arguing what is effectively an optimate case influenced by Livy's political standpoint, Machiavelli admits that what he has just said may appear inconsistent with his previous view that the hostility between senate and plebs maintained freedom through the legislation in favour of liberty to which it gave rise. None the less, he reasserts that earlier view, adding that the ambition of the *grandi* is so great that if it is not combated in various ways, a city soon becomes ruined. The struggle may have led to the enslavement of Rome after three hundred years, but this enslavement might well have happened much sooner, if the plebs with this legislation and their other appetites had not restrained the ambition of the nobles. He adds that the nobles were always more ready to make concessions about honours than about property and hence the plebs had recourse to extraordinary measures. As for the Gracchi, their intentions were more praiseworthy

[23] *Disc.* 1. 18.

than their prudence, retrospective legislation being particularly imprudent. A gradual approach will either delay or remove a misfortune that
is to come.[24]

Further evidence may be found of Machiavelli's positive view of the
plebs and the tribunes. He believes that the popular judgement is the
safest guide in the distribution of ranks and dignities, since the many are
less likely to deceive themselves than the few. Moreover, he takes issue
with Livy in arguing that the multitude is more wise and constant than a
prince. All the vices of the multitude are to be found in an individual.
While the Republic was uncorrupted, the Roman people was neither
deferentially slavish nor proudly tyrannical. It was the enemy of the
name of king and a lover of glory and the common good of the fatherland; it was not ungrateful like princes; it was rarely at fault in the
political decisions that it made and in its choice of magistrates. Moreover, popular rule leads to greater military success.[25] As for the tribunes,
they restrained not only the ambition that the nobles exercised against
the plebs, but also the ambition they employed in their own circles.
Ultimately, it was the organization of military command that was to be
as important a cause of the downfall of the Republic as these conflicts.[26]

We find, therefore, in Machiavelli an appreciation of the Roman
Republic which goes far beyond what he read in the pages of Livy, or in
the other ancient sources, and an interpretation which is highly percep-
tive, complex, and idiosyncratic. In particular, like Polybius, he subtly
makes a virtue out of the conflict between classes and institutions that
others considered a fatal vice and indeed he himself concedes to have
been at the root of the Republic's final downfall. This view in particular
will be seen to have had an important influence on later political
thought.

[24] *Disc.* 1. 37. The influence of App. *BCiv.* 1. 2, 7, 8 and 17 can be seen. For Appian's
availability see Sasso, 1978, 363.

[25] *Disc.* 1. 47. 27; 58, esp. 8, 10, 20, 24–6, 30. On the influence of Florentine political
history on Machiavelli's views see Bock, 'Civil Discord in Machiavelli's *Istorie Fiorentine*',
in Bock, Skinner, and Virioli, 1990, 181–201, showing that there is no serious inconsistency
between the thought in the *Discorsi* and the *Istorie*. It is at any rate clear that Machiavelli's
ideas about Rome were not based on preconceptions derived from the history of Florence.

[26] *Disc.* 1. 50. 6; 3. 24. F. Guicciardini in his *Considerazioni sui Discorsi del Machiavelli* (to
be found in *Opere Inedite*, i (Florence, 1857)) went through Machiavelli's main arguments
seriatim, not so much refuting them as providing an alternative anti-populist view. His
preferred mixed constitution would have had an elected monarch, a senate with long
tenure, and only limited reference to the people. He thought the *disunione* between patricians and plebs a disaster, which led to excessive concessions by the senate; for him the
nobles were better guardians of liberty, and the civil wars resulted not from long-term
commands but from moral decline.

The Antiquarians

From the mid-fifteenth century onwards humanist scholars devoted themselves in ever increasing numbers to the literary reconstruction of ancient Rome. One inspiration was the development of commentaries on literary texts, but more important was the influence of the monuments of Rome itself and other parts of the former Roman empire. Ancient buildings emerged from the redevelopment of Rome, even if some of them were destroyed in the course of that redevelopment, and so did sculpture and inscriptions. These sources, previously for the most part unexploited, together with coins made it possible to create a form of learning about Rome, which, although inevitably in part dependent on literary sources, had also an independent foundation, which in due course permitted a more critical approach to literary evidence.[27] Particularly striking was the effect of the discovery of the *Fasti Capitolini*, recording consuls and triumphs, at the foot of the Capitol in 1546 and their installation two years later in a new monumental setting designed by Michelangelo on the Capitol. They were transcribed by Bartolomeo Marliani, before being edited by Onofrio Panvinio and Carlo Sigonio, and subsequently *fasti*—not only the *Capitolini*, but those discovered elsewhere—became the second category of inscriptions in the manuscript epigraphic sylloges which are the ancestors of our current collections of Latin inscriptions.[28] The results of antiquarian research were not presented as historical narrative: the works were either commentaries or analytic studies of one or more aspects of Roman antiquity. In this second genre the pathfinder was Flavio Biondo's *De Roma Triumphante* of the mid-fifteenth century—a discussion of Roman religion, constitutional and administrative law, military organization, private life, and finally triumphs. Biondo also wrote an account of the topography of ancient Rome (*Roma Instaurata*), as well as a description of Italy and a history of Italy from the Gothic invasions in late antiquity to his own day. About a hundred years later there existed a considerable amount of published work, for example, Paolo Manuzio's *Antiquitatum Romanarum liber de Legibus*, Panvinio's editions and commentaries on the *Fasti*, Nicolas de Grouchy's *De comitiis Romanorum*; and, above all the works of Carlo Sigonio—his edition of the *Fasti*, *De antiquo iure Italiae*, *De antiquo iure civium*

---

[27] On the growth of antiquarian studies and the use of non-literary evidence see Momigliano, 1950; Weiss, 1969; Grafton, 1983, i. 153 ff., Crawford, 1993.

[28] Smetius, Naples VE 4; Aldo Manuzio the younger, Vat. lat. 5234, esp. ff. iii–vi.

Romanorum; De antiquo iure provinciarum; De iudiciis—not to his mention his broadsides on the *lex curiata*.[29]

The professed object of these works in general was to restore the knowledge of the most distinguished *res publica* and of the greatest empire that ever was and the dignity of Latin literature.[30] However, we find in Sigonio signs of a political agenda as well. The preface to *De antiquo iure Italiae*, stresses the remarkable Roman *disciplina* which allowed them to conquer and make subject to their laws not only Italy but remote parts of the world. This lay both in their devoted study of war and their methods of settlement after conflict. In the preface to the *De antiquo iure civium Romanorum* and in that to his commentary on the *Fasti* he applies Polybius' cycle of constitutions to the history of the Republic, though he argues that fundamentally constitutions have only two forms—one, when they are in the hands of one or a few, the other, when they are in the hands of many (when the artisans and shopworkers have full citizen-rights). The ideal constitution praised by Polybius and Cicero was fully achieved after the war with the Tarentines and Pyrrhus, that is, the period of the *lex Hortensia*. Sigonio portrays this as a sort of age of heroes, from which Roman history, both before and after, declined in excellence the further removed it was in time. He denounced the original domination of the patricians, seeing the founding of the tribunate as the necessary concession of a very sharp weapon to the plebs to protect their liberty and chastity: this was followed by the grant of intermarriage, admission to the patrician offices and priesthoods, and finally the *lex Hortensia* which made plebiscites binding on the whole people. He also derived a political lesson from the conflict between the patricians and plebeians about the desirability of avoiding exclusive castes in a citizen body. However, the tribunates of the Gracchi, in his view, marked the point where the balance of the mixed constitution was overthrown, and he follows the optimate tradition in Roman historiography in seeing the following period as an unjust domination of the people, in which all the tribunician legislation was designed to break the power of the optimates and strengthen the power of the plebs and their demagogues.[31] The *De antiquo iure civium Romanorum*, moreover,

[29] On these developments see esp. Weiss, 1969, 66 ff.; 145 ff.; McCuaig, 1989, and (on the *lex curiata*) McCuaig, 1986. On Panvini's unachieved project of 60 books of *Antiquitates Romanae*, surviving for the most part only in a manuscript epitome (Vat. Lat. 6783) see now Ferrary, 1996.
[30] See e.g. the prefaces of P. Manuzio's *De legibus Romanis* (1st edn. 1557) and Sigonio's *De antiquo iure civium Romanorum* (1st edn. 1560).
[31] *De ant. iure Italiae* (Venice, 1560), 3 ff.; *De ant. iure civ. Rom.* (Venice, 1560), 3 ff.; *In*

contains a chapter *de iure libertatis* (1. 6), which sought to define the essential components of liberty in the Roman view. These were, first, not being another's property (here Sigonio stressed the acquisition of *civitas*, when a freed slave acquired *libertas* at Rome); secondly, membership of a free *respublica*; thirdly, the protection from the magistrates associated with the *provocatio* laws and the provisions for capital trials; fourthly, the limitation on punishment for debt; fifthly, the secret ballot.[32] In some respects Sigonio is like Machiavelli: he sets up the Roman republic as a model of how to construct a community of free citizens, which also has the capacity to expand, and sees that the powers of the tribunes, the liberty of the plebs, and the participation of the plebs are essential features of this. However, he does not face up to the contradiction in the republic, whereby the opposition between the nobility and the plebs is both creative and destructive. He simply idealizes the central period of the Republic in a way which is arguably more generous than those of the ancient sources (even Sallust, who characterized the period between 218 and 146 by its very great concord). In this way Sigonio has helped to create the standard modern periodization, whereby the Conflict of the Orders ends in 287 and the decline of the Republic begins in 133, the intervening period displaying the constitution at its best.

In general, however, antiquarian research, which was carried out not only under the patronage of leading men in the Counter-Reformation but often by these men themselves (a classic example is Antonio Agustin), was not concerned with political thought, especially that which might suggest alternatives to the rule of one or a few.[33] A good illustration is a book which in many ways encapsulates humanist achievement—the *Annales Romanorum* of Steven Wynkens or Wynants, later Stephanus Vinandus Pighius, whose first volume was published in 1599, five years before the author's death at the age of 84, the two subsequent volumes appearing in a second edition edited and supplemented by Andreas Schott, the friend of Agustin.[34] This work neatly exemplifies the antiquarian combination of epigraphic, numismatic, and literary evidence by using the *Fasti* as the foundation for a sort of source-book on

fastos consularis ac triumphos Romanos commentarium (Venice, 1556), 1 ff.; McCuaig, 1989, 129 ff., with English translations of some of the central texts.

[32] McCuaig, 1989, 136–7, noting that the account is unsystematic, but probably one that would have been recognized by the Romans themselves. It is doubtful whether modern accounts have improved on its fundamentals. See e.g. Brunt, 1988, 281 ff.; Wirzubski, 1950; Bleicken, 1972.

[33] See especially the treatment of Agustin and his circle in Crawford, 1993.

[34] For Pighius' biography see Jongkees, 1954, esp. 148 ff.; de Vocht, 1959.

Roman history from the kings to AD 70 (the latter date was perhaps chosen because it was not only the date of the Roman capture of Jerusalem, but allowed the author to include the text of the *lex de imperio Vespasiani*). Within the annalist framework a number of sources are actually quoted, especially epigraphic texts: indeed the *Fasti Capitolini* appear in full at the beginning of Book II. The first two volumes are divided into books with names like *Tyrannifugium* and *Italiiuga* and this allows Pighius to give a brief explanation of his title by commenting on the historical significance of the period. However, no strictly political lessons are derived from the research. In the preface he stresses the importance of chronography and argues that his work was one way of demonstrating the permanence of Rome, especially Roman law, and that it amounted in effect to a history. The dedicatory address to Philip II is full of professions of loyalty to the Catholic faith and recommendations to the king to accept the vicissitudes of fortune as divine providence, while at the beginning of Book I he addresses Philip, saying that his account of the kings is intended to educate by example. We are a long way from Sigonio and even further from Machiavelli. By the time of the appearance of *Annales Romanorum* the field of political precepts had been largely occupied by the exponents of *Tacitismo*, who were exploiting a historian of the Principate and, as often as not, actually giving advice to monarchs on how to maintain their absolute rule.[35] The appreciation of the Roman Republic as a republic is next best illustrated in England.

The Roman Republic and the English Revolution

The influence of the concept of the mixed constitution can be detected in theoretical defences and discussions of the English constitution from the work of Sir John Fortescue, Henry VI's chancellor, onwards. However, in the fifteenth and sixteenth centuries what is in question is neither a mixed constitution in Aristotle's sense nor a system of checks and balances, as conceived by Polybius and endorsed by Machiavelli: it is the belief that the sovereign power in England, the king in parliament, was itself mixed, that the monarchy was constitutionally restricted. Reference was on occasion made to Aristotelian theory and classical precedents, but the actual structure of the Roman Republic was not

---

[35] Momigliano, 1977, 205–29, 'The First Political Commentary on Tacitus', expanding *JRS* 37 (1947), 91–100; P. Burke, 'Tacitism, scepticism, and reason of state', in Burns, 1991, 479–98.

relevant.[36] The situation changed when Charles I came into conflict with his parliament. In the chapter 'Of the liberty of subjects' in *Leviathan* Thomas Hobbes anatomized those who were deceived into thinking liberty to be their 'private inheritance and birthright, which is the right of the public only'. Those responsible for deceiving them were 'Aristotle, Cicero, and other men, Greeks and Romans', who derived these rights from their own popular governments, not from the principles of nature.

And, as Aristotle; so Cicero, and other writers have grounded their civil doctrine, on the opinions of the Romans, who were taught to hate monarchy . . . and by the reading of these Greek, and Latin, authors, men from their childhood have gotten a habit (under a false show of liberty,) of favouring tumults, and of licentious controlling the actions of their sovereigns; and again of controlling those controllers; with the effusion of so much blood; as I think I may truly say, there was never any thing so dearly bought, as these western parts have bought the learning of the Greek and Latin tongues.[37]

Interestingly, the theory of the mixed constitution was initially employed as an argument by Charles I against his parliament on the eve of the Civil War. *His Majesties Answer to the Nineteen Propositions of Parliament* (1642), drafted for him by Falkland and Sir John Colepepper, describes the English ancestral constitution as a mixture of the three kinds of government among men (absolute monarchy, aristocracy, and democracy), intended to give the conveniences of all three, without the inconveniences of any one. So far, this is good Aristotelian doctrine. However, the prophesy of the likely outcome of the concession of a greater share in government to the House of Commons has resonances of Polybius' portrayal of the triumph of the democratic element:

at last the common people (who in the mean time must be flattered, and to whom license must be given in all their wild humours, how contrary soever to established law, or their own real good), discover this *arcanum imperii*, that all this was done by them, but not for them, grow weary of journey-work, and set up for themselves, call parity and independence liberty, devour that estate which had devoured the rest; destroy all rights and properties, all distinctions of families and merit . . .[38]

---

[36] Nippel, 1980, 160 ff. provides a convenient overview of the contributions of Fortescue, Starkey, Aylmer, Ponet, and Cartwright.

[37] 2. 21. 9 (I have used the 1996 Oxford editon of J. C. A. Gaskin). The attack seems to embrace not only recent events in Britain but the activities of the 'monarchomachists' in the previous century, on whom see Skinner, 1978, ii. 302 ff.

[38] The relevant part of the text is conveniently available in D. Wootton, *Divine Right and Democracy* (London, 1986), 171 ff.; and J. P. Kenyon, *The Stuart Constitution: Documents and Commentary* (Cambridge, 1966), 21 ff. Cf. Pol. 6. 57, with Nippel, 1980, 258 ff., esp. 262.

The concept of a corporate sovereignty was to be developed by Philip Hunton in his *Treatise of Monarchy* (1643) and the basis was thus laid for the later doctrine of the sovereignty of the king in parliament.[39] However, the victory of the parliamentarians in the Civil War gave rise to more democratic constitutional proposals and the more explicit exploitation of the precedent of the Roman Republic, in particular its interpretation by Machiavelli.

James Harrington's work, *The Commonwealth of Oceana* (1656)[40] contained the formulation of an ideal constitution of a popular and representative type, grounded in a historical analysis of the evolution of armies and property-holding. It had one eye firmly set on the present in its concern to reconcile democratic aspirations with the claims of a national army and its portrayal of Cromwell as the 'Lord Archon' Olphaus who had the opportunity to create a new political system; the other ranged widely over English history and the ancient world, including material from the Old Testament, the history of Greece, especially Sparta, and the history of Rome. In discussing the Roman constitution, Harrington's argument becomes a dialogue with Machiavelli about the best form of a republic. The Constitution of Oceana is based on the ordered societies of the ancient world, comprising the Spartan military and political divisions and the Roman system of tribes and *centuriae,* including their age-groups and property-qualifications. The system assumes a limited citizenship of 5,000 based on the same number of lots of land and a maximum property holding of 2,000 pounds. The 'elders' (those aged 30 and upwards) in each parish are responsible for electing deputies from the parish and these deputies for electing military commanders and civil magistrates for varying lengths of office. Among these the 'knights' are to form the senate, electing from among themselves the supreme magistrates and members of the Councils of State in a system of annual rotation. There are *classes,* prerogative tribes, and four annual tribunes, two from the cavalry and two from the infantry, who were a kind of combination of the Roman *tribuni militum and tribuni plebis.* Legislation is proposed by the senate and decided by the people—following the practice of 'two silly girls', whereby one divides the cake and the other chooses.[41] Harrington believed that his constitution would maintain popular sovereignty without demagoguery and

[39] Wootton, 1986, 175 ff., for the text; Nippel, 1980, 269 ff.
[40] The text is fully edited and commented in Pocock, 1977.
[41] Pocock, 1977, 172 ff.; 210 ff., summarized in 333 ff.; note esp. 267 ff. and 335 on the tribunes.

would be both stable and militarily effective. He rejected Machiavelli's belief in the necessity of conflict, believing that what had happened at Rome could be avoided by having an equal society in the first place, that is, one in which there is an equal 'agrarian' and rotation in government. He answers Machiavelli's question, whether means could be found of removing the enmity between senate and people, by saying that internal equality is sufficient, whether a commonwealth is for stability or expansion.[42]

A more orthodox return to the principles of the mixed constitution and the precedent of the Roman republic can be found in a work called into being by the problems of the Restoration, but only printed posthumously after being a contributory cause of the author's execution—Algernon Sidney's *Discourses Concerning Government*. The author, who is making a riposte to Sir Robert Filmer's defence of absolute monarchy in the *Patriarcha*, defends the mixed constitution by the examples of the ancient Hebrews, the Greek cities, and Rome, as well as the contemporary instances of Venice, Genoa, Lucca, and the German cities. The Romans are important as a precedent for the overthrow of a monarchy. Sidney, moreover, repeats Machiavelli's arguments in the *Discorsi* in favour of Rome as a model. Security for a state must rest on expansion, which will be necessary anyhow to accommodate the increase in population that will result from good government: so this security will depend on the adequacy of the state's preparation for war. Moreover, tumult, war, and slaughter, though terrible scourges, do not necessarily imply the existence of the worst form of government. 'It is ill that men should kill one another in seditions, tumults, and wars; but it is worse to bring nations to such misery, weakness and baseness as to have neither strength nor courage to contend for anything.' Sidney then contrasts ancient and modern Greece to the former's advantage and follows the same argument in relation to Italy. 'When they [the peoples of ancient Italy] were free, they loved their country and were always ready to fight in its defence', whereas now 'the thin half-starved inhabitants of walls supported by ivy fear neither popular tumults, nor foreign alarms; and their sleep is only interrupted by hunger, the cries of their children, or the howling of wolves; . . . the fierceness of those nations is so tempered that every rascally collector of taxes extorts without fear from every man that which should be the nourishment of his family . . . the governors [of Rome] do as little fear Gracchus as Hannibal.' For Sidney the military strength of the ancient Italian cities was not only a defence against out-

<hr>

42 Pocock, 1977, 180 ff.; 272 ff.

side invaders but a guarantee against oppression by their own aristo-cracies.[43] Sidney, to be sure, is not much interested in the niceties of the Roman constitution, but he is concerned with the relationship between democratic liberty and military strength and the right of the poor to resist oppression from above.

Montesquieu and the Founding Fathers

Rome's combination of militarism and republicanism, however, was not so acceptable to the Enlightenment. In the work of Montesquieu we find the decisive steps towards the final abandonment of the Roman Republic as a model. His discussion of Rome in his *Considérations* works towards the conclusion that her example is no longer relevant to the contemporary political scientist. Rome for him is a society which from the earliest was focused on war: the city was a repository of booty as well as of agricultural produce; since it was a city without commerce and almost devoid of technology (*arts*), pillage was the only route for the Romans to personal riches, as it is in his own time for the Tartars of the Crimea; the change from monarchy to a republic led by annual consuls in fact meant an increase in the number of ambitious people eager for war. In an interesting variation on the Polybian *anacylosis*, Montesquieu suggests that if the Romans' conquests had been more rapid, they would have already reached decadence at the time of the arrival of Pyrrhus, since after reaching such a peak of wealth they must have degenerated into corruption. Machiavellian themes then reappear. The secret of power in ancient republics was the equal distribution of lands, as Tiberius Gracchus realized. The Conflict of the Orders and later struggles by the people were necessary for the plebs to achieve their rights. Nor could one expect a city of brave soldiers to be passive at home. In fact long-term service abroad eroded the citizen spirit of the armies, so that they ceased to be soldiers of the republic. It was thus *la grandeur* of the Republic which caused the trouble and turned popular tumults into civil wars. However, in a free state it is impossible to require men to be both daring in war and timid in peace. Every time one sees a so-called Republic in which all is at peace, one can be sure that there is no liberty there.[44] Thus, even if the development of commerce in Montesquieu's day had in his eyes outmoded war as an engine of expansion and prosperity so

[43] *Discourses Concerning Government*, esp. ch. 1, section 3; ch. 2, sections 16, 23, 26; Wootton, 1986, 417 ff.

[44] *Considérations sur les causes de la grandeur des romains et de leur décadence* (*Oeuvres* ii. 69 ff., 81–2, 111–19, ed. R. Caillois).

that the Roman model was no longer relevant, he none the less repeats the sympathetic assessment given by Machiavelli of the strife of the Republic.

The leading politicians who had to decide the future of the American states after their victory over George III were also children of the Enlightenment, conscious that they should be seeking new political solutions in the new historical conditions in which they found themselves. At the same time they were for the most part steeped in classical authors and classical history.[45] Individual Romans of course served as models of virtue or counter-examples of vice, but the constitution of the Roman Republic turned out to be a much more ambiguous example, a precedent which left traces in their writings, even when they sought to render it obsolete.[46] John Adams used ancient examples of mixed governments, including that of the Roman Republic, as a guide to the form of state government he advocated, including a representative senate as well as a representative assembly in order to avoid giving too much power to the democratic element. His reluctance to imitate Greek democracy too closely was based on belief in the fundamental imperfection of mankind, its greedy pursuit of self-interest and susceptibility to emotion.[47] James Madison, moreover, argued this same point strongly in *The Federalist*, when advocating the limitation on the number of representatives in the Congress and the creation of a federal senate. 'In all very numerous assemblies, of whatever characters composed, passion never fails to wrest the scepter from reason. Had every Athenian citizen been a Socrates, every Athenian assembly would still have been a mob.' '. . . History informs of no long-lived republic which had not a senate.'[48]

The Anti-Federalists remained attracted by the model of the self-contained face-to-face society of the classical city republic with its assembly, rotating magistracies, and citizen militia (the history of Rome showed what happened when a citizen militia was replaced with a standing army under a powerful executive). They wanted, furthermore, the kind of society that supported religion and the pursuit of virtue. In the view of some this entailed, among other things, the maintenance of a

---

[45] Richard, 1994, 53 ff.; Rahe, 1994, ii. 21 ff.; iii. 21 ff.

[46] Richard, 1994, 123 ff.; Rahe, 1994, 57 ff.

[47] J. Adams. *A Defence of the Constitutions of Government of the United States of America* (3 vols., 1787), esp. the preface and Letter 26 (Letters 27 and 30 contain respectively Machiavelli's *Discorsi* 1. 2 and much of Polybius 6 in English translation); Richard, 1994 123 ff.; Rahe, 1994, iii. 45 ff.

[48] *The Federalist*, nos. 55, 63, pp. 336 and 371, in I. Kramnick's Penguin edition (London, 1987).

homogeneous citizen-body through control of immigration and isolation from the corruption of European luxury.[49] The Federalists, however, held that it was possible to accomplish what the Roman Republic had failed to do—reconcile republican principles with a state of vast territory—by exploiting the principle of representation developed in seventeenth-century English political thought and the notion of a republic based on commerce rather than military expansion, propounded by Montesquieu.[50] Their checks and balances were to consist not only in the creation of competing and opposing constitutional organs but also in accepting and embracing the existence of factions, on the ground that these could not overthrow an enormous federal state but, on the contrary, their variety and potential conflict was a source of liberty and an insurance against any sort of tyrannical usurpation, in particular the domination that a majority faction could exercise in a small political community.[51]

The writings of Alexander Hamilton and James Madison in the numerous issues of *The Federalist* appear under the name of Publius, that is, Publius Valerius Publicola, the founder of the Roman Republic. Moreover, they use from time to time arguments drawn from the Roman Republic to substantiate the cases they are arguing. Hamilton appeals to the coexistence of the *comitia centuriata* and *comitia tributa*— the one, as he held, embodying the patrician interest, the other the plebeian—in order to justify the coexistence of legislatures in the states and the Congress. Madison uses the Roman tribunes, along with the Spartan ephori and Cretan cosmi, to illustrate the point that the principle of representation was not unknown in antiquity. 'The true distinction between these (sc. ancient political constitutions) and the American governments lies in the total exclusion of the people in their collective capacity from any share in the latter, not in the total exclusion of representatives of the people from the administration of the former'—a sentence which also makes plain his aversion to direct democracy. Hamilton, again, when arguing that the executive must be vested in a single magistrate, sets up the Roman consuls as one of the alternatives to be criticized.[52] One should also remember that Madison used Roman imperialism as an illustration of the dangers that their

[49] Richard, 1994, 78 ff. The sources are in H. J. Storing and M. Dry, *The Complete Anti-Federalist* (7 vols., Chicago, 1981, the first being a general introduction); a selection in J. R. Pole, *The American Constitution. For and Against* (New York, 1987).
[50] Rahe, 1994, ii. 22 ff.; iii. 39 ff.
[51] Madison, *Federalist* 10, 51 (Kramnick, 122 ff., 318 ff.).
[52] *Federalist* 34, 63, 70 (Kramnick, 227, 373, 403–4).

infant republic faced, in particular the history of an early exemplar of federalism, the Achaean League, and its ultimate overthrow by the Romans.[53] However, the overriding aim of Madison and Hamilton was to combine the strength and effectiveness of a united central authority with the liberty they had fought for, and here the division of powers in the Roman Republic (and in the constitution of classical Sparta) provided not so much a model as a mark to surpass. Here their acceptance, indeed presumption, of conflict between interests as a means of preventing any single authority in government exercising a tyrannical predominance owed much to the entrenchment of opposition between elements of the Republic at Rome, as it had been expounded by Polybius, Machiavelli, and their successors, even though Hamilton and Madison did not envisage in America the violent conflicts that had occurred at Rome and had no wish to encourage class-consciousness among their own plebeians. In short, perhaps the most enduring legacy of the Roman Republic to western political thought is the legitimacy and desirability of opposition and competition as constituents of liberty and stimulants of effective government.

The end of the eighteenth century marked a turning-point in the impact of the Roman Republic on later western thought. In France the revolution gave rise to much classical imitation in its rhetoric and striking of attitudes. Rome provided famous examples of republican virtue, fine models of republican oratory, and some useful political terminology. However, while Roman republican culture informed vocabulary and rhetoric, the political structure and ideology of the Roman Republic was an inappropriate recipe for the revolutionaries. Indeed, Sparta provided more compelling images of virtue, while Athenian democracy was to be in France a more enduring political ideal.[54] What followed in the next

---

[53] *Federalist* 18 (Kramnick, 161–4).

[54] See Schama, 1989, 169 ff.; Rawson, 1969, 268 ff.; Vidal-Naquet, 1995, 141 ff.

For the exploitation of classical precedent see for example in the writings of Lucie Camille Desmoulins (*Oeuvres*, ed. J. Claretie, Paris, 1874) a rejection of '*une loi agraire*' in *La France Libre*, (*Oeuvres*, i. 84), references to the *comitia centuriata* (with 181 centuries) (ibid. i. 87) and the '*loi Appia*' (= *Oppia*) (ibid i. 145), and a discussion of clemency in *Le Vieux Cordelier* IV (ii. 186–8) which invokes Brutus' letter to Cicero, Thrasyboulos, and the exploitation of clemency by Octavian. Robespierre himself was compared to the Cicero portrayed in Brutus' letter (*Oeuvres Complètes de Maximilien Robespierre* (Paris, 1912–) iii, letter 126). On 25 Sept. 1792 amidst suspicion of Robespierre's ambitions Danton proposed a decree invoking the death penalty against anyone proposing a dictatorship, tribunate or triumvirate (ibid. v. 29); Robespierre had to correct Vergniaud about who killed Tiberius Gracchus (ibid. v. 199); and Desmoulins' speech advocating the execution of the king included an ironical reference to the Convention as 740 Brutuses (ibid. v, 211–12).

century was a revival of the antiquarian studies that had been first undertaken by the humanists, this time in a period where the possibility of writing new ancient histories was fully understood. This was one element of the intellectual context from which Mommsen's *Römisches Staatsrecht* emerged. The link with contemporary events was not entirely lost. But in the nineteenth century and our own it has less been a matter of letting a given view of the Roman Republic influence contemporary projects as of recreating the Roman Republic in terms and concepts taken from the present. Polybius would have been happy that these studies continue, but he would have regretted that they had passed from the hands of practising politicians into those of academic historians.

Bibliography
of works cited, excluding those listed in Abbreviations

Aalders, G. J. D., 1968, *Die Theorie der Gemischten Verfassung im Altertum* (Amsterdam).

Accame, S., 1942, 'La legislazione romana intorno ai collegi nel I secolo a.C.', *Bull. Mus. Imp. Rom.* 13, 13–49.

Afzelius, A., 1938, 'Zur Definition der römischen Nobilität in der Zeit Ciceros', *C & M* 1, 40–94.

——1945, 'Zur definition der römischen Nobilität *vor* der Zeit Ciceros', *C & M* 7, 150–200.

Alföldi, A., 1965, *Early Rome and the Latins* (Ann Arbor).

Aly, W., 1943, '*Fragmentum Vaticanum de Eligendis Magistratibus: Vaticanus Graecus 2306*', *Studi e Testi* 104.

Arangio-Ruiz, V., and Pugliese-Carratelli, G., 1954, '*Tabulae Herculanenses IV*', *PP* 9, 54–74.

Astin, A. E., 1958, *The Lex Annalis before Sulla* (Coll. Latomus 32: Brussels).

——1964, '*Leges Aelia et Fufia*', *Latomus* 23, 421–45.

——1967, *Scipio Aemilianus*, Oxford.

——1978, *Cato the Censor*, Oxford.

——1982, 'The Censorship of the Roman Republic: Frequency and Regularity', *Historia* 31, 174–87.

Ausbüttel, F. M., 1982, *Untersuchungen zu den Vereinen im Westen des römischen Reiches* (Frankfurter Althistorische Studien 11: Kallmünz).

Badian, E., 1956, 'Publius Decius P. f. Subulo', *JRS* 46, 91–6.

——1958, *Foreign Clientelae* (Oxford).

——1959, 'Caesar's *Cursus* and the Intervals between Offices', *JRS* 49, 81–9, re-edited in *Studies in Greek and Roman History* (Oxford, 1964), 140–56.

——1965, 'M. Porcius Cato and the Annexation and the early Administration of Cyprus', *JRS* 55, 110–21.

——1970, *Titus Quinctius Flamininus* (Cincinnati.)

——1972, 'Tiberius Gracchus and the Roman Revolution', *ANRW* I. 1, 668–731.

——1996, '*Tribuni Plebis* and *Res Publica*', in Linderski, 1996, 187–213.

Balsdon, J. P. V. D., 1939, 'Consular Provinces under the late Republic', *JRS* 29, 57–73.

—— 1962, 'Roman History 65–50 BC.: Five Problems', *JRS* 52, 134–41.

Barnes, J., and Griffin, M. (eds.), 1997, *Philosophia Togata II: Plato and Aristotle at Rome* (Oxford).

Baron, H., 1966, *The Crisis of the Early Italian Renaissance* (2nd edn., Princeton).

Beard, M., 1990, 'Priesthood in the Roman Republic', in Beard & North, 1990, 19–48.

—— and North, J. (eds.), 1990, *Pagan Priests* (London).

Beloch, K. J., 1886, *Die Bevölkerung der griechisch-römischen Welt* (Leipzig).

Bertrand, J.-M., 1989, 'A propos du mot PROVINCIA: Étude sur les modes d'élaboration du langage politique', *Journal des Savants*, 191–215.

Bleicken, J., 1955, *Das Volkstribunat der klassischen Republik* (Göttingen).

—— 1959, 'Ursprung und Bedeutung des Provocationsrechtes', *ZSS* 76, 324–77.

—— 1962, *Senatsgericht und Kaisergericht* (Göttingen).

—— 1972, *Staatliche Ordnung und Freiheit in der römischen Republik* (Kallmünz).

—— 1975, *Lex Publica: Gesetz und Recht in der römischen Republik* (Berlin).

—— 1981, 'Das römische Volkstribunat: Versuch einer Analyse seiner politischen Funktion in republikanischer Zeit', *Chiron* 11, 87–108.

Bock, G., Skinner, Q., and Viroli, M. (eds.), 1990, *Machiavelli and Republicanism* (Cambridge).

Bonnefond-Coudry, M., 1989, *Le Sénat de la république romaine* (*BEFRA* 273: Rome).

—— 1993, 'Le *princeps senatus*: vie et mort d'une institution républicaine', *MEFRA* 105, 103–34.

Botsford, G. W., 1909, *The Roman Assemblies* (New York).

Brecht, Ch., 1939, 'Zum römischen Komitialverfahren', *ZSS* 59, 261–314.

Briscoe, J., 1981, *A Commentary on Livy XXXIV–VII* (Oxford).

Brown, F. E. 1974–5, 'La protostoria della Regia', *RPAA* 47, 15–36.

—— 1980, *Cosa: The Making of a Roman Town* (Ann Arbor).

Brunt, P. A., 1964, Review of Kunkel (1962). *TR* 32. 440–9.

—— 1971, *Italian Manpower* (Oxford).

—— 1982, '*Nobilitas* and *Novitas*', *JRS* 72, 1–17.

—— 1988, *The Fall of the Roman Republic* (Oxford).

Bucher, G. S., 1987, 'The *Annales Maximi* in the light of Roman Methods of Keeping Records', *AJAH* 12, 3–61.

Burckhardt, L., 1990, 'The Political Elite of the Roman Republic', *Historia* 39, 77–99.

Burns, J. H. (ed.), 1991, *Cambridge History of Political Thought 1450–1700* (Cambridge).

Carandini A. *et al.*, 1986, 'Pendici settentrionali del Palatino', *BCAR* 91, 429–38.

Carcopino, J., 1928, *Autour des Gracques* (Paris, repr. 1967).

Cassola, F., 1962, *I gruppi politici romani nel III secolo a.C.* (Trieste).

Catalano, P., 1960, *Contributo allo studio del diritto augurale*, i (Turin).

Cloud, J. D., 1971, 'Parricidium from the *lex Numae* to the *lex Pompeia de parricidiis'*, *ZSS* 88, 1–66.

Coarelli, F., 1983, *Il foro romano: Periodo arcaico* (Rome).

—— 1985, *Il foro romano: Periodo repubblicano e augusteo* (Rome).

—— 1997, *Il Campo Marzio* (Rome).

Cornell, T. J., 1975, 'Etruscan Historiography', *ASNSP* 3rd. ser. 6, 411–39.

—— 1979–80, 'Rome and Latium Vetus 1974–9' *AR* 1979–80.

—— 1995, *The Beginnings of Rome 753–263 BC.* (London).

Crawford, M. H., 1985, *Coinage and Money under the Roman Republic* (London).

—— (ed.), 1993, *Antonio Agustin between Renaissance and Counter-Reform* (Warburg Inst. Survey Texts 24: London).

Crifò, G., 1968, 'Attività normative del senato in età repubblicana', *BIDR* 3 ser. 10, 31–120.

—— 1970, 'In tema di senatus consultum ultimum', *SDHI* 36, 1–15.

Crook, J. A., 1967, *Law and Life of Rome* (London).

de Libero, L., 1992, *Obstruktion: Praktiken im Senat und in der Volksversammlung der ausgehenden römischen Republik* (Hermes Einzelschr. 59: Stuttgart).

Derow, P. S., 1973, 'The Roman Calendar 196–68 BC.', *Phoenix* 27, 345–51.

de Sanctis, G., 1907, *Storia dei Romani*, 4 vols. (repr. 1956, Florence).

Develin, R., 1975, '*Comitia Tributa Plebis*', *Athenaeum* 53, 302–37.

—— 1977, '*Comitia Tributa* Again', *Athenaeum* 55, 425–6.

de Vocht, H., 1959, *S. V. Pighii Epistolarium* (Humanistica Lovaniensia 15: Louvain).

Dionisotti, C., 1971, 'Machiavellerie', *RSI* 83, 227–63.

Drummond, A., 1978, 'Some Observations on the Order of Consuls' Names', *Athenaeum* 56, 80–108.

Dumézil, G., 1943, *Servius et la Fortune* (Paris).

Earl, D. C., 1960, 'Political Terminology in Plautus', *Hist.* 9, 235–43.

—— 1967, *The Moral and Political Tradition of Rome* (London).

Engelmann, H., and Knibbe, D., 1989, 'Das Zollgesetz der provincia Asia: Ein neues Inschrift aus Ephesos', *Epigr. Anat.* 14, 1–206.

Erskine, A., 1990, *The Hellenistic Stoa: Political Thought and Action* (London).

Farrell, J., 1986, 'The Distinction between *Comitia* and *Concilium*', *Athenaeum* 64, 407–38.

Fascione, L., 1981, '*Bellum indicere* e tribù', in F. Serrao (ed.), *Legge e società nella repubblica romana*, i (Naples), 225–54.

Ferrary, J.-L., 1977, 'Recherches sur la législation de Saturninus et de Glaucia', *MEFR* 89, 619–60.

—— 1982, 'Le idee politiche a Roma nell' epoca repubblicana', in L. Firpo (ed.), *Storia delle idee politiche economiche e sociali* (Turin), 723–804.

—— 1983, 'Les origines de la loi de majesté à Rome', *CRAI* 1983, 556–72.

—— 1984, 'L'archéologie du *De Re Publica* (2. 2, 4–37, 63): Cicéron entre Polybe et Platon', *JRS* 74, 87–98.

—— 1996, *Onofrio Panvinio et les antiquités romaines* (CEFR 214: Rome).

Fiori, R., 1996, *Homo Sacer: Dinamica politico-costituzionale di una sanzione giuridico-religiosa* (Univ. Roma pubbl.ist.dir.rom. 72: Rome).

Flower, H. I., 1996, *Ancestor Masks and Aristocratic Power in Roman Culture* (Oxford).

Fraccaro, P., 1911, 'I processi degli Scipioni', *Studi storici per l'antichità classica* 4 (Pisa), 217–414.

——1929, 'La riforma dell'ordinamento centuriato', in *Opuscula* (Pavia, 1957), II. 1, 171–90.

——1933, '*Tribules et Aerarii:* Una ricerca di diritto romano', in *Opuscula* (Pavia, 1957), II. 1, 149–70.

Fraenkel, E., 1960, *Elementi Plautini in Plauto* (Florence).

Frank, T., 1933, *Economic Survey of Ancient Rome*, i (Baltimore).

Frede, D., 1989, 'Constitution and Citizenship: Peripatetic Influence on Cicero's Political Conceptions in the *De Re Publica*', in W. W. Fortenbaugh and P. Steinmetz (eds.), *Cicero's Knowledge of the Peripatos* (Rutgers Univ. Studies in Class. Humanities VI: New Brunswick/London), 77–100.

Frederiksen, M., 1984, *Campania* (London).

Frier, B. W., 1980, *Libri Annales Pontificum Maximorum* (Rome).

Gabba, E., 1949, 'Ricerche sull' esercito professionale in Roma: i proletari e la riforma di Mario', *Athenaeum* 27, 173–209 = *Republican Rome: the Army and the Allies*, trans. P. J. Cuff (Oxford, 1976), 1–19.

——1958*a*, *Appiani Bellorum Civilium Liber Primus* (Florence).

——1958*b*, 'L'elogio di Brindisi', *Athenaeum* 36, 90–105.

——1987, 'Maximus comitiatus', *Athenaeum* 65, 203–5.

Gargola, D. J., 1995, *Lands, Laws & Gods: Magistrates and Ceremony in the Regulation of Public Lands in Republican Rome* (Chapel Hill and London).

Garnsey, P., 1966, 'The *lex Iulia* and Appeal under the Empire', *JRS* 56, 167–89.

Garofalo, L., 1989, *Il processo edilizio: Contributo allo studio dei iudicia populi* (Padua).

——1990, 'Il pretore giudice criminale in età repubblicana', *SDHI* 56, 366–97.

Gasperini, L., 1968, 'Su alcuni epigrafi di Taranto romano', *II Miscellanea greca e romana* (Rome), 379–97.

——1971, 'Ancora sul frammento "cesariano" di Taranto', *Epigraphica* 33, 48–59.

Gelzer, M., 1912, *Die Nobilität der römischen Republik* (Leipzig/Berlin) = *Kleine Schriften* (Wiesbaden, 1962), i. 15–135, trans. R. Seager, *The Roman Nobility* (Oxford, 1969), 1–139.

Giovannini, A., 1983, *Consulare Imperium* (Schweizerische Beiträge zur Altertumswissenschaft 16: Basle).

Gjerstad, E., 1953–73, *Early Rome*, 6 vols. (Lund).

——1962, *Legends and Facts of Early Roman History* (Lund).

Grafton, A., 1983, *Joseph Scaliger* (Oxford).

Greenidge, A. H. J., 1901, *The Legal Procedure of Cicero's Time* (Oxford).

Grieve, L., 1985, 'The Reform of the Comitia Centuriata', *Historia* 34, 278–309.

Griffin, M., 1997, 'Cicero and Matius on Friendship', in Barnes and Griffin, 1997, 86–109.

Gros, P., and Torelli, M., 1992, *Storia della urbanistica: Il mondo romano* (Rome–Bari).

Gruen, E. S., 1968, *Roman Politics and the Criminal Courts 149–78 BC.* (Cambridge Mass.).

——1974, *The Last Generation of the Roman Republic* (Berkeley and Los Angeles).

——1995, 'The "Fall" of the Scipiones', in I. Malkin (ed.), *Leaders and Masses in the Roman World: Studies in Honour of Zvi Yavetz* (Leiden), 59–90.

Guarino, A., 1988, 'Il dubbio contenuto pubblicistico delle XII Tavole', *Labeo* 34, 323–35.

Hall, U., 1967, 'Voting Procedure in Roman Assemblies', *Historia* 13, 267–306.

——1972, 'Appian, Plutarch and the Tribunician Elections of 123 BC.', *Athenaeum* 50, 3–35.

Hansen, M. H., 1987, *The Athenian Assembly* (Oxford).

Hardy, E. G., 1912, *Some Problems in Roman History* (Oxford).

Harmand, J., 1967, *L'Armée et le soldat à Rome de 107 à 50 avant notre ère* (Paris).

Harris, W. V., 1971, *Rome in Etruria and Umbria* (Oxford).

——1989, *Ancient Literacy* (Cambridge, Mass., and London).

——1990, ' On Defining the Culture of the Roman Republic: Some Comments on Rosenstein, Williamson, and North', *CPh* 85, 288–94.

Heikkila, K., 1993, '*Lex non iure rogata*: Senate and the Annulment of Laws in the late Republic', in Paananen *et al.*, 1993, 117–42.

Hellegouarc'h, J., 1972, *Le Vocabulaire latin des relations et des partis politiques sous la République* (2nd edn., Paris).

Heuss, A., 1944, 'Zur Entwicklung des Imperiums der römischen Oberbeamten', *ZSS* 64, 57–133.

Hölkeskamp, K.-J., 1988, 'Die Entstehung der Nobilität und der Funktions-wandel des Volkstribunats: die historische Bedeutung der *lex Hortensia de plebiscitis*', *Arch. f. Kulturgesch.* 70, 271–312.

Hopkins, K., 1983, *Death and Renewal* (Cambridge).

Hornblower, S., 1994, *Greek Historiography* (Oxford).

How, W. W., 1930, 'Cicero's Ideal in his De Republica', *JRS* 20, 24–42.

Jahn, J., 1970, *Interregnum und Wahldiktatur* (Frankfurter althistorische Studien 3: Kallmünz).

Jashemski, W. F. 1950, *The Origins and History of the Proconsular and Propraetorian Imperium to 27 BC* (Chicago).

Jolowicz, H. F., and Nicholas, B., 1972, *Historical Introduction to the Study of Roman Law* (3rd edn., Cambridge).

Jones, A. H. M., 1960a, *Studies in Roman Government and Law* (Oxford).

——1960b, '*De Tribunis Plebis Reficiendis*', *PCPS* NS 6, 35–9.

——1972, *The Criminal Courts of the Roman Republic and Principate* (Oxford).

Jongkees, H., 1954, 'Stephanus Vinandus Pighius Campensis', *Mededelingen van het Nederlands historisch Instituut te Rome* 8, 120–85.

Keyes, C. W., 1921, 'Original Elements in Cicero's Ideal Constitution', *AJP* 42, 309–23.

Kloft, H., 1977, *Prorogation und ausserordentliche Imperien 326–81 v. Chr.* (Beiträge zur klassischen Philologie 84: Meisenheim am Glan).

Kunkel, W., 1962, *Untersuchungen zur Entwicklung des römischen Kriminalverfahrens in vorsullanischer Zeit* (*ABAW* 56: Munich).

—— 1967 and 1968, 'Die Funktion des Konsiliums in der magistratischen Strafjustiz und im Kaisergericht', *ZSS* 84, 218–44, and 85, 253–329 = *Kleine Schriften* (Weimar, 1974), 151–254.

—— and Wittmann, R., 1995, *Staatsordnung und Staatspraxis der römischen Republik: Zweiter Abschnitt* (Handb. d. Altertumswiss. X. 3. 2. 2: Munich).

Lange, L., 1875, 'Die *promulgatio trinundinum*, die *lex Caecilia Didia*, und nochmals die *lex Pupia*', *Rh. Mus.* 30, 350–97.

Last, H., 1945, 'The Servian Reforms', *JRS* 35, 30–48.

Latte, K., 1936, 'The Origin of the Roman Quaestorship', *TAPA* 67, 24–33 = *Kleine Schriften* (Munich, 1968) 359–66.

—— 1960, *Römische Religionsgeschichte* (Munich).

Levick, B. M., 1981, '*Professio*', *Athenaeum* 59, 378–88.

—— 1983, 'The *Senatus Consultum* from Larinum', *JRS* 73, 97–115.

Linderski, J., 1990, 'Roman Officers in the Year of Pydna', *AJP* 111, 53–71.

—— 1995, 'Ambassadors go to Rome', in E. Frézouls and A. Jacquemin (eds.), *Les Relations internationales: Actes du Colloque de Strasbourg 15–17 juin 1993* (Univ. Sci. Hum. Stras. C. R. Pr.-Or. Gr. Ant. 13: Strasbourg), 453–78.

—— 1996, 'Q. Scipio Imperator', in J. Linderski (ed.), *Imperium sine fine: T. Robert S. Broughton and the Roman Republic* (Historia Einz. 105), 147–85.

Lintott, A., 1965, '*Trinundinum*', *CQ* NS 15, 281–5.

—— 1967, 'Popular Justice in a Letter of Cicero to Quintus', *Rh. Mus.* 110, 65–9.

—— 1968, '*Nundinae* and the Chronology of the late Roman Republic', *CQ* NS 18, 189–94.

—— 1970, 'The Tradition of Violence in the Annals of the early Roman Republic', *Historia* 19, 12–29.

—— 1971a, 'The Offices of C. Flavius Fimbria in 86–5 BC', *Historia* 21, 696–701.

—— 1971b, 'The Tribunate of Sulpicius Rufus', *CQ* NS 21, 442–53.

—— 1972, '*Provocatio* from the Struggle of the Orders to the Principate', *ANRW* I. 2, 226–67.

—— 1974, 'Cicero and Milo', *JRS* 64, 62–78.

—— 1976, 'Notes on the Roman Law inscribed at Delphi and Cnidos', *ZPE* 20, 65–82.

—— 1977, 'Cicero on Praetors who failed to abide by their Edicts', *CQ* NS 27, 184–6.

—— 1978, 'The *quaestiones de sicariis et veneficis* and the Latin *lex Bantina*',

Hermes 106, 125–38.

Lintott, A., 1981, 'The *Leges de Repetundis* and Associate Measures under the Republic', *ZSS* 98, 162–212.

——1982, *Violence, Civil Strife and Revolution in the Classical City* (London).

——1987, 'Democracy in the Middle Republic', *ZSS* 104, 34–52.

——1990*a*, 'Electoral Bribery in the Roman Republic', *JRS* 80, 1–16.

——1990*b*, 'Le procès devant les *recuperatores* d'après les données épigraphiques jusqu'au règne d'Auguste', *RHD* 68, 1–11.

——1997, 'The Theory of the Mixed constitution at Rome', in Barnes and Griffin, 1997, 70–85.

Luisi, N. D., 1993, 'Sul problema delle tabelle di voto nelle votazioni legislative: contributo all'interpretazione di Cic. *Ad Att.* 1. 14. 5', *Index* 21, 1–33.

Mackie, N., 1992, '*Popularis* Ideology and Popular Politics at Rome', *Rh. Mus.* 135, 49–73.

Mantovani, D., 1989, *Il problema d'origine dell'accusa popolare* (Dip. sci. giur. Univ. Trento 6: Padua).

——1990, 'Il pretore giudice criminale in età repubblicana', *Athenaeum* 78, 19–49.

Marshall, A. J., 1984, 'Symbols and Showmanship in Roman Public Life: the *Fasces*', *Phoenix* 38, 120–41.

Martin, J., 1970, 'Die Provokation in der klassischen und späten Republik', *Hermes* 98, 72–96.

Massa-Pauvant, F.-H., and Pailler, J.-M., 1979, '*Bolsena* V. 1—La maison aux salles souterranées' (*MAH* Supp. 6: Rome).

Mattingly, H. B., 1969, 'Suetonius, *Claud.* 24. 2 and the "Italian Quaestors"', *Hommages à Marcel Renard*, ii (Coll. Latomus 102: Brussels, 505–11.

Mazzarino, S., 1947, *Dalla monarchia allo stato repubblicano* (Catania; 2nd edn., Milan, 1992).

McCuaig, W., 1986, 'Sigonio and Grouchy: Roman Studies in the Sixteenth Century', *Athenaeum* 74, 147–83.

——1989, *Carlo Sigonio: The Changing World of the late Renaissance* (Princeton).

——1993, 'Antonio Agustin and the Reform of the Centuriate Assembly', in Crawford, 1993, 61–80.

McDonald, A. H., 1944, 'Rome and the Italian Confederation (200–186 BC.)', *JRS* 34, 11–33.

Meier, C., 1966, *Res Publica Amissa* (Wiesbaden).

Mertens, J. 1969, *Alba Fucens*, i (Brussels).

Meyer, Ed., 1922, *Caesars Monarchie und das Principat des Pompejus* (3rd edn., Stuttgart).

Michels, A. K., 1967, *The Calendar of the Roman Republic* (Princeton).

Millar, F., 1964, *A Study of Cassius Dio* (Oxford).

——1984, 'The Political Character of the Classical Roman Republic, 200–151 BC.', *JRS* 74, 1–19.

Millar, F., 1986, 'Politics, Persuasion and the People before the Social War', *JRS* 76, 1–11.

Mitchell, T. N., 1971, 'Cicero and the *Senatus Consultum Ultimum*', *Historia* 20, 47–61.

Momigliano, A., 1950, 'Ancient History and the Antiquarian', *Journ. Warburg and Courtauld Inst.* 13, 285–315 = *Studies in Historiography* (London, 1966) 1–39.

——1963, 'An Interim Report on the Origins of Rome', *JRS* 53, 95–121.

——1977, *Essays in Ancient and Modern Historiography* (Oxford).

Mommsen, Th., 1857, *Römische Geschichte* (2nd edn., Breslau).

Münzer, Fr., 1920, *Römische Adelsparteien und Adelsfamilien* (Stuttgart).

Namier, L. B., 1968, *The Structure of Politics at the Accession of George III* (2nd edn., London).

Niccolini, G., 1932, *Il tribunato della plebe* (Milan).

Nicolet, C., 1966, *L'Ordre Équestre à l'époque républicaine* (Paris).

——1974, 'Polybe et les institutions romaines', in E. Gabba (ed.), *Polybe* (Fondation Hardt: Entretiens sur l'antiquité classique 20), 209–58.

——1975, *Le Métier de citoyen dans la république romaine* (2nd edn., Paris).

——1976, 'Le Cens Sénatorial sous la République et sous Auguste', *JRS* 66, 20–38.

—— (ed.), 1983, *Demokratia et aristokratia. A propos de Gaius Gracchus: mots grecs et réalités romaines* (Paris).

Niebuhr, B. G., 1826–30, *Römische Geschichte*, trans. as *The History of Rome*, 3 vols. (Cambridge, 1828–42).

Nippel, W., 1980, *Mischverfassungstheorie und Verfassungsrealität in Antike und früher Neuzeit* (Stuttgart).

——1995, *Public Order in Ancient Rome* (Cambridge).

Nocera, G., 1940, *I poteri dei comizi e i suoi limiti* (Pubbl. ist. dir. rom. Univ. Roma, 15: Milan).

North, J. A., 1979, 'Religious Toleration in Archaic Rome', *PCPS* 25, 85–103.

——1990*a*, 'Democratic Politics in Republican Rome', *P & P* 126, 3–21.

——1990*b*, 'Politics and Aristocracy in the Roman Republic', *CPh* 85, 277–87.

Ogilvie, R. M., 1965, *A Commentary on Livy Books I–V* (Oxford).

Oliver, J. H., 1977, 'The Vatican Fragments of Greek Political Theory', *GRBS* 18, 321–39.

Ormanni, A., 1990, *Il 'regolamento interno' del senato romano nel pensiero degli storici moderni sino a Theodor Mommsen* (Naples).

Paananen U. et al., 1993, *Senatus Populusque Romanus: Studies in Roman Republican Legislation* (Acta Inst. Rom. Fin. 13, ed. J. Vaahtera: Helsinki).

Pailler, J.-M., 1971, 'Bolsena 1970', *MEFR* 83, 367–403.

——1988, *Bacchanalia: La répression de 186 av. J.-C. à Rome et en Italie*, (*BEFRA* 270: Rome).

Pares, R., 1953, *George III and the Politicians* (Oxford, repr. 1967).

Pelham, H. F., 1911, *Essays* (Oxford).

Perelli, L., 1982, *Il movimento popolare nell' ultimo secolo della repubblica* (Historica Philosophica 11: Turin).

Pieri, G., 1968, *L'Histoire du cens jusqu'à la fin de la République romaine* (Paris).

Pina Polo, F., 1996, *Contra Arma Verbis* (Heidelberger Althistorische Beiträge und Epigraphische Studien, 22: Stuttgart).

Plaumann, G., 1913, 'Das sogenannte *senatus consultum ultimum*', *Klio* 13, 322–86.

Pobjoy, M., 1996, 'Rome and Capua from Republic to Empire', unpublished Oxford thesis.

Pocock, J. G. A., 1975, *The Machiavellian Moment* (Princeton).

——1977, *The Political Works of James Harrington* (Cambridge).

——1987, *The Ancient Constitution and the Feudal Law* (2nd edn., Cambridge).

Pollock, F., and Maitland, F. W., 1968, *A History of English Law* (2nd rev. edn. Cambridge).

Pöschl, V., 1936, *Römischer Staat und griechisches Staatsdenken bei Cicero* (repr. Darmstadt, 1976).

Powell, J. G. F., 1994, 'The *rector rei publicae* of Cicero's *De Republica*', *SCI* 13, 19–29.

Purcell, N., 1993, '*Atrium Libertatis*', *PBSR* 61, 125–55.

Quaglioni, D., 1980, 'Un "Tractatus de Tyrannis": Il commento di Baldo degli Ubaldi (1327?–1400) alla Lex Decernimus, C. De Sacrosanctis Ecclesiis (C. 1. 2. 16)', *Il Pensiere Politico* 13, 64–83.

——1983, *Politica e diritto nel trecento italiano: Il 'De tyranno' di Bartolo da Sassoferrato (1314–1357)* (Il Pensiero Politico Biblioteca 11: Florence).

Raaflaub, K. (ed.), 1986, *Social Struggles in Archaic Rome* (California).

Rahe, P., 1994, *Republics Ancient and Modern*, 3 vols. (Chapel Hill and London).

Rawson, E., 1969, *The Spartan Tradition in Western European Thought* (Oxford).

Rawson, E., 1971, 'Prodigy Lists and the Use of the *Annales Maximi*', *CQ* NS 21, 158–69 = Rawson, 1991, 1–15.

——1973, 'The Interpretation of Cicero's *De Legibus*', *ANRW* I. 4, 334–56 = Rawson, 1991, 125–48.

——1991, *Roman Culture and Society* (Oxford).

Reynolds, J., 1962, 'Cyrenaica, Pompey and Cn. Cornelius Lentulus Marcellinus', *JRS* 52, 97–103.

——1987, *Aphrodisias and Rome* (London).

Rich, J. W., 1976, *Declaring War in the Roman Republic in the Period of Transmarine Expansion* (Coll. Latomus 149: Brussels).

——1996, 'Augustus and the *Spolia Opima*', *Chiron* 26, 85–127.

Richard, C. J., 1994, *The Founders and the Classics: Greece, Rome and the American Enlightenment* (Cambridge, Mass.).

Richard, J.-C., 1978, *Les origines de la plèbe romaine* (Paris).

——1982, 'Contribution à l'histoire de la préture', *RPh* 56, 19–31.

Richardson, J. S., 1983, 'The *Tabula Contrebiensis*: Roman Law in Spain in the

Early First Century BC', *JRS* 73, 33–41.

——1991, 'Imperium Romanum: Empire and the Language of Power', *JRS* 81, 1–9.

Ridley, R. T., 1986, 'The "Consular Tribunate": The Testimony of Livy', *Klio* 68, 444–65.

Rilinger, R. 1976, *Der Einfluss des Wahlleiters bei den römischen Konsulwahlen von 366 bis 50 v. Chr.* (Munich).

——1989, ' "Loca intercessionis" und Legalismus in der späten Republik', *Chiron* 19, 481–98.

Ross Holloway, R. 1993, *The Archaeology of Early Rome and Latium* (London).

Rouland, N., 1979, *Pouvoir politique et dépendance personnelle dans l'antiquité romaine* (Coll. Latomus 166: Brussels).

Rubino, J., 1839, *Untersuchungen über römische Verfassung und Geschichte*, i (Cassel).

Ryffel, H., 1949, *Metabolē Politeiōn: Der Wandel der Staatsverfassungen* (Berne).

Sabbatucci, D., 1954, *L'edilità romana, magistratura e sacerdozio* (Mem. Acc. Naz. Lincei vi. 3: Rome).

Sandberg, K., 1993, 'The *Concilium Plebis* as a Legislative Body', in Paananen *et al.*, 1993, 74–96.

Santalucia, B., 1984, 'Osservazioni sui Duumviri Perduellionis e sul procedimento duumvirale', in *Du Châtiment dans la cité: Supplices corporels et peine de mort dans le monde antique* (*CEFR* 79: Rome), 439–52.

——1998, *Diritto e processo penale nell'antica Roma* (2nd edn., Milan).

Sasso, G., 1958, *Niccolò Machiavelli: Storia del suo pensiero politico* (Naples; 2nd edn. Bologna, 1980).

——1978, 'Machiavelli e i detrattori antichi e nuovi di Roma: Per l'interpretazione di Discorsi I. 4', *Atti Acc. Naz. Lincei* Ser. viii. 22. 3, 319–418.

Schama, S., 1989, *Citizens: A Chronicle of the French Revolution* (London).

Schleussner, B. 1978, *Die Legaten der römischen Republik* (Vestigia 26, Munich).

Schmidlin, B., 1963, *Das Rekuperatorenverfahren* (Freiburg).

Schmidt, P. L., 1973, 'Cicero De Re Publica', *ANRW* I. 4, 262–333.

Schmitthenner W. F., 1973, *Octavian und das Testament Caesars: eine Untersuchung zu den politischen Anfängen des Augustus* (2nd edn., Munich), 39 ff.

Schulz, F., 1951, *Classical Roman Law* (Oxford).

Scullard, H. H., 1973, *Roman Politics 200–150 BC* (2nd edn., Oxford).

Seager, R. 1972a, 'Factio: Some Observations', *JRS* 62, 53–8.

——1972b, 'Cicero and the Word *Popularis*', *CQ* NS 22, 328–38.

Serrao, F., 1956, 'Diritto romano: Novità nel campo delle fonti romanistiche', *Stud. Rom.* 4, 198–202.

Shatzman, I., 1972, 'The Roman General's Authority over Booty', *Historia* 21, 177–205.

Sherwin White, A. N., 1982, 'The Political Ideas of C. Gracchus', *JRS* 72, 18–31.

Siber, H., 1942, 'Provocatio', *ZSS* 62, 376–91.

Skinner, Q., 1978, *The Foundations of Modern Political Thought*, 2 vols. (Cambridge).

Smith, C. J., 1994, 'A review of archaeological studies on Iron-Age and archaic Latium', *JRA* 7, 285–302.

—— 1996, *Early Rome and Latium: Economy and Society c.1000–500 BC* (Oxford).

Staveley, E. S., 1956, 'The Constitution of the Roman Republic 1940–54', *Historia* 5, 74–119.

—— 1972, *Greek and Roman Voting and Elections* (London).

Stein, A., 1927, *Der römische Ritterstand: Beitrag zur Sozial- und Personengeschichte des römischen Reiches* (Munich).

Stein, P., 1930, *Die Senatssitzungen der Ciceronischen Zeit (68–43)* (Münster).

Steinby, E. M., (ed.), 1995, *Lexicon Topographicum Urbis Romae*, ii, D–G (Rome).

Stibbe C. M. *et al.*, 1980, *Lapis Satricanus: archaeological, linguistic and historical aspects of the new inscription from Satricum* (The Hague).

Strachan-Davidson, J. L., 1912, *Problems of the Roman Criminal Law*, 2 vols. (Oxford).

Strasburger, H., 1960, 'Der Scipionenkreis', *Hermes* 94, 61–72.

Sumner, G. V., 1963, '*Lex Aelia, lex Fufia*', *AJP* 84, 337–58.

—— 1970, 'The Legion and the Centuriate Assembly', *JRS* 60, 67–78.

Suolahti, J., 1963, *The Roman Censors* (Helsinki).

Syme, R., 1939, *The Roman Revolution* (Oxford).

—— 1986, *The Augustan Principate* (Oxford).

Taiphakos, I. G., 1995, *Phantasia Politeias Isonomou* (Athens).

Taylor, L. R., 1939, 'Cicero's Aedileship', *AJP* 60, 194–202.

—— 1957, 'The Centuriate Assembly before and after the Reform', *AJP* 78, 337–54.

—— 1960, *The Voting Districts of the Roman Republic* (Rome).

—— 1962, 'Forerunners of the Gracchi', *JRS* 52, 19–27.

—— 1966, *Roman Voting Assemblies* (Ann Arbor).

Thomas, Y., 1981, 'Parricidium', *MEFRA* 93, 643–715.

Thommen, L., 1989, *Das Volkstribunat der späten römischen Republik* (Stuttgart).

Tibiletti, G., 1949, 'Il funzionamento dei comizi centuriati alla luce della Tavola Hebana', *Athenaeum* 27, 210–45.

—— 1953, 'Le leggi *de iudiciis repetundarum* fino alla guerra sociale', *Athenaeum* 31, 5–100.

Torelli, M., 1988, 'Poseidonia-Paestum', *Atti del XXVIIsimo convegno di studi sulla Magna Grecia Taranto-Paestum, 9–15 ottobre 1987* (Naples), 33–115.

—— 1993, 'Regiae d'Etruria e del Lazio e immaginario figurato dei poteri', in R. T. and A. R. Scott (eds.), *Eius Virtutis Studiosi: Classical and Post-Classical Studies in Memory of Frank Edward Brown (1908–1985)* (Cambridge, Mass., and London), 85–121.

Vaahtera, J., 1990, 'Pebbles, Points, or Ballots: the Emergence of the Popular Vote in Rome', *Arctos* 24, 161–77.

—— 1993a, 'On the Religious Nature of the Place of Assembly', in Paananen *et al.*, 1993, 97–116.

—— 1993b, 'The Origin of Latin *suffrāgium*', *Glotta* 71, 66–80.

Vatai, F. L., 1984, *Intellectuals in Politics in the Greek World* (London).

Venturini, C., 1969, 'La repressione degli abusi dei magistrati romani ai danni delle popolazioni soggette fino alla *lex Calpurnia* del 149 a. c.', *BIDR* 72, 19–87.

—— 1987, 'Concussione e corruzione', *Studi A. Biscardi* 6 (Milan), 133–57.

Versnel, H., 1970, *Triumphus: An Enquiry into the Origin, Development and Meaning of the Roman Triumph* (Leiden).

Vidal-Naquet, P., 1995, *Politics Ancient and Modern* (Cambridge).

Virlouvet, C., 1985, *Famines et émeutes à Rome des origines de la république à la mort de Néron* (CEFR 87: Rome).

Vitucci, G., 1953, 'Intorno a un nuovo frammento di Elogium', *RFIC* NS 31, 43–61.

von Fritz, K., 1954, *The Theory of the Mixed Constitution in Antiquity* (New York).

von Lübtow, U., 1955, *Das römische Volk—sein Staat und sein Recht* (Frankfurt).

von Scala, R., 1890, *Die Studien von Polybios* (Stuttgart).

von Ungern-Sternberg, J., 1970, *Untersuchungen zum spätrepublikanischen Notstandrecht: Senatus consultum ultimum und hostis-Erklärung* (Munich).

—— 1988, 'Überlegungen zur frühen römischen Überlieferung im Lichte der Oral-Tradition-Forschung', in J. von Ungern-Sternberg and Hj. Reinau (eds.), *Vergangenheit in mündlicher Überlieferung* (Colloquia Raurica 1: Stuttgart), 237–65.

—— 1990, 'Die Wahrnehmung des Ständekampfes in der römischen Geschichtsschreibung', in W. Eder (ed.), *Staat und Staatlichkeit in der frühen römischen Republik* (Stuttgart), 92–102.

Walbank, F. W., 1957, *A Commentary on Polybius*, i (Oxford).

—— 1967, *A Commentary on Polybius*, ii (Oxford).

—— 1972, *Polybius* (Berkeley).

Waltzing, J.-P., 1895, *Étude historique sur les corporations professionnelles chez les romains*, 2 vols. (Louvain).

Warren, L. B., 1970, 'Roman Triumphs and the Etruscan Kings: the Changing Face of the Triumph', *JRS* 60, 49–66.

Watson, A., 1974, *Law Making in the Roman Republic* (Oxford).

Weiss, R., 1969, *The Renaissance Rediscovery of Classical Antiquity* (Oxford).

Weston, C. C., 1991, 'England: ancient constitution and common law', in Burns, 1991, 374–95.

Willems, P., 1878, *Le Sénat de la République romaine*, 2 vols. and app. (Louvain), 1878–85.

Williamson, C., 1987, 'Monuments of Bronze: Roman Legal Documents on Bronze Tablets', *CSCA* 6, 160–83.

Wirzubski, C., 1950, *'Libertas' as a Political Ideal at Rome* (Cambridge).

Wiseman, T. P., 1971, *New Men in the Roman Senate 139 BC–14 AD* (Oxford).

—— 1979, *Clio's Cosmetics* (Leicester).

Wiseman, T. P., 1985, *Roman Political Life 90 BC–AD 69* (Exeter Studies in History 7: Exeter).

——1994, *Historiography and Imagination: Eight Essays in Roman Culture* (Exeter Studies in History 33: Exeter).

Wissowa, G., 1912, *Religion und Kultus der Römer* (2nd edn., Munich).

Yakobson, A., 1992, '*Petitio et Largitio*: Popular Participation in the Centuriate Assembly of the late Republic', *JRS* 82, 32–52.

Index of Ancient Sources Cited

General Index